THE SEVENTH HEAVEN

PITT LATIN AMERICAN SERIES

Catherine M. Conaghan, Editor

ILAN STAVANS

THE SEVENTH HEAVEN

TRAVELS THROUGH JEWISH LATIN AMERICA

UNIVERSITY OF PITTSBURGH PRESS

Published by the University of Pittsburgh Press, Pittsburgh, Pa., 15260

Copyright © 2019, University of Pittsburgh Press

Manufactured in the United States of America

Printed on acid-free paper

10 9 8 7 6 5 4 3 2 1

Cataloging-in-Publication data is available from the Library of Congress

ISBN 13: 978-0-8229-4585-7

ISBN 10: 0-8229-4585-1

Cover art: José Gurvich, *Javer and Javera,* 1974. Courtesy of the estate of the artist.

Cover design: Joel W. Coggins

To my beloved *chaver*, Sherwin B. Nuland (1930–2014)

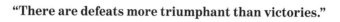

"There are defeats more triumphant than victories."

—Montaigne, "Of Cannibals" (trans. John Florio, 1603)

CONTENTS

THE SEVENTH HEAVEN

1   THE PULL

I was past fifty when the pull made itself apparent.

I had left Mexico, my place of birth, decades earlier and now lived a comfortable life elsewhere. Yet I had kept close ties with my family throughout the years. Then an unexpected rift took place among them, with immediate and far-reaching consequences. One consequence was that I suddenly felt uprooted.

This sense manifested itself in a bizarre, prophetic dream. In it I was walking in Colonia Copilco, the neighborhood in Mexico City where I grew up and to which I hadn't returned for ages. In the dream I looked for my old house, but block after block I couldn't find it. I became agitated by its absence. After a while, I finally stumbled upon it. A mysterious man was waiting at the door. He saw me but didn't make any gesture.

He was in his mid-sixties, disheveled. He wore thick glasses, a long, unkempt, salt-and-pepper beard, and a small hat that looked disproportionally large on his round bloated head. Under the hat I could see a yarmulke. There was something feminine about his lips. I had the vague feeling of having met the mysterious man before but I couldn't remember where. I was sure he wasn't Mexican. I approached him hesitantly. For some reason I don't understand, I decided to address him in French.

"Monsieur, voici ma maison." I explained that I had come from far away and needed to get into the house. He didn't budge. For a moment I thought he was mute.

When I was growing up, there was a small park around the corner from my childhood home. I walked toward it. It had changed tremendously. In fact, in the dream it was now an amusement park. There was a carousel, a Ferris Wheel, bumper cars, a rollercoaster, and some other attractions.

I found the ticket booth. An old lady was inside. I handed her money and told her I wanted to purchase a ticket.

"¿Pa' qué?" She spoke a working-class Mexican Spanish. "What for?"

I told her the ticket was to go to my old house. I hadn't seen it for a long time. I feared I was forgetting what rooms looked like, what it felt to be inside, how the morning light projected itself against the house walls.

She smiled and handed me a ticket and some coins. I walked back to my house. The mysterious man was still there. I showed him the ticket.

He looked bewildered and laughed euphorically. "Bienvenue au septième ciel," he announced. "Welcome to the seventh heaven."

At this point, I woke up . . .

I seldom remember my dreams. In fact, every morning as I wake up I go through a certain motion. Eyes still closed, I become aware I'm about to lose grasp of the images in the dream and futilely attempt to freeze them. I open my eyes and close them, in quick succession, but it is pointless. Throughout the day I also foolishly look for these images, again to no avail.

This particular dream was different. It was stamped into my consciousness, bouncing spiritedly from one corner to another. Interpreting it became a sport of sorts. I looked for photos of the façade of my Copilco house, the interior, the third-floor deck, a tree in the front yard. And I tried to retrieve the identity of the mysterious man. One thing became clear to me. The fact that I couldn't just reenter my childhood house meant I was now a stranger to it. More than a stranger, a tourist, because to get in I needed to pay the price of admission. In other words, my house was mine no more.

Plus, there was the expression *au septième ciel.* I had heard it at a dinner table just a few days prior, I believe for the first time. I remember being puzzled by it. The guest at the party had used it to refer to a mutual acquaintance whose life was somehow out of focus. "He is in seventh heaven . . ."

In any case, the dream became a kind of obsession. I thought about it constantly. Its deeper implications frightened me. It made me feel disconnected from my past.

Something else happened at the time. I had been reading a book originally written in Yiddish called *The Enemy at His Pleasure*. (The original title is *Khurbn Galitsye*, the destruction of Galicia.) The author was a folklorist called Shloyme Zaynvl Rapoport, who went by the penname of S. Ansky. He is best known for a classic theater piece, *The Dybbuk: Between Two Worlds* (1920), a haunting play about an exorcism. I have seen the play staged half a dozen times.

The action of the play takes place in 1882, in a shtetl in Miropol, Volhynia. In it there is a girl who is the daughter of a rich Jew. The father makes it difficult for suitors to satisfy his demands for his daughter's marriage. At the same time, a yeshiva student is in love with her. But in the father's eyes he is unworthy. Distraught, the student dies. Soon a match is made for the girl to marry a man who is finally approved by the father, though not before the yeshiva student's malicious spirit, known in Jewish folklore as dybbuk, takes possession of her.

Ansky was a socialist as well as a "Yiddishist" who believed that the soul of people was to be found in their language. He was from Chashniki, Belarus, which at the time was part of the Russian Empire. And he died in Otwock, Poland. In other words, he was from the so-called Pale of Settlement, the territory in the western region of imperial Russia where the Jews were allowed to live between 1791 and 1917.

He was appalled by the miserable conditions in which they lived in the region. Poverty was endemic. Anti-Semitic outbursts—called "pogroms"—were at a premium. This was the age of revolution. It was the age of large-canvas social engineering, of Communism, Anarchism, Nihilism, and other doctrines intent on remapping human interactions. And this was also the time when Jewish philanthropies were committed to relocating enormous masses of people to destinations such as the United States, Palestine, and Argentina.

Around the First World War, struck by a sense of urgency, Ansky headed an ethnographic expedition to towns in Volhynia and Podolia, which covered parts of Poland, Belarus, Ukraine, and Moldova. He took it upon himself to compile a multifaceted narrative (when first released, *The Enemy at His Pleasure* was in four volumes, the version I read in English being an abridgment) that offered a portrait—physical, psychological, and religious—of a society, the poor Jewish people of the Pale of Settlement as they struggled to make ends meet.

To accomplish this, Ansky and a set of teammates he assembled interviewed hundreds of people with a questionnaire of more than two thousand questions. They recorded five hundred cylinders of music and acquired photographs, manuscripts, and religious paraphernalia. From these he drew natural and supernatural stories, some of them about sheer survival, others about violence, and a few more about angels and demons and golems and goblins. The result, as I once saw it described, was "a Brueghel-like canvas" of a world on the verge of extinction.

In spite of this background, my reaction to *The Enemy at His Pleasure* was one of disappointment. It wasn't that Ansky's worldview was bleak. How else could he respond to the wretched conditions he and his team found surrounding this population? The world itself was against these Jews. But he wasn't really so interested in their economic and political situation per se as much as he was attracted to the way they steadfastly held to their beliefs. He was fascinated by folklore, which, as J. R. R. Tolkien believed, "keeps in memory what it was once needful for the wise to know."

What really troubled me was that Ansky didn't quite analyze his material as much as he simply collected it. This, in his opinion, was the role of an ethnographer: to observe and not judge. Consequently, the book, in my view, lacked insight. And whenever it did offer a viewpoint, it was to portray modernity as a threat, which was in and of itself disheartening, for I am one of those who think that progress is inevitable and that the best response to it isn't rejection but accommodation. Ansky idealized the spiritual qualities of the Jewish people he encountered, the way they embraced their redemption within, not beyond, the circumstances in which they lived. He admired that tenacity, never second-guessing it.

Yet I was in awe at Ansky's ambition. The book was a methodical exploration of the environment that Ansky himself knew well. He took his expedition not to a distant land but to the locale he himself inhabited. His findings are invaluable precisely because of this unfolding, this doubling of the self. It is easy to spot exotic traditions in a set of Polynesian islands, but to research one's own peers in an objective way demands humility.

He was at once a step behind the times in which he lived and stunningly prescient. Ansky embarked on his expedition between 1911 and 1914. As a result of pogroms and other xenophobic outbursts, Jewish emigration from that part of the globe had started in the last couple of decades of the nineteenth century. In the worst years, between mid-1903 and mid-1906, starting with the first of two cathartic pogroms in Kishinev, then the capital of Bessarabia, more than 250,000 Jews left the region. By the time Ansky concluded his fieldwork, 350,000 had abandoned Galicia alone.

He was right where the action took place. Had he not traveled around, we would have missed a rich multifaceted description by a chronicler who intimately knows the stuff on the ground. His oeuvre—along with Roman Vishniac's photographs of the ghettos of Poland, Romania, and other countries in Central and Eastern Europe between 1935 and 1938, allows us to glimpse a civilization as it vanished from the face of the earth.

All this to say that such occurrences—the unpleasant dream that I sensed had an oracular quality to it and my gut reaction to Ansky's ethnography— pushed me into an introspective mood, which in turn heightened a state of alertness. I began to feel that my responsibility was to explore my own roots more exhaustively. And not only my Jewish roots in Mexico but, more broadly, the labyrinthine path of Jewish life in Latin America as a whole.

Demographically, these communities are minuscule. Yet as a conglomerate they represent the third-largest concentration of Jews worldwide, after the United States and Israel and before France and Canada. Little is known about them and what is perceived through the prism of exoticism. In a region where democracy struggles to endure, where tolerance and pluralism at times become casualties, their history is a thermometer of society's overall health.

While I was languishing in my introspective mood, there were constant anti-Semitic surges in countries such as Ecuador and Bolivia. Dictators such as Venezuela's Nicolás Maduro regularly inserted anti-Zionist slogans in their rhetoric. In Montevideo a cemetery as well as the Memorial del Holocausto del Pueblo Judío were vandalized. Mexico and Colombia *secuestros express*, fast-paced kidnapping, regularly targeted Jews. And in Argentina, aside from periodic anti-Jewish statements in the media, a prominent Jewish prosecutor who accused the country's most powerful of a cover-up was found dead in his apartment. Not long after, a treasure trove of Nazi artifacts, including a magnifying glass allegedly used by Hitler on maps of Europe while he was strategizing with his commanders about the invasion of Poland and other countries, had been enshrined in a collector's apartment.

I grew up with these kinds of assaults. Like other Latin American Jews I learned how to cope with them, how to insulate myself from them. I remember reading, in my early twenties, Jean-Paul Sartre's diatribe *Réflexions sur la question juive* (*Anti-Semite and Jew*, 1943). Over time, its principal argument—anti-Semites need Jews as much as Jews need anti-Semites— has been consistently debunked by psychologists, historians, and others. (Sartre, I should add, wasn't Jewish, though in the latter part of his life, controversially, he underwent a spiritual conversion that brought him close to Kabbalah.) Still, all these years later, it continued to resonate with me. Anti-

Semitism is not the reason Jews remain Jews, I would tell myself. There is plenty more: love, friendship, learning, entrepreneurship . . .

I love the combination of Jewish and Latino. There is enormous joy in that encounter. Over several centuries Latin American Jews have thrived in multiple spheres, from economic well-being to the scientific, artistic, and educational realms. But the formula for success contains within itself the traps of ostracism. One doesn't need to be a catastrophist to realize that the region contains seeds of hatred and that Jewish life in general is fragile. All life is, of course, but as the diplomat and all-out Renaissance man Abba Eban once purportedly stated: "Jews are like everyone else—except a little bit more."

And so, after the rift with my family, recognizing that something inside had broken, I felt *the pull*—surreptitious, overpowering—to chronicle that life in a firsthand account, wandering from place to place just in case home too abruptly became susceptible to obliteration.

I have always enjoyed traveling. It is second nature to me. I like listening to people, getting the gist of a place, mapping its past. Travel, for that reason, is not only about relocating the body. It is, just as much, about opening up the intellect. And about looking for spiritual solace.

I never travel lineally. Instead, I twist and turn, allowing my itinerary to shape up spontaneously. Before I depart, I teach myself as much as possible about my destination. Then, once I'm there, I hunt for the type of information that is only available on-site: what people think about, how they see the world, their fears and desires. I know that information isn't knowledge; to become knowledge, it needs to be personalized. Someone has to own it for it to come alive.

For years Latin America has been one of my favorite destinations. I feel quite comfortable there. Some places I enjoy more than others. But each trip I make is autonomous. It is completed in a matter of days, a week at most. Whenever I zoom in and out, I don't keep a notebook in hand. Nor am I deliberately looking to make overarching connections.

For this endeavor I chose to make time more elastic. I gave myself roughly four years to accomplish the task, the same amount of time Ansky took for his tour of Galicia. Together, Volhynia and Podolia comprise about 40,000 square miles. That's the land Ansky surveyed. According to the famous 1911 edition of the *Encyclopedia Britannica*, the overall population before the First World War was approximately 5,500,000. In comparison, Latin America is 7,412 million square miles. In 2015 there were 626,741,000 people living in the entire region.

Healthwise, I was at the right moment: vigorous yet seasoned. My regular teaching gig allowed me substantial flexibility in terms of schedule. My children were older. I was happy.

The itinerary of my expedition wasn't fixed. I let my instinct take me where it wanted. In the end I zigzagged my way to countless different destinations, and sometimes to the same one several times over. Obviously, I had been to several places before. In this iteration I came across countless aspects I hadn't paid attention to before. I attended Shabbat services in Havana, Santiago, and other cities. I had extended dialogues with Crypto-Jews, whose Jewishness was kept in secret to avoid persecution. I visited the site where Adolf Eichmann was kidnapped by the Israeli secret service, Mossad. I looked at neo-Nazi literature and its followers. I roamed through ruined buildings used a long time ago as synagogues, schools, and ritual baths. I delved into the topic of Jewish self-defense groups. I went to cabarets and ball games and I drifted through cemeteries. I talked to families of the *desaparecidos*. I was in torture chambers maintained by the Argentine military junta and saw the instruments used to brutalize victims—not only victims of state violence during the Dirty War but those of Holy Office inquisitors in colonial times. I wandered in Israel in search of a Spanish-speaking diaspora that made *aliyah* (Hebrew for "ascendance"). And I was in the Amazon, searching for aboriginal communities that believe themselves to be descendants of the Lost Tribes of Israel.

Although I traveled alone for the most part, I never felt lonely. My wife and children occasionally came with me. As a result of my previous travels I had acquaintances in most places, with whom I kept in communication before and after my visits. Among others, I talked to vocal activists, engaging taxi drivers, despicable Holocaust deniers, retired postmen, enthusiastic soldiers, shrewd politicians, and perplexed Talmudic scholars. I also met with engineers, actors, lexicographers, curators, lawyers, photographers, students, entrepreneurs, journalists, academics, rabbis, teachers, artists, and translators. The composite picture ended up being intricate, elastic, and multifaceted.

Indeed, it was in the conversations, perhaps more than in the actual places, that I found meaning. A place is a place is a place. I feel galvanized when it has historical value. But it is the people who make my journey worth the effort. They give it depth. The way their words, the storytelling, and their reminiscences come to life through free association to me feels like an injection of adrenaline. That's what culture is about. And it was this culture that I desperately wanted to capture.

This and the angst I wanted to assuage, of being excluded from my childhood house and of meeting the mysterious man I saw in my dream, standing outside my childhood home.

2   YIDDISH GAUCHOS

1.

I first traveled to Argentina. I arrived with a sense of awe. Robert Louis Stevenson once said that "there is no foreign land; it is the traveler only who is foreign." I had been to Argentina before but never with enough time to dig deep into Jewish history, politics, and the collective psyche. Throughout my expedition, I returned to Argentina half a dozen times. It became my headquarters, so to speak.

This is the Latin American country with the largest Jewish population. It was also a crucial destination where individual philanthropists and welfare organizations targeted the relocation, between 1880 and 1920, of a vast number of Yiddish-speaking Jews from the Pale of Settlement. My intention was to do what Cuban novelist Alejo Carpentier, one of the masters of the Latin American novel, once called *un viaje a la semilla*, a trek back in time using the present as the point of departure.

Specifically, I went to El Once, the densely populated photogenic downtown neighborhood in Buenos Aires, known for its garment industry and retail businesses. It is ground zero, the place that Jews in Argentina are most commonly associated with.

El Once strictly speaking isn't a neighborhood, although *porteños*, as the dwellers of the nation's capital are commonly called, persistently refer to it that way. The real neighborhood is Balvanera, in which El Once is a small portion.

Argentina is one of the most multiethnic countries in the world. Aside from the Spanish, British, Italian, Portuguese, newcomers from Germany, Scandinavia, Poland, and Russia have settled in it. More recently, people from Africa, Korea, and the Middle East have also come in, along with immigrants from other parts of Latin America such as Bolivia, Peru, Paraguay, Chile, Uruguay, Colombia, Nicaragua, Guatemala, and so on.

In the nineteenth century Argentina was one of the two nations at the global level that received the most immigrants: it allowed in 6.6 million, second only to the United States, with 27 million. The country's constitution states that justice, welfare, and liberty apply "to all men who wish to dwell on Argentine soil."

Today most Argentinean Jews live in Buenos Aires and the cities of Córdoba, the country's second most populous city, on the foothills of the Sierras Chicas on the Suquía Rivera, and Rosario, in the province of Santa Fe, about 330 kilometers from Buenos Aires, on the shore of the Paraná River. In Buenos Aires itself, not all newcomers have passed through El Once. Still, the area is known for its pluralism and also for its relatively peaceful racial tolerance. Ashkenazi Jews congregated there at the turn of the twentieth century. It was home to them.

Before my arrival in Buenos Aires, I read profusely about the neighborhood. Most significantly I became acquainted with the hurdles faced by those early Jewish settlers—the drastic departure from their place of origin and the urgent need to learn the language and customs of the new home— through the poems of Eliahu Toker, who died in 2010 at the age of seventy-six. A child of Yiddish-speaking immigrants, he became a distinguished writer, scholar, and acclaimed translator of Yiddish literature into Spanish, including major authors such as Abraham Sutzkever and Jacob Glatstein. His evocative verses, including those in the collection *Lejaim* (*Lechaim*, 1974), were eulogies to butchers, seamstresses, scholars, and *cuenteniks* (as peddlers were called by Jews immigrants to Argentina).

I became familiar with El Once also through the work of another, substantially younger neighbor, Marcelo Birmajer. Born in 1966, he is a novelist, screenwriter, and columnist for the newspaper *Clarín* and the author of a popular novel called *Tres mosqueteros* (*Three Musketeers*, 2008) about a set of friends who, in the 1970s, joined the Montoneros, a left-wing Peronist guerrilla group. Birmajer translated Isaac Bashevis Singer's *The Death of*

Methuselah (2003) from English into Spanish. His credits include the script of *Abrazo partido* (*Lost Embrace* (2005), a Woody Allenesque comedy about a Jewish family whose members own a business in El Once. Along with *El décimo hombre* (*The Tenth Man*, 2016), this is the most textured depiction of Jewish life in Argentina that I have seen on film.

I met Birmajer years ago, when he and I engaged in a public conversation on humor and horror at the San Francisco Jewish Museum. We struck up a friendship. Soon after, he sent me a book-long reminiscence, *El Once: A Personal Journey* (2006), which I enjoyed a lot. It is built as an anecdotal tour through memory lane in the neighborhood's changing urban landscape: meandering alleyways, abandoned theaters, little-known restaurants, refashioned buildings, and so on.

It kept on bringing to mind the depictions of Delancey, Hester, and other busy streets in New York's Lower East Side, portrayals made at the beginning of the twentieth century in books such as Abraham "Abe" Cahan's *The Rise of David Levinsky* (1917) and Anzia Yezierska's *Bread Givers* (1925) and even in those descriptions marked with nostalgia by the next generation of Jewish American writers, such as Alfred Kazin's *A Walker in the City* (1951) and Irving Howe's *World of Our Fathers* (1976).

I love wandering around those streets. When I immigrated to New York City in the mid-1980s, the roughness of the place was overwhelming. The Lower East Side was an antidote to me. I lived on Broadway and 122nd Street, near the Jewish Theological Seminary (JTS). I would take the number 1 subway line to Canal Street. The multiethnic nature of the neighborhood was refreshing. Instead of the current residents (Asians, Africans, and Caribbeans), I would visualize the Italian, Jewish, and Irish tenants who settled on the area from the 1880s to the 1930s.

In my imagination the sidewalks were filled with busy Jewish merchants of all kinds, selling bread, fish, meat, fruits, and vegetables. Peddlers would announce their products in Yinglish, a mix of Yiddish and English. Yiddish theaters in nearby Villa Crespo would stage plays by Abraham Goldfaden and other classics, as well as adaptations of Shakespeare's *Macbeth*, *Hamlet*, and *King Lear*.

Although it was smaller in scale, I knew El Once had been a similar ecosystem, even though the majority of Jewish immigrants to Argentina didn't go directly to Buenos Aires. Instead, they settled in the countryside—in *colonias*, agricultural colonies in the Entre Ríos and Santa Fe provinces— where they worked the land and raised cattle.

Before my arrival I sent Birmajer an email, asking him if he would serve as my Virgil for a couple of hours. He generously complied. We ended up spending a long morning together. In a subsequent visit to Argentina, I would see him again. By then his life had taken a sudden tragic turn.

Of medium height, Birmajer is always in a T-shirt. He has short salt-and-pepper hair and a permanent five o'clock shadow, leaves his sunglasses suspended on his forehead, and has a relaxed demeanor. His columns in *Clarín*, read widely, touch on all sorts of topics, including the Middle East, and are unafraid to lash out against political correctness. It was a cold winter morning in June. Brimajer rented a small office space in an old apartment building in El Once, which he uses for writing. It was a tiny room with long windows, tall bookshelves, and all sorts of tchotchkes.

After a few pleasantries we left his place and began to wander around the neighborhood in a comfortable, jazzy way. On his iPhone, Birmajer brought up a map of Buenos Aires. He showed me how, given the way the city has grown over the past several decades, El Once, geographically as well as figuratively, is at the very heart of it.

The main artery is Avenida Corrientes. Another important one is Avenida Rivadavia, named after an Argentine president, Bernardino Rivadavia, whose mausoleum is also in the area. Although it is seen today as part of El Centro (downtown), in the nineteenth century Balvanera was a suburb. Its neighbors lived in *quintas*, country houses. It is impossible to escape its bucolic style, apparent in the sepia photographs that still survive. Nowadays that pastoral demeanor is gone. The intersection of Avenida Corrientes and Avenida Pueyrredón is one of the busiest in Buenos Aires. Thousands of people from all walks of life pass through this intersection on a regular basis.

Argentina is a relatively young country, yet history—a history of colonialism, of brutality, of relentless inequality—is tangible everywhere. The full name of El Once is Once de Septiembre (*Once* in Spanish is the word for the number eleven). This was the name of a railway station in the area that still functions today and around which sprawling retail stores of all kinds have sprung up. There is dissent among historians regarding the meaning of the name. Some believe it refers to the date when, in 1852, the province of Buenos Aires became an autonomous region. Others suggest that Once de Septiembre commemorates the death, on September 11, of Domingo Faustino Sarmiento, arguably the nation's most important politician, who served as president from 1868 to 1874 and who wrote one of the classic books in Argentine literature, *Facundo: Civilización y barbarie* (*Facundo: Civilization and Barbarism*, 1845). Among other things, Sarmiento's treatise argues in favor

of opening the doors to European immigrants, whom he considered civilizing forces that would ultimately help Argentina in its quest toward modernization. Another major political figure, Juan Bautista Alberdi, a theorist
and diplomat who was Sarmiento's contemporary and whose influence is
tangible in the drafting of the nation's constitution of 1853, stated, famously,
that "to rule is to populate."

Since the early wave of immigrants to Argentina came from Europe,
people in the country as a whole see the country as an extension of the Old
World in the New. Or at least they believe they are more "civilized" than
the other Latin Americans and that their culture is a continuation of the
intellectual tradition that produced Montaigne, Dante, Locke, Goethe, and
Schopenhauer. In the eyes of others in the region, this belief is false and the
source of Argentinean arrogance, an overinflated type of narcissism.

While I was growing up in Mexico, Argentines in popular jokes would
often be depicted as arrogant, conceited, and self-absorbed. And the same
opinion of them goes for the other countries in Latin America. The collective feeling is that Argentines see the rest of us as inferior. They see themselves as the most refined cosmopolites history has produced this side of the
Atlantic. While in El Once, one afternoon I talked to a man drinking beer
at a bar about *fútbol*, specifically about the two most celebrated Argentine
players: Diego Maradona and Leonel Messi. He was somewhat dismissive
of Maradona, arguing that wealth had turned him into "a fat cow." What he
said of Messi, on the other hand, made me laugh. I took it to be a perfect
example of the country's weltanschauung: "Messi is the best player in the
world and one of the best in Argentina."

Messi is of Italian descent, as is Pope Francis (Jorge Mario Bergoglio,
the first Latin American pontiff) and about 25 million other Argentineans—
more than 60 percent of the population. Italians are by far the country's
largest immigrant group. Jews come nowhere near. In 2015 they were estimated to be roughly between 180,000 and 220,000, down from 300,000 in
the 1960s. In a country of close to 45 million people, this represents less than
1 percent of the total population.

Still, the Jewish influence on Argentine culture is major. We talked of
the pianist and orchestra conductor Daniel Barenboim and of the composer Lalo Schifrin, who composed the theme of *Mission: Impossible*; Rabbi
Abraham Skorka who, along with Pope Francis when he was still bishop
of Buenos Aires, engaged in a Jewish-Christian dialogue that resulted in
a book; fútbol player Daniel Brailovsky, who played for the Club Independiente before moving to the Mexican league, then to the Israeli team Mac-

cabi Haifa, and who played for the Argentine and Israeli national teams in international tournaments; the literary critic Noé Jitrik; Rabbi Abraham Skorka, who published a book of Jewish-Christian conversations with Pope Francis; Daniel Burman, who directed *Lost Embrace* and *The Tenth Man*; as well as the filmmaker Damián Szifron, responsible for the masterful movie *Relatos salvajes* (*Wild Tales*, 2014), which in part is about Jewish life in Argentina; Ariel Dorfman, the playwright of *Death and the Maiden* (1989), who was born in Argentina, although he has Chilean citizenship; and the journalist Jacobo Timerman, author of *Prisionero sin nombre, celda sin número* (*Prisoner without a Name, Cell without a Number* [1981]), who was among the most recognizable voices against the dictatorship during the Dirty War (*La Guerra Sucia* in Spanish)—an ugly period from 1976 (although some put it half a decade earlier) to roughly 1983, in which a military junta, in power through coup d'états, had called for a *Proceso de Reorganización Nacional*, a process of national reorganization whereby dissident were "erased" from society through a variety of methods that included silencing, intimidation, torture, and disappearance.

Timerman's son Héctor Timerman, also a journalist, was part of the populist Justicialist Party, which is the largest component of the Peronist movement, and served in the left-leaning government of Cristina Fernández de Kirchner. Birmajer also mentioned León Rozitchner, a Marxist psychoanalyst thinker (in a country infatuated with Marx and Freud) who focused his attention on the effects of terror, the illusion of democracy, and the perils of submitting one's life to the rule of law.

I sensed displeasure in Birmajer with the politics of a few of these public figures, particularly Barenboim, who is known for his left-wing views and especially for his advocacy in favor of bringing Israelis and Palestinians together in a peaceful way that would end their decades-old conflict once and for all. And maybe also with the left-leaning views of Pope Francis. Catching his breath, he said it was possible to look at Argentina in the last 150 years through the prism of El Once.

"Labor unrest, economic stagnation, the oppressiveness of military juntas, a return to religious fervor. . . . The neighborhood is the lightning rod."

Interestingly, walking around it one doesn't get the feeling that History, written with capital "H," matters to the people here. Everyone is busy making a living. And the local authorities aren't particularly mindful of the way in which the past makes itself palpable to the present. Buildings have been redone without much regard for preservation. Depending on the various political winds, streets have occasionally been renamed. Worse, from scores of conversations I had with passers-by in El Once, the impression I got was that the average person didn't care about how the neighborhood had mutated over time. It was only when I engaged in conversation with restaurateurs, teachers, and lawyers that I was able to register a strong pride in the place as a habitat. One of them said to me, "It isn't city officials who keep El Once in good standing but the people who protect it from city officials." Another told me, "This is where the country's neurosis is at its happiest."

In Argentine Jewish history, El Once is the stage where *La Semana Trágica*, the Tragic Week, took place in 1919. This is the only pogrom in Latin America, although a few scholars interpret it less as an anti-Semitic outburst than as an anti-immigrant, labor dispute, in response to the rapid process of industrialization that Argentina was going through. President Hipólito Yrigoyen had been in power since 1916. Workers were organizing, and naturally immigration was perceived as a threat. Unrest took hold and Jews were attacked, according to some interpretations not because they were Jewish but because they were immigrants. Close to one hundred were killed in a matter of days, dozens were injured, and businesses and other sites were burned.

The neighborhood is also where prominent Peronist marches were organized in the 1950s. But unquestionably the most significant event to take place in El Once was the terrorist attack against the Asociación Mutual Israelita Argentina (AMIA), on July 18, 1994. Prior to that, in 1992, the Israeli Embassy, on Arroyo Street #910, on a posh side of Retiro neighborhood in the northeast end of Buenos Aires and quite a long way from El Once, had been the target of another suicide bomb. A group called the Islamic Jihad Organization, connected with Hezbollah in Lebanon and also with the Iranian government, claimed responsibility. It said the event was in retaliation for Israel's assassination of Abbas al-Musawi, Hezbollah's secretary general.

The AMIA explosion left the place in ruins. Eighty-five people were killed, sixty-seven in the building itself. The rest were passersby or in adjacent buildings. There were also three hundred injured.

I told Birmajer I remembered the AMIA explosion as if it happened yesterday. I was in New York City at the time. The attack took place on a Monday. The World Cup had just concluded, the previous afternoon, with an unimpressive match between Brazil and Italy, at the Rose Bowl, in Pasadena, California.

"With a score of 3–2 in penalties, Brazil became the world champion," said Birmajer. "Buenos Aires was just waking up to another week when an explosion shook it to the core."

He paused. "It was masterminded by Iran." The United States' National Security Agency had intercepted communication that proved Iran was involved in the Israeli Embassy case. It pointed to a Hezbollah terrorist cell on the border of Argentina, Brazil, and Paraguay, where a large Muslim community is located.

Without our realizing it the AMIA attack had become our sole focus of conversation. Up to that point, this was the largest terrorist attack ever to take place this side of the Atlantic Ocean. Birmajer and I tried to re-create the way people looked at things at the time. There was no particular reason for Argentines to look at news from the Middle East with more than a topical interest. At the end of the 1980s, the Palestinian National Congress had met in Algiers to unilaterally proclaim the State of Palestine. In 1991 a conference had taken place in Madrid that included Israel, Syria, Lebanon, Jordan, and a Palestinian delegation. A year later, a secret accord between Israelis and Palestinians had taken place in Oslo, Norway, and a declaration of principles was made public. And then, in February 1994, Baruch Goldstein, an American Israeli settler entered Al-Haram Al-Ibrahimi—the Cave of the Patriarchs, a religious site in Hebron—and with a machine gun massacred 29 Palestinians, injuring 125 more.

The state of alert in Israel was high. There was anger around the world. The sense that no diplomatic agreement could stop the bloodshed was exacerbated.

However, Latin American Jews were unconcerned. Their lives happened far away from the Middle East, in the periphery of Western civilization.

The AMIA detonation changed that forever.

"I called my mother in Mexico City," I told Birmajer. "'We've lost our innocence, Ilan,' I remember she said to me."

Weeks later, security in all the Jewish communities of Latin America was at a record high. I added, "A cousin of mine who lived in Miami Beach explained by phone that any foreigner who wanted to be part of Shabbat service in his synagogue needed to send a written petition beforehand with a copy of their passport." The situation made me recall a poem by Yehuda Amichai, the most important Israeli poet of the last fifty years. Born into an orthodox Jewish family in Germany between the two world wars, Amichai immigrated to British-mandate Palestine in 1935 and was a member of the Palmach, the strike force of the Jewish paramilitary organization that became the foundation of the Israeli Defense Forces.

Throughout his life he experienced violence firsthand. His poetry, how-ever, was about empathy. The poem I remembered was called "The Diam-eter of a Bomb." It is about the circles of pain that a bomb generates. The bomb's actual diameter might be only seven meters, Amichai says, but the suffering is far wider: the families of the victims, the staff at the nearby hos-pital, the gravediggers at the cemetery, the friends who were about to meet the victims at a café, and the strangers who heard about the tragedy on TV, on and on, forming "a circle with no end and no God."

The circles of suffering generated by the AMIA explosion reached far and wide. Synagogues, schools, and community centers from Mexico to Chile quickly implemented security checks. Before that point in time it was quite easy to be part of a minyan, a religious service, on Thursday morning or during Shabbat. All you had to do was show up at the door. After July 18, 1994, you needed to send a scanned copy of your passport beforehand. It was only after some research that you would be advised if the invitation was open.

After my trip to El Once in 2015, I spent a few days in Lima, Peru. Rabbi Guilermo Bronstein and his wife, Mónica, kindly invited me to dinner at their apartment afterward. Even on that occasion I needed to send proof of identity. After the service, he and I and a few others walked to his apart-ment, which was only a few blocks from the temple, Asociación Judía 1870, on Calle José Galvez #282, in Miraflores. Throughout we were protected by an entourage of guards dressed in civilian clothes. Likewise, in other cities from San Juan to Santiago, I needed to alert the synagogue's administra-tion in advance. Since it quickly became known that the perpetrators of the terrorist attack against the AMIA had been sponsored by the Iranian government, Argentine Jews felt especially vulnerable.

In a bizarre way the incident turned them into actors, albeit tangen-tial ones, of the Middle East conflict. The tragedy was a preview of the 9/11 attack against the World Trade Center in New York City. To intelligence services it became clear that Al-Qaeda operatives learned a lesson from the Buenos Aires event. For one thing, like the Twin Towers, which were seen as a symbol of American financial power, the AMIA in Buenos Aires was chosen because it represented Jewish interests. Striking against it was like hitting a restaurant in Tel-Aviv's trendy Dizengoff Street.

Birmajer said that, in the early 1990s, Argentina and Iran were hoping to develop a joint nuclear plant. Carlos Saúl Menem was Argentina's president at the time. Since he was of Syrian descent, it is believed that he was at the helm of the collaboration. Iran was already in the ascent as a significant ideological force in the Middle East. When Menem left office in disgrace in 1999 (years later, he was under house arrest on charges of illegal weapons sales but had immunity because he had once been elected senator, which didn't stop him fleeing to Chile), fingers were still being pointed in countless directions for both attacks. No tangible results came about.

A financial crisis at the beginning of the twenty-first century in Argentina contributed to muddying the waters. A quick succession of ad hoc presidents, some of them lasting only a few hours in power, put the AMIA attack on the back burner. This changed when Néstor Kirchner, from a left-leaning side of the Justicialist Party, refocused the attention by promising to solve the case. The effort was followed by his wife, Cristina Fernández de Kirchner. (They were the Bill and Hillary Clinton of Argentina, but he died of heart failure in 2010, having been expected to run for president again.) During her years in office from 2007 to the end of 2015 Cristina, as she was called, publicly pushed for a resolution, going as far as to arrange a deal with Iran that included allowing Argentine judges to travel to Teheran to interview potential culprits.

Rather than a breakthrough, the deal was seen by many as a betrayal. This view was supported by Alberto Nisman, then the country's chief prosecutor who was of Jewish descent. Nisman believed Cristina's agreement with the Iranians was a way to muddy the waters even more, so he prepared a dossier in which he blamed the president for being part of a criminal conspiracy to stall the AMIA case. But then, on January 18, 2015, shortly before my visit to Argentina and hours before he was scheduled to make public his findings before the Argentine Congress, Nisman was found dead in his Buenos Aires apartment.

His body was in a pool of blood next to one of the apartment's bathrooms. He had a bullet wound in his head. A .22-caliber gun was in his hand as well as the casting from the bullet. The death was said to be a suicide. Yet the circumstances were fishy. Nisman wasn't a depressed type. In conversations with friends and acquaintances, he had expressed excitement about the revelations he was about to offer in his meeting with Congress. Why would he die in such way?

For a while the Nisman case, which never acquired any anti-Semitic undertones, threatened to destabilize Cristina's government. She defended herself against charges of having ordered Nisman's execution and explained that, despite having been involved in an effort to silence him, she had provided evidence for him to build his case. Her arguments were contradictory. Public opinion was divided.

In the end, evidence was tainted, and detective investigations became more labyrinthine than an Umberto Eco novel. Political intrigue prevailed. No one was ever brought to justice. Nisman's case also resulted in impunity.

"You're right, Ilan. As in Amichai's poem, all sorts of aftershocks have been felt in different locations," said Birmajer. "But El Once is always the epicenter. This place is simultaneously peripheral and frighteningly global."

If you want to do a detailed people's history of Argentine Jews, he continued, just follow the exodus from the neighborhood. Thousands of descendants of the Yiddish-speaking settlers from shtetls in Eastern Europe moved not only to more financially solid areas in Buenos Aires but, as a result of political, economic, and social instability within the country, to the United States, Spain, and especially to Israel, where his brother Eduardo had done aliyah. This move essentially reversed the perception of Argentina as *un país de advenimiento*, a nation of plenty, portraying it instead, the way critics at times put it, as "an immigrant mistake."

Through the lens of El Once, one could also feel the temperature of the organized resistance against the military junta during the Dirty War. Since it is a working-class neighborhood, ideological upheaval was present in El Once, though the middle-class activists known for their involvement in opposing the dictatorship lived elsewhere in the city. A considerable number of Jews were among the kidnapped, tortured, and disappeared.

2.

Birmajer and I passed by synagogues, schools, bookshops, and delis. At one point we stumbled upon a store that sold all kinds of tchotchkes, knick-knacks, and ornaments. I stopped to look closely at its window. There was a swastika on display. Next to it was an old copy of Adolf Hitler's *Mi Lucha—Mein Kampf* (1925) in Spanish.

I told him I knew it was easy to buy copies of Hitler's autobiography in newsstands in Mexico City. "In Buenos Aires too," he said. "It circulates freely, to the point that *casi resulta desapercibido*, it is almost invisible. It isn't like Germany, where it is against the law to make it available."

Birmajer then pointed to a building that at one point had been a Yiddish theater and another one where a Yiddish newspaper was published. He said that for Passover and the High Holidays, people come to El Once to buy *pastrón*, *kreplaj*, and *varénikes*. As he talked, I saw stores that sold yarmulkes (skullcaps), *tallis* (prayer shawls), *mezuzas* (small parchment scrolls hung on doorways), liturgical books, Bibles, the Talmud, and other religious volumes. Birmajer connected all this with nostalgia. He reflected on the symbolic value of these types of ethnic enclaves. Secular Jews keep El Once at arm's length. They look at it as the cradle of Ashkenazic Jewish culture in Argentina. But there is also something kitschy about it. They want it to exist, to go on battling adversity, even though the majority of them would not be caught setting foot in the neighborhood.

We stopped at Sociedad Hebraica Argentina (commonly known as La Hebraica) on Calle Sarmiento #2233, the athletic and cultural facility—Birmajer called it "the people's center of gravity in the olden days"—around which Argentine Jewish life may be said to have revolved. It still does, though to a much lesser extent. A fourteen-story building, not all of which is used by the Jewish community any more, this is where classes are taught and lectures are given, where youth and senior groups gather, and an assortment of sports activities take place.

I walked into the building. I saw a cavernous eight-hundred-seat auditorium where a choreographic group was rehearsing *rikudim*, Israeli-style dances. There was a restaurant, a solarium, children's areas, and a library. I could imagine La Hebraica in its heyday, packed with Argentine Jews dressed in 1950s fashion. That splendor is now gone, though. The place looked like a Soviet-era social facility. I could understand why financially minded young Argentine Jews saw it as a symbol of the past. Birmajer said that, although the number of members of La Hebraica was probably close to sixty-five hundred, only about two hundred use this building on a regular basis. Although the leadership was considering another building in Belgrano, the fleeing families opted for a newer, more luxurious "country" branch called Sede Pilar, where activities take place on weekends and during holidays. This is on Avenida Sgto. Cayetano Beliera #1199 (people call it "Ruta 8, km 51.5"), in the Buenos Aires province.

I understood the mechanics well, because Mexico City also had an old Jewish neighborhood in downtown where, although in far fewer numbers, Jewish immigrants settled around the 1920s. There was a specific place on Calle Tacuba #15—near the Zócalo, Mexico City's main square, not far from the Palace of Bellas Artes—where for a few decades they congregated for all sorts of activities until the neighborhood became too shabby. To replace this center, a larger, state-of-the-art sports and cultural center, the Centro Deportivo Israelita (known as the CDI), was built near Ciudad Satélite, in the northern part of the city. In Argentina, at least the old Hebraica wasn't abandoned altogether. In spite of it no longer being a magnet, it continued to exist. This to me signified a continuity with the past, however tenuous that link might be.

"There's talk of closing it down," Birmajer said.

I told him that—while Jewish immigrants to Mexico from Poland, Russia, Ukraine, and other places had immediately gone from arrival ports like Veracruz, in the Gulf of Mexico, to the downtown areas in the country's capital—I knew that in Argentina their odyssey was more complex.

"Yes, before El Once, before we became full-fledged citizens, we were all gauchos," Birmajer responded sarcastically. "Yiddish-speaking gauchos."

He was talking about the agricultural colonias, the early Jewish settlements in Argentina at the turn of the twentieth century, which had initially taken root not in urban environments but in the Pampas. The word *pampas* comes from the indigenous language Quechua and it means "plains." It refers to the expansion of fertile lands covering almost 290,000 square miles on the border of Argentina, Uruguay, and Brazil. I told him I was scheduled to travel to the Pampas in a few days with a common friend of ours, Marcelo Brodsky, an internationally known photographer and a human rights activist. Specifically, I would go to Basavilbaso, Villa Domínguez, and other places in the province of Entre Ríos.

"If El Once feels a bit tacky, wait until you get to the land of the gauchos," he stated.

The conversation then turned to the Yiddish language. Birmajer didn't grow up speaking it. After the immigrant generation settled down, Argentine Jews didn't make Yiddish a language of instruction in Jewish schools. The case of Mexico was different. From kindergarten to high school, I attended the Yiddishe Schule in Mexique, Mexico's first Yiddish language and culture school. In other words, Yiddish had been an essential part of my education. And although for a while I rebelled against that instruction (as I assume everyone does at some point), with the years, I had come to see Yiddish as being an integral part of my identity.

From our original meeting in San Francisco, I knew that Birmajer was a fan of Isaac Bashevis Singer, the only Yiddish writer ever to win the Nobel Prize. He had read most of his stories as well as novels such as *The Magician of Lublin* (1960) and *Shadows on the Hudson* (1998). Years ago I edited a three-volume edition of Singer's collected stories, which amounted to some three or four hundred. Birmajer had that edition in his office. Throughout the day, he repeatedly praised the stories as a wonderful microcosm of Jewish life. In appreciation, he gave me a volume of Singer's stories translated into Spanish.

I mentioned a couple of stories by Singer that take place in Argentina and Brazil and one story in Miami that has a Jewish character. "They aren't very good," I said. "Lots of mosquitoes. Hypersexualized women. Cigar-smoking men. A constant threat of hurricanes. . . . You know, an abundance of stereotypes."

We agreed that stereotypes are like veils: they impede an appreciation of truth. Then Birmajer and I discussed truth in literature. "It isn't always factual," I posited. "The opposite of truth in science. In other words, for the writer reality doesn't need to reign tyrannically. As long as the depiction is genuine. . . . Truth is not what happened but what should have happened."

Other celebrated Yiddish writers had written about Argentina as well, I added. Most prominently in my mind was Sholem Aleichem, author of the classic *Tevye the Dairyman* (1894), which served as inspiration for the Broadway musical *Fiddler on the Roof*. Known as the grandson of Yiddish literature, Sholem Aleichem has a "railroad" story, part of a volume in which every tale is told on a train, as passengers board and then, a few stations later, get off again. This story is about the Zwi Migdal, an infamous cartel (the name of one of the ring leaders was Luis Zwi Migdal) that trafficked Jewish women from the shtetls in the Pale of Settlement and sold them as sex slaves in Buenos Aires, as well as to lesser centers in Brazil, Canada, China, South Africa, the United States, and South Africa. Part of the cast in the story, titled "The Man from Buenos Aires," also appear in *Tevye the Dairyman*.

Birmajer and I talked about the way Buenos Aires once nurtured a vi-brant Yiddish-language press. Novels, essays, stories, poems were churned out regularly. There was also a thriving theater scene. Klezmer music was ubiquitous. It is possible to understand the process of assimilation of Argen-tine Jews by looking at the transformation of those cultural manifestations.

For instance, there were tangos, *milongas, vidalitas,* and other traditional Argentine songs that were composed in Yiddish. Likewise, the famous play-wright Samuel Eichelbaum—the son of Russian Jews, immigrants that lived in Villa Domínguez, who died in 1967 at the age of seventy-three—wrote plays such as *Arón, el judío (Aaron, the Jew,* 1926) and *Underground* (1966) that were in a mix of Yiddish and Spanish that is essentially similar to to-day's Spanglish.

"*Casteidish*," Birmajer said. He was referring to a type of Yiddish that was native to Argentina, where it is also called Yidañol.

I added, "Words like *shmegege* for idiot, *putz* and *schmock* for penis, and *pipik* and *pupik* for belly button are examples of it."

I told him that when I was growing up in Mexico I was frequently exposed to a Mexican variety of Yiddish. Although in school I was taught "proper"

Yiddish, the generation of my grandparents would regularly switch from Yiddish to Spanish and vice versa, often in the same sentence. I put *proper* in quotes because the idea of propriety in Yiddish, in and of itself, is thorny, given that Yiddish is itself a bastardized language that sprang up around the thirteenth century in the vicinity of the Rhine River. It is a mixture, through code switching, between German and Hebrew, to which other ingredients were added as time went by.

In connection with Yiddish tangos, I mentioned Jevel Katz (better known by the Yiddish diminutive Jévele) who is one of the most successful Yiddish entertainers of all time in Argentina. I told Birmajer he was a favorite of mine. I have a tape of his music that was prepared for me by a friend of mine, Zachary Baker, a librarian at Stanford. Since then, I'm always eager to put my hands on anything connected to Katz, no matter the price.

I sang in Casteidish one of his famous stanzas:

> G'vald, yidn, *buena gente*,
> Ikh zukh a tsimer a *departamente*,
> Ver es veys, entfert mir *urgente*,
> Ikh muz zikh klaybn *inmediatamente!*

Making it understandable to non-Spanish and Yiddish speakers is a challenge because it loses its joie de vivre. Here is an attempt:

> G'vald, Jews, good folks,
> I'm looking for an apartment,
> If you know of one, answer me urgently,
> I've got to move immediately!

Jévele was known affectionately—but to his disliking—as "the Jewish Gardel," after Carlos Gardel, the French Argentine baritone who is the most important tango singer of all time. Like Jimi Hendrix, Katz always had a guitar with him. After his death in 1940, at the age of thirty-seven, the guitar was left to the Idish Wisnshaftlejer Institut (IWO; also known as YIVO, in English) in Buenos Aires. I might be wrong but I believe it was destroyed in the AMIA attack.

Tall and slim, with a charismatic smile, Katz would play in schools, in theaters, in bars. In the documentary *Jevel Katz y sus paisanos* (Jevel Katz and His Cohorts, 2002), Eliyahu Toker—who, like Birmajer, devoted his energy to celebrating El Once—remembered that, when he was a little boy, his father stormed into the house to announce, in sorrow, Katz's sudden death just as he was about to travel to New York City, in what promised to be a crossover tour to reach Jewish audiences in America. "Jévele has left us," Toker recalled hearing his father say.

He is buried in the Cementerio Judío in the neighborhood of Liniers, near Avenida Rivadavia, which is administered by AMIA. Years ago I saw a photograph of the funeral. I wondered, as I was talking to Birmajer, why Katz wasn't buried in La Recoleta Cemetery. If there is an Argentine Jewish icon, it is him. Later on I found out that there are no Jews buried in Recoleta. Katz passed away penniless. The cheapest tomb in Recoleta is substantially more expensive today than the minuscule apartment where he lived.

Birmajer said it made no sense. Katz might have been a jewel among Jews of the immigrant generation but he wasn't considered a national treasure.

Jévele had recently had an operation on his tonsils and had lost a lot of blood. At the time medical knowledge was limited and equipment was scarce and ineffectual. The doctor was unable to control the hemorrhaging, so during the funeral people called him a killer. Katz's tombstone has a guitar engraved on it, along with his photograph. Forty thousand people attended the service. I saw photographs of mourners at his funeral. Five years earlier Gardel had also died tragically, also at the height of his career, and his funeral also drew masses of followers. In his case it was an airplane crash. He was born in France but lived in Buenos Aires, on Calle Jean Jaures, near what is today the Abasto Shopping Mall (there's a street in the area named after him). His relationship with Argentina had always been difficult. Argentineans cried effusively the way only a lost hero is lamented. In the reports I've seen, the reaction to Katz was similar. "He wasn't only one of ours," a woman is quoted as saying. "Ketzele was us."

Unfortunately, he didn't record much. The pieces I've heard are often sung by other musicians. Katz adapted famous Spanish songs, not only tangos but also serenades, *rancheras*, fox-trots, vidalitas, and rumbas such as "La Cucaracha," "La Cumparsita," and "Manisero," originally from as far away as Cuba and Mexico. The songs describe the life of newcomers to Argentina finding a sense of place. One of them in particular, an early example and among his greatest hits, was "Ojo, mucho ojo." It was based on advice he had received when leaving Vilna for Buenos Aires, about, among other dangers, the Zwi Migdal organization. In the song Katz says, "Be careful, put *mucho ojo*, keep an eye open, so that you don't make a wrong move."

Other folk songs—like "De noche con un tranvía por Corrientes" (By night on a trolley on Corrientes Avenue), "Canning," "El gringo en la plaza,"

"Mi viaje a Tucumán" (My trip to Tucumán), "Un colono" (An agricultural settler), "Basavilbaso," and "Moisés Ville"—are all about agricultural landscapes in the hinterland. I expressed to Birmajer my enthusiasm with the connection: these songs now felt rooted to me. Like Bob Dylan, Katz was a *juglar*, the Spanish word for a minstrel. His travels took him from *pueblitos*, little towns in Entre Ríos, Santa Fe, far and beyond the country's borders. He performed as far away as Montevideo and Santiago de Chile.

In an essay Zachary Baker wrote called "The Streets of Buenos Aires: Jevel Katz and Yiddish Popular Culture in the Argentine Metropolis" (2004), the librarian looked for the singer's origins. He found them in the capital of Lithuania. Baker stated that "as many of his songs reveal, Jevel Katz owed a tremendous debt to the performance traditions of Jewish Eastern Europe, and more specifically, to the literary and theatrical heritage of his home town. Katz was after all a product of twentieth-century Vilna—a city that was steeped in the traditions of the Gaon, the *Haskalah* (Enlightenment), the Jewish labor movement, Zionism, and Yiddishism." He concluded: "Katz's trademark performance technique (drawing upon a wide gamut of the European vaudeville and cabaret traditions), the repertory that he created, the many genres and musical styles that he mastered and then parodied, the timbre of his voice, his use of multilingual rhymes and onomatopoeia, his choice of instrumental accompaniment—all of these together combined to create a uniquely Argentine Yiddish product."

"I don't know Yiddish as you do, Ilan, but Katz's Casteidish, like the Spanglish you love dearly, makes me think of Cocoliche," Birmajer announced.

I had heard the term *Cocoliche* before. It is used by Argentines to describe the pidgin language used by Italian immigrants and their descendants for approximately a hundred years, from 1870 to 1970. Birmajer mentioned Cocoliche terms that have made it into Argentine Spanish: *lonyipietro* (fool), *matina* (morning), *laburar* (to work), *salute* (cheers), *iguarda!* (look!), *facha* (face), *miti-miti* (half and half, fifty-fifty), *manyar* (to eat), and *fiaca* (laziness).

I told Birmajer that in New York City in the 1930s there had been something similar to Casteidish. It was called Yinglish. Upon first arriving from Warsaw and being exposed to it, Isaac Bashevis Singer purportedly suffered a writer's block. In interviews he claimed he couldn't write as a result of the language. He was extraordinarily prolific, and for him a writer's block didn't actually mean a complete shutdown. It is known that for a series of years Singer wrote for the Yiddish-language *Jewish Daily Forward* (in Yiddish, *Forverts*) all sorts of pieces under a variety of pseudonyms.

I asked Birmajer about Lunfardo, another Italian pidgin that was used by immigrants to Argentina. This was connected to the region of Lombardy. The *compadritos*—the working-class dwellers in the outskirts of Buenos Aires that Jorge Luis Borges (long my favorite Argentine literary figure and the reason I had been to Buenos Aires countless times before) uses as characters in his stories—communicate in Lunfardo.

"In the work of early Argentine Yiddish writers, a few speak in Yiddish, too," he replied.

We talked about a Borges story called "Emma Zunz," a tale of rape and revenge. The last words uttered by one of the characters before he is killed are in Yiddish. That character is Jewish—but not working-class, though. He is a well-to-do factory owner.

"Borges was a philo-Semite," I said. "He is the best Argentine writer and one of the best in the world. And though he wasn't Jewish, I think of him as the best Jewish Latin American writer. I have seen some of his work translated into Yiddish. In some sense these translations, and the ones I have seen of his books into Hebrew, are a way to fully bring Borges home—I mean, to a Jewish home."

Birmajer laughed.

"It would be funny," I said, "to encounter his oeuvre in Casteidish, don't you think?" But then I had a change of heart: "And make him sound like Jévele? Hmm. . . . Such is the precision of Borges's language in Spanish, maybe we should leave him as he is."

3.

It was close to noon when Birmajer and I made our way to the new, eight-story, modern AMIA building, built on the same site as the old one. I confess, this was the main purpose of my visit to El Once—to find the epicenter of ground zero. I had made an arrangement beforehand to visit it. I wanted to see how the facility had been rebuilt. I was particularly eager to visit its library.

Since Birmajer had errands to do, we said goodbye on Avenida Corrientes and Calle Ayacucho.

Before I made it to my destination, I stopped for a bite at a local restaurant. I ate an empanada, a *milanesa* (breaded beef) with French fries, and a flan with dulce de leche, along with a Quilmes, a local beer.

When time came to ask for the check, I asked the waitress if she knew how many blocks away the AMIA was.

"That terrorist attack was a shame," she said. Slim and coquettish, she looked to be in her late forties. "It will never get solved. Our corrupt politicians will go far away to protect their cover-up. *La impunidad*—impunity. As long as justice isn't served, it will happen again. But people don't care. It's Argentina, the land of thieves."

She asked me where I was from. I told her Mexico.

"Then you know how it feels," she responded. "Do you know how many times the Constitution has been rewritten in this country? Half a dozen times. Actually, I can't even tell you how many. The same people who re-write it are the ones who abuse it the most."

4.

The new AMIA building was built in 1999 to replace the one before. The administrative offices of the Argentine Jewish community are still found on these premises. Outside there is a memorial to the victims of the terrorist attack.

As I admired the premises, I couldn't stop the picture of the façade of the destroyed building from popping into my mind. I had seen black-and-white photographs of it countless times. The entrance originally had an imposing, wide, black-marble frame, on top of which was engraved a white Star of David. The large opening doors had an Art Deco style. I knew that, after the 1994 explosion, the ruins were disposed of in a number of places. Some were thrown into the River Plate, which divides Argentina and Uruguay and has major ports in their respective capitals.

The River Plate is also where the military junta disposed of a substantial number of the desaparecidos, while some of them were still alive. The military junta would tie a heavy object—a stone, a ball and chain—to one of the victim's feet before pushing them off an airplane. Years later, as part of the reconciliation period in which Argentina made an honest attempt to come to terms with the atrocities of the past, a memorial called Espacio Memoria was built on the edge of the river. The photographer Marcelo Brodsky, whose younger brother, Fernando, was among the desaparecidos, stewarded the creation of the memorial. During the construction, a few fragments of that Star of David from the AMIA façade were fished out from the river.

I had also seen an album with photographs of the faces of the eighty-five victims. They looked like people I knew in Mexico: cousins, schoolmates, old girlfriends. I was haunted by these images to such a degree that I felt as if the site was inhabited by ghosts. I could see them schmoozing near me, inviting me to follow them into corridors, smiling, never asking for pity. I was never frightened. On the contrary, seeing them gave me an inner peace. I knew that every year, on July 18 at 9:53 am, people hold a moment of silence in front of the AMIA. The next one would be in about a month from my visit. Maybe the ghosts were getting ready for the occasion.

People were friendly. I saw the executive offices, an auditorium, and different areas for children, young people, and the elderly. I am always impressed by the degree to which Jewish communities get organized. Compared to other headquarters throughout the continent, this was state-of-the-art.

In one office I went into I talked with a woman who handled a project called Villa 31. She said the name referred to a shantytown where Jewish and Catholic organizations cooperate on a soup kitchen. "Over two hundred people have meals there. It is a form of *Tikkun Olam*, meaning an effort to mend the world. The project also includes educational activities and pro-grams to stimulate community-based entrepreneurial projects."

On the fourth floor I spent some time at the Marc Turkow Center, which is devoted to preserving and disseminating archive material on Argentine Jews (Turkow was a journalist who wrote in Yiddish and Spanish). Among other things, the center has a visual archive of the agricultural colonias and an impressive collection of material related to the AMIA attack.

As it happened I came across a small exhibit, only a few illustrated pan-els, on Ansky's *The Dybbuk*. To an extent Ansky's efforts in *The Enemy at His Pleasure* was the forerunner of YIVO. This realization generated in me a feeling of confidence. My stroll through El Once isn't about tourism, I told myself, but about preservation.

After a few minutes of reconnaissance I chatted with a staff member, a librarian. I asked her about IWO—the center of research on Yiddish culture originally founded in Vilna, Poland, in 1925 (also known as YIVO)—whose focus was to study the language, religion, and history of Eastern European Jews. During the Second World War, the collection was looted by the Nazis. In response, the center relocated to New York. The Buenos Aires branch was established in 1928.

She told me that IWO wasn't far away, in the Casa Simón Dubnow, at Calle Ayacucho #483. I talked for a while about Samuel Rollansky. Known as the custodian of Yiddish civilization in Argentina, he helped create the IWO library at the old AMIA, which held the largest collection of Judaica in Latin America. He became its director until his death in 1995. I knew that he himself was the owner of a personal library with approximately thirteen thousand volumes.

I told the librarian that I found Rollansky to be a heroic figure. For this reason, before my visit to Argentina I had tried to put my hand on anything I could that related to him. I knew that he had been a columnist for *Di Prese* and *Di Idishe Zeitung*, the two Yiddish-language daily newspapers in Buenos Aires, and that he had combined this with his literary activity (writing novels, stories, and journalism) and his role as an educator. He established preschool Jewish programs and worked as a docent for almost forty years.

I knew that Borges was Rollansky's friend and that Borges telephoned him every year around Rosh Hashanah to wish him a happy new year and to talk for a few minutes about Baruch Spinoza, whom the two saw as the philosopher who laid the foundation of modern secularism. But Spinoza was also interested in algebra and in the science of optics. Borges once wrote a lucid poem about him polishing, alone in the darkness of his own room, one of the first lenses to be used to improve sight. And Borges used the mathematical infrastructure of Spinoza's *The Ethics* (1677) to craft a detective story called "Death and the Compass," which is set in a semifictional town with elements borrowed from Amsterdam, where Spinoza lived for many years. The story has an assortment of Jewish characters, including a few Hasidim. I could imagine the ways in which these works by Borges emerged from his telephone conversations with Rollansky.

A polyglot renaissance man, Rollansky was a child when, at the start of the First World War, the Germans invaded Warsaw, the city where he was born in 1902. They immediately imposed the teaching of German on the local population. For Rollansky this wasn't a form of opprobrium. On the contrary, it was a gift. It allowed him access to German literature, which left a deep mark on him. After each of the Hebrew lessons he took while preparing for his Bar Mitzvah, he would stop at a German bookstore to read Schiller, Heinrich Heine, and other German poets.

His immigration to Argentina came about circuitously. His mother wanted to send him to Brussels or Paris to study medicine, but Rollansky preferred to devote himself to letters. Having read somewhere that one of his idols—I. L. Peretz, a major Yiddish intellectual (when he died in 1915 a hundred thousand people attended his funeral, and Rollansky was among them)—had considered moving to Argentina, Rollansky became fascinated with the possibility too. Peretz never made good on the idea. Rollansky did.

At the end of the 1930s Rollansky had come to realize that the war in Europe would have terrible consequences for the Jews. He thought Yiddish was in danger. This fear remained with him all his life. Aside from the directorship of IWO, in 1957 he started his most ambitious project: the publication of the one hundred volumes of "Masterpieces of Yiddish Literature."

Nothing like it had ever been done anywhere on the globe. He fought against all odds, and in the end he achieved his objective. It was called *Musteverk*. In my house I have every single volume.

After I talked about them, the librarian brought out a few sample volumes, and we looked at them together. I told her that it was an uneven effort: the selection criteria were not always clear, and Rollansky almost never gives the original source of publication or why omissions or modifications were implemented. Still, taking into account the financial and logistical limitations he faced (he had to travel extensively to all sorts of countries, from the United States and Canada to France and Israel, to fund-raise as well as to gather material), the series is an astonishing achievement.

I added one more fact that I thought the librarian might enjoy. Throughout his life, Rollansky nurtured a love that is quintessential to any serious Argentine public intellectual: the love of fútbol. Having been exposed to the game by his brother-in-law, he was a lifelong ticket holder of the Club Atlético Independiente de Avellaneda. Even though he had a journalist's pass, he always preferred to watch the games from the stalls, where the real fans were to be found. And even though he always looked strange there, dressed as he was as a Polish dandy, with his impeccable suits and ironed shirts with starched collars, he exhaled a sportsmanlike *caballerosidad*, a gentlemanliness that was admired by many. If the rival made a good play, or if the opponent made a showy *gol*, Rollansky believed it was deserving of applause, no matter what. And he was convinced that proof you're a true fútbol fan is the fact that, when your team performs poorly, you have the guts to criticize it.

I had been told by Rollansky's grandson Eliezer Nowodworski, an interpreter who lives in Tel-Aviv and a close friend of mine, that the AMIA terrorist attack found Rollansky at home, recovering from a cardiac condition. Nowodworski described the moment to me. "I spoke with him minutes after the explosion. It was a few blocks away from his house. It had not yet been confirmed that the attack had taken place on Calle Pasteur. I was on line with him when the TV informed the world that indeed the target had been the administrative headquarters of the Jewish community. IWO was on the third floor and part of the fourth and my grandfather had his office there. It was wrenching. No doubt the attack would become the cause of his deteriorating health in the months to come. He died seven months later, before his ninety-third birthday."

The librarian stated that the collection at the IWO library in the old AMIA building had contained about seventy-five thousand items. It included volumes that had been brought secretly from Europe after the Kristal-nacht in November 1938, when Hitler declared war against the Jews, not only destroying synagogues and businesses but making bonfires in which thousands of Jewish books were turned into ashes. About half of the AMIA collection disappeared. Among them were about two hundred rare books, some handwritten and dated to the seventeenth century, others among the first books published in Yiddish in the New World. The explosion also destroyed posters and playbills for Yiddish theater in Argentina when its equivalent in New York was still incipient. There were letters from Jews attempting to escape Nazi Germany. And documents related to the Semana Trágica and to the Zwi Migdal of the type now in the archive of the Marc Turkow Center.

In response, Rollansky said to the *New York Times*, in what would be one of his last public statements: "Our history is burned without even a war. We are witnessing an inquisitorial act." (Nowodworski believes his grandfather was misquoted. The answer he really gave was "I was invited to my own funeral.")

The librarian told me that after the AMIA attack, some forty thousand volumes were recovered, thanks to the help of hundreds of volunteers. Between 2010 and 2013, the organization embarked on a project of digitization. "That way future generations would be assured access to the past," she said.

As I browsed through the volumes of the *Musteverk*, I thought of the history of book burning in Latin America. The region competes with any other in the world in this infamy. With the abundance of dictators (some of whom came to power through elections) from Rafael Trujillo of the Dominican Republic to Hugo Chávez of Venezuela, and even under General Francisco Franco in Spain, books, in spite of the fact that illiteracy is rampant, are seen as dangerous objects. In Barcelona, Franco's troupes burned the library of Pompeu Fabra, the lexicographer whose efforts contributed to the normative reform of the contemporary Catalan language. It is said that the burning took place while they shouted "¡Abajo la inteligencia!" (Down with intelligence!). In Argentina during Juan Domingo Perón's time, the library of Casa del Pueblo, a socialist organization, went up in flames. Jorge Rafael Videla, another Argentine dictator (he ruled from 1976 to 1981), was fond of burning of books. So was Chile's *líder* Augusto Pinochet. And in 2003, in Castro's Cuba, independent librarians were put on trial and their books burned because they were deemed counterrevolutionary. All of which made me see the destruction of the YIVO collection as an event of seismic proportions.

Either the librarian or me, I forget which of us, recalled what the German poet Heinrich Heine stated once: "where men burn books, they will burn people in the end."

Grateful for the encounter, I said goodbye. Outside, I stopped for a few minutes at a memorial for the AMIA victims. I wanted to put a pebble on it.

I looked around. A protective wall surrounded the new AMIA building. I hadn't noticed it when I arrived. There was a row of white cement cones separating the building from the street.

Suddenly a bystander uttered a few words. At first I couldn't understand her. "The white cones are mezuzah," she repeated. "They protect the sanctity of this site."

I found the idea intriguing. She added something that sounded like a Hasidic saying: *Siempre se puede estar peor*, You can always do worse."

"You mean Jews?"

"Suffering makes Jews sharper."

5.

I returned to El Once a week later. This time I was intent on exploring the Jewish religious life of the neighborhood.

During my earlier walks I had seen a number of orthodox Jews. Birmajer told me they were only one of the many different sects of Judaism in the area, including agnostics and atheists. He said these brands didn't always match the taxonomy used in the United States to describe Jewish affiliations: Orthodox, Conservative, Reform, and Reconstructionist. The most visible are orthodox and conservative, the latter containing various degrees of endorsement of traditional values.

In this regard it is important to note that Argentina has the only rabbinical school in Latin America where rabbis, cantors, and other religious leaders are ordained whose careers take them all over the region and beyond, from Lima and Havana to Boston, Houston, and Los Angeles. Called El Seminario, short for Seminario Rabínico Latinoamericano, it was founded in 1962 by an American, Rabbi Marshall T. Meyer, and it is the cradle of the Conservative Movement in the Spanish-speaking world. But El Seminario is in Barrancas de Belgrano neighborhood, not in El Once.

I had gone there a few days before and was amazed by the sophistication of the place. It is a multilevel building on Calle 11 de Septiembre #1669, with a sanctuary, a library, classrooms, and an assortment of offices. Still, for me, having studied at the JTS, which is made of a group of buildings taking over a considerable portion of a block on Upper Broadway not far from the

Hudson River in New York City, El Seminario seemed to me not only small but parochial.

The reason I was expecting a more grandiose facility is due, in part, to Rabbi Meyer's preeminence throughout Latin America. Truth is, I wasn't interested in the place itself but, rather, in the man behind it. He was born in 1928 and a graduate of Dartmouth College. Rabbi Meyer's stature in Buenos Aires is legendary. In 1983 when Raúl Alfonsín, the first democratic leader of Argentina after the dictatorship, took power, he organized a Comisión Nacional sobre la Desaparición de Personas, a commission endowed with investigating the fate of the desaparecidos. Rabbi Meyer was named a member. The result of that commission was a famous report released in 1984 called *Nunca más* (Never again). It opened the door for trials of the military junta.

Rabbi Meyer was also the founder of the Congregación Bet El, also in Belgrano, which is the model for other similar congregations throughout Latin America, including the one my family belonged to in the Mexico City neighborhood of Polanco in the 1970s. The original Bet El in Buenos Aires was affiliated to the Conservative Movement in 1935, but by the mid-1950s it had lost touch with its mission somewhat. In need of guidance, the leader asked Rabbi Abraham Joshua Heschel—a German-born philosopher who taught at the JTS in New York and who by then was already a significant activist in the civil rights movement—to send someone to Buenos Aires who could redirect the congregation. Rabbi Heschel sent Rabbi Meyer, who arrived with his wife, Naomi.

Rabbi Meyer was a defiant voice during the Dirty War, supporting families whose relatives had been kidnapped by the military and helping in the release of political prisoners. He also campaigned for the Mothers of the Plaza de Mayo. Years later I met him at B'nai Jeshurun, the synagogue in New York's West 88th Street, where he settled after he left Argentina and from where he continued to do activist work. Thanks to him, the ties between JTS and El Seminario as well as Bet El in Buenos Aires became strong. A few Argentine rabbis started to be ordained at JTS too. When I emigrated from Mexico, it was to do graduate work in Jewish philosophy at JTS. Several of my schoolmates were Argentines. A couple of them ended up as assistants at B'nai Jeshurun, and when Rabbi Meyer died suddenly of cancer in 1993, they succeeded him.

Unfortunately, Rabbi Meyer didn't publish many of his sermons and other pieces. Years ago I contacted Naomi with the hope of looking at his archive and with her permission bringing out a selection of his writing. I know I was not the first to conceive of the idea. But I thought at least I could make it happen. Naomi refused. I was told by several acquaintances that, in spite of Rabbi Meyer's illustrious career in Argentine, she may harbor negative feelings toward the Jewish community there.

In part, this is connected with the exact circumstances of Rabbi Meyer's departure from Buenos Aires, which are still surrounded in mystery. He generated animosity among the most traditional forces within the Argentine Jewish community, around 1961 and 1962 when he first tried to bring the Conservative Movement to a temple in Calle Libertad. The move promoted accusations of him being "the Communist rabbi" and a homosexual. The accusations were published by Nissim Elnecavé in the weekly *La Luz*. In the 1980s accusations of sexual misconduct were again leveled at Rabbi Meyer. This forced him and his family to leave in an atmosphere of scandal.

At B'nai Jeshurun I once heard him deliver a sermon during Kol Nidre, the most sacred of prayers in the Jewish calendar, delivered at the beginning of Yom Kippur. The sermon was stunning in both tempo and content. If memory serves me right, the prayer deals with man's responsibility to find God not only in acts of kindness but in efforts at social justice. Doing nothing when one sees a homeless person on the streets of New York, he said, is to become complicit in that man's misery. Man cannot navigate existence without a vision. In this sense man is God's envoy on earth. He quoted the Talmud and made reference to several Hasidic masters. To be Jewish is not to wait for the world to come. Ours is the only world that matters. I still look at this sermon as a turning point in my life: it made me want to devote myself to the study of Jewish sources.

Among the only pieces I've ever read by Rabbi Meyer is a speech called "Thoughts on Latin America," which is included in the anthology *The Scroll and the Cross: 1,000 Years of Jewish-Hispanic Relations* (2001). The speech was delivered to the American Rabbinical Assembly in the 1980s, just after he moved to New York. He describes himself as "a refugee in my own country at the present moment." These were the Reagan years. The United States and Latin America appeared to exist in altogether different realms. Rabbi Meyer talked of the misunderstandings among Americans concerning the "people down there" and, vice versa, the way Latin Americans simplified the complexities of Americans.

It strikes me that, in the absence of his work, the place to look for Rabbi Meyer's theology is in Heschel's canon. Heschel's theology was focused not on God's actions but on man. I once saw a TV interview with him where he was asked to explain the Judaic concept of man. He responded eloquently, offering an insightful interpretation of a crucial line in *Genesis*. His sentences are pregnant with meaning. Rabbi Meyer seems to have been attuned to that meaning.

"We start with the concept that God is involved in human life," Heschel said. "This means that the primary task of man is to realize that God has a stake in his life. We also believe that the Jewish people are not the same since Sinai. They are called upon to carry out the commandments of the Torah, the Law. Man is by his very being in travail with God's dreams and designs. In the Bible, we read about the creation of all other things: 'And then God said. And so it was.' But when God came to create man, He first had a vision of man. He said: 'Let us make man in our vision.' In other words, the vision of man preceded the creation of man. We may say that God has a vision or expectation of man. It is our task to recover it. That's why man is a messenger for God—*the* messenger. God is in our midst. Our most important problem is the problem of responsiveness, obedience to the Law, openness, listening to Moses, Amos, Rabbi Akiva, our privilege is being a part of the Jewish community, past and present."

I talked to a number of rabbinical students in El Seminario. They told me that most Argentine Jews who are affiliated to the Conservative Movement don't live in El Once. But a few still do business in the neighborhood, at times interacting, though not frequently, with the ultra-orthodox, who in recent decades have built yeshivas, children's schools, ritual baths, and other institutions in Buenos Aires, including in El Once.

Back in El Once, I stopped in a kosher butcher shop. Argentina is famous the world over for its *asado*. The word means "grilled barbecued meat." *Asado* denotes not only the wide range of grilling techniques used in the country (as well as in Uruguay, Paraguay, and Chile) but the social event attending a barbecue. In restaurants and in the countryside meat was cooked on a campfire, I had eaten delicious short ribs, roast veal, sweetbreads, and black pudding. One of my favorite delicacies was *choripán*, a simple sandwich made with just chorizo in a slice of baguette.

Before my trip I watched a documentary called *Everything about Asado* (2016). Inside the butcher shop, I spent a few minutes studying the way a couple of butchers talked with customers, cut the meat, and packaged it for them. One of them asked me if I needed help. I told him I was just looking.

"This isn't a theater. That's where people go to look!"

I told him I was in El Once as a tourist. That I was a Jew from Mexico City and I occasionally bought from kosher butchers there.

"No comparison," he stated. "Argentinean meat is the best."

"I know. . . . If you're kosher in Argentina, you probably can't eat all the varieties of *asado* available to the common folk."

"Well, not everything. The laws of Kashrut are strict for a reason. Most of what Argentines eat is unhealthy. Believe me, an Orthodox Jew in Buenos Aires eats very well. You should try different Jewish restaurants. Meshiguene. Al Galope. There's even a kosher McDonald's. Actually, don't eat in restaurants. Get yourself invited to a nice Jewish home. You'll dance with happiness!"

I asked if he had seen the documentary about *asado*.

"Yeah, it's for tourists like you. It shows too much. See this butcher shop? It's better if you forget it. The images aren't pleasant. And sight and taste go together. When you eat, you shouldn't be thinking about where food comes from. You should concentrate on what's on your plate. It will taste better!"

After I left the butcher shop, I wandered aimlessly, often touching on Avenida Corrientes. I remembered that Birmajer had talked about the intolerance of modern fashion among the ultra-orthodox. "They see secular Jews as lost souls on the way to perdition. That's why they proselytize. They believe the Messiah will only come when the lost sheep of the people of Israel come back—men dressed up in caftans, fur hats, the whole *meggileh*."

Birmajer said that mixed marriage was more common than ever and Jewish education in decline. Conversely, there was also a renewal in Argentine Jewish identity that pushed it beyond traditional ties to Yiddish, the Holocaust, and the state of Israel. He talked of a revival of Sephardic life—that is, an attempt by Ashkenazim to connect with the Jewish roots of Spain, including a growing interest in Ladino.

I found this interesting. As I looked at the people walking next to me, I wondered about their origins. Unlike Mexico, and in contrast to what historians such as Boleslao Lewin have suggested, Argentina didn't have a large Crypto-Jewish population during the colonial period. The explanation, I told myself, has to do with geographical location. The Virreinato del Río de la Plata, which is the foundation of modern Buenos Aires, was established in 1776 near the end of the colonial period. It was an insignificant town, and so was the branch of the Inquisition that functioned in it.

I thought of the countless ways in which Argentina and Mexico are dissimilar. Mexico City was perhaps the most colonial capital in the Americas. Its baroque architecture is extraordinary. And so are the ways in which indigenous and European customs became juxtaposed over time. Yet in contrast with Argentina, at the cultural level, the Jewish presence in Mexico is minuscule, at least to the naked eye. One needs to dig deep in order to find its roots.

I was about to call it a day when, approaching a police station, I was mesmerized by a sign outside that read "Policía" in three languages: Spanish, Hebrew, and English. I had never seen anything similar addressing a governmental entity in the whole Spanish-speaking world.

6.

Next day, I made my way to the synagogue on Calle Lavalle, which has a lovely stained-glass window depicting the biblical scene of Jacob's ladder. And, as I returned to Avenida Corrientes, I stopped to buy a soda. On the way out of the store, I met a Talmudic student. A mulatto, he was on his way to a class.

I had a copy of the Isaac Bashevis Singer book in Spanish that Birmajer had given me as a present. He saw it and asked if I was a tourist.

"Almost," I replied.

Red-haired, he was dressed in a black suit with a white shirt. His brown beard was long and tangled. *Peyes* (side locks) were rolled around his ears. I could see a velvet yarmulke under his black fedora hat. He gave me the impression of being in his mid thirties. His name was Shaul.

"What do you mean?" he said.

"I'm writing a book."

"What kind?"

"A travel book. About the Jews of Latin America."

"Where have you been?"

"I'm just starting. El Once is my first place."

Shaul told me he was originally from the southeastern city of La Plata, he had moved to Buenos Aires after studying engineering at the university. He had found the cycles of student life vacuous. He had been married but said he didn't have children. His parents, with whom he lived again for a brief period after his divorce until a few years ago, were Jewish but they described themselves as agnostic. Two of his sisters lived nearby. In his own spiritual awakening, Shaul had persuaded the entire family to light candles and, even reluctantly, to sing Musaf, Shacharit, Mincha, and Maariv, all prayers in the Shabbat liturgy. One thing led to another and soon Shaul found himself interested in rabbinical debates. He then met a proselytizing fellow in La Plata who fed him information about a Buenos Aires yeshiva, and that's where he ended up.

Shaul talked to me of the relevance of religious life for Argentine Jews.

He said the Southern Cone wasn't known for its theologians but this didn't matter because Talmudic debates, strictly speaking, were ahistorical. In other words, it mattered little where a rabbi was from.

"How many people know Rashi lived in France at the time of the Crusades?" He was referring to Shlomo Yitzchaki, the tenth-century exegete— arguably the most famous of the commentators of the Babylonian Talmud.

Shaul added: "These exegetes talk to one another as if they were in the same room. Truth is, they are separated by centuries."

He was excited about what he was telling me. He lambasted secularism. "It pushes people from the right path. People don't believe in anything anymore. They are incredulous. Miracles are reduced to scientific events. It's a shame!"

I wanted to ask him about being mulatto. It's not often one comes across a Jewish mulatto in Latin America—maybe in Venta Prieta, Mexico, or among the Jewish converts in Bello, near Medellín, Colombia. But I felt uncomfortable. In the United States race is a hot topic. It isn't the same in the Hispanic world.

After a pause, Shaul told me a story about the Ba'al Shem Tov, the founder of Hasidic Judaism in eighteenth-century Poland.

"Once a scientist went to the Ba'al Shem Tov. He told him: 'I know you're a holy man. But there is no holiness in the world. I know you believe the Shabbat is a sacred day. But all days are sacred. I know you're convinced the people of Israel crossed the Red Sea on their way out of Pharaoh's Egypt. And that the Red Sea opened up precisely at the moment they needed to escape. But such are the laws of nature that the Red Sea was meant to part just at that moment. Truth is, there are no miracles.' To which the Ba'al Shem Tov responded: 'Who created nature? And who decided to make it so that precisely when the people of Israel needed to cross, the Red Sea would allow them? Nature itself, its cycles, its coincidences, is the miracle!"

I asked Shaul if he knew of any important Jewish thinkers in Latin America. "Yes," he said, and he mentioned the work of a major Jewish thinker he considered Latin American, although he was from elsewhere and at the time of his death, in 1968, at the age of seventy-three, he had left no writing whatsoever, at least none that was accounted for.

Shaul didn't know his full name. He mentioned that the thinker had gone through the Shoah, French was his native language, although he spoke Yiddish, Hebrew, Polish, German, Russian, Romanian, Hungarian, Czech, and countless other languages. He was buried in Montevideo.

For some reason I had the premonition that maybe this sage was the man that showed up in my dream. I said I wanted to know more, but Shaul was evasive. He became suspicious of me, as if the information he was offering could be used against him and other ultra-orthodox Jews. This became clear when I asked him about the specific yeshiva he was a member of. The Yeshiva Guedola? Or Jafetz Jaim?

He changed the topic, wanting to know more about my book.

"Do you have an itinerary?"

"Not really. I want to visit all sorts of communities, some mainstream and others faraway. Do you know Ari Shavit, author of *My Promised Land: The Triumph and Tragedy of Israel* (2013)? Shavit is a columnist for the center-left Israeli newspaper *Haaretz* and was accused of sexual abuse in the early days of the #MeToo movement. The book is a comprehensive insider's history of Israel. Mine is along the same lines but for Latin America." I paused. "Or, using another coordinate, a bit like Benjamin of Tudela, the medieval traveler."

"He was from Navarra in Spain? Nathan Alterman wrote in Hebrew a poem about him." Shaul was referring to one of the foundational poets of the Hebrew renaissance.

"Benjamin of Tudela visited Asia and Africa in the twelfth century, before Marco Polo set sail."

"Where are you from?"

"Mexico."

"Why are you interested in the Jewish communities of Latin America? It would be better to leave us alone. We don't want unnecessary attention."

Then he switched gears. "Have you heard of Monsieur Chouchani?"

"No. Who is he?"

"He isn't anymore. Monsieur Chouchani died in the late 1960s. He is buried in the Jewish cemetery of Montevideo. He had a portentous memory. And was a boundless Jewish scholar. He had memorized the Mishna from the first letter to the last. He could quote any portion on the fly. I don't know why but maybe . . ."

"Maybe what?"

"Maybe you're looking for him without knowing it. He might be your man."

"In what sense?"

"I'm telling you that I don't know. I just sense it . . ."

At this point, it looked to me as if Shaul was showing signs of paranoia. He said he wasn't actually from La Plata but from Tucumán, in northern Argentina, about thirteen hundred kilometers from Buenos Aires. Couldn't

I detect it from his accent? I responded that it was easy for me to identify Argentine parlance but that fine-tuning the origin of a specific accent wasn't in my purview.

He laughed heartily. Then, abruptly, Shaul said that he was late. He was expected at a Talmud class and needed to get there as soon as possible. And, bam! just as suddenly as he had appeared, Shaul vanished into thin air.

7.

A few nights later I went to Teatro La Plaza, in Avenida Corrientes and Montevideo, to see some stand-up comedy with Roberto Moldavsky. A bearded fifty-five-year-old in a T-shirt, Moldavsky entertained the audience with jokes about circumcisions, *shikses* (gentile women), what one does in the shower, and corruption in Argentine politics.

Humor is an invaluable door to understanding culture. But it opens to a series of rooms that require patience to be appreciated in full. It is easy to think that everyone laughs at the same jokes. We don't. Jokes are culturally specific. This is particularly the case among Jews. For instance, Ashkenazi humor and Sephardic humor are different. The former is about angst, about the feeling of being displaced, of becoming a target. It is a humor that has much to do with the instability of modernity. And it is about the tension between the individual and the collective. Sephardic humor is less nuanced, more restrained. It is not about resignation but about compliance.

Stand-up in particular is an Ashkenazi trade. American Jews have perfected it. Its power is found in the act of reimagining the therapist's couch as a form of expiation and making that expiation public. The audience at Moldavsky's routine I assumed was made of third-generation Argentine Jews. If there were goyim, I didn't see them. Those present had an inside track that as an outsider I didn't. They understood his taxonomy. He talked about *bris* (circumcisions), about shikses, about fasting at Yom Kippur—all adolescent banter. Moldavsky could have been at a Bar Mitzvah. Or at a Jewish wedding. Maybe that's how the comedian made his living: paid by wealthy Jews to entertain the crowd on occasions that over time have lost their cultural meaning.

I felt as if I was wasting my time. Still, this type of performance, I told myself, is only possible in Buenos Aires, where the nation's pop culture makes room for a Jewish sensibility. It wouldn't be possible in, say, Mexico, Chile, or Cuba, where the Jewish presence is demographically insignificant. The gags made me realize that although the American Jewish stand-up tradition and its aftermath—from Jackie Mason and Woody Allen to Jerry

Seinfeld—have traveled successfully from the fringes of ethnic humor (what is known as the Borscht Belt) to the mainstream, no equivalent exists in the Spanish-speaking ecosystem.

After the show I met Daniel Divinsky for dessert. The founder and for decades (along with his then wife, Kuki Miller) the editorial director of Ediciones de la Flor, he was a veritable powerhouse in the Argentine publishing industry. And he had achieved his success without fully sacrificing his Jewishness. The backlist of Ediciones de la Flor included novels, memoirs, and other books by Argentine Jewish authors as well as translations of Jewish authors from around the world.

The most important items in Divinsky's catalogue were the works of Joaquín Salvador Lavado (aka Quino), the creator of *Mafalda*, which is arguably the best political cartoon in the Spanish-speaking orbit. Syndicated in newspapers between 1964 and 1973 and still serialized in dozens of them, Mafalda is a six-year-old girl who obsessively reflects on world affairs, politics, and philosophical issues. Such is her fame that in 2009 a life-sized statue of the character was installed in the neighborhood of San Telmo where Quino lived.

Except for the first five installments, Divinsky published all the Mafalda books: ten volumes, plus compendiums of the greatest hits and other commemorative editions. A lawyer by profession, he corresponded with me over the years. I knew he was already at the end of his career. And indeed not long after our meeting he was forced out of his company, by none other than his wife, with whom he got into a nasty divorce.

He reminisced about his life in the business, how difficult it was to make a profit, and yet how important it remained to keep quality humorous material on the Argentine book market. He had started in another publishing house called Jorge Alvarez, and he and Alvarez made a partnership to found Ediciones de la Flor. Pressed by the need for cash in an inflation-driven Argentina, Divinsky slowly took over as Alvarez sought better business opportunities in the world of rock music. Signing Quino was Alvarez's stroke of luck. Divinsky inherited Quino and subsequently signed up a slew of other illustrators such as Fontanarrosa, Caloi, Liniers, Sendra, and Maitena. During the Dirty War, the ideological content of his books meant he had to seek exile in Venezuela.

He said to me: "I don't know why but Jewish books don't sell in Argentina, even though Jews are among the most voracious readers in Argentina. It is different in the United States. And France. Of course, compared to other parts of Latin America, at least there's interest here, though the thermometer's needle doesn't move much. Maybe if there's a political scandal. Jacobo Timerman's memoir *Prisoner without a Name, Cell without a Number* is an exception. Is it that *porteño* Jews have figured out how to circulate the same copy a thousand times, like *Samizdat* literature under Soviet rule? I'm kidding. And it can't be libraries either because not even teachers use them. Again, I'm joking. But I'm also serious."

8.

My next chapter within Argentina was to go in pursuit of the places where Jorge Luis Borges—who, arguably, was Buenos Aires's most important citizen of the twentieth century—had spent most of his life.

As I had told Birmajer at one point during our conversations, Borges is the Latin American writer that I feel the closest kinship to. But this alone doesn't justify the trip. Throughout his life Borges was obsessed with Jewish themes, *lo judío*. He was friends with prominent Jewish writers in Argentina, lectured on a variety of Jewish topics, and inserted a variety of Jewish motifs and references, sometimes overtly and others tacitly, in his oeuvre. For all these reasons, in my estimation he is also the perfect way to explore Jewish Buenos Aires.

The first time I traveled to the city was in 1986. I was twenty-five. After a life of reading him, I wanted to talk to Borges personally. I would knock at his door. He was known to accept visitors. Having become blind around the age of fifty he would ask them to read for him from specific volumes in his library.

I remember the day perfectly. It was June 16, 1986. I woke up early and took a shower. Before I made my way to his apartment on Calle Maipu #994, I stopped by a newsstand on the corner of Calles Suipacha and Corrientes, near the modest hotel in the neighborhood of La Recoleta where I was staying.

Surprised, I read the unequivocal headlines: "Borges muere en Ginebra" (Borges dies in Geneva).

He had passed away the previous morning in Geneva, Switzerland, purposely far away from home, since he was disappointed with Argentina, a country that, at the end of the twentieth century, seemed to him parochial.

I was deeply disappointed. To cure myself of the grief, I retraced his tracks while reciting to myself lines of his work I had memorized a while back.

He himself had taken daily strolls through Buenos Aires with an assortment of companions—from his second wife, María Kodama, to students, friends, and editors.

Back in the city after almost thirty years, I decided to retrace my path, finding hints of him wherever I could.

It wasn't difficult. I first went to the San Telmo neighborhood where the old Biblioteca Nacional, the National Library, used to be. It was established in 1801 and located in Calle México #564, and Borges was the director of the library in 1955. It is now the National Center of Music.

Borges followed a distinguished line of directors before him that included the French-born writer Paul Groussac (who, like Borges, became blind) as well as two Jewish intellectuals, Héctor Yanover and Alberto Manguel, author of *A History of Reading* (1997). Some of the directors were acerbic anti-Semites, including Gustavo Martínez Zuviría (whom Borges loathed), the author of a couple of hideous books, *El cahal* and *Oro* (*Kahal* and *Gold*, both 1935).

I then took the subway to Plaza San Martín and walked a short block to the apartment building on Calle Maipú where Borges lived on the sixth floor for four decades, on and off.

And I made my way to Palermo, a neighborhood he frequently talked about in his lectures and conversations, and even in his own oeuvre. It was in a bookstore there that I came across and quickly purchased a copy of his 1955 two-volume anthology of gaucho poetry, which he coedited with his friend Adolfo Bioy Casares.

Borges wrote a number of moving pieces on Argentine history and culture. There is, for instance, the story "Man on a Street Corner," about a compadrito, a typical young man of modest means at the dawn of the twentieth century. A handful of poems deal with the tango, gauchos, and national heroes such as Sarmiento. And the famous story "The Aleph," with the climatic movement of it taking place in a Buenos Aires basement. But a lot of his work is about non-Argentine topics such as Homer's *The Odyssey*, Shakespeare's plays, *Don Quixote*, the Irish War of Independence, and Jewish themes, as in the case of the story "The Secret Miracle," about a Kafka-like playwright who makes a bargain with God.

Borges was among the first to translate Franz Kafka into Spanish. He wrote on Isaac Babel and Shmuel Josef Agnon. And he nurtured close friendships with several Jewish intellectuals, aside from Rollansky, including Alberto Gerchunoff, author of *Los gauchos judíos de La Pampa* (*The Jewish Gauchos of the Pampas*, 1910), who is considered the father of Argentine Jewish literature.

For Borges, Jews were at once insiders and outsiders in Argentine society. This wasn't a form of betrayal. Just the opposite. It allows them a certain objectivity that is useful in making innovations, because, as Borges argued in "The Argentine Writer and Tradition," "they act within that culture and at the same time do not feel bound to it by any special devotion."

There is a little-known mini essay he wrote that merits mention. It is called "I, a Jew" (in Spanish, "Yo, judío"), and it was published in the April 1934 issue of the Buenos Aires magazine *Megáfono*. In this essay he reacted, with enviable concentration, to an accusation in another journal, the rightwing magazine *Crisol*, that he was a Jew. It is worth quoting in full because it gives a taste of Borges's style:

> Like the Druses, like the moon, like death, like next week, the distant past is one of those things that can enrich ignorance. It is infinitely malleable and agreeable, far more obliging than the future and far less demanding of our efforts. It is the famous season favored by all mythologies.
>
> Who has not, at one point or another, played with thoughts of his ancestors, with the prehistory of his flesh and blood? I have done so many times, and many times it has not displeased me to think of myself as Jewish. It is an idle hypothesis, a frugal and sedentary adventure that harms no one, not even the name of Israel, as my Judaism is wordless, like the songs of Mendelssohn. The magazine *Crisol*, in its issue of January 30, has decided to gratify this retrospective hope; it speaks of my "Jewish ancestry, maliciously hidden" (the participle and the adverb amaze and delight me).
>
> Borges Acevedo is my name. Ramos Mejía, in a note to the fifth chapter of *Rosas and His Time*, lists the family names in Buenos Aires at that time in order to demonstrate that all, or almost all, "come from Judeo-Portuguese stock." "Acevedo" is included in the list: the only supporting evidence for my Jewish pretensions until this confirmation in *Crisol*. Nevertheless, Captain Honorario Acevedo undertook a detailed investigation that I cannot ignore. His study notes that the first Acevedo to disembark on this land was the Catalan Don Pedro de Azevedo in 1728: landholder, settler of "Pago de los Arroyos," father and grandfather of cattle ranchers in that province, a notable who figures in the annals of the parish of Santa Fe and in the documents of the history and the Viceroyalty—an ancestor, in short, irreparably Spanish.
>
> Two hundred years and I can't find the Israelite; two hundred years and my ancestor still eludes me.
>
> I am grateful for the stimulus provided by *Crisol*, but hope is dimming that I will ever be able to discover my link to the Table of the Breads and the Sea of Bronze; to Heine, Gleizer, and the ten *Sefiroth* in the Kabbalah; to Ecclesiastes

and Chaplin.

This is one of the most memorable pieces to be written in the Spanish-speaking world on why Jewish life matters.

At midday on a Wednesday I sat down at the bookstore café to read it. Borges was fascinated with the mythical role that gauchos played in the making of Argentine culture. The *Diccionario de la Real Academia*, the official organ of the Royal Academy of the Spanish Language, defines *gaucho* as "a mestizo who, in the eighteenth and nineteenth centuries, inhabited Argentina, Uruguay, and Rio Grande do Sul in Brazil, [and] was a migratory horseman adept at cattle work." In several respects this population of the lowlands is the equivalent of the cowboy in the United States.

Argentina's foundational book, similar in stature to Walt Whitman's *Leaves of Grass* (1855) or Mark Twain's *Adventures of Huckleberry Finn* (1884), is José Hernández's *El gaucho Martín Fierro* (*The Gaucho Martín Fierro*, 1872), a classic that has helped define what Argentine-ness is for many generations. Borges wrote eloquently about Hernández's book. He reimagines the life of one of Hernández's characters in a short story. And in other pieces he discusses on the value of gauchos as semi-primitive heroes whose life in the Pampas is about independence. In his view, this independent spirit permeates the Argentine collective character.

In part Borges was interested in the gaucho because his genealogical tree was divided: one line traced its roots back to England, another line to Argentina's War of Independence. Likewise, there were soldiers in his ancestry as well as intellectuals. He thoroughly admired men of action while depicting writers such as himself as cowardly.

Among the most insightful arguments he made on the topic is about the difference between *gaucho* and *gauchesco* literatures. At first sight, the distinction feels academic—but it really isn't as it makes an important point about authenticity in general. Bizarrely, the difference is also relevant for Jewish life in Argentina. Borges said that gaucho literature is the literature written *by* gauchos whereas gauchesco literature is *about* gauchos. The challenge is that gauchos themselves were primarily illiterate; thus, their tradition was, for the most part, oral. Hardly any portion of that tradition was written down. Gauchesco literature, thus, was produced by non-gauchos, a substantial number of them from urban centers, who invented gaucho plots and imitated the gaucho parlance.

Hernández's book is an example. He had Spanish, Irish, and French blood. He was a journalist (he founded the newspaper *El Río de la Plata*), a politician who was against immigration, and a federalist who opposed strategies to centralize the Argentine government. He was adamant against modernization as well as the Europeanization of the nation. In Borges's view, *The Gaucho Martín Fierro* is therefore an artifice, a falsification. This, in and of itself, is reason to celebrate it for Argentine culture, in his view, is at its best when produced by outsiders.

As it happens the first Jewish settlement in Argentina was in Moisés Ville, in the Santa Fe province. Other settlements took hold in Entre Ríos, which are the lowlands where gauchos lived for decades. Supposedly, the Jews in their interaction with the native population then became gauchos themselves. Gerchunoff promoted this view in *The Jewish Gauchos of the Pampas*. But Borges disagreed. He believed this was a misinterpretation. In one of his stories—"Unworthy," included in *El reporte de Brodie* (*Doctor Brodie's Report*, 1970)—he has a character state: "I don't know whether I've ever mentioned that I'm from Entre Ríos. I won't tell you that we were Jewish gauchos—there were never any Jewish gauchos. We were merchants and small farmers."

The statement seems innocuous, yet it is important in the history of Argentine Jews. Borges believed the poor, Yiddish-speaking newcomers from the Pale of Settlement never fully integrated into their surroundings. They didn't have enough time to accomplish the task. They moved to El Once within a short period of time after their immigration.

Toward the end of my pursuit of Borges, I walked toward Café La Biela, a historic restaurant in La Recoleta, on Calle Junín, opposite the Church of Nuestra Señora del Pilar and adjoining La Recoleta Cemetery. It is a café where Borges used to meet his friend and frequent collaborator, Bioy Casares. Together they edited anthologies and cowrote detective stories. Inside the restaurant there are life-sized statues of them seated at a table.

Before going in and asking for a table, I visited La Recoleta Cemetery, which is one of the most illustrious graveyards in the whole Hispanic world. I can't quite explain my attraction to cemeteries. They are always among the first places I visit when I arrive in a place. Maybe it is because cemeteries are never the places people think of when exploring a particular culture. Yet almost nowhere else, in my opinion, is that culture so clearly organized and in a state of exhibition as it is in a graveyard.

When it was built in 1732 by monks of the Order of the Recoletos, next to a convent and a church, La Recoleta was on the outskirts of Buenos Aires. Walking around makes the visitor feel that all the nation's history is squared into just fourteen acres. Tombs have Doric columns. They are in styles as diverse as baroque, Neo-Gothic, and Art Deco.

Bioy Casares is buried in these grounds, as are *gauchesco* authors such as Hilario Ascasubi and Estanislao del Campo. Even Facundo Quiroga, the legendary gaucho, is included.

The tomb of Evita Perón is a frequent attraction. It had fresh flowers when I stopped by. Nowhere was there any sign of the bizarre journey her embalmed corpse went through after she died. It was removed in 1955 in the wake of the coup that deposed her husband, Juan Domingo Perón, from the headquarters of the General Confederation of Labor, the largest Peronist trade union in Argentina. She was adored by millions but she was despised by the anti-Peronists, who saw her corpse as a symbol in need of elimination.

According to lore, the corpse was stored in various military intelligence sites, where, miraculously, flowers would suddenly pop up. It was then flown secretly to Italy and was buried under a fake name in Milan.

In 1971, when the country was struggling to normalize the political situation, the body was disinterred and flown to Perón, who lived in exile in Madrid with his third wife. A finger was missing and there were dents in the nose and one of the knees.

Perón was elected president once again in 1973, but he died suddenly soon after. His third wife, Isabelita, replaced him. It was she who brought Evita's embalmed corpse back to Argentina. It was put in a crypt in the presidential residency at Olivos, on the outskirts of Buenos Aires. It wasn't until 1976, more than twenty years after it was stolen, that it was finally buried by the military junta in La Recoleta.

Borges's father, Jorge Guillermo Borges, as well as his sister, Norah, are at La Recoleta too. Borges himself was supposed to be at La Recoleta also (he wrote a poem about it being his final destination), but his ambivalence toward Argentina resulted in his choosing to be buried in Geneva, Switzerland, instead.

The stroll made me think of Argentina's strong sense of *casticismo*, a word that is difficult to translate into English. The closest I can come is "purism," a sense that Hispanic civilization needs to be kept unadulterated. Much as I tried, I couldn't find any Jewish personality. Might I have missed any clues?

When I visited there were four different Jewish cemeteries in Buenos Aires: Liniers (where Jevel Katz's tomb is), Berazategui, Ciudadela, and La Tablada. At the AMIA, I asked someone if it would be at all possible to offer a combined estimate how many Jews have been buried in these four cemeteries. She told me that in an album that functions as a community portrait called *Retratos de la comunidad* (Portraits of community, 2005), she has seen a reference up to that point: 160,000.

9

At Café La Biela I was scheduled to meet Marcelo Brodsky for an espresso. My plan was to drive with him to Entre Ríos the following day. I have known him for years. He and I had an appointment with Edgardo Cozarinsky, a distinguished Argentine novelist, critic, and filmmaker, whose ancestors, immigrants from Ukraine, lived in the agricultural colonias.

Cozarinsky is named after Edgar Allan Poe, one of his mother's favorite authors. As a result of the Dirty War, he lived in France for years, where he made experimental films, including *La Guerre d'un seul homme* (One man's war, 1981), about the diaries kept by the right-wing German writer Ernst Jünger, which are contrasted with newsreels of the French Occupation. I first became acquainted with Cozarinsky's work through a sharp, incisive book he wrote on Borges and film. Then I read a novel, *Urban Vudú* (1985), which was praised by Susan Sontag and the Cuban writer Guillermo Cabrera Infante. Since then, I have read a number of his stories and essays, including *Sara* (2013), a gorgeous meditation on his mother.

Cozarinsky, like me, is a Borges fan. But what drew me to him on this occasion was a film I had watched called *Letter to Father* (2014), in which as an adult he returns to Entre Ríos, where his father grew up, to explore the landscape. In fact, it was Brodsky who directed me to it as a useful source for understanding the role that the agricultural colonias played in Jewish Argentine life.

Cozarinsky's father was an enigmatic figure with whom he had a troubled relationship, and his return to the colonias was an attempt to understand what had shaped his father. As the narrative evolves, it becomes clear that the elements dividing father and son were more than emotional. Cozarinsky finds out, by studying closely some remnants from his father's life, that he had joined the Peronists. This was a side of his father that he didn't know, ideologically the opposite side of what Cozarinsky himself stands for, and so the effort he spends in building a bridge across generations is more than personal: it is ideological, written against a large national canvas that pushed families in opposite directions.

I asked Cozarinsky specifically to reflect on his relationship with the colonias and about the myth of the Jewish gauchos against which Borges had reacted:

The whole affair about the Jewish gauchos should only be understood as a literary metaphor, proposed at the beginning with positive intentions. The very word *gaucho* evolved in such a way as to acquire alternative meanings. At the beginning it was used to refer to a bandit (outlaw, *hors-la-loi*) and, as such, those endorsing positivist thinking in the nineteenth century sought to exterminate it. As often happens, an early countercultural current consecrated it as a dissident, a libertarian, etc. Its anarchist figure was vindicated against that of the *hombre urbano*, the urban dweller. Thus, in Argentina we have an assortment of expressions connected with this ideological bent: *gauchada*, for instance, is used to refer to a disinterested favor. Or *fulano es muy gaucho*, so-and-so is very gaucho, refers to a good person, not venial.

Cozarinsky added: "I believe the expression *gaucho judío* was coined with the explicit intention of rooting Jewish life in the Argentina's national folklore. All of them were agricultural workers and little rural businessmen. None stole cattle or killed with a dagger in drunken matches."

10.

Cozarinsky's words were an important context for the trip I made the following morning with Marcelo Brodsky—to Villa Domínguez, in northeastern Argentina, about 365 kilometers from Buenos Aires. Thanks to Cozarinsky's words I felt I was well-equipped to understand what the landscape might offer me.

Entre Ríos (Spanish for "between rivers") is still known for its agricultural fertility. In Argentina and Uruguay, it is still affectionately referred to as "The New Mesopotamia" because it is in the intersection between the Uruguay River and the Paraná River.

The German philanthropist Baron Maurice de Hirsch was the force behind the resettlement. He founded the Jewish Colonization Association, which was in charge of acquiring lands in the Argentine, Uruguayan, and Brazilian Pampas. Baron Hirsch's father had been the first Jewish landowner in Bavaria, and his father was a banker to the Bavarian king, who in turn bestowed on him the title of baron. He himself worked in banking in Brussels, London, and Paris and amassed a large fortune, which allowed him to live opulently on the rue de l'Elysée in Paris.

Initially, Baron Hirsch gave generous amounts to the Alliance Israelite Universelle. But he began to feel this was enough. His interest was in Ashkenazi not Ottoman Jews, who were the focus of the Alliance. He wanted to change the conditions of shtetl Jews, which had become increasingly tenuous after the assassination of Tsar Alexander II in 1881. The event that triggered his philanthropic endeavors was a series of pogroms in Russia and other parts of eastern Europe between 1881 and 1884. In Baron Hirsch's view, the rioting and the ambivalent reaction to it from the Russian authorities—at times appeasing the vandals and at others encouraging them— was a sign that ordinary life for Jews in Central and Eastern Europe was coming to an end.

At first his solution was to offer two million pounds sterling to the Russian government to establish Jewish schools in the Pale of Settlement. But his proposal was received halfheartedly. Russia was ready to accept the offer of money but refused to allow a foreigner to dictate its educational policy. So Baron Hirsch came up with a different strategy. He created the Jewish Colonization Association in South America, to which he gave generous amounts of money throughout his life. Looking to foster commerce, technology, and education, the governments of Argentina, Uruguay, and Brazil offered land at a premium. After he died, his wife, Clara, continued the effort, expanding the capital to acquire more land in Argentina and Brazil, and also in Canada and Palestine.

The Jewish Colonization Association had the aim of conditioning the colonias in ways similar to a shtetl: building a synagogue, a cemetery, a *mikvah*, a school, and so on. These units quickly became magnets to immigrants. In 1889, less than 1,000 Jews had immigrated to Argentina. By 1920, there were 150,000 Jews living in the country.

While we were in the car I told Brodsky that to me Cozarinzky had seemed like a wanderer—a perfect example of the etherealness that Argentines are always eager to project. "You all are metaphysicians at heart," I said. "Curiously, that etherealness seems to be in sharp contrast with the rooted life of the Jewish *colonos*, who, having left behind a landscape in the Pale of Settlement where violence against them was de rigueur, they were eager to find stability, peace, and quiet."

I mentioned a story that was suddenly fresh in my mind by Roberto Bolaño, the Chilean author of *Los detectives salvajes* (*The Savage Detectives*, 1998). The story is called "The Insufferable Gaucho," about a Buenos Aires man who after a placid urban life decides to abandon the city in favor of the Pampas. It is a story that also springs from Borges's fascination with the gaucho. As the protagonist relocates to Entre Ríos, he witnesses a strange occurrence: the place is full of bunnies, which keep on reproducing at vertiginous speed. It's a bizarre tale that makes fun of magical realism. Bolaño pokes fun at the way we see the gaucho as an irrational, uncivilized character.

As I talked, I was struck by the fact that, no matter where in the landscape I looked, gauchos were completely absent. I couldn't see even one.

Brodsky laughed. "You'll probably only find bunnies, Ilan, because gauchos are a thing of the past."

At one point I saw a couple of well-built men riding horses but they looked like ranchers. I had a feeling that this was what Argentina in the twenty-first century was all about: a place deprived of its own autochthonous qualities—a Hollywood version of itself.

"The Gaucho is the ultimate renegade," Brodsky stated. "He runs away into the Pampa and only begrudgingly agrees to work for a *patrón*—he's a natural emblem of rebellion. Since you're an inveterate reader of Borges, you know its archetype is Martín Fierro, the quintessential '*forajido*' [outlaw] who ends up living among the native population, who kills with his dagger, and who survives outdoors on his own. That idealized character defines these '*tierras salvajes*' [savage lands]. The Gaucho is a referent for Argentina's rebelliousness."

With Brodsky at the wheel, it took us about four and a half hours to get to Villa Domínguez. (This includes a brief stop we made when a policeman handed him a ticket for going over the speed limit.) Brodsky had telephoned a number of acquaintances, all of whom were waiting for us.

Founded in 1890 Villa Domínguez is a small town—actually, in Spanish it is called a municipality—with less than two thousand inhabitants, in the department of Villaguay. I am told that José Néstor Pékerman, at one point the coach of Argentina's national fútbol team, is originally from Villa Domínguez. A hundred years ago, this was one of the main centers of Jewish life in the Mesopotamian colonias. Today it is almost completely deserted. Still, the place is absolutely beautiful, an assortment of rustic scenes (a stable, a county store, a dirt road) one is likely to catch in a period movie. Arriving in the town, though, the feeling one gets is of abandonment. Modernity seems to have been suspended.

This is still a fertile land of fields were rice, corn, wheat, sorghum, linen, and other items are harvested. The eyes extend unendingly to the horizon. The problem is that the technology one comes across looks outdated. Mules and horses are still used for traction, competing against tractors and other machinery.

We made it to a charming railway station, Estación Domínguez. It was built during an important period in Argentine history where the spread of the railway system was seen as the foundation for modernity. But as I made my way to the station, I could clearly see it no longer serves its original function. A señora in her sixties was waiting. She opened the door for us.

"¡Bienvenidos!" she said. "Entren, por favor." Please come in.

She showed us the inside of the station, which had been turned into a makeshift exhibition space. The smell was of humidity. The items on display (gaucho customs, pails, strings and lassos, cooking utensils, a pair of shoes, train tickets, newspaper clippings, and brochures) all attempted to showcase the last few decades in the region's history. It was a charmingly improvised effort, with no professional hand having touched it.

Brodsky conveyed to me the emotion his parents felt when visiting this same museum a few months before. They were products of the colonization endeavor. His father, who went by the name of Pocho, grew up in Coronel Suárez, in the southern tip of Buenos Aires province, where immigrant Jews also settled. On the museum walls were photographs of black clouds made of locusts devouring everything in their reach. He recalled the sound the insects made, the way they crashed against the windows, the darkness they brought with them. But he also invoked the Jewish weddings in the countryside, under the chuppah (canopy). And the determination of the new generation of Jews to settle in the Americas, to be free and happy, in their own land.

In contrast Sara, Brodsky's mother, had a more primal relationship with Entre Ríos. She had been born on the boat while her parents were sailing to Argentina and had lived with her grandmother in Basavilbaso. During the visit, her emotion was focused on the little objects displayed at the museum: furniture, lamps, Russian samovars, and so on.

After giving us a tour, the señora also told us about Osvaldo Quiroga. Brodsky had already talked to him. He was in charge of another improvised museum, this one specifically dedicated to Jewish life in Villa Domínguez. It was in a building that once had been the town's pharmacy.

I was struck by a coincidence, which I mentioned to Brodsky: the most famous nineteenth-century gaucho and the protagonist of Sarmiento's classic book is called Facundo Quiroga. I found it curious that our guide had the same last name. Were they related? I was intent on asking the moment we met him.

Brodsky and I drove along dirt roads. Stray dogs walked around near our parked car. A couple of young girls sitting at a door step watched our route with attention. A few children were playing fútbol in a yard nearby.

The grass was grown, making the passing of the ball difficult. The goals were made of sticks.

As I looked around, I suddenly imagined a centaur galloping in from the prairie. And not any centaur, but a Jewish one.

The image came to me courtesy of Moacyr Scliar, a physician and Brazil's most famous Jewish writer, who died in 2011. He and I became close friends. We maintained a correspondence that lasted a couple of decades. At one point in time we toured together through five cities in the United States, holding public conversations in theaters in which we discussed an array of themes, from writers such as Isaac Babel's *Red Cavalry* (1926) to Philip Roth's *Portnoy's Complaint* (1969) to gauchos and other myths roaming around the Jewish imagination.

Scliar was a magician with words. Although he was from a city, Porto Alegre, and more specifically from its Jewish neighborhood, Bom Fin, I frequently think of him as a gaucho.

Although he would have liked it (in Portuguese, those born in Rio Grande do Sul are called *gaúchos* and the nickname of Porto Alegre is *A capital dos gaúchos*), it is somewhat unfair to describe Scliar that way, given that he wrote about countless topics, from the Bible to indigenous tribes, from Crypto-Jews to the transformations of the Portuguese language. In his *Collected Stories* (1999) there are tales about Karl Marx, Samson and Delilah, Sigmund Freud, Hitler and the Holocaust, Scheherazade, the false Messiah Shabbetai Zvi, and Shakespeare's Shylock. Yet Scliar's most famous book is *O centauro no Jardim* (*The Centaur in the Garden*, 1980). A fantasy tale about a Jewish centaur called Guedali Tartakowsky who struggles to accept his physical features in a society prone to conformism, the novel allowed Scliar to reflect on segregation as a feature of Jewish history.

For him the centaur was a perfect metaphor for the bifurcated identity of Latin American Jews: part made-up animal, part modern-life denizen. It was ironic that I couldn't see any real gauchos but I saw Scliar's centaur come galloping toward me in the mountainside landscape of Entre Ríos, with a smile on his face—the same smile Scliar always had. It made me long for my conversations with him. For a moment, I felt as if I was inside, inhabiting, Scliar's fertile imagination.

In the car I recited to Brodsky a poem by Rubén Darío, the most important Latin American poet of the fin de siècle. He was originally from Nicaragua, but Darío's ideological views were opposite to those of José Hernández, the author of *The Gaucho Martín Fierro*: he was a cosmopolitan in favor of immigration. Darío's poem is called "Song to Argentina." In it he praises the arrival of Jewish immigrants to Argentina:

> Sing Jews of La Pampa!
> Young men of rude appearance,
> sweet Rebeccas with honest eyes,
> Reubens of long locks,
> patriarchs of white,
> dense, horselike hair.
> Sing, sing old Sarahs
> and adolescent Benjamins
> with the voice of our heart:
> "We have found ZION!"

As we came closer I started seeing a number of street signs in both Spanish and Yiddish. The only other time I have seen anything similar is not too far from where I live, in Hampshire College, on the premises of the Yiddish Book Center. And I have seen photographs of Birobidjan in Siberia, the place that Joseph Stalin designated as a Jewish homeland within the USSR. In Entre Ríos, these signs were obviously designed to impress tourists.

"Baron Hirsch is a mythical figure among Argentine Jews," Brodsky said. "Although he was behind the resettlement initiative, he never traveled to visit the country. This certainly contributed to the way he was idealized by thousands of people. The immigrant children nurtured another dream: "M'hijo el dotor." My son the doctor. Through higher education, the immigrants helped their offspring reach middle class and beyond. Entre Ríos was thus a springboard."

When Brodsky and I arrived, we found the place closed. Brodsky knocked at the door a couple of times. No answer. Finally, I saw someone walking from a block away. His gentle demeanor jumped out to the eye. "¡Perdón!" I heard someone apologizing. "I was at a meeting with a local *intendente*."

The man introduced himself—"Soy Quiroga!"—and allowed us in. A slim handsome man of about fifty, he said he wasn't Jewish. But he held a deep love for the Jewish history of Villa Domínguez.

My immediate impression of the place was of a cabinet of wonders. There were artifacts everywhere: newspaper clippings, yellowed photographs, theater bills, a phonograph, gaucho boots, a horse saddle, equipment for milking cattle. I couldn't walk around carefully enough, not to bump into something fragile that might break.

As for the exhibit at Estación Domínguez, it was clear there were scant resources behind the effort but enormous goodwill. Items were on shelves, in glass boxes, on tables, on the floor, hanging from the ceiling. There were posters, a dentist's chair, dolls, a Yiddish playbill, photographs, books, diaries, photographs.

They were all exposed to humidity. A few were also touched by the sun. I felt I was in a novel by Bruce Chatwin.

Quiroga showed us a backroom. It had tons of boxes, a bookshelf filled with volumes, and piles of Xeroxes. This, he said, was where he did his work. I saw an old computer.

I asked if he knew Yiddish.

He didn't. "Do you?" He asked me in return. When I said "Yes," he asked me if he could show me a few documents and if I could give him an overview of what they were about.

"Are you a relative of Facundo Quiroga?"

He laughed. "I wish. But people in Villa Domínguez aren't of any famous stock," Quiroga said.

He added that, on occasion, he got an intern who speaks English and Spanish. He and whoever wants to offer a hand help compile a database of all the items in the museum. On a couple of the walls in the pharmacy are still the wooden drawers and glass windows used to store medicine. Inside them are now postcards, family albums, diaries, and correspondence in Yiddish, Hebrew, Russian, and Spanish.

Later on Brodsky told me he found Quiroga exemplary. "Without knowing much about Jewishness," he stated, "he rescued the past from oblivion. I can't think of a more worthy mitzvah. That's why his lack of resources is unfortunate. The impact of his actions could be infinitely larger."

Quiroga said donations arrived on a regular basis. They helped him sustain the museum, which he had been doing practically on his own for some time. He described how new items were arriving all the time. "Once someone passes away, the relatives of the colonos deliver things in boxes. These belongings tell a history," stated Osvaldo. "At one point, there were approximately two thousand Jews living in Villa Domínguez. They were all settlers from Russia. There are none left now."

That evening Brodsky and I spent the night in a nice hotel nearby, which took us a while to find. It was run by a German woman in her forties and her parents. The woman's children were also around. She told me her ancestors were from the German region of the Volga River.

The hotel had been the house of Miguel Sajaroff, one of the most important leaders of the colonization enterprise in Entre Ríos. He studied agronomical engineering in Wittenberg, Germany. He emigrated to Argentina in 1899 and was a settler on this small farm granted to him by the Jewish Colonization Association.

A visionary, Sajaroff committed to improving the life of the colonos by creating a cooperative called Fondo Comunal Villa Domínguez in 1904, which, with him as president, advocated cooperation with other agricultural cooperatives created earlier in the Santa Fe and Corrientes provinces. Sajaroff's cooperative grew to become an administrative system—a federation—throughout Entre Ríos that advocated for long-term credit to farmers, insurance mechanisms, a coordinated effort in the production throughout the region, and strategies of experimentation.

Quiroga showed me several of Sajaroff's accounting books. He had kept them meticulously. Even more interesting was the fact that Sajaroff had written an autobiography of his life in Entre Ríos. Quiroga found a volume in a cabinet and gave it to me to browse. He also told me that, without knowing, on the way from Buenos Aires we had passed through a town called after Sajaroff.

It was hot. The hotel had a swimming pool. Brodsky and I took a dip. In the evening we drove around in search of a restaurant where we could have dinner. There were only a couple of places, one of them was a pizzeria. The owner told us she could heat us up a few empanadas and prepared us Argentina's national drink, yerba maté.

Accompanied by Quiroga, Brodsky and I visited a cemetery nearby and what looked like a day school. They were in ruins.

Quiroga then led us to a building that was at some point used as a synagogue. Although the walls were crumbling, we made our way in. It was cold, distant, not a living space. The emptiness took my breath away. It may have been a hundred years since practicing Jews congregated here.

Suddenly, a father and a son walked by.

"¿Les gusta?" said the father. He wanted to know if we liked it.

Brodsky smiled.

"The Jewish God once lived in this house," said the son. "But He left. He lives somewhere else now."

11.

The following morning we drove to Basavilbaso, another municipality and also the name of a city that, during the age of colonization, was a trading center. I had seen some black-and-white photographs of the place in the Marc Turkow Center.

Brodsky knows a few people in town. At one point we stopped at a woman's house. She was famous for her baked goods. Her husband was sick, she said from behind a fence. But if we returned in about an hour, she could have a full *leikaj* for us and a couple of pounds of *pastrón*.

As we waited, Brodsky and I drove around Basavilbaso. It was a modest, unassuming town of about ten thousand people, about thirty-five miles from the border with Uruguay. (The locals refer to it as "Basso.") A worker at a gas station told me the area had sprung to life in 1892 thanks to the Entre Ríos Railway. He said his grandfather remembered the first train that ever arrived, on June 30, 1887. "When I was a child, my grandfather would mimic the prolonged sound that train made. Everyone was in awe. Rrrrrrr. . . . It used to scare me to death." The comment reminded me of a crucial scene in García Márquez's *Cien años de soledad* (*One Hundred Years of Solitude*, 1967), when the first train makes its appearance in Macondo.

In the car Brodsky talked to me about Jewish cuisine in Argentina. "In this country there are all kinds of Jews: orthodox, secular, agnostic, what have you. The fights among them are internecine. Yet one thing unites us all: Ashkenazi food, from the shtetl as well as from Russia. 'My mother's knishes are the best!' everyone says. Borscht topped with cream, latkes, *varénikes*, kreplach, *mandalakh*, strudel, *gehakte leiber* (chopped liver) mixed with egg. . . . At one time, there used to be plenty of Jewish restaurants serving these dishes. Unfortunately, only a handful survive in El Once or Villa Crespo, a by-product of acculturation."

Brodsky talked about his Grandmother Rosa—La Babita, his father's mother—and how whatever she touched in the kitchen turned into a delicacy. "She was from Kajovka, between Russian and Ukraine. A Russian teacher, she emigrated to Argentina in 1914. Her chicken *varénikes*—which we Italianized into *capelletis de pollo*, were truly out of this world. Although she never gave up her Russian tongue, she never used it to communicate with her children because she wanted them to be Argentine."

He added: "For a while, she taught Russian to Roberto Arlt, the classic author of *Los siete locos* (*The Seven Madmen*, 1973)."

I became nostalgic for Mexican Jewish cuisine, especially for the latkes with mole and apple sauces that my wife prepares for Hanukkah. Or the tacos of chopped liver. Or gefilte fish with mango salsa.

From there we proceeded to visit the remnants of another agricultural colony, Colonia Lucienville, next to the Gobernador Basavilbaso Station. Colonia Lucienville was founded in 1894, in honor of Baron Hirsch's son Lucien, who died a few years later, in 1897. If in Villa Domínguez the infrastructure of Jewish life in the past was crumbling, in Lucienville, where one of the cooperatives organized by Sajaroff was established in 1907, there is almost nothing left for the visitor today.

I wanted to go to Moisés Ville, which houses a museum that, on the face of it, looks to be more sophisticated than what Osvaldo Quiroga built over time. But it was far away and we didn't have the time. Time has turned Moisés Ville into the most famous of the Jewish colonies. It houses the Museo Histórico Comunal y de la Colonización Judía "Rabino Aarón Halevi Goldman," which apparently has a more institutionalized, better-financed exhibit than the one in Villa Domínguez.

Either way, the impression of the colonias that I was left with was that the colonization enterprise orchestrated by Baron Hirsch was an astonishing endeavor.

Talk of Moisés Ville brought to mind a canonical figure in Argentine Jewish intellectual history, Alberto Gerchunoff, and we talked about him while we drove back to Buenos Aires. Brodsky knew his work. I said I was a passionate reader of Gerchunoff. If ever a literary figure serves as a center of gravity, Gerchunoff is it. Through his work it is able to understand the impact the colonization effort had on everyone.

Before him one is able to find sketches, poems, vignettes, and chronicles of immigrant life, written by Jewish refugees in Russian, Polish, Hebrew, Yiddish, and at times a rudimentary Spanish. But it is his beautiful and meticulously measured Castilian prose in *The Jewish Gauchos of the Pampas* (translated into English in 1955), a book deeply influenced by Cervantes, that he gave birth to a literature that is distinctly Jewish in Argentina.

In 1891, when Gerchunoff was seven, his father traveled from Russia to the Pampas, and the family followed him. Agriculture and raising cattle were the jobs designated for the shtetl dwellers, and hard labor was their lot. As expressed in his 1914 autobiography, *Entre Ríos, mi país (Entre Ríos, My Country*, 1950), Gerchunoff admired the capacity for hard work of his fellow Argentines. His family was first stationed in the colony of Moisés Ville, but when his father was brutally killed by a gaucho, they moved to another colonial called Rajil. This tragic event and Gerchunoff's later adventures in the new settlement were the inspiration for his early work.

An admirable aspect of Gerchunoff is his multilingualism. Most immigrants improvised a "survival" Spanish during their first Argentine decade. Gerchunoff not only learned to speak perfect Spanish as a child, but by 1910, when he was twenty-six, his prose was setting a linguistic and narrative standard. Reading him today, it is possible to discover in his work a stylistic cadence later developed by his followers, among them Borges, who praised him as "the writer of le mot juste," a distinction seldom awarded to an immigrant.

Gerchunoff was like Rollansky. He arrived with little resources but an unstoppable traction. He didn't have any family, friends, or acquaintances. Soon he decided that in order to fulfill Peretz's legacy—to make Yiddish cosmopolitan—he needed to attach himself to the Jewish community. Gerchunoff got a job as a Yiddish teacher in one of Argentina's provinces. For a while he taught in Corrientes and Moisés Ville, which allowed him to get a sense of *la Argentina profunda y rural*, Argentina's deep, rural landscape.

A few years later, Gerchunoff moved to Buenos Aires and, beginning in 1902, contributed regularly to newspapers, among them *La Nación*. Even after the tragic loss of his father, Gerchunoff stubbornly went on believing that Argentina was a true paradise. He saw the province of Entre Ríos and the cosmopolitan Buenos Aires as a diasporic "holy land" of sorts, where the contribution of the Jews would always be welcome in shaping the national culture and where all manifestations of anti-Semitism would ultimately vanish.

But the Semana Trágica turned things sour for Gerchunoff. It affected him deeply. For a while he didn't offer any public comment. Fifteen years later, this view was ultimately shattered when Hitler ascended to power in Germany. By then Argentina had imposed restrictions on Jewish immigrants. This, in Gerchunoff's eyes, was unacceptable. Refugees were in desperate need. At the same time, a rise of anti-Semitism in the country made him feel isolated. The promise of Argentina as "a European jewel in the Southern Hemisphere," as it was often represented, turned into unrest.

I remembered a couple of lines Gerchunoff wrote in 1937 and recited them to Brodsky: "What should we do? Jews and Argentines, we should protest, fight, and expose the policies of cowardice." And "The Jew anywhere is irreplaceable." Juan Domingo Perón, a populist general, soon would work the masses into a type of hysteria about the nation's potential.

"A prophet," commented Brodsky. "Gerchunoff smelled what was coming . . ."

I added: "The end of his career is marked by even more reticence. He wrote about Spinoza and Heine. He had stopped portraying Argentina as a land of plenty. And he turned into a Zionist, advocating for a Jewish state where Jews would no longer be pariahs."

Pariahs? This made me recall that, a week earlier in my conversation with Edgardo Cozarinsky, I had asked him about Gerchunoff. He described him as some self-made literati who collaborated in *La Nación* and was a friend of Borges. "He was famous for his verbal ingenuity. To a high-class Señora who asked him if he was really Jewish, he responded: 'Señora, puedo poner la prueba en su mano.' Proof of it can be placed in your hand."

Cozarinsky didn't think Gerchonoff would survive, "although [his work] may be consulted as documents of an epoch, for example of a sentiment naively Zionist that didn't foresee the consequences of implanting a Jewish state in Palestine territory. Nevertheless, his loyalty was with the province of Entre Ríos, perhaps a childhood idealization, just like the one my own father had, who was born in Villa Clara."

And when I asked Cozarinsky if he saw himself as a descendant of Gerchunoff, who to this day is considered the most important Jewish Argentine writer, he responded in blunt terms: "No tengo idea de una literatura judía argentina, debe existir sin duda. Pero no me manejo con esa clasificación. A lo sumo literatura con temas judíos. Hasta por ahí nomás" (I don't have any idea of a Jewish Argentine literature. It might unquestionably exist but no one cares to use those classifications. At best there is a literature with Jewish themes but little else).

12.

My trek through El Once and other Buenos Aires neighborhoods and through the agricultural colonies founded by Baron Hirsh left me in a state of rapture. In physical terms I never came across a gaucho, let alone a Jewish gaucho. Yet the enormity of the myths was overwhelming. They shaped a nation. They shaped an essential chapter in the sequence of Jewish diasporas in history.

Back home, after I settled back down, I reread Roberto Bolaño's story "The Insufferable Gaucho." It acquired new meaning for me. The first time I encountered it, it seemed to me to be a meditation on the elusiveness of the gaucho spirit. But this time it seemed also a depiction of Argentina as a game of mirrors. "Argentina's like a novel," Bolaño states at one point, "a lie, or make-believe at best. Buenos Aires is full of crooks and loudmouths, a hellish place, with nothing to recommend it except the women, and some of the writers, but only a few. Ah, but the pampas—the pampas are eternal. A limitless cemetery, that's what they're like."

Yes, Argentina, the nucleus of Latin American Jewry, was astonishing in its spread. It was also packed with contradictions, a promised land that remains a precarious labyrinthine dream. Jews in it are at once an integral part and outsiders whose presence is questioned at every turn. Is the duality avoidable? In my impression, this was precisely what made Argentine Jews what they are: amphibious creatures, nervous, always on the alert, hyperconscious of their own condition.

As an antidote I decided to travel next to Mexico and the American Southwest. Immigration has also defined this region, although in dramatically different ways. What shapes the place is a mestizo identity that, roughly speaking, is the by-product of a double rejection: of the indigenous past and of an oppressive European presence. Argentina looks outward to find its true soul whereas Mexico looks inward.

That inwardness, in the words of Octavio Paz, is a labyrinth.

3   KAHLO'S EYEBROWS

1.

Frida Kahlo's eyes are always looking at you. Her thick, wide eyebrows shelter those eyes, making them look intense. There's something non-Mexican in those eyebrows.

Kahlo was Caucasian but you could be forgiven for not remembering that, since her intent was on dressing like a true Mexican. Not like any Mexican and certainly not like the modern Mexican women of the upper middle class in the 1930s, to which she belonged. She dressed like a Mexican Indian. More specifically, like a Tarahumara Indian, from the Tehuantepec Isthmus in southern Mexico. In her self-portraits she regularly wears bright colors—whites, oranges, blues, greens, and browns.

For a woman of her background to dress like she did and to look into your eyes with that deep, unmistaken glance is an act of rebellion.

Kahlo's father was German, her mother mestiza. This bifurcation is the source of her art. Nowhere is it more tangible than in the painting "The Two Fridas" (1939), in which the heart of a European-dressed Frida is tied through an artery to an indigenously dressed Frida.

The children of immigrants are frequently given to represent their identity as divided. Where do I belong, they ask? To this land of plenty or to the place my forebears came from?

About her father, Kahlo claimed he was half-Jewish. She maintained he was Hungarian. Both claims are false. His full name was Carl Wilhelm Kahlo Kaufmann. He was born in Pforzheim, Germany, known now as Baden-Württemberg, and was the son of a jeweler. German historians have mapped a genealogical tree. They believe he was a Lutheran who probably came from a family in Frankfurt.

If this is true, why did Frida Kahlo insist, as she repeated throughout her life, on perverting the truth? More intriguing for me, what prompted her to describe him as Jewish?

Wilhelm (in Spanish, Guillermo) Kahlo went to Mexico in 1891, in part because he had a fraught relationship with his stepmother. He liked it there and applied for citizenship three years later. In 1891 he set up a photo studio, working for newspapers such as *El Mundo Ilustrado* and *Semanario Ilustrado* at a time when photographs served as the conduit for people to look at near and distant places. He mostly photographed buildings, churches, monuments, and other public spaces. All photographs are in black and white. Color was still not available yet.

One might say that Wilhelm Kahlo's daughter emphasized color in opposition to her father's black and whiteness. Everything in her world is in sparkling color. Her lips, for starters. They are always bright red.

That Frida Kahlo by the end of the twentieth century had become the ultimate Mexican icon is emblematic. Such is her influence in art, fashion, and architecture that one might say, thanks to her, Mexico is nothing but a multicolored fiesta.

Likewise, Kahlo chose her father's Jewishness because it fitted her life-long project to make art out of suffering.

She spent most of her childhood and adulthood in the same house, known as La Casa Azul, the blue house. It is in Coyoacán, a borough (in Mexican Spanish, *delegación*) on the southern part of Mexico City that is known as a cultural hub. She contracted polio at an early age, and at the age of eighteen she was seriously injured in a traffic accident, which caused her enormous pain throughout her life. She underwent surgery countless times.

As an adolescent Kahlo had contemplated going to medical school. The accident forced her to abandon her plans. She required a lengthy recovery. It is in this period that she decided to become an artist.

Most of her paintings are self-portraits. One painting shows her in bed.

In another one we see her naked strapped in a corset, with a metal structure inside her in lieu of her vertebral column, and with nails all over her body.

In a metaphorical sense Kahlo's art might be said to be the forerunner of the selfie. She is always at the center of the image. Except that, unlike selfies, her facial expression is always flat, stoic, and unafraid. This is in sharp contrast with the suffering showcased in the rest of the painting.

That's the reason why Kahlo's oeuvre is embraced in Mexico as the nation's favorite symbol. Colonialism, economic disparity, political corruption: the country sees itself exactly in the same way as Kahlo did—injured, overshadowed, yet enduring in its vision.

In Mexico, Kahlo was my point of entry. I wanted to explore the complex issues related to her claim of being part Jewish, which in my eyes was a form of impersonation. She was married (another source of suffering) to Diego Rivera, one of *Los Tres Grandes*, the three muralists that defined Mexican public art in the twentieth century. The other two were José Clemente Orozco and David Alfaro Siqueiros. Intriguingly, Rivera also claimed to have Jewish blood.

In reaction to my dream of a few months earlier I wanted to visit my old house in Colonia Copilco. Vividly in my mind I still had the picture of the mysterious man at the door, forbidding my entrance. The reference to someone like him by Shaul, the Talmudic student I met in El Once one afternoon, made me curious.

Argentina and Mexico are strikingly dissimilar. To the point that they might be said to function as polar extremes. The second most populous country in the region, Mexico (the population in 2015 was over 125,000,000) has also consistently opened its doors to successive waves of immigrants, although their overall influence is comparatively smaller. The country, instead, is known for its *mestizaje*, a mix of Spanish and indigenous elements. The most recognizable theoretician of this racial synthesis is José Vasconcelos, the author of *La raza cósmica* (*The Cosmic Race*, 1925). Vasconcelos, who happened to nurture pro-Fascist and anti-Semitic beliefs, argued that mestizos are called to lead the world.

Mexico is the core of Mesoamérica, a name still in use. The name refers to a cultural area that flourished before the arrival of the Spanish conquistadors in the sixteenth century, which reaches to Central America and includes states in the American Southwest such as Nevada, Arizona, Colorado, and New Mexico.

My objective on the next leg of my voyage was precisely to delve into

Mesoamérica, looking for traces of Jewish presence. I settled down in a hotel next to Perisur, a fancy mall in the intersection of Anillo Periférico and Avenida Insurgentes right next to Universidad Nacional Autónoma de México (aka UNAM), one of the largest institutions of higher learning in the Americas. Then I spent a whole day in Coyoacán. I wanted to visit Kahlo's La Casa Azul as well as two other museums—one dedicated to Rivera; the other dedicated to their mutual friend, the Russian revolutionary Leon Trotsky.

I have always loved Coyoacán. Only about thirty blocks, it's a small neighborhood in comparison to most others in Mexico City. For a while it was known as Villa de Coyoacán, but people have shortened the name. *Coyoacán* in Nahuatl means "the place of coyotes." In Aztec times this section was a village on the shore of Lake Texcoco. In 1523 Hernán Cortés and his Spanish soldiers used it as their headquarters in the conquest of Tenochtitlán, as the city was known. According to lore, it was in Coyoacán that Cuauthémoc, the last of the Aztec emperors, was tortured. Cortés—unsuccessfully—burned Cuauthémoc's feet to make him confess where the Aztec gold amassed by his empire was hidden. And it was also in this neighborhood that the first Catholic mass was celebrated in Mexico. Cortés and La Malinche, his mistress and translator, prayed in it.

Today there's the charming Plaza de Santa Catarina at the heart of Coyoacán with a fountain that features coyotes drinking and howling. Next to the plaza is another public space, Plaza Hidalgo, with a central kiosk where mariachi bands and other musicians perform regularly. In the area is the parish of San Juan Bautista. Not far are beautiful arches that give visitors a taste of how the area looked in the colonial period. All around are cantinas, cafés, restaurants, ice-cream parlors, elementary schools, banks, a market, a theater, and a park.

It is fitting that Kahlo is identified with the picturesque neighborhood. Everything in it is quaint and full of character. On the sidewalks are dozens of street vendors selling balloons, *elotes con queso y crema* (grilled corn with white cheese and cream), *chicharrones con limón* (fried pork belly with lime juice), *esquites* (little corn cups), cotton candy, and *artesanías* (tourist souvenirs).

I started in Sanborns, a famous restaurant chain with a branch in Coyoacán. The branch was on Parque Centenario #5. Inside the restaurant there was a pharmacy and a store that sells all sorts of items—from toys to music, jewelry, and books, newspapers, and magazines. I looked around. There were more than two dozen books on Kahlo. I also saw masks, posters, greeting cards, matchboxes, wallets, key chains, and other stuff with her face on them. I even found "mini-Fridas," thumb-sized dolls of her.

There were almost as many items on Rivera, but customers seemed to pay less attention to them.

Surprisingly, in the magazine section I stumbled upon a copy of an old comic-strip superhero, *Kalimán*. I hadn't seen one in a long time. I bought it, sat down to eat at the restaurant, ordered Swiss enchiladas (one of Sanborn's staples), and proceeded to study it.

When I was growing up, this was the superhero I most admired. I liked that the comic strip was utterly autochthonous—by which I mean it was locally conceived, produced, and distributed. This is important when one considers that, in the 1970s, the most ubiquitous of all comic-strip products were those of Walt Disney, Hannah Barbera, and the like, which, in Mexico and throughout Latin America, were mass-marketed in full color in Spanish versions. Compared to these products, *Kalimán* was a modest affair. The price per issue was lower.

Not that it was a makeshift affair. The series had started in 1963 as a radio drama created by a pair of artists, Rafael Cutberto Navarro and Modesto Vázquez González. Its popularity had grown by the time I became a reader, allowing it to branch into a number of derivatives that included books and a couple of B movies. Many of my friends read it as well. Later on I found out that every comic strip with him as hero had a printing of 100,000 copies. It often needed to be reprinted. The series ran for twenty-five years, from 1965 to 1991, with a total of 1,348 weekly issues. The pages were made cheaply in sepia, although color was introduced at a later stage. Ads in the inside covers were for Mexican food.

It is crucial for me to describe Kalimán as a character. He wasn't a mestizo. Instead, he had Caucasian features, including blue eyes. He wore a turban with a jewel-encased red K in front. A sleuth capable of solving strange cases (murders, kidnappings, thefts, international plots to control the universe) with bravado, he was known for his erudition and self-discipline and also for his superpowers: he could levitate at will, hypnotize others by quickly focusing his sight, communicate through telepathy, and heal himself magically after suffering a major injury. He was capable of moving objects through telekinesis.

In other words, he was neither indigenous nor mestizo. He was said to be from India (the place, by the way, Columbus originally intended to reach when he set sail in 1492, in order to escape a Turkish blockade of the Mediterranean Sea), although I don't remember his origins ever being fully explained. His force was the result of his knowledge of Eastern religions. At times he even looked Arabic.

None of his qualities were related directly to anything recognizably Mexican. Still, the settings of his adventures were recognizably Mexican. More than anything else, he fought for us and, thus, was one of us, too.

I recalled seeing, years ago, one of the movies based on the strip: *Kalimán, el hombre increíble* (Kaliman, the incredible man [1972]). An expensive production, the movie had an international cast and was filmed in Egypt. It was based on the story "Los profanadores de tumbas" (The gravediggers). Kalimán was played by a Canadian actor, Jeff Cooper. His voice was dubbed into Spanish by the popular TV host Luis Manuel Pelayo. It was a melodrama that made me realize how cheesy and unsophisticated the whole thing was. The fact that I wasn't yet ready to outgrow my devotion to the character was due in large part to my need, and surely that of a sizable audience, to embrace Mexican myths on their own terms while rejecting foreign entertainment as extraneous.

Finding *Kalimán* in Coyoacán was a coup. I was excited. I paid the bill at Sanborn's and made my way on to the museums.

I went to Casa Trotsky, on Avenida Río Churubusco #410. Trotsky, who was born Jewish, was one of the essential leaders of the Bolshevik Revolution. In a power struggle after Lenin's death, Josef Stalin forced him into exile. He went to Kazakhstan, then to Turkey. Rivera, Kahlo, and other left-wing Mexican artists convinced the country's government to give him asylum. That's how he ended up in Coyoacán. His Mexican friends secured him his own place. It is now the museum.

The building is a beautiful colonial structure. It has a stunning garden with a monument that features the Soviet hammer and sickle. In one room there's a gallery with posters, photographs, and glass-covered boxes that feature books open to relevant pages. Trotsky's unassuming office showcases his desk with a typewriter on top. On top of the desk are piles of working documents. There are a few small wooden tables nearby, a bookshelf, and a large map of Mexico on the wall. There's a simple dining room in which a table is covered with a yellow tablecloth. This is where he was assassinated, on August 21, 1940, with an ice pick, by Ramón Mercader, a disgruntled Spanish exile and probably a Stalin spy.

As is common, on the way out, the visitor comes across a bookstore. When I was there it featured works on political philosophy, Communism, and the Soviet Union. And plenty on Frida Kahlo.

Nowhere in the entire museum was there any mention that Trotsky was

Jewish. Granted, it wasn't an aspect that he himself stressed. But it is impossible to understand his odyssey as a thinker and a twentieth-century revolutionary, and even his feud with Stalin, without acknowledging this.

My father remembers how, when he was a little boy, my grandfather took him to the Palacio de Bellas Artes in downtown Mexico City, where Trotsky's body was laid out in an open casket. There was a long line of people waiting to see it.

I always have the same eerie reaction when visiting an illustrious person's house. I leave the place saturated. There is something creepy, even grotesque about these sites. It is as if everyone has agreed to engage in a breach of privacy. These are no longer personal chambers. They now belong to all of us. That's what the culture of celebrity is about.

The Casa Museo Estudio Diego Rivera is equally droll, though it is designed to satisfy a consumerist hunger. One learns little about the artist (his full name was Diego María de la Concepción Juan Nepomuceno Estanislao de la Rivera y Barrientos Acosta y Rodríguez) and his world. Not in Coyoacán per se but in a nearby neighborhood, San Angel Inn, the museum is in a street called after Rivera. It has no identifying number. I took a taxi to get there.

Compared to Trotsky's the house is modern. Painted in blue and red, it has large windows and an outdoor staircase. A line of cacti separates the building from the street. Inside the visitor finds puppets, canvases, and all sorts of tchotchkes.

Rivera was a large man and a larger-than-life artist. In his drawings, paintings, and murals he sought to include all aspects of Mexican history. Nothing in the museum gave me any feeling of his harsh, abrasive, at times even abusive personality. Institutions like this one sugarcoat the famous person's reputation. At times Kahlo described him as intimidating. Rather than respond to her, he left her for long periods and often had affairs with other women. It's the Mexican husband's default response.

The two spouses were studies in contrast. It's enough to look at their attire. He was as conservative as she was exhibitionistic. He was often photographed in dark suits, with a white shirt and a tie, unless he is in his overalls, working in his studio or standing on a scaffold working on a fresco.

Kahlo's hyper-Mexicanness, in my view, is an antidote to Rivera's subdued profile.

In any case, Rivera's place reminded me of Pablo Neruda's three homes in Chile's capital, Santiago—Isla Negra, La Chascona, and La Sebastiana—except that Neruda's homes give the visitor a better taste of his style.

Rivera imagined himself a descendant of *conversos*—a term that refers to
Jews who in the sixteenth century converted to Catholicism, often in order
to escape the might of the Inquisition. In an interview he said a few were
accused of being *judaizantes* (Judaizers). I was struck by his use of the term.
Rivera believed that a few of his relatives had been persecuted by the Holy
Office (El Santo Oficio de la Inquisición, the Inquisition) and had died at
the stake. This autobiographical element—chained martyrs dressed up in
Sanbenitos, surrounded by inquisitors—is a motif in his oeuvre, including a
few of his murals.

That ancestry is not unlikely. The museum made no mention of it.

Of the three sites, the Kahlo's La Casa Azul, located on Calle Londres
#247, is the most popular. And there is good reason. A museum since 1958,
four years after Kahlo's death, it isn't far from the Vivero Coyoacán, a park
known in Mexico as *pulmón verde*, a green lung. The sense of design is im-
maculate. The walls are white and blue. Tables, chairs, and bookshelves are
painted yellow. All sorts of artisan ceramics and other Mexican popular art
are on display. Kahlo wasn't a collector per se, but she obviously enjoyed
surrounding herself with beautiful objects. High above a dining room were
designs of doves and signs that read "Diego." There's an adobe fireplace.
When I was there, dresses like the ones she wore were on display. The outdoors is full of semitropical vegetation.

This paraphernalia made me think about genuineness. There is a saying
in Mexican Spanish: *Hacerse el indio.* It means "to play the fool." The saying
is full of prejudice. In Mexico, where the indigenous past is an essential element, *indio* (Indian) is a pejorative term. In Spain the word *gitano* (gypsy)
has a similar connotation. It can mean "sly," "conniving," and "deceitful."
A *gitaneada* is a mean, contemptible trick. And *gitanear* is the verb for "to
wheedle" or "to cajole."

In some crafty way Kahlo *se hizo india*—she molded herself, through incessant performance, into an indigenous woman. It is an act of defiance that
upsets the concept of "playing the fool." Actually, she refashioned what *el
indigenismo mexicano* (Mexican indigenousness) is all about, turning it into
a bold defiant political attitude. The fact that she was a woman in a macho
culture made her message all the more powerful.

Kahlo was bisexual. She probably had an affair with Trotsky. And an
affair with the Italian photographer Tina Modotti. All of this emphasizes
her appeal.

I confess that, while looking at the exhibit material, I periodically caught
myself focusing on the other visitors. It was enlightening to see them utterly

hypnotized. Kahlo revolted against the bourgeois aesthetics of her time. It is ironic that, all these decades later, she is now at the center of those aesthetics.

While wandering around, I remembered a thought-provoking essay by Borges called "El escritor argentino y la tradución" ("The Argentine Writer and Tradition"). In it he wonders why the Koran features no camels in its narrative. According to Borges this is a significant absence rather than an oversight. He argues that were the Koran written for foreigners it would be packed with camels because camels are the most recognizable animal connected with Arab civilization. A native, however, doesn't need to be reminded of camels. Why point to an element that is everywhere in the region anyway?

The same goes for Kahlo. Why overemphasize Mexicanness in Mexico? To compensate for a bifurcated identity.

Still, there was little mention of her father's German heritage. And none about her claim that he was Jewish.

I thought to myself: reclaiming Jewish ancestry in Mexico is a fraught affair. More than anything else, for Kahlo and Rivera it was a kind of fad, I believe, in part because neither of them socialized, at least not overtly, with the Mexican Jewish community. On the contrary, they kept themselves at arm's length from it. For them their Jewishness, real or invented, made them renegade artists and bohemian apostates.

That their respective estates ignore this claim is not surprising. I knew from growing up there that Mexico didn't openly acknowledge its Jewish heritage.

I left La Casa Azul and made my way to the Mercado de Coyoacán on Calle Ignacio Allende. It is a splendid fruit and vegetable market, as authentic as it is possible to find nowadays in Mexico City. You can buy all sorts of things there: cloth, kitchen utensils, CDs, piñatas, electronics, and so on. Walking through the aisles is a treat.

2.

Coyoacán is only a few miles from Copilco. I had made up my mind to visit my childhood home. But I got cold feet. In part this was because of a telephone conversation I had with my sister, Liora. She lives in the Santa Fe neighborhood, on the northern side of the city.

She told me she had heard that Copilco was no longer a viable place to live. When I was little, the area was perceived to be remote in regards to where the action was. But it was now overcrowded. Years ago, the municipality built a metro station that connected Copilco with the rest of Mexico City. It had also brought along crime, prostitution, and other ailments.

"Why go there?" my sister said. "You'll be disappointed."

Added to this was a vision I had while looking at a picture book—it made me think of Maurice Sendak's *Where the Wilds Things Are* (1963)—in El Parnaso, a bookstore on the corner of Santa Catarina. In the book, a boy is in his own house when it suddenly breaks away from the piece of land it is on and ends up in a small island made only for it to stand. It is a drifting island, not a static one, and it moves around the ocean in search of a new location to be in.

The picture book—I only browsed through it—seemed to be about finding one's own place in the world. But to me it was about a rootless, peripatetic house with no clearly solid ground underneath. I don't know exactly why, but the narrative made me feel uneasy. The thought of reentering my old house was no longer appealing. What was the point? What would I achieve? Maybe it's better to leave the past in the past. None of my relatives had been in it for decades. In other words, the house was no longer mine. Why cling to it?

At this point I also recalled a photograph I had seen a long time ago, that my mother showed me once. It was of the lot where that childhood house was built in the early 1960s. The lot was empty. It had a couple of sickly short trees and lots of grown weeds all over. I remember the thought I had when I saw the photograph: this is how the place looked while it was waiting for me.

After closing the picture book, I felt the opposite feeling than I had experienced when I had my dream. My old house was no longer waiting for me.

Yet I had explicitly come to Mexico City to visit my house in Copilco. Somehow it was a task, maybe even a mission. I wasn't going to forgo the opportunity.

I made arrangements the following morning. I was staying in a hotel in Colonial Condesa. I called a taxi, which took me all across Avenida Insurgentes. There was heavy traffic. A drive that was meant to take forty-five minutes took an hour and a half, in part because I wanted to see the UNAM campus. In my early years, I spent a lot of time there: playing soccer, biking, and other activities.

We passed by—sometimes near, sometimes not—a number of famous murals I remembered fondly by artists such as Rivera, Siqueiros, Juan O'Gorman, José Chávez Morado, and Francisco Eppens Helguera. Then we took Avenida Universidad and turned right on Avenida Copilco.

The block where my old house stood was on Calle Odontología #85. Even before we reached it, I was shocked by the degree to which the neighborhood had changed. When I was growing up, the area was bucolic. It was also considered remote. My maternal cousins in the northern part of the city never wanted to come play because they thought the drive was too long. Reaching Copilco by public transportation was even harder. Bus routes took students to UNAM but not to my neighborhood. After being dropped off from the bus, you had to walk a couple of miles to reach it.

My parents built the house a few years after I was born. The area was sparsely populated. I remember a lot of empty lots. There was an abandoned factory nearby where my two siblings and I would spend long hours. And there was a sweet small park with a fountain, swings, and a slide. It had a drinking fountain near where I was told Spanish conquistador Hernán Cortés's horses rested on their way to conquering the heart of Tenochtitlán around 1521.

The factory was gone. There were no empty lots. The park was filled with itinerant vendors. Most of all I was overwhelmed by the density: of people, of automobiles, of buildings, of stores. Metro Copilco, a subway station a few blocks away, was an unending well from which masses swelled onto the street's sidewalks. The station was surrounded by taco vendors and an array of other merchants pushing products of all kinds: dolls, soda, cotton candy, notebooks, T-shirts . . .

I asked the driver to drop me off on the corner and wait for me. I walked half a block until I was in front of my old house. It had a sizable fence along the roofline. The fence immediately made me uncomfortable. The first image that crossed my mind was the portion of fence I have seen in various parts along the United States–Mexican border. I also thought of the wall in Jerusalem separating Israelis and Palestinians. I have walked portions of that wall on various trips I have made to Israel. When I was little nothing of its kind was needed in Copilco. Given the amount of people pullulating around, the current owners of the house had probably decided to build it in as visible a way as possible in order to keep burglars away.

A beautiful tree that used to live on the sidewalk was gone. The garage door had been changed from iron to a material resembling wood. On the ground floor there was some graffiti painted with chalk. I couldn't understand it in full: something about the corrupt policies of the current UNAM chancellor. A few of what had been my neighbors' residences were now dental dispensaries, stationery stores, and other businesses.

I felt dislocated. I was alien in my own surroundings. My heart was trembling.

For a few seconds, I hesitated to ring the bell. When I did, I told myself I was courageous. Why go back to the past? Or at least to this particular past? From now on, I would remember Copilco not by what it was like, back in the 1960s, but by what I was looking at right now.

I waited for a few minutes. No one answered. I tried ringing again for a longer time.

A woman said something through the intercom. I told her I was an old tenant and that I wanted to see the house again.

"No hay nadie," she stated, "There's nobody here." I smiled. Her words reminded me of a line in Octavio Paz's *El laberinto de la soledad* (*The Labyrinth of Solitude*, 1950), his classic study of the Mexican collective psyche. At one point, when he and his first wife were just married, they hired a maid. One night they heard noises in the kitchen in the middle of the night. Paz went to see who was in there. From the hallway he asked who it was. "Nadie, señor," answered the maid, "It's just me." In the book Paz writes of a feeling of inferiority he recognized in the Mexican people, whose initial view of themselves is as nobody.

I asked again—gently—if I could see the house.

"No," she said again through the intercom. Disheartened, I started to make my way back to the taxi, and then I heard someone calling me. A woman at the entrance door called me back and asked who I was. I told her my name and that I was raised in the house. My father, Abraham Stavans, was a telenovela actor. I now lived between Boston and New York but was in Mexico for a few days on a short visit that included, hopefully, a visit to my old house. Politely, I wondered if I could take a quick look at the inside and began describing the first-floor layout.

"Será un placer," the woman said, "With pleasure." She only had a few minutes before she needed to run out. And the second floor was in disarray. But I was welcome to see the first floor with her. Coming back to a place where one lived such a long time ago must be difficult, she said. Everything will probably look strange. "Please come in, though."

As we made our way into the house, I asked her about the fence. She said thieves entered a bunch of years ago and at gunpoint stole numerous things. The neighborhood in general was dangerous. Police didn't patrol it the way they should. Or else the police were probably in cahoots with the burglars.

Once inside I reached an immediate conclusion: the house was much darker than I remembered it. And nothing, absolutely nothing, reminded me of the past. I knew the architectural design, but the kitchen, dining and living rooms, and hallway had no resemblance to the places I held in my memory.

I wanted to be gentle. "Sí, es igual y diferente," I told the woman, "It's the same and different."

Most significantly was a deodorant I sensed as I wandered around. It was pleasant yet unlike anything we ever used when cleaning. It must be a new brand, I told myself. Generally, I have a good sense of smell, although, like most people, I can't bring back the memory of a specific smell I've been exposed to. I tried invoking the original smell of the house. Or better, the smell of different rooms. The kitchen, for instance, I remember smelling like my father's pleasant aftershave lotion. And my brother's room for some reason in my mind is connected with baby powder. Unfortunately, much as I tried I couldn't invoke these smells. And that saddened me.

The woman told me a few things about her and her husband, where they were from, what they did for a living, but I don't remember anything at all. Physically, I was next to her but mentally I was elsewhere.

Overall, the strongest emotion I experienced was discomfort. It probably was a mistake to come back. I should not have paid any attention to my dream.

I walked through a couple of rooms, look at the patio, the garden in the back, and then thanking the woman profusely I made my way back to the front door. I told her a taxi was waiting for me on the corner.

"When is a place no longer yours?" I asked.

She sighed.

Maybe the dream I had was a premonition: once you leave a place, you're a total stranger to it. The best you can do is keep it in your memory. That version of it is yours forever.

3.

Rivera's claim that his ancestors were judaizantes inspired me to look up the word on my iPhone, just to see how it was defined. I also thought it would be a good idea to look it up in a biography. Or maybe in a biographical encyclopedia, which wouldn't be too difficult to find at the Librería Gandhi, a first-rate bookstore on Avenida Miguel Ángel de Quevedo #222, not far from where the taxi dropped me off after my tour through Copilco.

After I had lunch at a nearby VIPS, a restaurant chain I like, I walked back to Librería Gandhi to browse through the section of lexicons, encyclopedias, and other volumes about languages. I learned that the word *judai-*

zantes was used in the Spanish-speaking world up until the mid-nineteenth century, in demeaning ways, to accuse Jews of undermining the Christian faith. In fact, the word denoted an unabated rejection of all things Jewish, linking Jews to the devil.

The *Dictionary of the Spanish Language*, published under the aegis of the Royal Academy in Madrid, is the most authoritative source. The first edition of the dictionary appeared in 1780. That edition gives the Latin root, *iudaizāre*, then defines the word: (1) *abrazar la religión de los judíos*, To embrace the religion of Jews; and (2) *Dicho de un cristiano: practicar pública o privadamente ritos o ceremonias de la ley judaica*, Said of a Christian: to practice, publicly or privately, the rites and ceremonies of Jewish law.

I also learned that the word was first recorded in Sebastián de Covarrubias's *Tesoro de la lengua española o castellana* (1611), which is regarded by scholars as the foundation of Hispanic lexicography. Covarrubias, whose family was of Jewish stock, compiled his thesaurus with the support of the Inquisition. In the climate of intolerance, someone like him needed to be *más papista que el Papa*, more zealous than the pope himself.

Along with *judaizar*, Covarrubias, in the entry on *judío*, includes the adverb *judaizante*. In this entry he describes Jews as the Chosen People, calling attention to their continuous life in Spain for centuries, and at this point he argues that, as a result of their *insolencias, embustes*, and *codicia* (insolence, lies, and greed), Jews were thrown out from the country. His tone endorses such punishment. Covarrubias lists two strategies engaged in by the Inquisition before the expulsion to distinguish Jews from the rest of the population. One, in 1370, was the use of a sign, similar to the yellow Star of David used by the Nazis, stamped in their clothing. As a result of this, he called them *judíos de señal* (Jews with a sign). The second strategy, imposed in 1405, was the use of a more prominent identifier: a red circular cloth, featured on the right shoulder. Tangentially, Covarrubias affirmed that the same practice was also used with cattle.

Of course, I didn't need any lexicon to know that in twenty-first-century Spanish the word *judío* remains culturally charged. Among Jews it is a day-to-day noun. But non-Jews use it in derogatory ways.

The lexicographic search made it clear to me that what I had seen in Argentina, and what most attracted me, was the merging of Jewish and Hispanic elements in Latin America. Not separate but juxtaposed. That's what my exploration on the Yiddish gauchos was about. And Jevel Katz's Casteidish.

Something inside inspired me to focus my attention on the colonial times in Latin America, specifically the Inquisition, Crypto-Jews, and whatever intermingling took place between Spanish conquistadors and missionaries of Jewish descent and the indigenous population of the New World.

In El Once, I heard that Buenos Aires never had a large Crypto-Jewish population during the sixteenth century, but in contrast, I knew that Mexico and the American Southwest did. I also knew there were communities of so-called *Indios judíos* (Indian Jews) in various parts of Latin America. In fact, I had visited several of them on different occasions. But I had never attempted to understand what characterized them. In what sense were they "Indian" and in what sense "Jewish"?

When I returned to the United States this time, I called upon a number of acquaintances, including Isaac Goldemberg, to help me imagine this part of my journey. I have known Goldemberg ever since I moved to New York City in the mid-1980s. He and I lived in adjacent buildings. One of the last times I had seen him he told me about a documentary film he was embarking on about the Indian Jews.

Goldemberg and I met at a café in the Upper West Side. Born in Chepén, on Peru's Pacific coast in the country's north, in 1945 and now on the faculty at Hostos Community College in the Bronx, he is one of the most important Jewish writers from Latin America. And, also, a vivid incarnation of *mestizaje*.

His father was Ashkenazi and his mother Catholic. He is the author, most prominently, of *The Fragmented Life of Don Jacobo Lerner* (1976), about the search for definition of a protagonist who is very much like Goldemberg. The title itself insinuates the answer he comes across: the self as a succession of fragments.

Goldemberg writes exclusively in Spanish, which isn't easy when you live on a day-to-day basis in an English-language ecosystem. I asked him why he had left Peru in his teens. "Basically, I left because I wanted to see the world. I felt divided."

As a result of his mixed blood, he didn't fit in with the mainstream Jewish community. He felt ostracized. But then he made peace with himself.

"Jews are hybrid creatures," added Goldemberg. "In that sense, our Latin American Jews are unique, different from European Jews, American Jews, and so on. We're a unique mix in which language plays an essential role. It makes us part of our countries of origin, it shapes us physically as well as philosophically. But it is juxtaposed with Hebrew, Yiddish, Ladino. That juxtaposition is in our genetic chart."

He added: "I was Peruvian before I was Jewish. For me, to be Peruvian meant being Catholic. All my mother's family were Catholic. This was in Chepén (which, in Moche language, means 'house or mother of sand'). I moved to Lima, where my father was, at the age of eight. Until then I didn't know he was Jewish. I began asking questions: who I was, what I was. I didn't want to *quemar las naves*, to burn one's ships," he stressed. (Interestingly, the expression in English is "to burn one's bridges.") He went on: "I kept my ties with Chepén as well as my mother. Back and forth, back and forth."

Goldemberg paused. "Chepén's main mountain became Mount Sinai, the *acequia* (irrigation ditch) across it the Jordan River, and the surrounding desert my biblical Judea. I decided that being Jewish like my father meant being Peruvian without refuting my Jewish roots, and that being Peruvian like my mother meant being Jewish without rejecting my Peruvian roots. That's how I ended up with a double identity. Today, I find enormous satisfaction in being *el otro de mí mismo*, my self's other side."

This time around I had caught Goldemberg just back from Lima, where he was in preproduction on the documentary. It was called *Los incas judíos* (the Inca Jews). With about half of the budget in hand and the rest expected from a couple of investors as well as the Peruvian government, he had interviewed, in the country's capital and in Cajamarca, a major city in the northern Andes with a population of approximately two hundred thousand, a number of Cajamarcan Indians (around three hundred) who had converted to Judaism in the 1990s. "I'm passionate about the topic," he told me. "I want to show the Jewishness of Peruvians and *la peruanidad*, the Peruvianness of Jews. I'm eager to make a movie based on a detective novel I wrote, *Remember the Scorpion* (2015). I'm hoping the documentary will serve me as a springboard."

I prompted him to reflect on the beliefs of Spanish chroniclers and missionaries during the colonial period about the biblical origins of the pre-Columbian people in the Americas. "As you know, several of them where converso descendants," Goldemberg posited. "This genealogical link likely contributed to them planting the hypothesis that the indigenous population were descendants of the Lost Tribes. One of them, the Dominican friar Gregorio García, in his book *Origin of the Indians of the New World and the Occidental Indies* (1607), sought to prove this thesis by offering a series of resemblances between the Incas and the Jews. For instance, that the two used sandals and dressed similarly, that the two made offerings to their deities of the first harvest, that they followed the custom of returning their dead to their original lands and they bury them in hillocks, that they had equivalent physiognomic features, that the Inca regal title '*Manco*' is derived from the Semitic root '*Malek*,' which means king, that they frequently referred to themselves as brothers even when they weren't, that the two peoples would subject themselves to torture without resistance, and so on."

I asked Goldemberg if he thought the Spanish chroniclers and missionaries were in the business of propagating these ideas. He responded: "On one hand, in the case of Fray Gregorio García, who wasn't a descendant of conversos, it was justifiable to colonize the Indians in order 'to fulfill the divine punishment against the Jews described by biblical prophet Isaiah.' On the other hand, in the face of the most important question of the time (Was there proof that the indigenous population was human? Should these individuals be considered beasts of burden?), it is possible that some religious leaders endorsed the thesis so as to grant the Indians a humanity that had been put in question by society at large, since being Jewish was unquestionable proof that such a population was indeed human."

The conversation with Goldemberg left me inspired. I recalled that, years before, I had read a novel by the Peruvian Nobel Prize–winner Mario Vargas Llosa, *The Storyteller* (1989), that kept my fantasy alive. Saúl Zuratas, the book's Jewish protagonist, is an anthropology student of Sephardic descent who, in an attempt to harmonize his Jewish and Peruvian selves, decides to abandon scientific research and become a storyteller for the Machiguenga, a tribe in the Amazon. To tell stories, and to use them as repositories of ancestral memory, is Zuratas's way to help the Machiguengas survive—and to help him make his own fractured identity whole.

This isn't one of Vargas Llosa's most accomplished books yet to me it is among the most significant. It explores the topic of cultural nomadism, which is what the Jewish diaspora is all about. In an interview when it was released Vargas Llosa insinuated that the divided self of the protagonist, Saúl Zuratas, was loosely inspired by Isaac Goldemberg's quest.

Even if *The Storyteller* is sheer fiction, the fact that people associated Goldemberg with it and with indigenous cultures in Latin America granted him a special aura. Truth is, Vargas Llosa's novel isn't the only one that at once nurtures this type of nostalgia for the region's aboriginal roots and predicates the idea that the Jews are another group of people who also hold important secrets about Latin America's origins. Sometime in the early 2000s, Moacyr Scliar—my Brazilian friend whose Jewish centaur I saw in the Argentina Pampa—had given me a copy in Portuguese of his own novel *A majestade do Xingu* (1997). It has a similar theme. In this case the plot is about a real person: Noel Nutels, a Ukrainian Jew who emigrated to

Pernambuco, Brazil. He had studied medicine in Recife and practiced as a physician. But Nutels was a fervent lefty. Using his skills as a doctor needed to be connected with the ideological causes he practiced. And so, in 1931 he began to work for the Serviço de Proteção ao Índio—a federal organization later on transformed into the Fundação Nacional do Índio—devoted to helping the country's indigenous population.

The more I thought about these two books, the more they became linked in my mind to a single concept: surrender. In Vargas Llosa's novel there is an actual rejection of Western values, whereas in Scliar there is an attempt to keep these values in use while inserting oneself into Indian civilization.

I decided to return to Mexico City. But first I spent time researching the myth of the Lost Tribes of Israel. As Goldemberg suggested, it is a myth that plays a considerable role in Latin America. And not only there: as late as the nineteenth century, travelers all over the globe engaged in the practice of spotting these tribes in all sorts of distant lands, from Afghanistan and Azerbaijan to Burma (Myanmar) and Kurdistan, from Kashmir, China, and Japan to Zimbabwe, Mozambique, and Uganda.

Goldemberg was right. The source of the myth in the New World dates back to the fifteenth century. Almost from the moment Columbus set foot in Hispaniola and when the encounter between Spaniards and the indigenous population took place, speculation among missionaries and others on the origins of the aboriginals became hotly contested.

Fray Bartolomé de Las Casas was the sixteenth-century "defender of the Indians" and arguably one of the most influential thinkers in Latin America (although he was born and died in Spain, most of his life was spent in Latin America). Las Casas believed the indigenous people in the Americas were descendants of the ten Lost Tribes. These are the biblical tribes, identified by the names of Joseph's siblings—Asher, Dan, Ephraim, Gad, Issachar, Manasseh, Naphtali, Reuben, Simeon, and Zebulon—who, after the death of King Solomon in 928 BCE, created the Kingdom of Israel, which covered most of the central and northern Land of Israel. The other kingdom, the Kingdom of Judea, was made of the remaining two tribes, Judah and Benjamin. This kingdom spread on the Judean highlands.

When the Kingdom of Israel was conquered by the Assyrians in 721 BCE, the inhabitants of the central and northern kingdom were deported. What exactly happened to them is unknown. Among Jews themselves there was a debate. Rabbi Akiva, for instance, a much-admired sage connected with the Mishna, believed they were lost forever, whereas his intellectual opponent, Rabbi Eliezer, was convinced they would indeed be found. This discussion also thrived among non-Jews. It remained active in the European imagination at the end of the fifteenth century.

In *A Short Description of the Destruction of the Indies* (1552), Las Casas argued that the language of the Island of Saint Domingo was "corrupt Hebrew." He also claimed that the indigenous population found by Columbus was acquainted with Adam and Eve and the books of the Old Testament, "which likewise was a Hebrew doctrine."

Similar views were presented by other chroniclers such as Father Diego Durán, author of *The Aztecs: The History of the Indies of New Spain* (1571). Perhaps more prominent was the work of Fray Bernardino de Sahagún, who stated that the original Mexicans borrowed from the moral code of the Jews. And the Spanish historian Gonzalo Fernández de Oviedo y Valdés, in *General and Natural History of the Indies* (1557), argued that the Indians in Nicaragua refrained from working on the Sabbath.

I discovered that the myth is embedded in a baroque tapestry of historical references. According to Eldad ha-Dani, a Jewish traveler in the ninth century, he spotted the missing tribes beyond the rivers of Abyssinia. His geographic coordinates weren't particularly sharp. Abyssinia may refer to modern-day Ethiopia. Or, in the medieval imagination, "Abyssinia" may refer to any landscape beyond the European confine. Ha-Dani also made mention of the famous Sambatyon River, a Jewish stream, which, he argued, stopped running and came to a still on the Sabbath. The reference is as much a myth as his vision of having located the "Lost Tribes." Likewise, Benjamin of Tudela, the Jews of Persia (in today's Iran) believed that four of the ten lost tribes—Asher, Dan, Naphtali, and Zebulon—lived beyond the River Gozan, in the towns of Nizzabur, located in a mountainous region.

Fast forward to the seventeenth century, when Menasseh ben Israel (aka Manoel Dias Soeiro), a major Jewish scholar in Amsterdam who founded the city's first printing press and was a teacher of Baruch Spinoza, argued in his book *Esperança de Israel* (Hope of Israel [1640]) that the lost tribes lived in Brazil. Indeed, he planned at one point to emigrate to the Americas in order to see its members with his own eyes. Ben Israel also pleaded to Oliver Cromwell in 1655 to allow the resettlement of Jews in England, using the argument of the lost tribes as proof that the return had biblical undertones.

A few years back, while passing through Colombia, I went for a couple of hours to a small community of Jewish coverts called Bello that is near Medellín, the country's second-largest city located in the central region of the Andes. In total, there were about three hundred Jews. Their leader had once been a priest in a congregation of three thousand who converted to Judaism, and he now leads a community of about seventy Jewish families. Tradition was what kept the people together. There was also a kosher bakery, a children's Hebrew school, and other communal institutions. A busy yeshiva trained many of the men in the art of Talmudic exegesis.

It was a spectacle to behold. I was greeted like a sibling. I talked to various members about their daily routine. I got a feeling of dislocation, though. A few Bello dwellers approached me with proselytizing zeal, intent on recruiting me into their religious activities. They made me feel like an apostate. This often happens with converts. They end of being more devout than Jews who were born Jews.

Their case wasn't unique. In fact, there are about half a dozen fringe communities of this kind in Latin America, if not more. I describe them as "fringe" because, regardless of their authenticity, in all cases the central *Kehila* rejects their claim. They are portrayed as impostors of various kinds whose attachment to Judaism is only skin-deep.

For instance, in Ecuador there is a group that seeks to "return" to Judaism through the guidance of a Brazilian American rabbi called Jacques Cukierkorn. And on the Brazilian side of the Amazon River, in Belém, about 150 kilometers from Manaus, I know of a community of about one thousand. This one started with the immigration to the region, made predominantly of men, who traveled all the way from Morocco between 1810 and 1910 as part of the boom in the region's rubber industry. With time, these Ottoman immigrants intermingled with Amazonian women. The "Indian Jews" of Belém adapted to the customs of the area while retaining an assortment of elements from the Jewish religion.

Likewise, after my trip to El Once and the agricultural communities of Entre Ríos, I stopped for a few days in Lima where I came across yet another manifestation of this peculiar type of Latin American Judaism. Unfortunately, I only got to appreciate *el judaísmo charapa*, the Jewish Indians of Peru, through hearsay. I was invited for Shabbat to the household of Rabbi Guillermo Bronstein. He is the religious leader of Peru's largest synagogue, Asociación Judía de Beneficencia y Culto de 1870. Before dinner, I prayed at his temple. The synagogue has about 225 families and is located on Calle Libertad #375.

Over lasagna and salad in his house Rabbi Bronstein told me of three different groups of Indian Jews in Peru, where the total Jewish population was about three thousand. One of these groups was the community in Cajamarca that Isaac Goldemberg was including in his documentary. Rabbi

Bronstein said it was also possible to connect with a few of them living in Israel's Occupied Territories.

Then he described the community of *judíos charapas* in Iquitos, in the Peruvian Amazon, on the east side of the Andes. He mentioned a book by Ariel Segal, a scholar who taught in Lima, Peru, and whom I had met decades ago in his native Caracas. The book was called *The Jews of the Amazon: Self-Exile in Earthly Paradise* (1999). Rabbi Bronstein talked about it. He also offered me a few contacts and suggested that I go there. I was intent on it, but other activities came in the way. Then I left it for another occasion, but that occasion never materialized. Rabbi Bronstein said that, in practice, the judíos charapas engage in a mix of Jewish and Catholic rituals, that scores of charapas had emigrated to Israel after converting to Judaism, including about 150 people between 2013 and 2014. The conversion was done under the advice of his brother, Rabbi Marcelo Bronstein, of New York's B'nai Jeshurun, the same synagogue that Rabbi Marshall Meyer had reinvigorated in the 1990s. Marcelo Bronstein was one of his two successors.

And as the third group in Peru, Rabbi Bronstein mentioned the community of B'nei Moshe, north of Lima. He said it was founded in 1966 by a local man called Villanueva (he couldn't remember his first name) who apparently decided at some crucial point in his life to convert to Judaism. Like the charapas, the "Inca Jews" were mostly flown by the Israel government to the West Bank, in Kfar Tapuach.

4.

Truth is, I didn't need to go to Colombia, Ecuador, Brazil, or Peru to come face-to-face with the so-called Indios judíos. In my own native Mexico there is a group of them who live in Venta Prieta. They serve as a perfect example of the misunderstanding that surrounds these groups.

I was first in Venta Prieta in my twenties. And on a return trip to Mexico City, after the one where I visited my childhood house, I went back to it. It is a fascinatingly complex community. While they have been rejected time and again by the country's Jewish mainstream, they plow on unencumbered.

In Spanish the word *venta* means sale. In the early twentieth century, when the name Venta Prieta apparently originates, *ventas* were road stands on the Camino Real de la Plata, as the road from Mexico City was known, and the name of Venta Prieta comes from the itinerant vendors who used to offer fruit, vegetables, and other goodies for sale to those traveling along the road. I heard it said, although it seems improbable, that *prieta*, which means dark, is a reference to a method of smoking their meat and other dishes these vendors would sometimes use. Or else, to the way they liked their food well cooked.

They live in Pachuca, a city of about half a million people in Mexico's central state of Hidalgo. The road that goes from Mexico to Venta Prieta is about sixty miles long, though the traffic always makes the trip feel much longer. In total, there are about 150 Venta Prietanos. They live within a few dense blocks. I had been told that other folks fantasized Aztec stereotypes (wearing feather panaches, painted faces, and pierced noses and ears). I had also been told that the Jews of Venta Prieta aren't really Indians but, rather, mestizos. And they are tired of being treated by tourists as part of a freak show. The pervasiveness of the stereotypes has turned them inward. They would rather be left alone.

The town is nondescript. Not until you look closely into their habitat do you realize the way they have organized their life around Jewish rituals. Venta Prieta has a large cinder-block building that is the synagogue, and quite imposing, given the surroundings. It is called Templo Negev, on Calle Benito Juárez. Neighbors live modestly in community. There is a cemetery nearby.

The origin of the community is lost in legend. The patriarch of the place was a man called Ramón Jirón. I have heard rumors that he ran away from an abusive father, or else from the obligation to become a priest.

Around 2005, a dispute took place at the heart of Venta Prieta. A portion of the community expressed interest in becoming more devout. The feeling was that commitment to the faith needed to be more complete. The option was orthodoxy. But others disagreed.

And, in typical Jewish fashion, a new synagogue was formed, one committed to conservative principles.

As in the case of the community in Cajamarca, Peru, to consider the Jews of Venta Prieta as Indians is ridiculous. As a community it seems they organized around 1920. In other words, their history is relatively recent. It matches a series of articles published by the Hungarian ethnographer Raphael Patai, a polymath interested in folklore and alchemy and in the Bible and the life of Jews in Arab lands who collaborated with Robert Graves, in 1964, on the book *Hebrew Myths: The Book of Genesis*. After visiting the place Patai believed the birth of Venta Prieta was actually due to a Protestant proselytizer who converted the people of Venta Prieta, first to the Iglesia de Dios and only later to Judaism.

The whole affair is often an uncomfortable topic for the Ashkenazi community in Mexico City whose members look at Venta Prieta less as a legitimate source of historical debate than as a nuisance. While in Mexico, I talked to various staff members of the Kehila on Calle Acapulco #70. Their response was dismissive. This rejection was interpreted by some to be racist. The mainstream stand is corroborated by the Spanish version of *Encyclopedia Judaica*.

> Beside the religious congregations of the Sephardim and Ashkenazim, there is a group of proselytes who are called Indian Jews. The members of this group are no more Indians than the remainder of Mexican citizenry. There has also arisen a pretension, with all the exaggeration of sensationalism that this group consists of descendants of the secret Jews of the sixteenth century. This is an exaggeration.

> The Jewish group to which we refer came in great part from the Protestant sect, Iglesia de Dios, who began their activities in Mexico during the past century. Part of the members of this sect consider themselves spiritual Jews, circumcised in their hearts, and venerate Jesus of Nazareth, neither as a God or son of God, but as a prophet. As a consequence of disputes and for other reasons, some affiliates of the sect decided to consider themselves Jews and have lived as such for some two decades. Their children learn to read Hebrew, and the cult uses the Jewish devotionals.

The name "Indian Jews" is polemical. The community dislikes it. For decades they had no rabbi, no *mohel*, and few prayer books. They were also uncertain about mortuary rituals. Their customs were, loosely interpreted, halfway between reform and conservative, although a lot felt improvised. They felt adrift.

That changed with Rabino Samuel S. Lerer, an American conservative rabbi, who moved to Mexico in 1968 to lead the English-language Congregación Beth-Israel in the country's capital. Once he had established his name, he became a liaison for the Venta Prieta community, which he first visited in the 1960s, officiating in rituals such as circumcisions and Bar Mitzvahs, preparing the congregation for the holidays, and becoming a personal friend.

Lerer means teacher in Yiddish. Born in Palestine in 1915 before the British Mandate, Lerer was known among Mexican Jews of all persuasions for his liberal views. Rabino Lerer was ordained as an orthodox rabbi in 1938 by Rabbi Abraham Isaac Kook, the first Ashkenazi chief rabbi in British Mandate Palestine (he went by the Hebrew acronym of Haroeh) and one of the most influential rabbis of the twentieth century. Rabbi Kook had an enormous impact on him, which is seen in his strategies with the

Venta Prieta people and other Mexicans interested in becoming Jewish. A major thinker at the crossroad between Zionism and Jewish orthodoxy, Rabbi Kook believed the messianic era had already started and Zionism was part of its plan. Basing his beliefs in Jewish law and biblical prophecy, he was apolitical, refraining from membership in political parties. What mattered to him was reaching out to outcasts because his belief was that all Jews together would bring along redemption. Not surprisingly, Rabbi Kook had empathy toward nonreligious groups among the Jewish people.

Rabino Lerer took Rabbi Kook's teachings to heart. Before coming to Mexico, he led congregations in Montgomery, Alabama; Hollywood, Florida; and Akron, Ohio. He was also on the faculty of the University of Iowa for three years. But it was in Mexico where he left his mark. By the time he retired in 1999 and moved to San Antonio, Texas (he died in 2004, at the age of eighty-nine), he had converted approximately three thousand people, including my sister-in-law and a friend of mine who was at one point married to a former teacher of mine at the Yiddishe Shule in Mexique. Rabbi Lerer even advised my friend how to get circumcised at the age of thirty-seven.

A bunch of the converts belonged to the Venta Prieta community. And Rabbi Lerer converted members of another "Indian Jewish" community in Puebla, Mexico, who had a stronger belief, in contrast with their Venta Prieta counterparts, of their Crypto-Jewish ancestry. By the year 2000 there were eight families in the town. Rabbi Lerer had converted them all. He also converted people in the port of Veracruz, on the Gulf of Mexico, with whom he became involved in the 1970s.

A record of Rabino Lerer's connections with these communities appears in the documentary *Ocho candelas* (Eight candles [2002]), directed by Sandro Halphen. It centers on the Jews of Veracruz, who eventually created the Comunidad Beth Shmuel, with approximately thirty families. In interviews they describe their coming to Judaism through marriage. But there are a few that describe their converso life dating back to the expulsion of the Jewish from Spain in 1492.

Since Rabino Lerer's death, a rabbi from Mexico City goes for Shabbat services. A few of the members of the community have moved to Israel, paid for by the Israeli government.

Rabino Lerer's conversions weren't recognized by the Kehila. They might be linked to Rabbi Kook's messianic drive. The return of Crypto-Jews is connected with a larger vision of redemption. Only when all Jews (those who openly acknowledge their faith and those who have been forced to keep it in hiding) reemerge as a single nation, a tribe made of many tribes, will the world be mended. That messianic era will therefore include the Jews of Venta Prieta.

5.

In that second trip to Mexico I decided to focus on the Inquisition. I knew that near the Alameda Central, the main park in downtown Mexico City, there had been the place where autos-da-fe took place. I asked one of the waiters. To my surprise he knew all about it. "It was called Plaza del Quemadero," he said. "The plaza of the burnings. It is in the western section to the Alameda. Jews, witches, homosexuals, and other deviants were sacrificed in public offerings."

An elegant man in his seventies, the waiter used the expression *No quisiera estar en su pellejo*: "I wouldn't want to be in their shoes." He also pointed me in the direction of the Palacio de la Inquisición. "I don't know much about the building, though," he confessed. "I know it has undergone different kinds of renovations."

The waiter gave me a brochure. It included a listing. The Palacio was included.

I walked a few blocks. Unfortunately, he was right that the building had been renovated. On the corner of Calle República de Brasil and República de Venezuela, the building faces the Plaza de Santo Domingo, where, among other places, the Holy Office of the Inquisition once performed autos-da-fe. Yet the site is no longer connected to the Holy Office of the Inquisitions, also called *Tribunal de la Santa Fe* or *El Santo Oficio*, in Mexico.

After repeated pleas I convinced a guard standing at the door to let me have a peek inside. It was clear it still retained its former grandeur. It is possible to imagine the *audiencias* taking place in its chambers. This, after all, was the bureaucratic headquarters. Decisions were made by the official inquisitor, Fray Pedro Moya de Contreras, and his staff.

I pointed to the listing that the waiter had given me. The guard didn't have a clue what I was talking about. Nor did anyone else. Then, after I kept insisting, an old lady told me of a current exhibit on the Santo Oficio, this one on Calle Tacuba #5, in a place called Museo de la Tortura y de la Pena Capital.

As it turns out the focus wasn't at all on the Tribunal de la Fe in Mexico. In capital letters, a marquee outside highlighted the word *tortura*. I made my way in. Inside I found grotesque artifacts with a variety of historical origins from the French Revolution to the USSR. These artifacts included garrotes, *brodequin*, and *turcas*. A scene explained what the *muerte por garrote*, in which a victim was supposedly locked on the neck and made to asphyxiate. Another showcased a *potro*: a long table where a person was physically stretched to excruciating degrees in order for the inquisitors to extract the "truth." As I turned around, I saw pathetic-looking, blood-spilling human-sized mannequins.

It all felt like a Madame Tussauds attraction. I found out it was all an itinerant exhibit, from Florence, Italy. It was in Mexico City only temporarily. No reference was made to famous cases of autos-da-fe during the colonial period in Mexico. Nothing about the roots of the Inquisition.

I wasn't surprised. Open discussion on the Inquisition in Latin America is scarce. In Spain and Portugal too. School textbooks skim over the theme. The rigidity of the Catholic Church, still connected in people's mind to the Franco dictatorship, is a topic of discussion. But anti-Semitism isn't addressed head-on. In fact, one might say that Spain and (to a lesser extent) Portugal are illustrious examples of countries where anti-Semitism thrived without Jews since they were expelled in 1492.

Although the Tribunal Inquisition was formally established in Mexico in 1571, priests with inquisitorial duties arrived as early as 1524—that is, shortly after Hernán Cortés's conquest. A monastery where the Inquisition administered its affairs was built on the Plaza de Santo Domingo.

I was upset by the utter disregard for historical seriousness. It was systematic, though. Hispanic civilization as a whole looks at this period with neither interest nor respect. One could notice this at the level of language, not only Mexican Spanish but the Spanish language in general. To what extent was it impregnated with Jewish presence as a result of *La Convivencia* (early eighth to late fifteenth century), the period of more or less harmonious cohabitation in Spain of the three major Abrahamic religions—Judaism, Christianity, and Islam—in spite of occasional violent outbursts and tense theological disputes? And what happened after the expulsion of the Jews in 1492?

I walked into another Sanborns like the one I had been to in Coyoacán. This one was at Avenida Francisco I. Madero #4 and is called the Casa de los Azulejos (the house of tiles). It has a majestic tile façade and a memorable courtyard. After the American brothers who created Sanborns bought the building in 1917, they asked Orozco, one of Rivera's friends, to paint a small mural in it.

Rivera painted a number of murals in downtown Mexico City, in places such as the Palacio Nacional, in Plaza de la Constitución, as well as in the

Secretaría de Educación Pública. Depending on the period, Kahlo would go visit him. They would hold court at the Sanborns. They spent time there with friends such as Tina Modotti, Edward Weston, Carlos Mérida, and others.

Two of their friends were Jewish. One was Anita Brenner, who was Kahlo's junior by a couple of years. An influential public intellectual whose work defined the way Mexico was perceived throughout the twentieth century, Brenner commissioned Modotti and Weston to travel around Mexico documenting the country's diverse array of art and architecture. Their work resulted in hundreds of photographs that Brenner included in her book on Mexican art, *Idols behind Altars* (1929). These black-and-white photographs serve as a stunning archive of the tension between nature and society and provide a record of a nation making its way uncomfortably toward industrialization. The book reads as a composite that pushes hard to celebrate the mythical side of Mexico.

Likewise, in *The Wind that Swept Mexico* (1943), which follows the ups and downs of the Mexican Revolution from 1910 to almost the end of the Second World War, Brenner offers a bracing photographic history assembled from journalistic sources by George R. Leighton, helped by Walker Evans who made prints from historical negatives at his studio. Brenner organized exhibitions and wrote children's books inspired by folktales such as those of the Nahua indigenous people, like *The Boy Who Could Do Anything and Other Mexican Folktales* (1942), illustrated by Jean Charlot.

In her role as interpreter Brenner influenced policy. One example is her involvement in convincing the Mexican government to open the door to Jewish refugees during the war. Another example is the instrumental role she played, along with Rivera, in persuading President Lázaro Cárdenas to allow Trotsky to come to Mexico from Norway as a refugee fleeing from Stalin. Some fellow advocates belonged to the Trotskyist Young People's Socialist League in the United States. These Jewish public intellectuals, mostly children of Yiddish-speaking immigrants, formed a crucial bridge between European political and cultural thought and American audiences.

At Sanborns I imagined Brenner conversing with Kahlo over coffee and *arroz con leche*, at a time when Mexican art was dominated by still lifes and scenic images of volcanos.

Kahlo shows her some photographs of her work. The critic looks at the artist's paintings with a dismissive gesture.

"Frida, I honestly don't think there's a market for this type of self-representation, especially by a Mexican woman."

At the core the two disliked each other. Brenner was in the business of selling Mexico to outsiders whereas Kahlo was about refashioning it altogether.

For Brenner, Kahlo's statement that her father was Jewish was another symptom of the artist's desire to reinvent herself from head to toe.

Another visitor at the Casa de los Azulejos was Isaac Berliner, author of *Shtot fun palatzn* (1936), Yiddish for *City of Palaces*, a collection of poems in which he showcased his first impressions of modern Mexico City.

In fact, the day I visited the Sanborns I had a copy of the Yiddish book with me. A new edition with English translations was published in 1996. I wanted to read it while trekking through the area where Berliner had lived.

The poems themselves are less lyrical than impressionistic, the by-product of a newcomer's reaction to these exotic lands where pre-Columbian myths are juxtaposed with European influence. The imagery is rigid, pre-dictable. Berliner talks of mute churches made of stone, pious nuns, armor-clad bronzed bodies, and of a sea of parishioners committed to a millennial faith.

Berliner was born in Lodz. He was already collaborating with a number of publications in Poland when, in 1922, at the age of twenty-three, he sailed toward Mexico, where he soon became a pioneer in local Jewish cultural life. He wrote for numerous magazines in Warsaw, New York, Toronto, and Buenos Aires, as well as on Mexican Jewish periodicals such as *Di Tsayt*, *Di Shtime*, and *Undzer Vort*.

My sense is that his book would have been utterly forgotten were it not for Berliner's chance encounter with Rivera. Years ago I saw an anonymous newspaper photo, dated 1934, depicting the two men dutifully looking at the camera. An obese fifty-eight-year-old Rivera, white shirt, pants belted above the waist, striped tie, wearing his customary working jacket, has his right arm laying around the shoulders of the other man, a stern, smoking thirty-five-year-old Yitskhok (Yiddish for Isaac) Berliner. I visualize Berliner entering Casa de los Azulejos—not a place Jewish immigrants socialized in. A few days earlier an acquaintance had put him in touch with the world-renowned painter Diego Rivera. In ungrammatical Spanish, he tells the painter about his collection of poems. In turn Rivera, sparked by his own self-created Jewish ancestry, empathizes with this foreigner. He knows that

Yiddish is the language of the downtrodden in Europe who are victims of pogroms. Their suffering is his as well.

Berliner wonders if the master would be willing to illustrate a Mexican edition of *Shtot fun palatzn*. In a moment of impromptu friendship, Rivera consents to the request.

In a short time Rivera produces a series of simple drawings, including one in which—bizarrely—he depicts himself as an inquisitor of the Holy Office. These drawings are all of archetypal images: a mother with a wrapped-up child on her back, a peasant with sombrero and serape, a shirted man asleep on a footstep with his head bent down. These silhouettes display an extraordinary plasticity capable of invoking an entire people in a few masterful strokes.

In his introduction to *Shtot fun palatzn*, Moisés Rosenberg, founder of the newspaper *Der Veg* (where, starting in 1949, Berliner would become the literary editor), posited that the poems "reveals to us the most intimate recesses of the Mexican soul." To which Tibol, a Mexican art historian, in a book called *Diego Rivera: Great Illustrator* (2008), adds: "Not a festive soul; in the land of the sun the poet saw the solitaries, the sick, the sad, the poor, and expressed his vision in strong, melodious verse."

A fascinating feature of the book is the glossary appended at the end. It features an array of Spanish words like "manyanitas" (greetings), "pulkeria" (bar), "soropes" (serape) that are clearly being integrated into Yiddish for the first time. As in the case of Jevel Katz, in that sense this collaboration is a living time-capsule to appreciate the linguistic gestation of what is known as Casteidish. To me the fact that Berliner's Yiddish and Rivera's drawings are companions is a lesson. The Jewish immigrants from the Pale of Settlement didn't arrive in a vacuum. Even though they formed a close-knit community, they interacted with the environment.

That evening I called Angelina Muniz-Huberman. Polite, generous, and enormously erudite, she is the daughter of refugees of the Spanish Civil War who were staunch atheists. Her mother came from a Crypto-Jewish family. She showed her daughter to make *el signo de los levitas*, the Levite's sign. Muniz-Huberman's mother's maiden name is Sacristán. "It's a Spanish translation of *Shamash*," Muniz-Huberman said to me.

Today she is one of Mexico's most prominent Jewish writers, a prolific author of fiction, poetry, and scholarship, especially on Sephardic civilization. Her books include *The Confidants* (2009), *A Mystical Journey* (2011), and *Dreaming of Safed* (2014). Her husband, Alberto, a wonderful man, is a doctor as well as a biochemist and a translator.

As is often the case when I'm in Mexico City, she invited me next afternoon to have tea and cake in her apartment. The place is in Delegación Benito Juárez, not far from where I went to high school. We sat in her living room, which is illuminated by a large balcony full of plants.

At age eighty Muniz-Huberman is limited in her mobility. She has been walking with a cane for thirty-five years, a sign of Progressive Systemic Sclerosis. For years we have maintained a conversation on Jewish and Hispanic themes, about 1492, about Crypto-Judaism, about defining oneself as a Jew in the face of adversity. I see her as a continual source of inspiration. She in turn has always been generous with clear-headed vision and intellectual support. This time round we also talked about politics and literature before the topic became the Inquisition.

I asked her why there is such little talk about the Inquisition in the Hispanic world. "For two reasons," she answered. "Because it was a shameful act that is better not to remember and because it went against conversos and '*indios forzados*,' the indigenous population forced to convert. These were '*seres prescindibles*,' dispensable beings who questioned the Catholic faith. As a result, Jews are still being stigmatized by the enormous weight of Christianity, which doesn't endorse the views of the *Nostra Aetate* declaration of Vatican II, which exonerates Jews from Jesus Christ's death."

She added that while the act of remembering is a Jewish imperative—the first line of the Kaddish is "Shema Israel!" (Hear, O Israel!)—in Hispanic civilization this duty is seldom stressed.

We talked about Henry Kamen's *The Spanish Inquisition* (1965), which argues that although the initial target of the Inquisition in 1480 and 1834 were conversos—that is, Jews who converted to Christianity—in truth it was a political instrument against all manner of dissidents, heretics, blasphemers, and other deviants. We also talked about Benzion Netanyahu's *The Origins of the Inquisition in Fifteenth-Century Spain* (1995), which proposes the theory that conversos were less numerous than is frequently suggested. Netanyahu was the father of Israeli prime minister Benjamin "Bibi" Netanyahu. Netanyahu also argues that the true rationale of the Tribunal de la Fe was racial, not religious.

We talked about how the Inquisition didn't target Jews and about how the most famous auto-da-fe was for Luis de Carvajal the Younger, in 1595. His was among a number of prominent inquisitorial cases in the Americas, which were never as many as in Spain. Many of the cases were more political than religious, although in truth it is difficult to differentiate between these two realms. For instance, a political plot by Martín Cortés, the son of

Hernán Cortés, to seek independence from Spain generated Inquisitorial wrath. In other words, the Tribunal was endowed with persecuting seditious individuals. After their arrest, they were tortured, even decapitated, and their houses flattened.

I asked her what in her view defined Jewish Latin American identity, a frequently labyrinthine topic. She answered by pointing at what she described as "situations" and she referred to two: "The first situation is that of conversos who made it to the Americas in the sixteenth century, settling in places remote from urban centers in order not to be caught. Today their descendants are seeking a way to reincorporate themselves back into Judaism. The second is the Eastern European immigration at the beginning of the twentieth century, either as a result of persecution or for economic reasons. These Jews didn't go through the conversion process. Their identity was well-defined."

I asked her if she could find a metaphor to describe these situations. "For conversos, the chameleon. For Yiddish-speaking Jews, migratory birds. And for women writers, she-lions. For Holocaust survivors, I would use the phoenix as a metaphor, since they reemerged from the ashes."

Muniz-Huberman concluded: "Another distinction is the presence in the Sephardic world of tenacity and stubbornness, which is how Inquisitors often described their victims, particularly women. Or Ashkenazim, linked to a tradition that renewed them. In all cases, what characterizes these groups is the importance of heritage."

At this point, she gave me to read a beautiful autobiographical essay called "La niña en el balcón" (The girl on the balcony). It starts with a scene that takes place in 1942, on the balcony of a house in Mexico City's Condesa neighborhood. In the piece Muniz-Huberman, aged six, is on the balcony with her mother, who reveals to her a crucial snippet of family information, one transmitted from generation to generation, always through the matrilineal line. Her mother tells her that, although they are Republicans who went to France (where Muniz-Huberman was born), escaping General Francisco Franco's forces in Spain, and from there bounced to Cuba and finally to Mexico, they are in fact Jewish with roots in Spain that go back prior to 1492. "La luz del conocimiento ilumina el balcón y ahora sabe que pertenece al pueblo de Israel," she writes. "The light of knowledge illuminating the balcony, she now knows she belongs to the people of Israel."

The essay also talked about discovering the pleasures of reading. Her mother would give her books, including the Bible in the Spanish-language version of Casiodoro de Reina and Cipriano Valera, a couple of "enemies of the Holy Office" because of their conversion to Protestantism. The essay described the anti-Semitism she experienced. And how, while she was growing up, that anti-Semitism solidified Muniz-Huberman's Jewish identity. Muniz-Huberman offers the anecdote when a drunkard once called her "¡Güereja judía!" (Jewish blondy). Or when in Mexico City someone shouted at her: "gachupina" (Iberian invader) o "refugacha" (Iberian refugee), insults designed to make her feel guilty for sharing the sins committed by the Spanish conquistadores during the colonial period in Latin America.

Our conversation then shifted to language. I told her about Diego Rivera's use of the term *judaizar* in an interview to discuss his Jewish ancestors and of my lexicographic search for the term. And I mentioned Antonio de Nebrija, the first Spanish grammarian, and his path-breaking *Gramática* (1492), the book that gave the Spanish language its legitimacy in intellectual, political, and social circles.

"He was a converso," Muniz-Huberman said.

I had been a fan of Nebrija for a long time, though I know his limitations. "The *Gramática* doesn't have the dry humor you find in Doctor Johnson's *A Dictionary of the English Language*, yet it is a triumph of populism over elitism," I said.

I told Muniz-Huberman that during a trip to Madrid I had stopped at the Biblioteca Nacional, near Plaza Colón, and I had held a first edition in my hands. "The book was published the same year Columbus crossed the Atlantic for the first time," I continued. "And the year when the Jews were expelled from the peninsula. In his dedication, Nebrija tells Queen Isabella that Spanish is meant to be the language of the Spanish Empire in all its glories. It strikes me as astonishing that a former Jew would be the visionary announcing such a glorious future."

I paused. "Glorious as well as oppressive."

We talked of three distinctive modalities of anti-Semitism, which in the Hispanic world have a distinct metabolism. These modalities are often interconnected, to the point that unscrambling them might seem a hopeless endeavor. Yet each modality displays unique characteristics. They include one sponsored by the Catholic Church that portrays the Jews as Christ killers. The sources are plentiful, significantly the teachings of Paul, among the most influential source in the tortured history of church-sponsored anti-Semitism. In his epistles Paul portrays the Jews as being caught in a double standard: on one hand they bore witness to Jesus's passion, and on the other they betrayed him, in the character of Judas, and need to be punished accordingly. Paul's argument streamlines this ambivalence: "ridicule them, abuse them, but do not kill, for their presence in time is tied to Christ's life and teachings" (*Epistle of Paul*, 17:25–26).

Still active, this modality had its expansion during the colonial period from 1492 to 1810. The second modality isn't so much religious as ethnic, although religion cannot be altogether extracted from it. It looks at Jews as being stingy moneylenders. The sources are texts like Shakespeare's *The Merchant of Venice* and *The Protocols of the Elders of Zion*, the latter a hoax published as a pamphlet in Russia in 1903 describing a Jewish plan for global domination. This modality prevailed with the Ashkenazi and Sephardi immigration at the end of the nineteenth century. And the third modality results from the creation of the state of Israel in 1948 and the impact of Zionism on Israel's Arab neighbors. Regardless of their ideological persuasion, Jews in Latin America are seen as being enablers of Israel.

After we mentioned Luis de Carvajal, I told Muniz-Huberman that a year earlier I had been an actor, albeit in a supporting role, in the Carvajal saga.

Carvajal was a Crypto-Jew in sixteenth-century colonial Mexico. *Crypto* in Latin means "hidden" in English. (A derogatory term used to describe these Jews is *Marrano*s, from the Spanish for "pork.") Born in Spain, Carvajal emigrated to the New World when his uncle—Luis de Carvajal the Elder, who was governor of the northern Mexican state of Nuevo León—invited the family to join him. His suggestion was that life in the New World was easier for secret Jews.

Carvajal the Younger took advantage of this opening. He began to proselytize, encouraging other Crypto-Jews to come over from Spain. Having previously been unacquainted with the Hebrew Bible, he now read it voraciously. He also adopted a new name, Joseph Lumbroso, and circumcised himself in order to make the covenant of his faith. And he began to write about his newly awakened identity.

Judging from his writing Carvajal was probably bipolar. Eventually the Inquisition caught up with him. He was imprisoned. This didn't deter him. His mother and sister were also imprisoned. While in his cell he would communicate with God. He would also send secret messages to his mother and sister in the peel of the food the guards would bring to him, which he would reject, asking them to forward it to his family. The guards intercepted the message. Instead of stopping him they encouraged Carvajal to continue, using the communication as proof of his disloyalty.

The inquisitors set him free because they thought he would lead them to other heretics. While free Carvajal wrote an extraordinary document: his autobiography, written in the third person and detailing his ordeals in prison. Sometime later, he was imprisoned again for the second and final time. He was burned at the stake in the Plaza del Quemadero, on December 8, 1596.

His plight is an invaluable prism through which to look at the crossroads where politics and individual freedom meet in Mexico. It would take until the War for Independence in 1810—led by a Catholic priest, Padre Miguel Hidalgo y Costilla, in his secessionist drive from Spain—before a debate on civil liberties could be embraced nationwide. In Nueva España, persecution of dissidents, in this case a subversive "hidden" Jew with biblical aspirations, is an occasion to explore the survival of minorities in a tyrannical atmosphere.

I first became exposed to the Carvajal story through Arturo Ripstein's film *El Santo Oficio* (1974), known in English as *The Holy Office*. I saw the movie at the *filmotèque* CUC (Centro Universitario Cultural) when I was still living in Mexico City. After working as an assistant for Luis Buñuel, Ripstein (himself a Jew) had taken off on his own, becoming an important Mexican director. This was, if my recollection is right, his second feature-length film, the first, *El castillo de la pureza* (The castle of purity, 1973), was about a mental asylum. My father had a small role in that one.

I didn't like *El Santo Oficio* then, and I don't like it now—it is slow-moving and needlessly obscure. Still, I applaud its director's courage in trying to address religious persecution in Mexico when the topic seldom makes it into the public sphere. Persecution not only against the Jews either. In the late 1920s Catholics were targeted by secular revolutionaries in what came to be known as La Cristiada. Graham Greene's novel *The Power and the Glory* (1940) is an excellent book about this period.

The movie gave me a sense that my own experience as a Jew in Mexico somehow needed to be told on-screen for a larger audience. There has been a plethora of plays, paintings, and biographies about Carvajal the Younger. In fact, I myself did a graphic novel, a detective story of sorts called *El Iluminado* (2012), about Carvajal's journey of self-discovery. I used *The Holy Office*, among other sources, as a compass for historical accuracy.

An effort to unearth other elements of Carvajal the Younger's story and those of other conversos has been steadily growing in recent years. For instance, Katia Skolnik, a former classmate of mine, directs the Centro Carvajal Sefarad in Monterrey, Nuevo León. After I returned from Mexico City, I talked with her via Skype. She told me she devotes her time to recording oral histories in interviews with people who are convinced they have Jewish roots. A short time ago she identified a *mikva*, tombstones under Monterrey's Catholic Cathedral, and other sites. She also taught classes (*un diplomado*) on the Inquisition.

This was welcome news to me. According to Skolnik the stories that Monterrey was founded by Jews are actually true. As she walks around, she comes across hundreds of people with stories about quiet, secret devotion. She said she was preparing an illustrated book with photographs of people and places in Monterrey and Saltillo, Coahuila.

Skolnik claimed that members of the Ashkenazi communities in Mexico City, Monterrey, and other major cities were unhappy with the awakening of Crypto-Jews, fearing that a mass of new conversos to Judaism would suddenly invade their temples.

The way Carvajal the Younger's story again infringed upon my life involved his autobiography. It was written by him in a miniature book, sewn together with a couple of other items, including a liturgical volume and Maimonides's Thirteen Principles of Faith.

Somehow, his miniature book, along with other material related to the Inquisition, made its way to the Archivo General de la Nación, the nation's historical archive located in Mexico City. It sat there for centuries. The Archivo is poorly administered and lousily kept. Not surprisingly, a number of important items have been stolen from it.

Apparently, in 1931, Joaquim Nesbit, a Brazilian Jewish scholar who was also a professor at Northwestern, walked away from the Archivo with the miniature book in his possession. According to various versions, he and another scholar, Alfonso del Toro, were rivals. Nesbit and del Toro were both preparing scholarly work on Carvajal the Younger. There is a suggestion that it wasn't Nesbit but del Toro who actually stole the manuscript and then blamed his colleague. Years later, del Toro would publish his biography of the family, *La familia Carvajal* (1944). In it, he accuses Nesbit.

After the robbery, the autobiography disappeared from sight. The Archivo listed it as missing.

Then, in June 2016, the item was finally put up for sale at Swann Auction Gallery. It was described as an "Early transcript of Inquisition victim Luis de Carvajal's autobiographical *Memorias* with devotional manuscripts . . . manuscript leaves in an unknown hand 3 volumes." The price estimate was from fifty to seventy-five thousand dollars. The catalogue said: "the present volume clearly dates to not long after Carvajal's lifetime (sixteenth century). Provenance: owned by a Michigan family for several decades."

I was contacted by Leonard Milberg, a wealthy book collector attached to Princeton who wanted my opinion. I told him it was probably the stolen item. I recommended that he proceed with caution and that he alert the authorities.

The FBI was contacted, from where the case was transferred to the US Attorney General's Office. Swann Auction Gallery took the information down. The Mexican government was contacted as well. The item was authenticated by two experts in Mexican early material, a Philadelphia book dealer and Ken Ward of the John Carter Brown Library. In the end Milberg made an agreement with them: he would repatriate Carvajal the Younger's autobiography to Mexico as long as the item was allowed to be reproduced and placed in an exhibit called "The First Jewish Americans: Freedom and Culture in the New World," at the New York Historical Society, in October of that year.

Three copies were made: one for the Princeton Library, one for the New York Historical Society, and one for Shearith Israel, the Spanish-Portuguese New York synagogue close to Columbus Circle. Then it would be returned to the Archivo General de la Nación in Mexico in honor of the Mexican Jewish community, where it would be displayed to the public.

The return of the autobiography to Mexico generated conflicted emotions in me. On the one hand I was thrilled it was returning to its original home. But I also wondered if the loss and return would become a lesson to Mexican archivists. This and other items could be stolen again. Better security would need to be established.

Happily, Milberg's present to the Mexican Jewish community was seen as a beneficial occasion. The arrival of the item was turned into an official function. Its display would take place under secure circumstances and the general public would be invited to see it. Eventually, I would write about all this in *The Return of Carvajal: A Mystery* (2019).

Muniz-Huberman was taken by the conclusion of the story. The repatriation of Luis de Carvajal's precious manuscript was good news, since it belongs to Mexico.

"Hopefully security at the Archivo General will be better now and no one else will run away with it again," I said.

I said goodbye. As I prepared to leave Muniz-Huberman's apartment, I was overwhelmed by a feeling of gratitude. Spending time with her always grants me a sense of inner peace.

6.

After Mexico City my next stop was New Mexico, specifically Santa Fe and Albuquerque. They are the hub for a wave of Crypto-Jewish reawakening over the last few decades.

To me New Mexico not only feels like an extension to Mexico into the United States; it actually gives the impression of being proto-Mexican. It didn't become the Forty-Seventh state until January 6, 1912. When Mexico declared its independence from Spain in 1821 (the War of Independence started about a decade earlier), New Mexico was part of Mexico. After the Mexican-American War, it was purchased by the United States as part of the Treaty of Guadalupe Hidalgo. And in 1853 New Mexico acquired its present size through the Gadsden Purchase.

An oasis in the desert, Santa Fe manages to be simultaneously premodern and utterly hip. Founded in 1610 by Spanish colonists, this is the oldest capital city in the United States. What makes it enchanting are its buildings of warm terracotta colors. Its full name—La Villa Real de la Santa Fe de San Francisco de Asís—is emblematic in that it denotes a simultaneous loyalty to both Crown and Church, a partnership that proved deadly for those deemed *indeseables* (undesirables) during La Reconquista, a period in which Spain cleansed itself of Jews and Muslims in the hope of establishing a nation under a single religious banner. By all accounts, this was a deadly, misguided proposition.

Santa Fe in Spanish means "Holy Faith." And St. Francis of Assisi, the ascetic religious figure it reveres, withdrew from world affairs to search for his true calling. Somehow the city makes that withdrawal its own feature. Whenever I walk through its streets, I have the impression that the clock runs slower here, as if I was in 1809, the year before Mexico fought for its independence. A journalist, historic preservationist, activist for indigenous rights, and Harvard dropout called Charles Fletcher Lummis moved to New Mexico in 1888 when it was still a territory. A few years later he wrote an autobiographical account of the area. He called it *The Land of Poco Tiempo*—the land of little time, or maybe, the land a little while ago.

My first destination was the St. Francis Cathedral Basílica. The story of its construction is part of Willa Cather's novel *Death Comes to the Archbishop* (1927). It was built between 1869 and 1886 by Jean-Baptiste Lamy, the archbishop in Cather's novel whose statue is prominently displayed outside the building. It replaced a couple of previous Catholic buildings on the same site, an adobe church called La Parroquia and, before it, an older church that was destroyed in the Pueblo Revolt of 1680.

I had heard unsubstantiated accounts that the earlier buildings were constructed by secret Jews wanting to prove their commitment to the Catholic faith and that Archbishop Lemy, who was born in France and was appointed by Pope Pius IX to head the newly formed Apostolic Vicariate of New Mexico, wanted to exert all his power to squash any impression that Jews were behind not only the shaping of the central Santa Fe church but also the establishment of the early colonial settlements. And yet that is what the origins of the Santa Fe community are purportedly all about. As a result of its geographic coordinates, Santa Fe was a place deemed so remote that the influence of the Inquisition might be more lenient there and less pernicious to the refuse expelled from Spain in 1492.

These are all rumors, yet rumors are an engine for the imagination. The St. Francis Cathedral is a beautiful massive building in the Romanesque Revival style. The panels on the bronze door tell spectacular stories about the history of Santa Fe. Restored in the early 2000s, the interior is kept handsomely. Its welcoming interior has arches and Corinthian columns. The nave is majestic. In its center there is a baptismal font. And in the chapel, known as La Conquistadora, behind the altar a large altarpiece displays depictions of the lives of various saints.

What made the St. Francis Cathedral emblematic to me was a stone at the top of the entrance with the Hebrew Tetragrammaton, the four letters of the divine name, engraved in it. Although this isn't the only cathedral with these letters, the fact that it is in Santa Fe is crucial. Some believe it was a way for Archbishop Lemy to thank the Jewish donors for their contributions to building the Basílica.

Upon looking at the Tetragrammaton, I had a couple of questions. The first is Why would Jewish philanthropists donate money for such a cause? It might have been a way for the makers of the cathedral to pay tribute to the Jewish foundation of the previous buildings that stood there beforehand. The second question is Why would the Jewish donors, if indeed they were the ones who partially funded the endeavor, call attention to their donation at a time when acknowledging one's own Jewishness was a danger? The answer might be that the Tetragrammaton, as such, was enigmatic enough to simultaneously announce and hide the Hebraic origins of its philanthropists.

The presence of the Tetragrammaton might be a cold fish. As mentioned before, a number of ecclesiastical buildings worldwide display it as well: Our

Lady Church in Aschaffenburg, Bavaria; the Ukrainian monastery Pechersk Lavra in Kiev; the Carmelite Monastery in Ghent, Belgium; and the dome of St. Mary Abchurch in London.

For me the presence of the four Hebrew letters of the divine name on St. Francis Cathedral in Santa Fe was a sign of arrival. Standing at the building's façade, I studied the inscription for a while. Then I visited the New Mexico Museum, where a bookstore includes Judaica. The titles here were about the Sephardic liturgy, the Kabbalah; there were children's book about New Mexico and autobiographical memoirs from Crypto-Jews in the Southwest.

I ran into Ron Duncan Hart and his wife, Gloria Abella Ballen, at the New Mexico History Museum in Santa Fe, just a few steps from the Spanish colonial plaza of that historic city. They are the publishers of Gaon Books, which concentrate on Sephardic themes from Spain to Latin America, including Crypto-Judaism. To my knowledge this is the only publishing house in the United States with such a focus. Hart is extraordinarily accomplished. He is an anthropologist with a doctorate from Indiana University who specializes on medieval Jews in the Andalusian culture, with a focus on the exchange between Spain and Morocco. For a while he worked for the Ford Foundation and UNICEF and was a dean of academic affairs. Abella Ballen is a renowned visual artist from a Sephardic family in Colombia who has won multiple international awards.

We went for a pleasurable walk through the streets of downtown Santa Fe. I asked them about their connection to Crypto-Judaism. They mentioned first having experienced it while they were living in Colombia, when a friend and fellow anthropologist from Antioquia—a province in the country's central northwestern part with a narrow section that opens to the Caribbean Sea—began to explore his family's Jewish roots. Hart at the time was doing research on the Inquisition during the Spanish colonial period in the city of Cartagena. He realized that some Crypto-Jews had retreated to the interior of the country, especially Antioquia, and that their descendants were living in that region today. He told me that, like his friend, he and his wife were acquainted with more than a thousand people from Colombia, Peru, Brazil, Mexico, and the American Southwest who over the last few decades had begun to search for their Jewish ancestry. One of the goals of Gaon Books was "to provide an outlet for the voices of people of B'nei Anusim—for example, folks of Crypto-Jewish background—who were exploring that past."

The New Mexico History Museum, where we met, was the site of the famous arrest by the Inquisition in 1662 of the Spanish colonial governor of Santa Fe and his wife for Judaizing. In 2016 the museum had a widely attended exhibition entitled "Fractured Faiths: Spanish Judaism, the Inquisition and New World Identities," which documented their history from Spain to Santa Fe. Hart collaborated on the exhibition and was coeditor of the bilingual exhibit catalogue.

We talked about the extent to which, like the tortured labyrinthine history of Crypto-Jews, information about and from that community tends to be passed on by oral tradition from one family circle to another. Since oral history is ephemeral, Hart and Abella Ballen thought they needed to capture it on film. They added to Gaon Books a web component now called Gaon Web, which features a range of educational films about Crypto-Jews, pondering their self-rediscovery as well as their connections with Israel and the Ashkenazi and Sephardic communities. "It is an ongoing project," Hart said. "It draws on Jewish experiences from Spain, Morocco, and the Americas. After family lifetimes of identifying as Catholics, an individual suddenly confronting a Jewish family background might find it surprising. It might be exhilarating for some and deeply disturbing to others. It might be a welcomed spiritual path, or it might forecast conflict."

Later on in my hotel room, I watched some testimonials. One film by Miguel Flores Zúñiga was about a decades-long Torah study group in Juárez, Mexico, near El Paso. Another film by John García described how, without any previous knowledge, at age eighteen he was told that his family belonged to the Sefaradim. I found these stories enthralling.

Hart and Abella Ballen invited me to dinner with Crypto-Jewish friends, but I already had a dinner engagement for the next day.

Speaking of food, they mentioned a kosher taco truck art project organized in El Paso by a city councilman, Peter Svarzbein, who is of Argentinian heritage. Aside from having superb brisket in the menu, the truck gives information about the Crypto-Jewish experience.

Thinking how good those tacos must be, I remembered seeing the menu of a similar Los Angeles–based endeavor called Takosher that included on its menu latke tacos and that, fittingly, didn't open on Shabbat.

I told Hart and Abella Ballen that I was of the impression these trucks were a manifestation of a cultural need that started in that periphery of American Jewish culture but slowly has moved mainstream. Given the increasing closeness between Jews and Latinos in cities across the United States—from Miami to Chicago, San Francisco, and Houston—maybe in a few decades this type of cuisine will cease to be so exotic and become just normal.

Hart responded that he wanted to catch the wave before it broke. "The B'nai Anusim might be seen as living on the fringe these days. But their odyssey will become more central. That's why the desire is to build a memory bank. It isn't exclusively for those searching today. It is also for future generations."

7.

That afternoon I went to visit the Chicano poet Jimmy Santiago Baca, whose lyrical verses I have admired for years. Baca spent time in prison when he was young. It was there that he found his voice as a poet.

Baca was born in Santa Fe in 1952. Abandoned by his parents when he was a child, he lived with relatives for a while and ended up in an orphanage. In his teenage years he got involved in drugs, which led him to get arrested. He served six and a half years in prison. He corresponded with Denise Levertov, among others, who encouraged him to write. I love his book *C-Train and Thirteen Mexicans* (2002). It explores the underbelly of cocaine addiction as well as the connections that Chicanos create in order to cope with the xenophobia of the Anglo environment they inhabit.

Not surprisingly, when you spend time with Baca the entire American Southwest is seen from the prism of those denigrated by history, without access to power. Everywhere we went the locals, Anglos, knew him and wanted to share an anecdote with him. In his exchanges he consistently sprinkled his conversation with elements *en español* to make a larger point. And he was also close to Hispanos (as people of Spanish descent are known in New Mexico—at one point, someone even described them, awkwardly, as "Amerindian Hispanic") and listened to their every word with compassion.

Baca first took me to a special restaurant for *champurrado* and *pan dulce*. *Champurrado* is a chocolate-based *atole*, a warm thick Mexican drink, prepared with a dried version of lime-treated corn dough, corn flour, *panela*, milk, and a bit of cinnamon on top. *Pan dulce* are Mexican pastries.

"The *mexicanos* in Santa Fe are true Jews, in metaphorical terms," Baca said as we talked. "I'm not referring to Crypto-Jews, a couple of whom I know you'll be meeting. Nor about the *nuevo mexicanos*, the old Mexican families in New Mexico that have been here since before 1848, when the Treaty of Guadalupe Hidalgo was signed. I'm talking about the recent arrivals. They work as maids, cook, gardeners. . . . The *nuevo mexicanos* don't relate to them. It is all about class, *manito*. The *mexicanos* have no money.

They come without means. A few of them are undocumented. Society sees them as scum, just as Jews were seen in the Middle Ages."

Baca and I also talked about how Santa Fe has changed over the last few decades. He drove me around parts of the city he loved that were off the beaten trail. In the evening Baca and his family drove me to Ojo Caliente, about fifty miles from Santa Fe, a spa of mineral waters discovered by the Spaniards in the 1500s as they traversed the region in search of the Eternal Fountain of Youth.

Baca and I, in bathing suits, sat for about half an hour in one of those hot springs. He talked to me about being of Apache and Chicano descent, about controlling his anger outbursts, and about always feeling like a misfit.

I had dinner with his family at the restaurant in Ojo Caliente. That night I stayed over in an enchanting cottage Baca had booked for me that was connected at one point with the painter Georgia O'Keefe. I had a dream in which I entered a dark cave and inside was a fawn. I wanted to touch it but the fawn was frightened of me. When I extended my left hand and offered it an apple I had with me, the fawn came closer but a noise in the back of the cave frightened it. I then looked up and saw at the mouth of the cave Baca dressed up as a prison inmate. His face was bright red. He looked at me angrily.

When I woke up from the dream, I was overtaken by an epiphany: I'm always the protagonist of my own dreams, yet I never see myself in them. Oddly, I don't think I've ever seen my face in one of my dreams. I didn't see it in this dream either. This might be because I take the role of the camera— that is, I'm an observer. I wondered at that moment if other people see their faces in dreams.

I meant to put this question to Baca, but when we saw each other briefly in the morning for breakfast, I forgot.

8.

I rented a car and took Route 25 to Albuquerque, about an hour southwest, to visit the impressive building of the Jewish Community Center (JCC) of Greater Albuquerque. Around twenty-five thousand Jews live in the state of New Mexico. Many of them are transplanted from other parts of the country. In fact, I was told that only about 13 percent are native New Mexicans. The vast majority, Ashkenazi, are now liberals. It wasn't always that way. Some of their forebears moved to the area with the opening of the Santa Fe Railroad in 1879, which brought along an economic boom. Other families have come more recently. To what extent did the Ashkenazim interact with the Crypto-Jews? The answer is little known, because the kind of "reawakening" that is evident these days didn't exist at the time. Being Jewish was a stigma, not an asset.

Truth is, even today, the interaction isn't close between the conversos and the Ashkenazi Jews who are part of the mainstream community. They surely do more than tolerate each other, but ties aren't particularly strong. There seems to be some mistrust, even suspicion, regarding the Crypto-Jews, although these feelings aren't formalized in any fashion. From several conversations I've had with educators, it appeared that Crypto-Jews to a large extent were not formal members of the JCC.

Among the sites I wanted to visit in New Mexico were graveyards. I drove to Fairview Cemetery near University Heights, which goes back to 1881. It has an adjacent section for Jewish interments. I wanted to see the tombstone of Francisco Perea. The Pereas, I read, were an influential nineteenth-century New Mexican family. José Perea was a Presbyterian minister. Francisco Perea was his uncle and, judging by where he is buried, he probably was a Crypto-Jew. It appears that this Perea (the genealogical line could be linked to Perera, a name that, along with the names Pardo, Penhas, and Peretz, denoted Sephardic ancestry) was a delegate in Congress. He defended Albuquerque against Texans who volunteered in the US Civil War and appears to have been in the theater, in Washington, DC, when Abraham Lincoln was assassinated.

The tomb was old and hadn't been kept up. I was the only one in the cemetery. In fact, the place didn't appear to be a magnet for visitors. I didn't see flags, flowers, or other offerings near the tombstones.

Years ago I read an illuminating autobiography called *The Cross and the Pear Tree*, by the Guatemalan journalist Victor Perera. In it, he explored his family tree back to Spain before 1492 and the way the last name Perera (from Spanish *pera*, "pear") mutated over time. Perera spelled his last name with the added "r." Was this the same genealogical tree? Wanting to know if the Pereas and the Pereras intersected, I looked for a graveyard keeper. None could be found. After a few more minutes walking around reading the inscriptions—for some macabre reason, the tombs of infants attract me—I decided it to call it quits.

Before my trip a number of acquaintances had offered me suggestions for cemeteries with Crypto-Jewish families buried in them. Fairview Cemetery was one of them. Also, years back, my eyes fell on a book by *New York Times* photographer Cary Herz (1947–2008) about the Crypto-Jews in New

Mexico. A generous portion of Herz's black-and-white photographs are of tombstones. Other photos are of Crypto-Jews in the act of praying, surrounded by family and friends, and so on, yet those of tombstones were the ones that caught my attention.

I visited a number of other cemeteries. I needed to educate my eye in order to identify the tombstones. A few showed a discreet, underplayed juxtaposition of Jewish and Christian symbols: two lions, a Star of David, and a *hamsa* (an open right hand, with the index and middle fingers joined and separated from the ring and baby finger). In most cases, though, these references will be absent, in which case the guesswork you need to do involves detective work connected with names, genealogies, and so on.

This juxtaposition, when it does occur, is an expression of "double-consciousness," a term immortalized by W. E. B. Du Bois in his book *The Souls of Black Folk* (1903). Du Bois uses the term in reference to the way that blacks in the United States deal with white culture. And that's what looked to me to be the strategy: they stated, in no uncertain terms, that although on the surface, in public, they were Catholic their private life was organized around alternative motifs. Those motifs reached way back to Jewish ancestors who passed on those beliefs from generation to generation, usually in silence, away from public scrutiny.

9.

Next I decided to drive as far as Las Vegas, New Mexico, about 120 miles from Albuquerque, a remote place in San Miguel County. This is where Congregation Montefiore Cemetery is located. Montefiore is a name associated with a Sephardic family. Moses Montefiore (1784–1885) was a prominent British financier, and his grandchild Claude Montefiore (1858–1938) was a famous Jewish philosopher and the founder of Anglo-Liberal Judaism. This Montefiore graveyard was the place where, in 1985, Herz started her project of photographing Crypto-Jews. The graveyard houses the tombs of descendants of the Montefiore family, although not those who came here via the United Kingdom.

During the second half of the nineteenth century, the Southwest for most Jews was still terra incognita: a land to conquer, a place to make a profit. The Treaty of Guadalupe Hidalgo that concluded the Mexican-American War was signed in 1848. The treaty established that the Southwest was now a property of the United States—bought for five million dollars. But these territories were not unpopulated. Mexicans, creoles, mestizos, indigenous people, and others inhabited them. The doctrine of Manifest Destiny projected a "civilizing" mission and invited adventurers to relocate to the newly American territories. These adventurers included relatively recent arrivals from the Pale of Settlement who, thinking the Lower East Side in New York City was too crowded, ended up with Nevada as their home.

The Montefiore Cemetery was built in 1881. This is the first Jewish burial ground west of the Mississippi. At some point the site was desecrated, although I haven't been able to place the event within specific dates. The graveyard was abandoned for a while, but in recent decades it has been fixed up. Ashkenazim were buried in this soil, mostly merchants from Germany. In histories of Jewish immigration to New Mexico, I had seen lists of "pioneers" settling in waves that were organized around 1830–1849, 1850–1869, and 1870–1879. I came across names such as Spiegelberg, Zackendorf, Staab, and Freudenthal.

The inscriptions I saw were sparse: names, followed by dates, almost nothing else. It was on this holy ground that I found what Herz had seen. I came across a Star of David and even a Kabbalistic sign but it was a struggle to locate them. (Not too far away there is a Masonic cemetery where the absence of overt religious symbols is even more emphatic.)

After all, this is a Jewish site, meaning that the few Crypto-Jews interred here have been "allowed to return." They rest next to dozens of other Jews who lived their life as such. For instance, the stones for the Levy family, most of whom appear to have been entrepreneurs, include those of Henry A. Levy (whose name is misspelled Levey), Carolina Levy, Henry Levy, buried next to his wife, Jennie, and daughter, Pauline, and the younger Jacob Levy, who (I found out later) drowned on September 10, 1905, at Kroenig's Lake. Reports claim that he "had pushed out a few feet from shore in a leaky skiff with a piece of board for a paddle. The current carried him out and when 200 yards from shore, he stripped off his clothes and attempted to swim in. He was sized with cramps and went down. His sister was a witness to the tragedy. His body was found 25 feet under water."

There is a remote possibility that some in the Montefiore Cemetery might have been descendants of those who were expelled from Spain in 1492 by King Ferdinand of Aragón and Queen Isabella of Castile. Nevertheless, it is unlikely that their ancestors came directly from the Iberian Peninsula. More plausibly, a few of these arrived via Brazil, as did the first Jews to settle New York. Or perhaps from Italy, Amsterdam, and the Balkan portion of the Ottoman Empire.

The Americas, I told myself while I walked around, are sprinkled with Jews from disparate origins such as these. If one were able to make threads from their place of rest to their place of origin, the lines between the Old World and the New, and within the Americas, would construct a multifarious web. For there is something kinetic about Jewish lives. They move around constantly. It is a desire to "make it," to see the world, to create connections. It is the need for education, which almost always brings along the impetus to break away from one's old confines, to acknowledge the restlessness of the spirit as a mission in life. And, of course, there is the nervousness—call it animosity!—of the environment that sees them as threats.

I saw several tombstones that Cary Herz had photographed in San Miguel County, Sandoval County, and Torrance County. One had the Star of David engraved on top of an angel. Another said *Nasio Israelita* (born an Israelite). I saw the Hebrew letter shin featured inside a flower. And a six-pointed lily that serves as a proxy for a Star of David. And then, again guided by Herz, I came across graves with Jewish names: Rebecca, Abraham, Esther, Salomón, and Moisés (acute accents were often missing), as well as—emblematically—Adonai.

This made me recollect that the names of the Jewish divinity aren't prohibited in Spanish. When I was growing up in Mexico, my father had an acquaintance called Adonai. I also knew someone with the name Elohim. And Jesus is a ubiquitous name in the Spanish-speaking world. In the English-speaking world, this is bizarre until one remembers that the Greek word *Iēsous* is a rendition of the Hebrew *Yeshua*, with the variants Jeshua and Joshua. I have a son called Joshua.

My visit to these graveyards left me with a wholesome sensation of having communed with the dead. Santa Fe is somehow an auspicious place to establish such communication. One gets the sense (at least, I did) that the line between the Here and Now and the Hereafter is thinner in Santa Fe than in other places. Maybe this is because of the landscape. As one travels around New Mexico, the sky feels so close it's almost within reach. I was happy I started my travel in a place that to me feels like it is frozen in time and following its own beat. In *Death Comes to the Archbishop*, Willa Cather says that, in other places, "men travel faster now, but I do not know if they go to better things."

10.

One evening in Santa Fe I met Isaac Pérez (this is a pseudonym) for dinner at Amaya, the restaurant of the Hotel Santa Fe where I was staying. We started with drinks, after which I had a delicious wilted spinach and apple salad and a glazed duck breast with a maple flavoring. Pérez had a stuffed *chile poblano.* For desert, we had spiced apple-raisin strudel and a poached pear in gingerbread crumble.

As it turned out, our vigorous conversation, which ended up lasting almost two hours, along with the explorations I had done in prior days, made me confident that the travels I was embarking on had begun on the right foot.

I had been corresponding for a while with Pérez, a handsome, slender, mestizo man, about sixty, with a Pancho Villa moustache. He had retired a few years before from a job with the postal service. Our relationship started when he sent me a letter in appreciation of a book I had written about growing up a Yiddish speaker in Mexico and then switching to other languages such as Spanish, Hebrew, and English. For a short while we became correspondents.

Growing up Catholic near Cañada de los Alamos on R-25, he discovered his Jewishness through a close-knit community of people for whom the coming to Judaism was a return to ancient ways. Through the genealogical research done by his wife, who is from Nayarit, Mexico, Pérez reached the conclusion that his family ancestry predated the fifteenth-century expulsion from Spain.

In his description of the personal search he had embarked on, at one point Pérez mentioned a mythical key. Pérez's aunt kept it in a box. "It apparently opens the door to the abandoned house left behind when my ancestors were forced to leave," Pérez said to me. The aunt showed the key to only a small number of relatives as proof of lineage.

In the past I had heard repeated references to family keys in Crypto-Jewish families. I had also read about them in David Gitlitz's book *Secrecy and Deceit* (2002). Basing his research on Inquisitorial records as well as rabbinical rulings, correspondence, and eyewitness accounts, Gitlitz describes countless customs shaping the religion of some of these families. Their ancestral customs include activities performed under duress and at times surrounded in mystery connected with hygiene, cuisine, clothing, education, and prayer. In Pérez's family, males generally had biblical names. His mother stayed home on Saturday instead of Sunday. And certain themes of the Old Testament (which he now called the "Hebrew Bible") kept on returning in home discussions.

Pérez had memorized several Hebrew liturgical passages. English was his native language. He seasoned it with occasional Spanish terms, although his Spanish skills were tentative. By his own account, he understood more than he could speak.

Not long before our dinner the Spanish government had announced its decision to grant citizenship to the descendants of Sephardic Jews who, like Pérez's forebears, were thrown out of Spain by the Alhambra Decree of 1492. I had written a *New York Times* op-ed about it, and Pérez sent me an email sharing his views. It was expected that there would be some 150,000 applications and that the criterion for approval would not be "overly strict." Applicants wouldn't be asked to relocate to Spain, nor would they need to renounce their existing citizenship.

On the surface the invitation to repatriation looked like a conciliatory move, the result of deep national soul-searching in Spain. In reality, it was just another chapter in Spain's ambivalent relationship with its Jewish past.

Thinking about modern Spain's conflicted relationship with its Jewish past I recalled that in 1905 a Spanish senator, Ángel Pulido Fernández, published a book called *Los españoles sin patria y la raza sefardí* (Spaniards without homeland and the Sephardic race). This was not too long after the Spanish-American War of 1898, when the Spanish Empire, which had been crumbling for a long time, finally gave up its last breath, losing control of Cuba, Puerto Rico, and the Philippines. Pulido, in autobiographical mode, describes how—a couple of years earlier, when he and his family were sailing from Belgrade on a boat—he met Dr. Enrique Bejarano, a learned man and the director of a Sephardic (Pulido calls it "Israelita Española") school in Bucharest. Dr. Bejarano was a savvy storyteller. But what mesmerized Pulido was his language. The senator had never before heard anything about Ladino, let alone been exposed to it. The grammatical structure was similar to Spanish, yet it was different.

Dr. Bejarano talked to Pulido about the nostalgia of Sephardic Jews for Spain. It was a nostalgia more spiritual than anything else. The two reflected on "la Sefarad kerida" (the beloved Sefarad), the name by which Spain is mentioned in the *Book of Obadiah* (1:20), although its location is uncertain. Such were the Sephardic Jews' roots that even after generations they still longed to return one day. They had their own customs, their own language, and their own sense of community. Yet they still belonged to Spain—even while Spain ignored them.

It was during this conversation that Pulido understood that those whom Spain had expelled in 1492 had remained, willy-nilly, the country's Jews. Soon the senator inaugurated a campaign for Spain to reverse its edict of expulsion. He proposed a series of efforts, diplomatic and otherwise, to energize the liaison between Spain and the Sephardic Jews of the Balkans. These efforts reminded me of another one in 1655, a petition to Oliver Cromwell by the Dutch Jewish rabbi and scholar Menasseh ben Israel, who was a teacher of Baruch Spinoza. Ben Israel became convinced that the American Indians were descendants of Jews and petitioned Cromwell to repatriate the Jews who had been expelled from London.

Needless to say, Pulido (like ben Israel) was perceived as being out of his mind. *Los españoles sin patria y la raza sefardí* was placed in the Index Librorum Prohibitorum, the list of forbidden books kept by the Inquisition, which was still active—anachronistically—in the early years of the twentieth century.

Still, Pulido didn't give up. Thanks to him, that same year an organization called Unión Hispano Hebrea was created in Morocco (at the time a Spanish protectorate). The organization had as its mission to create a sense of belonging among Moroccan Jews. And in 1915, a *cátedra*, an endowed chair on Hebrew Studies, was established at the University of Madrid.

Pulido might have been defeated. But he set the seeds for future change. Pérez wasn't thinking of applying for a Spanish passport. He was an American through and through. It was difficult enough to profess a commitment to a faith that wasn't part of your upbringing. The reaction to his search among his siblings had resulted in much tension. "Some in the family don't want to have anything to do with this resurgence," he told me. "We were all raised *castizos* and my siblings are happy that way. One of them is active in St. Edwin, in south Albuquerque. They think wanting to be Jewish all of a sudden is hypocrisy."

Castizo is a difficult word to translate: it might imply "pure" or "authentic." It might also be taken as "traditional," to the point of being reactionary.

The tension had made Pérez uneasy, even insecure. Some of his lifelong friends shunned him, whereas new ones were linked with his reawakening. He wanted to be careful not to imperil their relationship.

Pérez had not done a DNA test but a few acquaintances had. He said the results for the most part had come back positive. Some in Pérez's circle also believed that Columbus was Jewish, as were a few crew members in the *Niña*, the *Pinta*, and the *Santa María*.

I said that modern Spain had made apologies to the Jews before. In fact, the Alhambra Decree was officially revoked in 1968. In 1992, as part of the festivities of the Quicentenario, the events commemorating the arrival of Columbus in the Americas, Spain publicly portrayed itself as a penitent nation paying for its sins. King Juan Carlos, wearing a yarmulke, prayed at a Madrid synagogue alongside Israel's president, Chaim Herzog.

The country was ripe for reconciliation, the king proclaimed: Sephardic

Jews had a place in Spain's present. No doubt this was a charged statement. The truth is that the Jews left Spain in 1492 but Spanish anti-Semitism stayed behind, mutating in countless ways. Indeed, the country is a prime example of a nation that fosters "anti-Semitism without Jews," a phenomenon often marked by dualist attitudes. Take the dictatorship of General Franco from 1939 until 1975, for example. Some Jewish refugees were saved by various consuls and other diplomatic administrators with Franco taking the credit, yet his fascist forces regularly used anti-Semitic motifs in state propaganda. During my first visit to Spain in 1982, just as when I was visiting El Once decades later, I came across swastikas, copies of Hitler's *Mein Kampf* in translation, and Nazi stuff (swastikas, flags, manuals, badges, and so on) for sale.

Although the idea of granting citizenship to Sephardic Jews as circulating at the time, the country was in the middle of a financial bonanza. Since it did not "need" the Jews the proposal came to nothing—until this recent announcement. Now Spain finds itself mired in the worst financial crisis in memory. Suddenly the idea of reconciliation has legs.

"Funny how we've gone from being filth, scum, to being perceived as an engine of progress," Pérez posited. "Rejection is at times good. I know about that. Those who reject you think you'll always be the same when in truth the rejection is a cleanser for the soul. Rejection makes you stronger."

I found Pérez's comment enlightening. It made me think of an expression in Spanish that I find curious: *cargar con el muerto*. It literally means "to carry the dead," the equivalent in English of "to be left holding the bag." Who is the real loser in a rejection, the rejected or the person who rejects?

Truth is, the majority of New Christians who made it to the Indies were Portuguese, not Spanish. The Jews were expelled from Portugal in 1497, five years after the same event in Spain. Spain has always had a far smaller population (approximately one million around the time of colonization). The impact of the Portuguese Inquisition, while pervasive, was smaller in scale and less epic in scope. Quite a few *cristãos novos* (New Christians) participated in various efforts connected with the Portuguese Empire, such as the domination of Macau, Ceylon, and Angola. Scores of crucial figures in the shaping of Brazil were of Jewish origin. Gaspar da Gama served with Pedro Cabral in the expedition that discovered Brazil.

In physical terms, the oldest surviving synagogue in the Americas is in Willemstad, the capital of Curaçao. It is called the Snoa (short for *esnoga*, in old Portuguese), though its real name is Mikvé Israel-Emmanuel Synagogue. It is a colonial building, painted yellow with white edges and clean white columns inside. The door and the elegant furniture are made of mahogany. There are windows in the walls. And an imposing candelabra hanging above. The floor is made of sand.

I have never seen it full. It doesn't quite feel real. It is more of a museum piece. The temple has Hebrew inscriptions on the arch entrance. Of an overall population in Curaçao of around 150,000, the number of member Jews is less than 300, although this number depends on whom you ask and at what time of year, since a number of them are merchants with addresses in Miami and elsewhere in the Caribbean.

The site dates back to 1674, although the current temple was built in 1703. There is another synagogue in Sint Eustatius, a municipality of the Netherlands, and one more in Suriname. All these islands in the Caribbean were settled by Portuguese Jews.

I told Pérez that according to Spain's minister of justice, Alberto Ruiz-Gallardón, this new legislation was an attempt to correct "the biggest mistake in Spanish history."

"From anti-Semitism to philo-Semitism," I continued, "it is all quite fluid. The terms always depend on what the Jews are needed for." I mentioned Isaiah Berlin, the liberal thinker, Oxford philosopher, and one of my heroes. In one of his famous essays he expounds on the duality between the hedgehog and the fox, which, according to Berlin, represent the two ways of approaching the world: one boiling down everything to a single idea, the other looking at things eclectically. Berlin spent his life thinking about the limits of freedom and about the place of tolerance in a pluralistic society. The challenge of freedom, he thought, depends on not curtailing the rights and privileges of others. History is full of examples where such limits are breached—to disastrous consequences.

As he had done in our electronic exchange, throughout our conversation Pérez showed substantial interest in the Jews of Latin America. Aside from me, he didn't know any Jew from the region. I told him I was at the beginning of a journey that hopefully would take me as far as Patagonia, the Caribbean, and the Amazon jungle, and to Spain itself. He wanted to know how different the Spanish- and Portuguese-speaking Jews were from American Jews and from Jews elsewhere on the globe. Were they more politicized, given the history of dictatorship and repression in countries such as Argentina, Chile, Paraguay, and Cuba?

"Do they all go back to Spain before 1492?" Pérez pondered.

I responded that, as a matter of fact, roughly two out of every three Latin American Jews were Ashkenazi—that is, their ancestry traces back to Poland, Russia, Ukraine, and other parts of Central and Eastern Europe. Maybe the ratio was closer to three out of four. In the second half of the nineteenth century, these Jewish immigrants were courted in Argentina, Colombia, Mexico, and elsewhere as being harbingers of modernity. And then came the refugees of the Second World War, and not only to these countries. The region of Sosúa, on the northern coast of the Dominican Republic, was allocated for Jewish refugees from the Holocaust by General Leónidas Trujillo of the Dominican Republic in the hopes that they would push the underdeveloped region forward. On the other hand, those described as Sephardic (that is, originally from Spain) actually came from Turkey, Syria, Lebanon, and other parts of the Ottoman Empire. In Israel and elsewhere, they were called *Mizrahim*, a word in Hebrew meaning "eastern."

"They were Levantine Jews. Some might have come from Spain but it is difficult to say. More likely their ancestors' move was connected with the diaspora in Babylon that resulted from the destruction of the First Temple on Tisha B'Av, the ninth of the Hebrew month Av, in 587 BCE. *The Book of Lamentations* mourns that destruction. Some Levantine Jews came back when the Temple was rebuilt but others stayed in Babylon."

We had finished the main course. I asked Pérez if he knew about the testimonials that Ron Duncan featured on the Gaon Books webpage. I thought it was fitting that it was based in Santa Fe. Pérez had heard of Duncan, though he didn't know him in person. He expressed disinterest—though not disdain—for those Crypto-Jews who went public with their stories. For him this was a private affair.

Isaac Pérez wanted to know if I thought it appropriate to define the wave of Crypto-Jews who settled in the New World after the arrival of Columbus as "a Jewish immigration." I responded that I didn't think it was appropriate. Officially, a number of them were no longer Jewish but New Christian. As for the Crypto-Jews, in my mind I perceived them as being runaways though, again, several never reconnected with their Jewish faith. Those that did at times returned by happenstance, after something reignited their curiosity. They weren't separatists like the pilgrims of the *Mayflower* who escaped religious persecution by looking for a promised land where they could profess their faith. As a general rule, the Crypto-Jews were apolitical—until and unless they came to terms with their Jewish past.

"By virtue of the secretiveness, we shall never know how many Crypto-Jews came to the Americas," I said. "The Inquisition—El Santo Oficio de la Inquisición—made arrangements to establish branches in the colonies. The headquarters were in the Kingdom of New Spain, later on known as Mexico, and the Kingdom of Peru. The one in Mexico was established in 1571. These individuals arrived surreptitiously. And they kept a low profile. . . . In contrast, we know that the number of New Christians was rather high. The majority of them never reverted to Judaism. Indeed, they came to be seen as a class onto themselves, establishing relationships among themselves, protecting their common turf, and so on. In my view the emergence of trans-atlantic capitalism (marine routes pushing merchandize into the colonies) was, in large part, a by-product of this weltanschauung."

Soon the conversation shifted to the topic of Jewish self-loathing. We talked about Woody Allen. Pérez wanted to know why I thought Jews liked to ridicule themselves in public. I wasn't sure what he was asking. "Do you think those returning to Judaism need to engage in this practice?"

"I don't know," I answered. "Maybe it's a survival mechanism. If the environment dislikes you, if the environment in which you live is anti-Semitic, sometimes a reaction is to preempt such hostilities by turning the attacks onto yourself through laughter. Then again, there is no such thing as a blanket definition of anti-Semitism and Jewish self-hatred. The anti-Semitism sponsored by the Catholic Church is different from left-wing anti-Semitism. And US anti-Semitism is different from German anti-Semitism, French anti-Semitism, Hispanic anti-Semitism, Arab anti-Semitism, and so on."

I remembered a famous quote: "Anti-Semitism is the hatred of Jews more than is strictly necessary," which I once saw attributed to Isaiah Berlin, though I doubt it really came from him. I told Pérez that Angelina Muniz-Huberman, the prominent Mexican intellectual, had said to me that Hispanic anti-Semitism is the result of ignorance. Maybe, although I'm not sure she's right. All hatred is based on ignorance. But that truism doesn't take us very far. We all are to some degree ignorant, and often consciously so. Ignorance has always been an engine of progress as well as regression. Muniz-Huberman also said that Jewish self-hatred "is a way to put oneself on the side of the good guys."

Pérez had mentioned Columbus on a few occasions. At this point it was clear to me that he wanted to talk about the possibility that the Genoese admiral was in fact Jewish. Pérez had read a lot on the subject. He mentioned Columbus's birth in 1451 in Italy. His language was a hodge-podge of Italian, Spanish, Portuguese, and other tongues. His signature is seen by some as having elements associated with Hebrew writing. Yet there is no concrete evidence of any Jewish ancestry.

"To me it is sheer speculation," I said. "Actually, more than the question itself to me it is more interesting why people keep looking for clues." I said that the loci of Columbus in history is that of a pathfinder. "In poetry, theology, and rabbinical response, [the year] 1492 is often equated with the exodus of the Jews from Egypt. Columbus is a kind of accidental Moses. The admiral himself seems to me to have been a rather limited figure, a naïve sailor whose role it was to help circumvent a blockade by the Turks of a crucial route in the Mediterranean Sea to bring merchandize to India. Thus the onomastic confusion: the lands that Columbus stumbled upon are called Las Indias. His understanding of the indigenous population he encountered was also simplistic. Still, his actions were unquestionably enabled by Jewish contributions. Funds came from Queen Isabella, who in turn received a few of them from Jewish investors and philanthropists. And the technology Columbus used was made possible in part by Jewish inventors. Among them was Abraham Zacuto, known for building the astrolabe that is still used in marine voyages to this day. Still, there is no tangible evidence that Columbus was Jewish. What is fascinating is the degree to which his place in history is pregnant with meaning."

Pérez and I then discussed the complicated relationship between Latin America and Columbus. There are statues of him all over the place. These statues are frequently the target of protest. They are defaced, spray-painted. People threw stones at them. The most famous statue is in Hispaniola, the island made up today of Haiti and the Dominican Republic. This is where the Genoese admiral first set foot and the first land he named.

Pérez told me that he and a niece had been to New York City for their first time recently. He went to the Empire State Building, the Statue of Liberty, and the 9/11 Memorial. He had seen the cityscape dozens of times in movies and on TV, and it felt familiar when he was actually there. But he was also puzzled by all sorts of things. For instance, he was intrigued by the statue of Columbus on Columbus Circle and Fifty-Ninth Street, on the edge of Central Park. He was shocked by how beautiful that part of town was and by the degree to which everyone took the statue for granted. He did research on it: the statue, by the Italian sculptor Gaetano Russo, was erected in 1892, to commemorate the four-hundredth anniversary of Columbus's first voyage.

Pérez asked me if I had heard of any protests against it.

"Maybe some rallies took place in 1992 but I can't recall anything significant," I answered. I told him about the different ways in which October 12 was commemorated north and south of the Rio Grande. "In the United States, it is Columbus Day. In some places in Latin America it is called Día de la Raza, the day of race. In others it is Día de la Hispanidad, the day of

Hispanic civilization. And in still others it is a kind of Día de los Muertos." I added that when I was in Caracas, Venezuela, the main statue of Columbus in one of the city's main arteries had been decapitated. "Down there he is undoubtedly a villain."

Soon Perez and I were talking about the expulsion itself.

"How many Jews were expelled?" he asked.

I told him that as far as I knew the number was elusive. Truth is, no one knows for sure. He said he had heard historians talking of as few as eighty thousand and as many as two hundred thousand. The routes of exile led them to the Netherlands and all across the Mediterranean basin, from Greece and the Balkans to Italy, northern Africa. A few, of course, made their way to what centuries later would become Latin America, too.

"They were asked to depart with their sons and daughters and servants. It didn't matter if they had been rich or 'lesser folk.' They were not in any manner allowed to return 'under penalty of death.' And 'they shall not dare to return to those places, nor to reside in them, nor to live in any part of them, neither temporarily on the way to somewhere else nor in any other manner.' Sounds biblical, doesn't it? Like the *Lekh-Lekha*, the 'Go for you!' Abraham gets from God in *Genesis*."

"I'm not sure," I replied. "You know that this wasn't the first edict that expelled Jews in Europe: Italy threw them out in 855. England, in 1290. Koln, now in Germany, in 1381 and again in 1420. The Netherlands, in 1442. In Sicily, which was associated with the Kingdom of Aragón, in 1492. Five years after Spain, in 1497, Portugal also followed suit. Jews occupied prominent places in that country's political and economic life. Yet King Manuel I, in marrying Isabella, Princess of Aragón, agreed by contract to force the Jews either to convert to Catholicism or to leave. The end result was the same, though. Jews weren't welcome. Simple as that!"

Dessert came in. I said that the original post-1492 Sephardic communities flourished across the Mediterranean, eventually extending to the Middle East, the Americas, Turkey, the Netherlands, the Balkans, Northern Africa, and Italy. Sephardic Jewry has a distinct liturgical tradition, a unique cuisine, music, and literature that became a staple of the Ottoman Empire. Ladino, a hybrid tongue close to fifteenth-century Spanish and originally written in Hebrew characters, mutated into regional dialects. While it never had the unifying centrality that Yiddish had among Ashkenazi Jews, Ladino fostered continuity.

Today's Sephardic Jews are, for the most part, educated, entrepreneurial, and deeply engaged in their own countries. The collapse of the Ottoman

Empire in the twentieth century reconfigured these communities, as it did the societies in which Sephardic Jews lived.

I told Pérez that what seemed ironic to me with the effort at repatriation in Spain was that the country wasn't at the same time opening its doors to another element of its Ottoman-era heritage and another expelled community—the Moors. Between 1609 and 1614 the Moriscos (as Muslims who had converted to Christianity were known) were thrown out of the kingdoms of Aragón and Valencia. That blow consolidated the project known as La Reconquista, Spain's attempt to build a unified identity based on a single religion and ethnicity.

The continuity of Morisco culture is less defined. There were indeed concerted efforts at the time to push the Spanish government to make a similar invitation to descendants of Spanish Moors. It is doubtful whether this will happen, however, because, as in other parts of Europe, anti-Muslim sentiment in Spain is rampant. Behind the veil of Spain's philo-Semitism thus lies an unmistakable tinge of Islamophobia.

Equally certain is that the new repatriation law was not about Spain's rediscovery of its Sephardic heritage, I added. In my eyes, that cultural inheritance was treated carelessly, judging by the country's approach to Jewish sites.

11.

Purposefully, I had not talked to Isaac Pérez in detail about the controversy surrounding Crypto-Jews in New Mexico because I thought it might upset him. In 1981, while working as a state historian, Stanley M. Hordes had begun hearing stories about them, sometimes from hearsay, others directly from the families. In 2005 he published a book about it entitled *To the End of the Earth: A History of the Crypto-Jews of New Mexico*, an in-depth exploration that traces the ups and downs of this population from before the expulsion in 1492 through various periods, such as the first Crypto-Jewish settlements in the state from 1579 to 1591, the establishment of the First Permanent Colony in New Mexico in 1595–1607, through the adjustments to Anglo-American culture in the period of 1846 to 1950, and up until the vestiges of Crypto-Jewish life in the twenty-first century.

Today a portion of the Hispano community (*Hispano* is a term used by the Hispanic community of New Mexico) look at the debate surrounding the Crypto-Jews with suspicion. Another front of criticism comes from academic circles. To some extent, Hordes's volume was an attempt to make an argument to debunk academic critics. It hasn't succeeded, at least not fully. The leader of the doubters is Judith S. Neulander, a lecturer in the Department of Religious Studies at Case Western Reserve University, in Cleveland, whose research focuses on religion, arts, and related sciences through a folkloristic lens.

Her doctoral dissertation at Indiana University, "Cannibals, Castes, and Crypto-Jews: Premillennial Cosmogony in Postcolonial New Mexico" (2001), describes as "demonstrably unfounded" the ancestry of the Crypto-Jews in the region, as groundless as the claims of a group of Chinese Jews living in Kaifeng, once the capital of the Chinese Empire, or India's northeastern states of Manipur and Mizoram, all of whom allegedly descend from the biblical Lost Tribes of Israel. Neulander has also published pieces in support of her argument in the journal *Jewish Folklore and Ethnology Review*.

Other critics suggest that Crypto-Jews are a phenomenon of orientalism and that they are examples of "prompted" memories not unlike those of Jerzy Kosiński, author of the novel *The Painted Bird* (1965), and Binjamin Wilkomirski, responsible for the autobiography *Fragments: Memories of a Wartime Childhood* (1995), who falsely pretended to have gone through the Holocaust. These critics put in question the authenticity of the personal testimonials of the Crypto-Jews because, in their view, the testimonials are based on fragile memory, often ancestral, passed down from one generation to another. In other words, these are cases of invented identities.

I myself take these opinions seriously. Ethnographers at times see themselves as private eyes looking for a missing connection to the past. However, identity for me is less scientific. The story of the Crypto-Jews for me is less about authenticity—no doubt it is a kettle of fantasies and invented possibilities—than it is a manifestation of a particular trend in the history of the Jewish people to find connections to a long-lost fountainhead of genealogies.

A while after my dinner with Pérez, Spain indeed passed its repatriation law. The early response by the Sephardic diaspora to the new legislation had been understandably enthusiastic in troubled spots such as Istanbul and Caracas, where Jewish communities felt vulnerable. After all, a free passport to the European Union doesn't come every day. Other corners of the Sephardic community were also weighing the possible benefits. While it would be foolish to think of Spain's self-interested offer as the end of that diaspora, I had read that about two hundred million Jews had applied for repatriation.

Keeping in mind that the numbers are abstractions, this, as I had told Pérez, was about the largest number that historians speculated might have left Spain with the Alhambra Decree. In particular, I had heard from Venezuelan friends exhausted by the economic debacle that their country was suffering, in 2016, under Nicolás Maduro, the inept president who the belligerent Socialist leader Hugo Chávez had before his death chosen as his successor. One of my friends confided that among those applying were scores who until then had never acknowledged any Jewish ancestry. An acquaintance even posted a selfie on Twitter of the line outside the Spanish Embassy in Venezuela.

I was incredulous. To me it sounded like an astronomical number, though there was irony in it. More than five hundred years later, a return of sorts was indeed taking place. And this return proposed an altogether more relaxed conception of nationhood. As I told Pérez those applying for repatriation didn't need to move to the Iberian Peninsula. They could if they wanted to. But they could also stay where they were. They would become an integral part of Spain without having to live within its confines. This means that Spain wasn't limited by its own borders.

I love this conception of citizenship. It is, well, quite Jewish. You can be part of a people without being in the same space with most of them. That is, you can be landless, *aterritorial*. It looked to me as if, with a quick stroke, Spain was making itself abstract.

Pérez said he hadn't been to Spain yet. The trip to New York City had been expensive. He wished he could travel there one day, hopefully not too far into the future. But even if his ancestors were from there, he felt ambivalent about it. He didn't like soccer. His favorite sport was American football. It was a pity New Mexico didn't have its own team.

"This is one of the poorest states. Not enough money for a franchise here."

He didn't feel like Spain would be welcoming to him. It wanted a different type of Jew. Rich Jews. He wasn't rich.

I said that I was scheduled to travel there soon. We even talked about how Spain was in the middle of what looks like a Sephardic cultural revival. Classes on the topic were being taught at universities and community centers. In Israel, a series of Ladino singers were popular. For instance, I had a colleague who was writing a book on the Jews of Salonica, Greece. In Seattle and Los Angeles, where the Sephardic community was numerous, there were festivals, poetry events, other cultural activities. I had been at religious services in a synagogue where the rabbi delivered part of his sermon in Ladino. And young people were also embracing Ladino, hoping to revive it.

As we said goodbye, Isaac Pérez said he expected to fully convert to

Judaism soon. He talked of regularly attending Shabbat services. He then described, in detail, how moved he was last year when, in Albuquerque, he heard during Yom Kippur the prayer Kol Nidre being intoned. To him it felt as if had the capacity to touch God's heart.

He said Kol Nidre was like a key that opened a door inside him.

We embraced each other in the hotel lobby. The conversation had been enormously stimulating. Pérez wanted me to write with news after my trips to Spain and Latin America. "I feel I'm part of a chain . . ."

12.

After my meal with Isaac Pérez, in a fancy store not far from Plaza of the Governors in downtown Santa Fe at one point I caught sight of a stand selling T-shirts. Among them there were a few with reproductions of Kahlo's paintings. I suddenly noticed the abundance of flowers. She habitually has a flower crown on her head.

I noticed a T-shirt that made her look like the Virgen de Guadalupe, aka La Virgen. Her eyes were looking at me attentively. And her eyebrows— those weren't Mexican. They reminded me of the eyebrows of Ashkenazi Jewish immigrants to Mexico in the 1920s.

La Virgen, as people call her, is Mexico's patron saint. It is possible to argue that, in the country's theology, she is more important than Jesus Christ. She is perceived as everyone's mother. And it goes without saying that Mexicans have a fixation with the mother. Proof can be found in all sorts of linguistic expressions: *A toda madre!* means "wonderful!" *Chinga tu madre!* means "Go fuck yourself." *La puta madre!* means "Oh my God!" And so on.

That Kahlo has been turned into a mother figure—she who as a result of her physical handicaps was never able to get pregnant—is in itself miraculous.

"How much?" I asked the store owner.

She quoted me a price.

"Frida as La Virgen? That's funny," I said. "What's next?"

I handed her the money. "Do you have any of Diego Rivera as Christ?"

"No, that's not possible," she replied.

"Why?"

"He really didn't suffer. Actually, he made everyone else suffer . . ."

4   **PARADISE LOST**

1.

Minutes after we landed at the José Martí International Airport in Havana, Cuba, the charter plane emptied into a hangar. About 120 passengers put on their hats and sunglasses. You could sense the steaming heat outside.

Since I was in the front row I descended first. It was a couple of years before President Barack Obama proposed doing away with the US embargo instituted in 1962. His argument: after decades it was clear that American policy of pushing the Cuban economy to the brink of collapse had only made the island's government and its people more resilient.

After drifting through Mexico I decided to go to Cuba. Arguably no place in Latin America generates as much curiosity. In part this curiosity is the result of the island's strategic location. In the colonial period it was the port of arrival in the mercantile route from Europe to the New World.

For a long time sugar and tobacco were the island's essential source of income, to such a degree that one of the canonical books is Fernando Ortiz's *Contrapunteo cubano del tabaco y el azúcar* (*Cuban Counterpoint: Tobacco and Sugar*, 1940), an ethnographic study suggesting that these two products were not only agricultural commodities but cultural characters.

Fidel Castro's revolution at the end of 1958 established a break with the way the island had always been a kind of US backyard, a favorite spot for gangsters and high-fashion prostitutes. That is what Castro's entourage of bearded guerrilla fighters, the *barbudos*, fought against: the tendency to see the island as a banana republic. He had fought against Fulgencio Batista, one of the dozens of Latin American dictators backed by Washington. It took Castro a while, until the early 1960s, to declare his loyalty to the Soviet Union's model of Communism. This defiance turned Cuba into a source of pride all over the region.

But the US embargo put the country on the brink of disaster, undermining its economy. It was always dependent on foreign aid—first from the Kremlin and other Soviet countries, then from oil-rich Venezuela. Full-fledged independence was a delusion.

My flight left Miami very early. It only took about forty-five minutes.

Ruth Behar, *una jubana*, a Cuban Jew and a cultural anthropologist and writer, was traveling with me. She had agreed to serve as my personal guide and introduce me to people in the Jewish community of Habana. She also offered to connect me to contemporary writers not yet published in English in the United States whose work could be considered for my imprint, Restless Books. Born in Havana in 1956 Ruth has Sephardic Turkish, Ashkenazi Polish, and Russian ancestry. Her family left the island after Castro came to power. She often returns and made a documentary called *Adio Kerida* (2002) about her longing for Cuba.

Although it was a short flight and I'm a frequent traveler, I'm rather afraid of flying. Every time there is turbulence I hold on to whatever is near me and recite the prayer Adon Olam. I seldom pray otherwise. And although I am constantly in conversation with God, I'm also a skeptic verging on atheist. Indeed, whenever I find myself mumbling to myself the Adon Olam, I laugh. What good will it do a lapsed believer? Yet I'll do it again next time, maybe as an expression of superstition.

The flight was uneventful. We landed promptly at ten o'clock in the morning. The plane included descendants of Cuban exiles who had never been on the island since their parents left in the early 1960s. I talked to a couple in Miami. They were anxious. The older generation family members weren't altogether happy with their trip. But after years of opposition, they had finally found it in their hearts to look past those objections and make the trip anyway.

I quickly found myself in a dimly lit room. My shirt was now decorated with an archipelago of sweat spots. The small fan hanging from the ceiling barely alleviated the heat discomfort.

Straight lines formed next to ticket-booth windows that were part of tiny cubicles made of metal and glass. Inside were customs officials dressed in uniform. Another flight had landed a few minutes after ours, this one from Canada, and its passengers were now mixed in with us. From the languages that surrounded me, I gathered a few visitors were Dutch, Norwegian, German, and French.

As it turned out, my queue ended up being slower than the rest. From a distance I could discern the silhouette of the customs official, an attractive young woman around twenty-five years of age who looked at each passport mechanically, with an expression of absolute disinterest.

There were at least fifteen people before me. Darn it! I was on my way to meet a tortoise.

But at least I wasn't alone on this journey. Ruth Behar and I have known each other since the early 1990s. At the University of Michigan, where she has been on the faculty for three decades, she founded a study abroad program in partnership with Casa de las Américas, Cuba's leading organization in charge of fostering social, cultural, and economic relations with—and among—Latin American countries. The program organizes courses, lectures, workshops, and symposia and also publishes magazines, books, and other materials.

Part of Behar's arrangement while leading the study abroad program was the availability of an apartment next to Casa de las Américas, on Calle 3ra, in El Vedado neighborhood, near the US Embassy. She had wintered in Havana for three years and knew the city well, in addition to having traveled back and forth to the island since 1991.

By sheer luck, or maybe because she knew the system better, Behar ended up in a faster lane than I did. She soon disappeared into the luggage area, though not before she smiled politely after her passport was handed back to her by the customs official. I was left to fend for myself.

I was getting anxious. In these situations, I look for ways to entertain myself mentally. I thought, for starters, that disorder is the lay of the land in Cuba. And in the Hispanic world in general. I was comparing these types of lines with the way people organize themselves in the United States. There is a semblance of efficiency there, although in truth, situations like this one generate as much disorder there as well.

Or else, a different kind of order. That's where my mind settled in—the difference between the approaches to order and chaos in the Anglo and Hispanic worlds. To me they are essentially different. In Latin America, disorder isn't called that way: it is simply seen as an alternative kind of order.

Then I thought about how ridiculous passports are: bogus certificates of membership. I recalled that the Spanish film director, Luis Buñuel, in his memoir *The Last Breath* (1983) talks about the moment, in the early twentieth century, when passports became official. He would stop in front of a customs official and say, "Here I am! Why bother with a piece of paper? This is my face, these are my hands, this is the real me." That explanation didn't pass muster. And it surely doesn't do the trick today, in the age of terrorism. Who cares who you really are?

About twenty minutes later I finally stood before the tortoise. She stared at me with deference, carefully studying my US passport, my visa, and a letter of invitation I had been asked to provide to enter Cuba.

A sudden expression of perplexity overtook her face. She started asking me a thousand questions, first the ones that standard protocol calls for: Where are you from? What time did the flight leave? Where are you staying in Havana? These were followed by an onslaught of ridiculous ones: Why are you traveling alone? Who do you work for—the US government?

The first questions came in English. Unfazed, I responded in Spanish, hoping this might expedite our encounter.

Suddenly, she wanted to know how come my passport said I was born in Mexico, yet I was traveling as an American. Then she stopped on a passport page stamped by Israeli customs. "Why have you been to Israel recently?"

I had traveled to Israel to give a lecture a couple of years before. I was planning to return soon.

Soon I told myself: next time, it might be good to take my Mexican passport as well. And what if I applied for a Polish passport? Recently the Polish government was extending an invitation to the descendants of those who left the country. If my application was granted I would have three passports. Would that upend the very idea of what a passport is: an international document tying the individual to one particular nation?

Claiming my Polish citizenship was disingenuous, though. Not because of the Polish government but because of me. I don't feel any love for Poland. It was the place my forebears were forced to abandon because of the pogroms.

Does one need to love the country whose passport one carries along, I asked myself?

I told the woman I was a scholar.

"An Israeli scholar? What about Israeli arms sales to Latin American dictatorships? Are you Jewish?"

Never before had anything similar happened to me. What right did this bureaucrat have to ask such questions?

She must be an officer in training, I told myself. It is therefore essential that I remain calm.

Soon a supervisor was called in. He politely asked me to follow him to an adjacent room.

There was nothing official in the supervisor's demeanor. He was wearing civilian clothes: a cheap green Polo shirt, blue denim pants with a black belt, and a Baltimore Orioles baseball cap.

He talked to me in a more calculated way. Before I had time to answer his first question, he reached out to a garbage bin and rescued a piece of paper. He took out a fountain pen and scribbled some notes on the paper.

Things moved much faster with him. He wanted to know what hotel I was staying at in Havana, when I had made my reservation, the precise nature of my trip, any Cuban acquaintances I might spend time with. I was methodical in my replies.

Not finding any fault, he got tired of me and said I could go.

"Bienvenido a Cuba! Y disculpe las molestias," he said, "Apologies for the inconvenience."

Apologies for the inconvenience? The whole affair at the Havana airport had gone on for about forty-five minutes. All the other passengers were long gone.

I left with a sour taste in my mouth. "Gracias, compañero," I replied sarcastically, almost immediately regretting my imposture.

2.

Strictly speaking, there are few taxis in Cuba. In most cases one simply hires a driver. The typical automobile on the island—a hulking DeSoto, Plymouth, or Ford—is from the 1950s. People improvise all sorts of charming ways to keep these clunkers on the road.

Behar and I chose a driver and settled on a price. After we dropped her at Casa de las Américas, the driver took me to the Hotel Meliá Cohiba in the Vedado neighborhood, on Avenida Paseo right by El Malecón, Havana's gorgeous coastline.

My itinerary in the next week was tight. Behar had made arrangements for me to visit several Jewish sites, including a Holocaust exhibition, a small Sephardic synagogue I had heard about, a kosher butcher shop, and a couple of cemeteries.

At its height before the revolution, Cuba had some 15,000 Jews. Depending on whom you ask, there are between 750 and 1,500 Cuban Jews in the nation today. A great many of them are converts or products of mixed marriages who identify as Jews.

There was also a science-fiction writer I'd heard about, who was the author of a trilogy. I hoped to learn more about him, and Ruth Behar knew of another science-fiction writer she wanted to introduce me to. And I wanted to browse through antique bookstores.

Behar told me that the blue building, the Hotel Riviera, next to the Meliá Cohiba had been built by Meyer Lansky, a Jewish mobster known as the "Mob's Accountant" who had been close to the dictator Batista. A wealthy amoral entrepreneur, for a while he was the unofficial gambling minister. He built a casino empire that included new buildings, the conversion of old ones, and even the making of luxury suites at the Hotel Nacional, which overlooked an old fortress, El Morro, defending Havana's harbor. Ernest Hemingway, another Havana habitué, objected to the casinos, to no avail.

I looked at the Lansky building from afar, then went to my room to relax.

The first order of the day was to exchange money, which I did at the hotel desk. Cuba had two currencies: one for the locals and another one for tourists. The latter was exponentially high-priced. The intention was clear. After sugar and tobacco dried up as the island's exports, and with the embargo constraining most international transactions, tourism was the number-one source of income. Establishing a tourist currency was thus a way to multiply this source of income.

I also tried to get a code number to access the Internet at the hotel's business center. The one-hour pass was astronomically expensive. I tried to log in. It took me about fifteen minutes. From there on the connection was tenuous at best. In the end sending a quick email took about half an hour.

I walked along El Malecón for about a mile until I reached Old Havana. I wanted to get a peek at it. I hadn't been on the island for a while. News of its decaying state reached the United States in the form of videos. But the reality was much worse. Except on a portion of El Malecón, buildings in the city were in a state of utter decay. The sewer system was practically unusable, and the Saudis had generously given the Cuban government a grant to redo parts of it in Old Havana. This meant that a number of streets were closed. They were being dug up in order for new sewers to be installed.

I walked back to the hotel and had a bite at the restaurant next to the swimming pool.

That afternoon Behar took me to visit El Patronato, the headquarters of the Jewish community. The address is also in El Vedado, a quiet residential neighborhood in Havana.

Our point person was Adela Dworin, an elegantly dressed woman in her late seventies. She isn't only the community leader but the depository of the Jewish community memory. She and Behar have known each other for years. Dworin even had memories of Behar's family from the 1950s. Behar introduced me politely, explaining that I was writing about Cuban Jews.

Dworin spoke in what seemed like a calculated tone. She asked that I call her Adela. Spanish felt like her native tongue yet her English cadence reminded me of the way Jewish refugees from the Second World War formulated their sentences in English using the Yiddish syntactical pattern.

As she took me around the administrative offices, she talked about how Cuba has for centuries been an economic, social, and cultural gateway thanks to its strategic position in the Caribbean, a port of arrival and transit for European merchandise to the Americas. As part of the Spanish Empire from the early colonial period it was also a destination for the *Cristiano nuevo* (New Christian), a term that refers to a converted Jew whose ties to the Catholic Church in the fifteenth century and beyond was rather recent.

I visited the library at El Patronato. It had a healthy collection of American novels, especially best sellers, translated into Spanish. I saw copies of Leon Uris's *Exodus* and *Mila 18*. I also saw a couple of books by Isaac Bashevis Singer.

We finally settled in Adela's office. She talked to us while some of her staff worked on old-fashioned computers. Another one was attending to the books, although it didn't look to me as if any were in circulation. My impression was that the volumes too were donations.

Cuba's strategic position meant that merchandise such as ice machines or automobiles arrived there before anywhere else in Latin America. And along with merchandise came the Jews.

Much later, in the early twentieth century, a Yiddish-speaking Ashkenazi immigration wave arrived, making Havana a hot spot for literary, artistic, and musical exchange. The official date that Cuban Jews give for their arrival on the island is 1906. Actually, the first Jews, according to lore, were American. Less than a decade after the Spanish-American War of 1898, several American Jewish officers, part of the Liberation Army of Cuba, got involved in the sugarcane and railroad industries. Soon they had founded the United Hebrew Congregation.

In the 1910s and 1920s Sephardic Jews came from Turkey and Syria, and in the 1920s a large migration arrived from Poland. In the 1930s and 1940s more European Jews came, in flight from the Nazis, even as America shut its doors to them.

By the time Castro drove with his convoy into Havana, the Jewish community was thriving not only in Havana but also in other cities such as Santiago de Cuba and Camaguey. Castro's determination to make Cuba a Communist paradise followed. Fear spread like wildfire among the middle and upper classes that the government was about to take possession of small and large businesses. This set off an exodus of tens of thousands of middle-class Cubans, including many Cuban Jews (about 90 percent of the Cuban Jewish community) to Miami and elsewhere.

Yet Cuba's Jewish life didn't perish. It survived, albeit radically shrunken. During the first couple of decades Castro saw religion, in Karl Marx's words, as "the opium of the people." But later on it seems he changed his mind. Religious societies resurfaced, and Jewish ones among them.

In fact, the reinvigorated Jewish community thrived. Adela said that, relatively speaking, the Jews of Cuba probably enjoyed an abundance of riches. She asked an assistant to show me the pharmacy on the upper floor of the building where El Patronato is housed. I was told it was better stocked than any other in Cuba. Medicines of all types came in the form of donations, especially from American Jewish groups visiting the island. These groups brought clothes, prayer books and other religious paraphernalia, and anything else people thought might be scarce in Cuba.

Indeed, the pharmacy at El Patronato was famous all over the country. Not only Jews but people of all backgrounds used it.

I asked Adela if this overt generosity fostered envy or even anti-Semitism. "Aquí no hay antisemitas," she adamantly replied—and repeated thereafter. "There is no anti-Semitism in Cuba."

My reaction was ambivalent. Indeed, at no point in my previous and future visits to the island did I come across any overt anti-Semitic comment. Yet everything has to do with how anti-Semitism is framed.

The substance of my reaction to Adela's comments involved another dimension, however. Whenever she talked I got the feeling she was in need of protecting her comfortable position as *La Jefa*, which entailed benefiting from government patronage that allowed her and her entourage, for instance, to receive medicines and other donations from American Jews. Why would she want to jeopardize such comfort?

In other words it may be true that Cuba isn't anti-Semitic. Faiths and ethnicities apparently coexist in harmonious ways—but as change arrives, so does resentment.

On the other hand, it is true that Cuba never was a home to the kind of anti-Zionist campaigns that were prevalent in other parts of Latin America. Castro resisted Soviet pressure to break off relations with Israel after the 1967 Six-Day War, when most of the rest of the Soviet bloc cut its diplomatic ties with the Jewish state.

Cuba cut off formal relations with Israel only in 1973, after the Yom Kippur War. The Zionist Federation of Cuba was closed down by executive order three years later. But other Jewish cultural institutions continued to operate even as Cuba denounced Zionism ever more harshly in the international arena. Religious institutions including synagogues were repressed and restricted as part of the officially atheist regime's broader campaign against religion.

After the fall of the Soviet Union in 1989, informal ties gradually returned. Cuban Jews have quietly been allowed to emigrate to Israel for many years. And it was an Israeli firm that established the first foreign investment enterprise in Cuba's citrus industry, in 1991. Israeli tourists have long visited Cuba freely, and Cuban artists and intellectuals have visited Israel regularly.

At the end of my visit to El Patronato I gave Adela one hundred dollars. It was a *donación*, a donation. Beforehand, Behar had made it clear to me that this was how the Jewish community in Havana survived: through Adela's improvised lectures.

"Muchas gracias," said Adela. "Many thanks."

She invited us to Shabbat services in a couple of days.

Outside her office on our way out, next to the restrooms, there was a man in his eighties, senile, sitting on an antiquated sofa. I looked at him attentively. He seemed to be lost in thought, although he followed the action around him with his eyes. No one paid attention to him.

I approached him and said hello. He smiled. I tried to make small talk but he was incoherent. His memory was faulty. He couldn't tell me his name. I got the impression I was looking at the town's fool.

Adela was no longer available. I asked one of the staffers. She told me his last name but I have forgotten it: something like Señor Sefsovitch. She wasn't sure what he did or where he lived. "He's always here. He keeps us company!"

Maybe he was a Holocaust survivor. Or an old revolutionary. Or a janitor. Or a teacher. Maybe he had family in Florida but he didn't want to move to another country and become a stranger.

That evening we went to a fine *paladar* nearby called Restaurante Porto Habana. Paladares are impromptu restaurants. A few years before the Cuban government had given permission for people to get into private business. This paladar was on the fifth floor of an apartment building. It had floor-to-ceiling windows.

We ate *sopa de mariscos*, green salad, and fish. I was delighted with the quality of the food; it was fresh, flavorful, well cooked. I asked Behar if she thought entrepreneurship would ultimately change the face of Communism in Cuba.

"It's a peculiar experiment," she responded. "Private enterprise is allowed. As are a number of small businesses. People used to look at you with suspicion if you dreamed of opening a paladar. But now they are common. Some have actually grown a lot. Calling them paladares is no longer accurate. They are fancy restaurants. In fact, some of them are as good as anything you will find in Paris."

"There must be a limit, though. Otherwise, it is no longer Communism."

"That's the question. How much individualism will the authorities tolerate? One option is that progress will be slow yet steady. Another option is that at some point the ruling party will say 'Enough!' and Cuba will go back to the limitations of the Cold War years. To me that model is no longer tenable. The Soviet Union isn't around to offer a free hand. Nor is Venezuela, which used to have a seemingly endless reservoir of oil."

Soon the owner brought us dessert. It was pastel de tres leches. I had never tasted a more sumptuous kind.

3.

A day later Behar and I visited two Jewish cemeteries, about twenty-five kilometers east of Havana. It would take about thirty minutes each way through the Carretera Central de Cuba and the Primer Anillo.

Adela had arranged for a driver to take us. His name was Juan Pablo Escovedo. He picked me up at the hotel. From there we went to Behar's apartment. Since she wasn't outside I rang the bell, but it didn't work. A neighbor allowed me into the building.

Her place was on the third floor. When I arrived a very old woman was sitting on a sofa, watching a baseball game.

I said hello. She told me Behar was in the bathroom.

The place had no air-conditioning. It was steaming hot.

A few minutes later, Behar came out. She hadn't been in the bathroom but reading in the bedroom. We talked about the apartment. She said she wanted to take me to Casa de las Américas before we left Havana.

We went down the stairs. The Casa de las Américas building was practically next door. She took me around, showed me the exhibit areas, introduced me to scholars, students, and staff, and showed me the small bookstore.

The organization has a larger-than-life reputation in Latin America. It organizes semi-annual literary contests and sponsors conferences that bring in academics and intellectuals from all over the world.

The president is Roberto Fernández Retamar, a recalcitrant theorist whose work I read years ago. His principal claim to fame is an argument that feels loosely inspired by Edward Said's Orientalism. Latin America, he argues, is seen as barbaric in Western civilization. This barbarism goes back to Shakespeare's last play, *The Tempest* (1611), in which the character of Caliban, imprisoned by the magician Prospero, is shaped by sheer impulse. Caliban's name is inspired by the Caribs, a Caribbean tribe that generated much curiosity in Europe in the seventeenth century after a series of travelers purportedly spent time with the tribe.

Behar suggested we meet with Jorge Fornet, the director of the institution's literary research activities. He has been interested in Latinos in the United States for some time and I enjoyed speaking with him.

Behar and I then looked for our driver. He had been sleeping in the car, a 1957 turquoise-colored Chevrolet Bel Air convertible.

Soon we all were on the road. Juan Pablo was a charming thirty-two-year-old mulatto, an engineer by training, but it was easier for him to make a living in Cuba these days as a taxi driver because of the two currencies. Tourists think in dollars—and no matter what the government says, Cubans think in dollars too.

Juan Pablo told us he had two children, a girl and a boy, aged twelve and nine. His wife was a doctor. He had never been outside Cuba.

We engaged in conversation. He told us he was from Santiago but had been living with his sister in Havana for several years.

"Are you Jewish?" he asked.

We told him yes. Behar explained that she had been born in Havana. Her family left when she was little. She returned frequently and was in touch with her childhood *nana* as well as with scores of other people in the Jewish community.

Juan Pablo said he was friends with some Jews at El Patronato. The building, in the El Vedado neighborhood, is also the headquarters of the city's Jewish community and where Temple Beth Shalom, built in 1952, is located. Juan Pablo said El Patronato gets the best philanthropic donations. "Specially medicine. American Jews send antibiotics, aspirin, syringes, cough syrup, skin ointment. . . . You can't get that stuff anywhere else."

His mother had become sick some months ago. Diarrhea. It wouldn't go away. Pharmacies in Havana were depleted, so the doctor recommended the Jewish community. They only open the dispensary twice a week. And you have to wait on line. But where don't you have to make a line? Her prescription was filled. A few days later she was feeling better.

Guanabacoa is a colonial town where the first African guild was created to alleviate the plight of slaves in Cuba. It is a somewhat improbable home for not one but two Jewish cemeteries, one Ashkenazi and the other Sephardic, both of them more than a century old. They are not the only places where Jews are buried on the island but their strategic location, a short distance from the capital, makes them the most prominent.

About halfway there Juan Pablo wanted to know if any of our relatives were buried in Guanabacoa. Behar said yes and I said no. She wrote a poem about her relative called "The Jewish Cemetery of Guanabacoa." I read it and told Behar it was the first place I wanted to go when we arrived in Cuba.

During the drive I said that decades ago a great-uncle of mine, Abel Eisenberg, played first viola in Havana's Orquesta Filarmónica. This was in the 1940s. He soon left the island to become conductor of the Sinfónica Nacional in the Dominican Republic. He died in 1996 and is buried in Mexico City.

Juan Pablo asked what we did for a living. Behar said she was an anthropologist and a writer. I said I spend my life around books: writing them, teaching them, making them. I suggested that cemeteries are not like books, which tend to be organized with some sort of logic. There is seldom any logic in a graveyard: no alphabetical rule of thumb. No chronology either. Burials take place on a first-come-first-served basis, depending on when the lot was acquired. The result is deliberately haphazard. In other words, whatever guiding principle there might be, you need to find it on your own. People sometimes end up close to their loved ones but next to others they probably never met. Yet that's what they end up being for all eternity: neighbors.

"Are Jews buried in elegant clothes?" he asked. "Because Jews like elegant clothes, right?"

They aren't dressed when they are laid to rest, Behar said. I mentioned that a while back I had written a novella called *Morirse está en hebreo* (2006), which was made into a film called *My Mexican Shiva* (2007), about the death of an uncle of mine. I included in it the ritual bathing of the corpse before the burial. In order to be accurate I had attended a session in Mexico City, at the Ashkenazi cemetery. During the ritual performed by the *Chevra Kaddisha*, the ears, the nails, everything was cleaned while prayers were intoned. It was all about purity. And a raw egg was cracked, its contents spilled on the belly.

With Behar near me I felt at ease. I mentioned that my interest in cemeteries dates back to my teens. I lost a dear friend before we reached the age of twenty. His name was Marcos Reznik. He had an aneurism. He had just dropped his girlfriend off at the airport and was sitting down to have breakfast. Truth is, I don't remember attending the funeral. I probably was too distraught. But I have visited his tomb dozens of times. He is buried in the Cementerio Judío on Calle Constituyentes, the same cemetery where I attended the ritual of the Chevra Kaddisha. My ancestors are buried there. And my parents acquired a lot for themselves in it.

"Whenever I find myself there," I continued, "I think of a line from a sonnet by the Spanish Golden Age poet Francisco de Quevedo: Vivo en conversación con los difuntos, / Y escucho con mis ojos a los muertos, I live in conversation with those gone, / and listen with my eyes to the dead. However, I have to confess: what makes these grounds holy I can't fully wrap my mind around."

"Well, I don't believe in God," said Juan Pablo. "But people that do swear that graveyards have a direct line to God. What do you think? What I think, if you ask me, is that these grounds are as common as any other, yet they are holy because those that left are holy. And because our beloved one are believed to be with God, graveyards are the bridge between the here and now and the hereafter."

Somehow what Juan Pablo was saying made me think of a line by Samuel Beckett: "The end is in the beginning and yet you go on." I have never been able to sort it out, and this, precisely, is what attracts me to it.

"Do Jews believe in the afterlife?" asked Juan Pablo.

I said it was complicated. Orthodox Jews believe that when the Messiah comes, the dead will be resurrected and an enormous caravan will walk toward Jerusalem.

"Do you believe in the afterlife?" Juan Pablo clearly wanted to know what I thought.

"I don't," I said. "You die and that's it, you're dead. The fact that people want to be buried with their kin is done less for the dead than for the living. Who cares where you're buried? Those who love you. Truth is, I very much care where I will be buried: next to Alison, my wife. Otherwise, I will be lonely."

"Do you care where? Does it need to be in Mexico?"

"No, probably not in Mexico. I no longer feel at home there, though I don't know where. Maybe in Israel, although Alison doesn't care much for that. Most likely where I live, in Amherst, Massachusetts, which is where we have spent the best years of our lives."

I was amazed by how personal the conversation had become. Behar talked about her repeated visits to Cuba, the closeness she felt to the island. Most of her work, in one way or another, was about those ties.

Juan Pablo talked about how his own wife, as a doctor, witnessed death all the time, "in a matter-of-fact way." He also said that one of his daughter's friends died from diphtheria.

"I thought diphtheria was eradicated," Behar affirmed.

"So did I," said Juan Pablo. He added that his own father was buried in Santiago, "where Fidel Castro is from." And he said that burials in Cuba are done uniformly by the government. "There isn't much to it. For instance, lots of people he knew have been cremated. 'La Revolución' dismantled any certainty there might have ever been about the afterlife."

He paused, then directed his next question to me. "Do you read the inscriptions of gravestones when you're in cemeteries?"

"Yes. I use them to come up with the story behind them. I look at the spellings of the words. And at the symbols, the icons, and other graphics. Once in a while, I find a typo . . . or what I believe is a typo. Honestly, while I often visit Jewish cemeteries, I'm more ecumenical. During a trip to Buenos Aires, I went to La Recoleta, the site where the nation's founders are laid to rest: Rosas, Domingo Faustino Sarmiento, Perón's wife, Evita. Had Borges, the Argentine I feel closest to, been buried in his native Argentina, he would in all probability be in this graveyard. Yet he had a conflicted relationship with Argentina, which made him choose Switzerland, where he spent precious years in his youth. I don't know why but graveyards are a magnet to me."

"You'll be enthralled with Guanabacoa," Juan Pablo announced.

"Why?"

"Well, I'd rather you see it with your own eyes . . ."

The cemeteries in Guanabacoa sat next to each other. The largest, Centro Macabeo of Cuba, is used mostly for Ashkenazim. It was founded in 1906 and erected in 1910. Its façade reads "United Hebrew Congregation," which points to the American funds with which it was built.

The other graveyard is the Cementerio Sefardí, once serving the Sephardic community of Havana.

Some portions of the perimeter of the cemeteries were made of walls and others of fences. I saw an entryway with a Star of David.

We walked around while the Chevrolet Bel Air was parked outside. For about ten minutes nothing happened. Then a young man came running toward where we were. He was the graveyard keeper. I was glad to see him. Behar knew him and reminded him she is a friend of Adela Dworin at El Patronato. Someone from El Patronato was supposed to call in advance to let the cemetery keeper know Behar and I would be visiting.

No one did, but he said there was no problem. He would be pleased to show us around. He found a key in his pocket to open a padlock attached to a chain that closed the main entrance.

Juan Pablo announced he would wait for us outside. "I hope you aren't upset."

I took out a yarmulke I'd brought with me and made my way in. The cemetery keeper followed us a few steps behind. He asked if we wanted water. It was around eleven o'clock and it was hot.

I wandered around. It didn't take any time for Behar to spot her relative's tombstone.

I found a small memorial to the Holocaust victims. It wasn't far from the tomb of one of the most important leaders of the Jewish community of Cuba. I read the inscriptions: they were mostly in Hebrew and Spanish. On occasion I came across a line in Yiddish.

In some ways the sorry state of these Jewish cemeteries in Cuba might be viewed as a reflection of the abandonment and reduced circumstances experienced by Havana's remaining Jews during decades under Castro's Communist Rule—at least until the 1990s, when the government lifted many of its restrictions on religious communities and allowed Cuba's Jews to travel freely to Israel and permitted American Jews to visit them.

I noticed some tombs had been remodeled. The cemetery keeper told us that these were redone when a family member, usually in Miami, made a special request and sent the funds directly to El Patronato.

Nearby, I saw some small graves and told myself they must be of infants.

Then, as I got deeper into the cemetery, I was horrified by what I found. A number of the tombs were in ruin—but not from natural decay. They had been vandalized. This was what Juan Pablo was referring to when he said he hoped we weren't distressed.

The marble stones were broken into pieces, their fragments put back in place. Inside, bones had been stolen.

I asked the cemetery keeper if the damage was something new. He told me it looked visibly worse than on previous occasions. Nor was it exclusive to Jewish cemeteries. He mentioned that some desecration had taken place at the Cementerio Colón, the main graveyard in Havana, also located in the Vedado neighborhood and built in 1876. But the acts of vandalism there were minor in comparison. More cases occurred in Chinese cemeteries.

He confessed that the Jewish tombstones had suffered substantially in recent times.

I inquired into the cause, and Behar and the cemetery keeper between them came up with three possible explanations, though it quickly becomes clear that only one was true.

First, he said that there was the popular suspicion that Jews bury their dead with jewelry.

This made me think back to the question that Juan Pablo had asked while we were driving to Guanabacoa: if Jews are buried in elegant clothes.

I knew that Castro's revolution organized nationwide educational programs that had paid off. The percentage of illiteracy was minuscule compared with other Latin American countries. Equally, state-run efforts to eliminate poverty, in cities as well as in the countryside, had been effective. Still, the country's economy was in shambles. It once survived as part of its loyalty to the Soviet Union and later on was dependent on oil and other products delivered from Venezuela out of political empathy. But that had dried up as well. Thus, searching for treasures in tombs, especially in Jewish ones, might not be accidental.

The second explanation from the cemetery keeper was far less believable. Since Raúl Castro had been president of the Council of State of Cuba and the president of the Council of Ministers of Cuba from 2008 to 2018, that is, since he took over the reins of the government from his ailing brother, Fidel, private enterprise had tentatively emerged on the island, with paladares opening up, real estate being sold, the construction industry widening, and so on. Marble was a commodity with marketable value.

The challenge to this explanation was that, as far as I could assess, the tombstones, while broken, were not missing much marble.

The third explanation—the obvious one as well as unquestionably the most worrisome—had to do with religious practices in Guanabacoa. In the 1920s the town had several Jewish garment businesses, including Sedanita, owned by an American Jew from the Lower East Side. But the town was best known for Santería, a syncretic Caribbean belief that combines West African elements with Christian motifs. Less well known was another religion with African roots that took hold in Cuba; it's called Regla de Palo Monte, or simply Palo Monte.

One of the rituals of Palo Monte required the use of bones from nonbaptized people. These bones came from Jewish and Chinese graveyards. The Jewish bones were the only ones used to ward off the Evil Eye.

This last explanation left me stunned. I asked if the Cuban government did anything to stop the practitioners of Palo Monte. The graveyard keeper said they were part of a colonial-era religion with a growing number of followers in the country, and the authorities were unlikely to undermine the practice since it plays a central role in the nation's collective identity.

But should that collective identity be built on dishonoring the dead of other faiths, in this case the Jews?

I then reached the Sephardic cemetery. The situation there was a bit less extreme. It looked like the Ashkenazi cemetery was easier to reach for the vandals.

All this left me in a state of disbelief, not to say disquiet.

I talked to Behar, who had written about the desecration in her book *An Island Called Home* (2007).

As I made my way back to the Chevrolet Bel Air, I gave the cemetery keeper his *propina*, a contribution for his time, thanking him on Behar and my behalf for the information.

Juan Pablo was sitting in the driver's seat. He stared at us. Tolerant as one should be of other people's cultural practices, I still couldn't quite appease my indignation. He said the desecration was mostly seen as a local affair.

I told Juan Pablo the issue should become a national referendum. I added that I wanted to write something about it.

"You should," he said. "These are *your* dead. You have every right to protect them."

On the return trip to Havana, we talked about all sorts of things, including the US embargo and the attitude of Cuban exiles toward Havana. "You know, they used to be called *gusanos*." In Spanish the word means "worm."

"Honestly, nowadays people don't talk about them anymore. And if they do, it isn't in derogatory terms. You know, everybody makes choices in life. You love or you hate. You laugh or you cry. You're ambitious or you're asleep. You stay or you go. Who am I to judge why they left? I was tempted myself a number of times. My aunt lives in New Jersey. And I have cousins in Florida. But my wife and children are here. Can you just pick up the suitcases and leave? It's much harder than that, which is why I give credit to those who do it. You need *cojones*. Particularly if you're going on a raft. Chances are you'll be eaten by sharks. And if you make it to the other side, other kinds of sharks are waiting there."

4.

As if to prove her point that paladares in Cuba could rank as high as any five-star restaurant in Paris, one night Behar made reservations at La Guarida on Calle Concordia #418. The place literally took my breath away. It is located in a section of Old Havana where my eyes could only see architectural structures in a sorrowful state of decay, in a crumbling building where Tomas Gutiérrez Alea and Juan Carlos Tabío shot their celebrated movie *Strawberry and Chocolate* (1993), about a romance between a gay man and a straight man.

As you climb the stairs to the second floor you see that within the ruins is a luxurious paladar. The walls are filled with photographs of local and international stars. The interior decoration, with fancy chandeliers and an assortment of antique furniture, with all sorts of peculiar artifacts on display in different corners, might be described as postmodern baroque. The bread was sublime. I ate seviche, a lobster dish, and an unforgettable apple dessert.

Behar had invited a Cuban friend of hers, Luisa Campuzano, a feminist literary critic who taught at the Universidad de La Habana. The friend said that the price of a single dinner at La Guarida was the equivalent of six months' salary for a pediatrician.

During the dinner conversation Campuzano asked what I was doing in Havana. I told her in detail about the trek I was making through Latin America.

She wanted to know where I had been already. I told her I had spent time in various corners of Argentina, mostly in Buenos Aires and in the province of Entre Ríos. I described El Once. I told her about the colonias that Baron Hirsch had funded for Yiddish-speaking shtetl Jews to settle in the Pampas. I also mentioned I had explored what used to be called Mesoamérica.

"Nobody calls it that way anymore. Only anthropologists and maybe ethnographers," Campuzano said. "Didn't Miguel León-Portilla, widely known for his studies on pre-Columbian cultures, always use that term? I heard him speak in Mexico City. He said the idea of Mexico and Guatemala and so on is rather recent. Before that, there was the great expansion of the Aztec Empire, which went from central Mexico to parts of what today is considered Central America."

I said that traveling across the Latin American republics, I was frequently struck by how heterogeneous they are. Of course they have a lot in common. But they are also quite different. Cuba, for instance, feels like certain parts of Mexico; like Veracruz, in the Gulf of Mexico; but not like Sonora, which is on the side of the Pacific Ocean. Likewise, the social composition of Bolivia, with its Aymara culture, is dramatically different from Uruguay, which resembles Argentina in genetic disposition.

I mentioned that I had been in Venezuela a couple of times. And in Colombia, Bolivia, and Panama. As the conversation progressed, the three of us found ourselves wondering if there is something that makes Latin America coalesce as a coherent entity. It clearly isn't language, for aside from Spanish and Portuguese, the languages spoken are French, English, Dutch, myriad indigenous languages, and an assortment of creoles, including Spanglish. Nor is it religion, for in these lands there are Catholics, Santeros, Muslims, Protestants, Macumbas, Jehovah's Witnesses, Jews, Buddhists, Candomblés, Hindus, Jews for Jesus, and others, as well as atheists and agnostics. No matter what the answer to these questions might be, the consensus for better or worse is that Spain and Portugal are the matrices, the fountain of *lo hispánico y lo portugués*, all things Hispanic and Portuguese.

Campuzano argued that Europe, as a composite, is also an abstraction, perhaps even a more extreme one. "An even bigger number of languages (German, French, Italian, Spanish, Portuguese, Romanian, Czech, Polish...) are spoken there," she stated. "And the national agendas are dramatically different as well, defined by diverging historical pasts. Still, Europe— perhaps because of the shared horrors it inflicted on itself in the twentieth century—managed to coalesce around a fragile, yet more-or-less unified, sense of collective purpose. Latin America has never come close to such a feat. In political, economic, and social terms, it remains a discombobulated collection of parts."

In response I said that my visit to Bogotá coincided with a fútbol match between Colombia and Ecuador, which I ended up watching in a bar. I was struck—and I had often been in similar situations in the past—by the animosity of the two sides toward each other while the game was taking place. At one point, a few people, after screaming all sorts of obscenities at each other, even got into a fight. Yet the moment the match was over, they started hugging again in typical Latin American style.

"It seems to me that when we need to show our own patriotism, we'll go to any justifiable extent. Yet if we face a foreign enemy—say the Argentine and German soccer teams face each other—by default we'll automatically support Argentina because it's our continental neighbor. That, to me, is what being a Latin American is all about."

Behar said she could imagine that some readers might be skeptical of my approach. They would probably say that, given the difficulty of establishing what made Latin America whole, it might be better to write a travelogue about Argentina, or about Mexico, or about Cuba—that is, surrender the ambitious idea of a transcontinental journey and instead focus on specific and well-defined nations. But then you would forfeit the opportunity of daring to speak of what made the America on the other side of the border from the United States an America in its own right.

"E pluribus unum," I said. "That's how the United States sees itself. Does it apply to us too? Interestingly, politicians have repeatedly come up with programs to unite the region, but they always fail. Yet think of literature. We talk of Borges, García Márquez, Fuentes, Cortázar, Onetti, and others as Latin American writers that belonged to a movement called 'El Boom.' Yes, they were from Argentina, Colombia, Mexico, and so on. But people thought of them as *latinoamericanos*. It's all in one convenient concoction."

"Why convenient?" Campuzano wondered.

"Because there's power in unity. It has marketing possibilities. It sells books."

By the end of the evening's conversation at La Guarida, over shots of liqueur, the feeling I was left with was that it is precisely the abstract nature of Latin America that made it such an enthralling place to explore. In truth, I was mapping out a world that existed not in real life but in people's minds.

5.

During the conversation in La Guarida, Campuzano asked me about my impressions of Venezuela. She wanted to know what I thought of Hugo Chávez and his successor, Nicolás Maduro. The way she framed the question, it was a matter of honor. Cuba is often portrayed as a "repeating island." This means, in part, that what happens in it spreads to other parts of Latin America. Not bad for a place that covers only 42,500 square miles.

Cuba's influence is best appreciated when pondering Fidel Castro's evangelical view on Communism. From the 1960s onward Castro's regime worked exhaustively to replicate the model elsewhere on the European continent. Perhaps his most famous ambassador was Ernesto "Ché" Guevara, a Quixotic freedom fighter from Argentina who ended up high in Castro's regime. His desire to spread the gospel of the revolution made him give up everything he had achieved in Havana in search of a mightier goal: turning the entirety of Latin America left. He was killed at the age of thirty-nine by United States–backed Bolivian forces on October 9, 1967, in La Higuera, Bolivia.

This didn't stop him from remaining, for the better part of three decades, an incubator of Communist ideals. By the 1990s the Communist bug jumped to Venezuela, where the military figure Hugo Chávez, born into a working-class family, eventually orchestrated an unsuccessful coup d'état. After spending a couple of years in prison, he founded the Fifth Republic Movement and went on to be elected president in 1998.

I told Behar and her friend that the last two times I had been in Venezuela was in 2005 and just before Chávez died, in 2013. I knew he had repeatedly come to Havana for medical reasons. I also knew that his regime had been generous with Cuba, offering cheap oil and helping its economy in other ways. In exchange, Cuba sent doctors to some of Venezuela's poorest neighborhoods.

When I arrived in Caracas in 2005, anti-Semitic vitriol in the country was at a record high. At the time the country registered as one of the most dangerous countries for Jews in the Western Hemisphere. This was in sharp contrast with the period before Chávez was first elected president. Venezuela then wasn't known as a place where Jews felt threatened. It was a country that was famous for its conviviality and joie de vivre and for its love of melodrama. After Mexico and Brazil, soap operas produced there are among the most popular as well as among the most exported throughout Latin America and beyond.

My trip was geared toward research. I wanted to know the situation of Venezuelan Jews. Its population was estimated at ten thousand. That was down from between fifteen and twenty thousand in its heyday, made up of Yiddish and Ladino speakers from, among other places, Romania, Poland, Bessarabia, Syria, Greece, and Turkey. And the ten thousand were quickly shrinking, with a solid wave of emigration in search of refuge going to Florida and to a lesser extent other American states.

I knew that a bit before my visit the Tiferet Israel Synagogue in Caracas's central Maripérez neighborhood was assaulted, at around half past four on a January afternoon. Its members were not the only ones who had felt shaken, so did minorities all across Venezuela.

Chávez had recently given an incendiary speech against Israel. As he had done before, the maneuver was his way to distract attention from the internal problems facing Venezuela: incessant poverty in spite of the country's rich oil reservoir, rampant urban violence, and a fractured electorate in which the concept of civil peaceful dialogue was quickly eroding. Chávez portrayed Israel as a genocidal state that manages to survive only because a cabal of wealthy Jews in the United States, through the media, control the world's public opinion.

Photos of the attack spread widely via the Internet. Apparently, several intruders entered the synagogue, but not with the intention of robbing it, since nothing of value was taken. Instead, religious paraphernalia were spilled out of the *Aron ha-Kodesh*, the Holy Ark in which Torahs are kept, into the ceremonial gallery. The number 666 was painted on walls, accompanied by swastikas and Stars of David. The synagogue's security fence was cut, and several office desks were looted.

Portions of the media tried to represent the incident as just another example of urban violence. But others charged the Chávez government with culpability.

In fact, the Caracas Jews I talked to at the Tiferet Israel Synagogue and elsewhere offered myriad opinions on Israel, from cautious support to unabashed outrage. As far as I was concerned that's how it should be in a democracy. The question for me was What kind of democracy was Venezuela under Chávez?

Chávez was quick to denounce the synagogue attack. And he rejected the suggestion that he or any of his supporters might be tied to it. He went on to suggest that political opponents plotted the attack to reduce his chances in a then imminent referendum on a constitutional amendment that would allow him to stay in office after his term ended.

The incident in Maripérez wasn't isolated. There have been other anti-Semitic events in previous years, including two Venezuelan police searches of the Hebraica, the Caracas Jewish community center. The police claimed to be on the lookout for explosives and other weapons. These searches occurred as Chávez began to talk about Mossad, the Israeli secret service, as an intrusive entity in Venezuela.

A few days after the Tiferet Israel Synagogue was attacked, another small synagogue in La Florida neighborhood was targeted. But public opinion coalesced around the Maripérez incident, and a campaign in support of Venezuelan Jews took place inside the country and beyond. It included a manifesto published with eight hundred signatures.

During the 2005 trip, I had breakfast with various leaders of the Venezuelan Jewish community at the Unión Israelita de Caracas, the city's kehillah. Among my concerns was how such a small minority would be able to cope with state-sponsored animosity amid such polarization. What was an acceptable response? Was Chávez as blatantly anti-Jewish as he was anti-Zionist? Did he make an effort to distinguish between the two terms? How far could things go? Could the menace reach a violent scale where human lives could perish?

What I heard was dismay. There are about twenty synagogues through-out the country. But the situation in other cities like Maracaibo and Valencia was less worrisome because Venezuela, with its centralized approach to politics and culture, filters everything through the capital. It was the Caracas Jews who felt the heat.

This heat was never from *El Líder* himself. Manipulation was among his best talents. At one point he would allow anti-Holocaust propaganda to be used in Chavista rallies, portraying the Shoah as a myth. Then, at another point, he would show sympathy for Venezuelan Jews. Along with Brazil's president, Luiz Inácio Lula da Silva (aka Lula), and Argentina's Cristina Fernández de Kirchner, at one point Chávez even signed an accord against regional anti-Semitism.

The consequences of this dance were not always clear or direct. An air of uncertainty permeated everything. Abraham Levy Benshimol, president of the Confederation of Israelite Associations of Venezuela, told me the Jews in Venezuela defined themselves as "a community under threat."

Among the troubling incidents that happened in the roughly eight years between my trips were the attacks against the social club Hebraica and the animosity surrounding the revival, in a commercial theater, of the Broad-way musical *El violinista sobre el tejado*, the Spanish version of *Fiddler on the Roof*. In early 2009, after the attack on the synagogue in Maripérez and two weeks before the premier of the play, the Orquesta Sinfónica Gran Mariscal de Ayacucho notified the play's production company, Palo de Agua Producciones, that because of its Jewish theme they would abstain from performing in the show.

The reason, a person involved in the decision later told me, was that their budget depended on subsidies from the federal government and participating in the show would put in question the continuity of that subsidy. The same director, Michel Hausman, and the theater producer, Yair Rosenberg, had staged Spanish-language adaptations of Mel Brooks's *The Producers* (1967) and Andrew Loyd Webber's *Jesus Christ Superstar* (1971), both of which also openly address Jewish topics. Together these plays have been seen in Venezuela by more than eighty thousand spectators.

The Venezuelan magazine *Zeta* investigated the incident and found that the orchestra's conductor hadn't received any direct orders to stop its partnership with Palo de Agua but that the atmosphere of fear that prevailed in Caracas after the Maripérez incident prompted him and his musicians to play it safe by disconnecting themselves from the show, a maneuver that, in the conductor's eye, wouldn't put in jeopardy the orchestra's government subsidy. In the end, the musical was staged with players, many of them from Gran Mariscal de Ayacucho, hired on an individual basis. But it left a deep feeling of discomfort, not to say alarm, among those involved in the production.

The next time I visited Caracas, in early 2013, things had deteriorated visibly. Chávez was mostly out of sight, in the middle of a series of cancer treatments. Talk about succession was incessant. By then the number of Venezuelan Jews had dwindled. I heard all sorts of numbers. I had the impression that the total was less than one thousand. Still, Chávez had always claimed to have plenty of Jewish friends and that an anti-Semite was the last thing he was.

In a dialogue I had with the librarian of the Biblioteca Leo y Anita Blum in Unión Israelita de Caracas, which survived from donations, she told me that she's able to speculate how large the Venezuelan Jewish diaspora is from the increasing number of gifts the library receives from people about to leave the country for good. In other words, the Biblioteca was growing in volumes and shrinking in readers.

I told Behar and her friend that I had recently had an insightful conversation with Martha Shiro. In my eyes, her story was emblematic of the plight of Venezuelan Jews connected with educational institutions. She lived in Miami, where a large number of exiled Venezuelan Jews relocated after they left in disagreement with Chávez. Of course, that's the same setting where Cuban Jews had rebuilt their lives from the 1960s onward.

A prominent linguist originally from Romania, Shiro had lived in Caracas for many years. For a considerable portion of that time, she was affiliated with the influential Instituto de Filología "Andrés Bello." Shiro told me that, in 1999 when Chávez began his first presidential mandate, she, together with a number of highly qualified and motivated colleagues—some following in the footsteps of Ángel Rosenblat, a world famous philologist of Polish descent, who grew up in Argentina but whose first language was Yiddish, others opening new paths in language studies—were responsible for designing, developing, and expanding teaching and research in the area of linguistics. Her university stimulated all these activities.

Everyone understood that Venezuela's political and social crises didn't

start with Chávez. In truth, his electoral victory was due to the general dis-
content, caused by a series of events that pushed the country's population to
reject the political class, whether they were part of the current government
or of past ones enmeshed in corruption scandals. As Shiro put it to me,
Chávez's election generated much enthusiasm and hope in those around her.
The growing consensus was that Venezuela was ready for a new political
era in which the future needed to be kinder, more inclusive, to the poor in
Venezuela.

Shiro shared that hope too, though she was skeptical of the lofty
promises—the *borrón y cuenta nueva*, the idea of starting from scratch—
that Chávez was offering, because she remembered perfectly well the same
political discourse in Romania under the Soviet Union, before she as an
adolescent emigrated to Venezuela with her family. The slogans and empty
promises flowing from Chávez's mouth and those of his followers were
almost identical to those repeated incessantly during her childhood and
early adolescence: "Let's fight for peace!" "¡No volverán!" a chant against
oligarchs and counterrevolutionaries, and "¡Patria o muerte! ¡Viva Chávez!"

As an educator and a specialist in language development, Shiro didn't
have much confidence in the "innovating" programs to make the country
literate that were promoted by the Chávez administration. These programs
were imported from Cuba and paraded on TV; elderly people were put in
front of the camera to explain how they had managed to learn to both read
and write in a matter of days or hours. Shiro was acquainted with previous
efforts by researchers in universities, schools, even government institutions,
all of whom tried to improve the teaching of reading and writing.

Her own research had similar goals. She knew the complexity of the
problem. She knew that literacy skills could not be reduced to decipher-
ing the letters in a word. It was about being able to understand written
discourse at various levels according to the readers' needs and purposes.
When the Venezuelan government asked UNESCO to declare the country
"free of illiteracy," everyone knew it was a farce—another empty slogan.

Shiro's skepticism turned into complete rejection when the Chavista government declared that public universities—especially the Universidad Central de Venezuela—were nests of oligarchs, enemies of the people, because
both faculty and students had voted against the Chavista party. This was the
reason that Chávez created a parallel and privileged university, Universidad
Bolivariana, where the Chavista doctrine reigned and where neither faculty nor students who had voted against Chávez were admitted. The Lista
de Tascón was an unforgivable, unconstitutional act, because it served the

purpose of blacklisting the names of the people who, like her, had signed a referendum in favor of revoking the president; as a result, government institutions didn't give jobs, contracts, or credit to those who appeared on the list.

In this heated political climate there was a fierce campaign against the "enemies of the People, of the Revolution, of Peace, or of Justice," who were blamed for every political failure. The list was growing, as new scapegoats appeared. It started with the "Fourth Republic" (the governments prior to Chávez, from Betancourt onward) and it was followed by a litany of "enemies," such as the empire (that is, the United States), the oligarchs, the traitors, and a long list of etceteras.

The polarization between Chavistas and anti-Chavistas was being felt everywhere, including at the Universidad Central. Each year under Chávez's regime the division between these groups would become more accentuated. In the School of Humanities and Education, where Shiro was working, the majority of faculty and students were not supporters of the government. The divisions between those who supported and those who opposed the Chavista government were felt all across the university, but the proportion changed from department to department, from school to school. There was one school in particular where the majority of faculty and students were hard-line Chavista. They used to make their position known with all sorts of clashes and provocations against the rest of the community. They organized marches and boycotted certain guests or lecturers who were considered to be anti-Chavistas. They also protested, sometimes with violence, the decisions taken by the majority with which they disagreed.

Moreover, a series of budget cuts took place at public universities as well as restrictions to their overall autonomy and to the academic activities and research they were carrying out. The Universidad Central de Venezuela, the largest and oldest university in the country, was being asphyxiated, and Shiro felt the need to escape in order to breathe freely.

All this was very similar to the political discourse she could remember from her childhood in Romania. The big difference was that Chávez would repeatedly declare himself a devout Catholic. The great heroes he quoted were Bolívar, in first place, and Jesus ("the first revolutionary"), a close second. Thus, in Chávez's long and frequent speeches, you couldn't miss references to the Jews as Christ killers.

As the years went by Chávez's government established close relations with Iraq, Syria, and especially Iran. High-ranking government figures under Chávez allegedly collaborated with organizations like Hezbollah and

Hamas, which resulted in stronger anti-Israeli and anti-Semitic sentiment.

The Jewish community in Venezuela was threatened and at times van-dalized as in the attack against the Synagogue of Maripérez and the aggres-sion against the social club Hebraica. Later on, diplomatic relations with Israel were broken off, with difficult consequences for the Jewish commu-nity, which harbored a strong pro-Zionist sentiment. Many members of the community (Shiro's husband included) were Israelis by birth and had rela-tives in Israel. As a result of the breaking off of diplomatic relations, Israeli citizens couldn't visit their relatives in Venezuela because it wasn't possible to obtain a tourist visa to enter the country.

At La Guarida over dessert, I told Behar and her friend that Shiro men-tioned to me the influence of Norberto Ceresole on Chávez. Ceresole was an Argentine political scientist whose career was spent building a theory of anti-Jewish influence that touched on a number of Latin American coun-tries, from his own country to Peru and Venezuela. What Shiro didn't know was to what extent those ideas were dangerous. She had heard Ceresole's name a bunch of times. It was only when she browsed through one of his books that she found out how he emulated the ideas presented in *The Proto-cols of the Elders of Zion*, stating that the Holocaust was a hoax.

An agnostic Jew and the daughter of Holocaust survivors (her parents lost their entire family, their parents, grandparents, siblings, uncles, and cousins), Shiro felt very affected. She remembers an anecdote with a stu-dent in one of her graduate classes. The class was on discourse analysis, and among the students there were some working for a government ministry where they had the responsibility to analyze public opinion in the national press. At one point, one of the students, without her permission, was taping everything that was said in class. When she noticed it, she allowed him to continue but showed displeasure for not having been informed from the beginning.

Her classes included discussions on how to analyze different types of dis-course, including political discourse. At the time there were already official declarations on how the Holocaust was an invention by the Jews in order to gain the world's sympathy. She made reference to this point, saying that, just like her, there were thousands or millions of witnesses, children of sur-vivors who grew up with no grandparents, uncles, or cousins because they had been massacred in concentration camps. After the class was over the student came to her and said that, in order to protect her, he had stopped taping while they were discussing this topic. She was surprised because she thought there was nothing to hide in regards to her position connected with the Holocaust, but the student believed that this position could bring problems if it became known outside the classroom.

This is how the anti-Jewish policies played out and how certain themes not on the official agenda or not aligned with ideas supported by the government would become very delicate, even censurable, and people would begin to feel afraid of expressing freely what they thought or believed.

Shiro's decision to leave Venezuela was due to a variety of different reasons that were intimately linked among themselves. The political situation, the general sense of insecurity, the gradual censorship of ideas, and the high rate of street crime were all affecting her work at the university as well as her personal life. As a consequence of the crisis and insecurity, her two children had already left Venezuela and were raising their families elsewhere since they didn't see a future for themselves in the country where they were born.

In the year 2010 when Shiro was already a professor emerita she decided to leave Venezuela, the country that so generously had opened its doors for her. She opted to move away from but not to sever ties with "my Alma Mater, where I was formed, where I became an adult. That tie is impossible to break. I still proudly belong to *la universidad que vence las sombras*, the university that vanquishes shadows."

"What a shame," I remember Behar's friend saying. "Without its Jews, Venezuela will have no traction. The same happened to Cuba."

6.

After a few days in Cuba I had made friends with Juan Pablo Escovedo. I liked his demeanor. When time allowed, he and I enjoyed talking about salsa, merengue, *bachata*, and other Latin music. He was a lover of jazz. When I told him Paquito D'Rivera was a close friend of mine, he screamed with excitement. At one point he left for me at the hotel reception a CD with music of young Cuban *salseros*.

At one point I asked Juan Pablo if he had time to travel with me alone to towns not farther than a couple of hours from Havana. He was thrilled. We negotiated a price. Given the nation's two economies, the amount he quoted me was insignificant. I offered him twice that amount.

On one of my days on the island Juan Pablo took me on a trip to the town of Trinidad. Originally called Villa de la Santísima Trinidad, it is a town in the province of Sancti Spíritus, in central Cuba, that was founded in 1514 and where Hernán Cortés, on his way to Mexico, recruited men for his expedition.

It is a bucolic place that is a popular tourist destination. It has an extensive market of local crafts and wonderful paladares. In Trinidad I visited Palacio Cantero, also known as Museo de Historia Municipal. With a neoclassical architectural style, the museum is located in the house, built in 1828, of Don José Mariano Borrell y Padrón, who in the first half of the nineteenth century was one of the town's richest men. A converso, he left signs of his Jewish faith in the Stars of David and other Jewish symbols that he used in the interior frescos. They are visible in the plasterwork of the mansion's main hall.

A guide at the Palacio Cantero told me that, although Jews, Muslims, and other non-Christians were forbidden from traveling to the newly discovered Indies after being expelled from Spain in 1492, in fact a number of islands in the Caribbean became magnets, especially for Jews. He quoted a statement from the bishop of Cuba in 1508 that "practically every ship arriving [in Havana] is filled with Hebrews and New Christians." I asked him if the people in Trinidad knew that Borrell y Padrón was a Crypto-Jew. "Of course," she replied. "It wasn't a secret. Conversos were involved in finance. The sugar trade was developed by them. Slaves were first brought to Cuba in 1513. We have records of a large group of slaves arriving in 1520. Jews were slave owners. Slavery was abolished in the island in 1886, almost twenty-five years after Abraham Lincoln's Emancipation Declaration in the United States."

She added that, in 1827, Borrell y Padrón's *ingenio*, his refinery, was the biggest producer of sugar in the world.

Later on, Juan Pablo drove me to Cienfuegos, a city of about 165,000 people in Cuba's southern central coast. I had been told about a minuscule Jewish community living there. I visited the home of Rebeca Langus. Located in one of the main arteries, her home had a nondescript entrance—5001 A—that was difficult to find. What finally enabled me to find it was a white Mezuzah hanging on the upper right side of the door frame.

To reach her small apartment I needed to climb a staircase. David, her son, opened the door. The place had numerous bookshelves packed with religious books in Hebrew, as well as Menorahs, framed diplomas, and several Jewish paintings done by David of Israel, a country he had visited a number of times: the Wailing Wall, a pair of orthodox Jews in the act of praying, and so on.

I talked with Rebeca for about half an hour. She described to me the challenges of raising a Jewish family in a remote place like Cienfuegos. "It is easier if you're a musician or a singer. Do you know María Conchita Alonso? She was born in Cienfuegos. Benny Moré? Or if you're a ball player.

Cristóbal Torriente? José Abreu? Joe Azcue? They all played in the Major League. If you're Jewish, it's harder. You have to keep at it, do it in spite of the countless forces from the environment persuading you to go astray."

She celebrated Shabbat and the High Holidays. On occasion she and the few other Jews in Cienfuegos needed some help from Havana. But mostly they were helped by tourists who donated all sorts of items. Clothes, medicine, books. "And money. Their money keeps our faith on track."

7.

"Chances are you'll be eaten by sharks." The line by Juan Pablo echoed in my mind the next afternoon as I was hunting for old books in Old Havana. I was talking to booksellers whose telephone numbers circulate only among a select group of collectors, when I came across a middle-aged woman from Jamaica.

In her mid-forties, she spoke fluent Spanish with a Cuban accent, although it was clear she was a foreigner. It turned out she was an academic based in Atlanta whose areas of expertise included pirates in the Caribbean in the seventeenth century. Someone had recommended to her a Mexican novel by Carmen Boullosa. She asked me if I knew the author, who lived in New York. I said I did.

Later on that day, I happened upon her again, this time in Casa de las Américas. For some reason we ended up in the same waiting room, scheduled to meet different cultural functionaries. To kill time I asked her if she had heard about the Jewish pirates of the Caribbean.

Her answer was fascinating. Jamaica was a private fiefdom that, in 1494, King Ferdinand and Queen Isabella awarded to Christopher Columbus for his achievements in sailing across the Atlantic and landing in large expanses of land that were quickly turned into colonies of the Spanish Empire. People would continue to debate forever if Columbus was of Jewish ancestry or not. However, it is beyond any shadow of a doubt that Jamaica in the sixteenth century quickly became a Jewish safe haven. "They hid their identity, promoting themselves as Christians." But it was *un secreto a voces*, a well-known secret, that most of these entrepreneurs nurtured a Hebraic faith. "You can trace their path in the archives of Jamaica's national library. Or you can take an easier path: just talk to people."

In 2009, the Jamaican academic said, it was announced that some of the oldest tombstones (about 360) in Hunt's Bay cemetery outside Kingston had Hebrew letters. This is Jamaica's oldest graveyard, with some of the graves dating back to 1672. These tombs also had skulls and crossbones. Question:

How hidden is this secret? She said there was some controversy about these tombs. It could be that the skulls and crossbones were added later on the stone. Yet even if this is the case, the truth is that in the eighteenth century 20 percent of the Kingston overall population was of Jewish descent. By the end of the nineteenth century, approximately two thousand Jews lived in Jamaica. That's a far cry from today, when only about two hundred are still living there.

I asked her if she was Jewish. She didn't think she was. "Maybe there's a remote ancestor on my mother's side, but I haven't been able to prove it. I immigrated to New York City when I was eight. The family then moved to Maryland. I didn't want to have much to do with Jamaica until I got to college. I took a class on baroque literature in the Spanish Caribbean. Then another one in anthropology. It took me a while to find out that what I really liked was history."

"Jamaica was a refuge," she posited. After the expulsion from Spain in 1492, a small adventurous group turned to piracy, pushing back against the Iberian fleets. "Jewish pirates were part of a larger net of forces attacking Spanish fleets in the hope of destabilizing the political and financial prowess of the nation that had pushed out their ancestors." One famous pirate was Yaakov Kuriel, about whose life it is difficult to find much accurate information. Apparently, he descended from Crypto-Jews and his family converted to Christianity. A ship's captain, Kuriel was captured by the Inquisition but was set free because a number of his captors were Crypto-Jews like him. Another pirate was in Hayreddin Barbarossa's fleet, which also attacked Spanish ships. He might have been involved in the defeat of the Spanish fleet in the battle of Preveza in 1538. Other Jewish pirates of the Caribbean became privateers that, in mercenary fashion, worked for the Netherlands.

When I was back home a few weeks later, I found a couple of books, one called *The Other Within: The Marranos, Split Identity, and Emerging Modernity* (2009) by Yirmiyahu Yovel, which focused on the role of Marranos in the development of trade in early modern times, and the other called *Jewish Pirates of the Caribbean* (2008) by Edward Kritzler, a groundbreaking exploration of Jewish life among corsairs and buccaneers about which I knew almost nothing. Several ideas mentioned to me by the Jamaican academic became seeds of an expanded meditation on how conversos had developed a trade across the Caribbean that was patently developed in these volumes. For instance, I found out that, at the end of his life, Kuriel emigrated to Jewish Palestine where he became a Kabbalist in the circle of Isaac Luria, one of the Jewish leading mystics, who went by the acronym Ha'ARI and died in Safed in 1572.

The strategic growth of the Caribbean islands as essential trading posts was an attractive feature for enterprising Crypto-Jews and other rejects. Cuba benefited tremendously, and so did Jamaica. Kritzler writes: "*Conversos* with the aptitude and capital to develop colonial trade, comfortable in a Hispanic society, yet seeking to put distance between themselves and the homeland of the Inquisition, made their way to the New World. No licenses were required for the crew of a ship, and as many were owned by *Conversos*, they signed on as sailors and jumped ship. Servants also didn't need a license or exit visa, so that a Jew who obtained one by whatever means could take others along as household staff."

That night in my room at the Hotel Meliá Cohiba, while suffering from insomnia, I looked out my window. I could sense a tempest in the vicinity through a certain quietude, a feeling of foreboding that nature allows itself before the storm. The Caribbean Sea was in a turbulent state, the waves crashing furiously against El Malecón, inundating the street, almost reaching the buildings on the edge of the island. The spectacle was energizing. In the last few days I had marveled at the ways in which these buildings have slowly been restored by a historical commission dedicated to safeguarding the patrimony of Havana. The structures had deteriorated overtime as a result of seawater salts.

In the darkness of night I imagined myself in a humid dungeon, the prisoner of Barbary corsairs. It was a silly image, yet it kept popping into my mind, in large part as a result of the dialogue I'd had with the Jamaican academic.

I hadn't asked what her name was. I hadn't given her mine either. She became a silhouette in my mind, a figment of my imagination.

Jewish pirates? More than a Disneyland character, Johnny Depp's Jack Sparrow with a straight historical agenda: to pillage Iberian ships in order to once again bring down the Spanish Armada.

On El Malecón a few old automobiles attempted to crisscross the enormous puddles. I looked attentively at the water: the vastness, the enormity of it. In the Caribbean, water is the mother of everything. It comes from below and from above and from every side. The islands form an archipelago. They are interrupted masses of land. Each of these islands is a world unto itself. There are more than seven thousand of them in an area of about one million square miles. A large number of the islands are minuscule. They remain uninhabited. The large ones make a total of thirteen different sovereign nations. There are also twelve territories—dependent on France, England, the Netherlands, or the United States. They are separated by a handful of common languages.

For those escaping absolutism, the archipelago was the perfect sanctuary. Who would care to look for relapsing Jews in this maze, amid this amount of water? To this day the region feels as if it was left unfinished at the time of creation. Some countries are more developed than others, yet the sense of despondency is difficult to shake. This could be the best place to practice a mystical type of religion devoted to the Ten Sephirot as well as Guematria—the belief that Hebrew words, since they are made of Hebrew letters each with a numerical value, have a hidden mathematical meaning.

At some point in my long stretch of nostalgia, the electricity in the neighborhood went out. The Hotel Meliá Cohiba and all the surrounding buildings all went dark. Suddenly, any noise from refrigerators, air conditioners, elevators, and other appliances disappeared. It was substituted by silence: inscrutable, bottomless, abysmal.

Only the ocean was present. The ocean and me.

8.

While in Havana, I took time to talk to people of all walks of life about one of the most famous incidents in Cuba's history, as well as in the history of its Jewish community: the case of the MS *St. Louis*.

At one point in my conversations with Juan Pablo, he said he wanted me to read a book. Next day, he brought me a copy of *Heretics* (2013), a detective novel by Leonardo Padura, one of Cuba's most important intellectuals. It was his latest book. I had read some of Padura's other work—thrillers, a novel about Leon Trotsky's assassination in Mexico, a few essays on what makes Cuban baroque literature unique—but not this one. I started reading it right away. It dealt to a large extent with Jewish apostasy. There were sections on the Spanish Inquisition on the island. And the topic of the MS *St. Louis* was central in the early chapters. In fact, I found Padura's description of the ordeal generated by the boat in the Port of Havana to be absolutely enthralling. It was clear he understood its relevance in Cuban Jewish history.

The story of the MS *St. Louis* is a narrative of hope—a quest for a promised land, regardless of location—for those in desperate need of salvation. It serves as a metaphor of the plight of European Jews seeking refuge in the Americas under Nazism. Cuba features as corrupt and untrustworthy, a place where politics are unpredictable. But the United States is also misguided, not to say cruel. President Franklin Delano Roosevelt turned a blind eye to the fate of these refugees.

Before going to Cuba I had researched the topic as much as possible because I knew it would come up in conversations. I wanted to be prepared. While on a trip to Jerusalem, for instance, I had seen the name of Captain Gustav Schröder—who commanded the MS *St. Louis* and who died in Hamburg in 1959—inscribed at Yad Vashem, the Holocaust remembrance center, as one of the Righteous among the Nations. I also knew that Germany had given him the Order of Merit posthumously.

Yet when I first asked around in Cuba, I found little about Captain Schröder. I was told there is no plaque, no statue, no acknowledgment that commemorates him in Havana, which is where he spent, it is possible to say, the most harrowing six days of his life. I mentioned this to Adela Dworin. She said people of a certain age did know about him. The best approach was for the Communists just not to get their hands dirty with this episode.

Captain Schröder was in charge of the German ocean liner when it set sail from the port of Hamburg on May 13, 1939. It was carrying 937 passengers, and most of them were Jews. All of them were escaping Hitler's might. They had been repeatedly harassed in Europe because of their religion. Taking the boat to the Americas was their only hope. The majority of them had acquired the necessary transit documents, including visas, that were required for them to enter the Port of Havana. Unfortunately these papers proved not to be enough.

By all accounts the journey of the MS *St. Louis* across the Atlantic had been generally pleasant. The passengers were treated like "privileged tourists." But upon docking at the Port of Havana, at four o'clock in the morning of May 27, 1939, things took a turn for the worse. Cuba's president, Federico Laredo Brú, refused to open the doors to the refugees. The decision appeared to come out of the blue. They weren't allowed in either as tourists, because the regulations for a tourist visa in the country had recently changed, or as refugees, because no law had been considered in the senate that would welcome them in the country in spite of their dire situation.

Their arrival took place less than four months before the Second World War began. No sooner was the ocean liner docked than frantic negotiations were taking place between Cuban diplomats and US government figures. Henry Morgenthau, who was then US secretary of the treasury, sought to convince his Cuban counterparts to allow the almost one thousand people in. So did the US secretary of state, Cordell Hull. And there were efforts by members of the American Jewish Joint Distribution Committee. All these attempts were futile. The Cuban government didn't yield. The president at the time was Federico Laredo Brú. He changed his mind a number of times. Brú's principal political opponent was Fulgencio Batista, who would become a long-time right-wing dictator. Batista didn't rescind power until Fidel Castro orchestrated an uprising and brought him down in 1958.

In the end, only twenty-nine of the Jewish refugees were allowed to disembark. Twenty-two were Jewish. They were given permission because they appeared to be the only ones to have appropriate US visas. As negotiations reached a stalemate, the impasse turned into an international scandal. It was front-line news in newspapers in the United States, Europe, Palestine, Latin America, and elsewhere. Eventually, the liner sailed toward Florida, circling around the coast. Then to everyone's surprise US Secretary Hull persuaded President Roosevelt not to allow the refugees into the United States either. And so the MS *St. Louis* returned to Europe, where its passengers were disseminated among various countries that allowed them in: England, France, Belgium, and the Netherlands. Their voyage of redemption had become a political Ping-Pong.

British writer Julian Barnes's *A History of the World in 10 ½ Chapters* (1989) has a chapter on the episode. It is one of dozens of depictions of the episode, real as well as fictional. There is also an atrocious Hollywood movie depicting the story, *The Voyage of the Damned* (1976), with Faye Dunaway, Ben Gazara, and Orson Welles, among others. Aside from being stiff and unspired in almost every way the screenplay serves as a thermometer of the kinds of plots Hollywood believes its audience wants to hear: tales of endurance. Except that in this case, no matter how much you sugarcoat the narrative, its conclusion is devastating.

At any rate it was the scene of those six fateful days in which the *St. Louis* was docked in the Port of Havana that, when I found people to finally share their opinion on the incident, truly felt like an open wound. At the time there had been close to fifteen thousand Cuban Jews living in Havana. A large portion had come mostly from the Pale of Settlement after 1924. Scores of them still spoke Yiddish. Others had begun to assimilate into the native culture. Within hours, certainly after a day, a few hundred gathered in the Port of Havana to show support for those in transit to the United States. Given the way negotiations were taking place, the general feeling was that the stalemate would be resolved soon. Most people thought Cuba would probably open its doors to a few refugees. It seemed others would unquestionably end up in Miami, New York, or elsewhere in the United States. No one actually foresaw the damnation that was about to occur.

Soon more than a thousand Cuban Jews were at the port. They wanted to send messages of support to the refugees, offer them food, water, and shelter, send them greetings from family members elsewhere in the world. A small number were relatives of those onboard.

But at the port there were also *falangistas*, right-wing forces connected with Spain's General Francisco Franco who had recently come to power after a bloody civil war and whose regime articulated anti-Semitic sentiments such as those of Hitler, Mussolini, and other European leaders, even though there were no racial laws in contemporary Spain and, in fact, the lives of tens of thousands of Jews were saved as they crossed Spanish territory on their way to the New World. And there were socialist protesters, too. They argued that accepting the Jewish refugees would curtail jobs for Cuban natives.

An old man I spoke to in El Patronato—I believe his name was David—told me he remembered being at the Port of Havana with his mother. He also recalled the adults in the family reading articles and opinion pieces on the MS *St. Louis* in *Diario de la Marina* and other local newspapers. He told me a small fleet of rented boats had tried to get to the MS *St. Louis*, bringing relatives and other interested people close to the refugees. But the government ordered police boats to control the onslaught.

"It wasn't a confrontation," David said. "The police boats simply blocked the way."

He added that tension was in the air. "There was news of suicides. And of attempts of refugees to throw themselves into the waters. They were ready to do anything in order to swim to land."

On another occasion, while we were having supper at a paladar, I asked Ruth Behar for any details she knew. Maybe there was a connection to her family. As a student of Cuban Jewish history, she was the most authoritative voice in the matter.

She told me this is a topic people hold dear to their hearts, in Cuba as well as in the United States. "It isn't true that people hardly speak of the episode. Each time I give lectures, someone invariably raises the topic. In fact, sometimes it is the only thing people know about the Jews of Cuba. They don't often know that the United States also rejected the Jews on the *St. Louis*."

She lamented that Cuba gets such a bad rap with the MS *St. Louis*. "The perspective of the Cuban Jewish community, both on the island and in Miami, is that Cuba in general has been a refuge for the Jews. Cuba kept an open door toward the Jews during the Second World War. There were many who used the island as a 'trampoline,' in order to later on make it to the United States. But this was different. It resulted from a conjunction of factors that unfortunately brought out the worst in people. As far as I know, the Jewish community in Cuba at the time was very conscious of what was happening with the *St. Louis* while the crisis was going on in 1939. I heard from my maternal grandmother, who was Polish and the family's most intellectual woman, that the Jews in the community went out on the streets to protest. They felt hurt, insecure, and powerless. Keep in mind the Jewish community was very newly established at the time. Almost all were Ashkenazi. This means that protests must have been limited. Protesters sympathized with the refugees while they also didn't want their status as immigrants to be in jeopardy. It was only a few years before this that my grandmother had managed to bring her own mother and siblings from Poland. Like other Jews she was plagued by legal, social, and emotional uncertainty. Perhaps that's why they were unable to save the Jews on the refugee ship."

After talking to David, Behar, and others, one morning I took another walk along El Malecón. I was going somewhere, I forget where, but got lost in my own thoughts. Looking at the Bay of Havana, it became obvious to me how small the entire place is. It is a rather narrow inlet divided into three main harbors: Marimelena, Guanabacoa, and Atarés. All sorts of historical incidents have taken place in this area. In 1898 the U.S. battleship *Maine* sank. This became the trigger for the Spanish-American War that ultimately pushed Spain out of the Caribbean Basin and decimated its shrinking dreams of remaining a global empire. And in 1960 the French freighter *Le Coubre* exploded, killing approximately one hundred people. The ship was carrying seventy-six tons of Belgian munition. It is believed that the CIA, which was trying to bring down Fidel Castro's government, was involved in the incident.

The uproar caused by the MS *St. Louis* must have felt enormous in such a small theater. I imagined the world's attention converging on this bay. I imagined various groups organizing in the three harbors, trying to get President Brú's attention and those of Roosevelt and other crucial players. I imagined Captain Schröder frantically keeping his passengers hopeful, feeding them whatever he was able to get from the local authorities as he received telegrams and other messages from Germany, Havana, Washington, London, Paris, Brussels, and other places. And I imagined Cuban Jews auspiciously hoping to provide help.

I felt frightened.

9.

The tragic story of the MS *St. Louis* and my conversation with Behar made me recall a parallel Second World War incident about bondage that is equally cathartic yet far less known. It happened on a Caribbean Island 550 miles east of Cuba.

As early as 1935 Rafael Leónidas Trujillo Molina, the dictator who led the Dominican Republic from 1930 through 1961, suggested that his country welcome as many as one hundred thousand refugees from Europe.

This sounds like a far-fetched idea. But Trujillo's strategy was the same as countless other Latin American politicians, particularly during the nineteenth century: he wanted to "whiten" the population of the Dominican Republic through European immigration. He looked down on his own mulatto population. His dislike for Haitians was even more pronounced than the aversion he felt toward people of color in his own country. Haiti and the Dominican Republic, let it be remembered, share the same island, a fact that infuriated Trujillo. Among countless other things he is infamous for the so-called Parsley Massacre. On October 1937, as he was insisting on bringing Jews and other immigrants into his country, his troops, carrying out his orders, killed all the Haitians in the Dominican Republic. The number of victims is a matter of intense debate. It ranges from 550 to more than 12,000.

The atrocities made Trujillo an international pariah. The following year, at the Evian Conference he insisted on his invitation. Opening the doors to refugees from Nazi Germany was a way to redeem himself. No one else wanted these Jews. Certainly not Franklin D. Roosevelt. Although Trujillo's target of one hundred thousand never materialized, the Dominican Republic issued visas to about eight hundred German and Austrian Jewish citizens. All arrived between 1940 and 1945.

Families received eighty-two acres of land, ten cows plus two additional ones per child, a mule, a horse, and a ten-thousand-dollar loan.

Trujillo's intention was to create a place in the Dominican Republic specifically for them. He chose Sosúa, in San Felipe de Puerto Plata, in the country's northern shore, about 130 miles from Santo Domingo. Today Sosúa is a tourist attraction because of, among other things, its sex trade. But the synagogue still stands. And there is a museum where the Jewish presence of almost a century ago is commemorated. Still, the place feels remote.

From the start, Sosúans were welcoming. From my own experience I'd say Dominicans almost always are. They interacted with the newcomers, doing business with them, and striking up friendships. The relationship was fruitful. Over time it resulted in a strong collaboration and, in some cases, even marriage.

The whole experiment is reminiscent of Entre Ríos, Argentina. In the mid-twentieth century Sosúa was more rural than it is now. When the Jewish refugees arrived they worked together with cattle, along with a few Dominican natives. A few of them drove tractors. The place was a *comuna* like Moisés Ville, Villa Domínguez, and others that were sponsored in the Argentine Pampa by Baron Hirsh.

"No maps were in existence," a settler, Félix Bauer, wrote in his memoirs. Another, Barbara Steinmetz, described Sosúa as "just a piece of land with a few buildings on it . . . and very sparsely populated." And a third refugee, David Kahane, stated: "There were two barracks and a few shacks. No electric lights, and the mosquitoes were humming."

This episode in Jewish Latin American history fascinates me. I have talked with numerous Dominican Americans. In general they have scant knowledge of it. The descendants of the refugees seem to be almost the only ones aware of the episode. And scholars too, obviously.

A few months before my trip to Cuba I went to Bowdoin College in Maine. I met there Allen Wells, a professor who wrote an exploration of Sosúa called *Tropical Zion* (2009). He is the child of Sosúan Jews who eventually settled in the United States. The family used to take vacations in the Dominican Republic.

We talked about other subjects, including the historical context of Gabriel García Márquez's masterpiece *One Hundred Years of Solitude*, a book I adore. But soon we settled on Sosúa. Wells's father lived in the colony between 1940 and 1947. "Growing up in Sosúa always had seemed like a fairy tale, replete with heroes and villains, told by my father who seldom tired of relating his experiences," he stated in his account. His father, Heinrich Wasservogel (the name was later on Americanized to Henry Wells), recalled: "No one wanted us. . . . He [Trujillo] was *the only one* who took us," his resonant voice punctuating those three small words for added emphasis.

Wells gave me a signed copy of *Tropical Zion*. I asked him to what extent the Parsley Massacre actually had an impact on the foundation of the Jewish colony in Sosúa. He said Trujillo was a racist obsessed with Haitians crossing the border to the Dominican Republic. Yet he was an opportunist in that he rescued Jewish refugees who themselves were the target of racism in Europe.

"What an irony!"

Within Jewish groups there was infighting among those sponsoring a line that brought refugees to British Mandate Palestine. That is, between Zionists and non-Zionists.

Another irony is that while Roosevelt closed the doors of the United States to Jewish refugees, yet he encouraged Spanish-speaking countries in the Americas to embrace them and, in the case of Sosúa, he sanctioned the enterprise. This, in Wells's view, was the foundation for the relationship between Washington and dictators in Latin America.

Wells believes it to be "one of history's small ironies that a man so feared and despised by many of his fellow Dominicans—and by neighboring Haitians—was admired by these immigrants." In his book he quotes yet another Sosúan resident, Martin Katz, who remained in Sosúa after everyone else had left. Katz had full knowledge of Trujillo's atrocious record on human rights. And of the Parsley Massacre of Haitians in the Dominican Republic. "He was a bad man who killed many, many people," Katz stated. "But to the Jews he opened his country."

All in all, the Dominican Republic today has a community of approximately three thousand Jews. Most of them live in the capital. A minuscule fraction of them still have ties to the Sosúa episode. Intriguingly, one of the country's most distinguished politicians, Francisco Hilario Henríquez y Carvajal, a doctor, lawyer, writer, and educator, was of Jewish descent. He served as president for only a few months in 1916, prior to the occupation of the island by the United States. His children—Pedro, Max, and Camila—are considered the most important Dominican intellectuals of the twentieth century. Pedro Henríquez Ureña delivered the Charles Eliot Norton Lectures at Harvard and was one of Borges's closest friends.

10.

In Cuba, I was magnetically attracted to the Sephardic component of the Jewish community. As in other parts of Latin America this component is often eclipsed by the Ashkenazi presence. Yet it has an enviable vigor I found alluring. As an Ashkenazi Jew, I find at times there is the temptation to fetishize the Sephardim, to make them seem mysterious.

A day after my visit to the harbor, I visited the Centro Hebreo Sefaradí de Cuba. I spent a long time with its president, Dr. Mayra Levy, a lively and engaging conversationalist. She told me that approximately 65 percent of the total Jewish population of the island today are Sephardic. She mentioned that the first Sephardim came in 1907 or 1908, more or less when the Union Hebrew Congregation was created. And the first Sephardic organization was launched in 1913. Called Chevet Ahim, it was located in Old Havana, on Calle Inquisidor, between Calle Luz and Calle Santa Clara. It was affiliated to the American conservative movement. It is the oldest Jewish organization in the island.

The Sephardic community soon built a center that became a magnet for Sephardic families. It included a Chevra Kadisha at the cemetery, a welfare society called Bikur Cholim that cared for the ill, and a school named after the founder of Zionism, Theodor Herzl.

Aside from the Sephardic Jewish Center in Havana, there are a couple of Sephardic synagogues: Hatikvah in Santiago de Cuba and Tiferet Israel in Camagüey. And there are also groups of Sephardic Jews in Guantanamo, Manzanillo, Campechuela, Cienfuegos, Santa Clara, Caibarien, and Sancti Spiritus.

Cuba isn't alone in its Sephardic presence. At the turn of the twentieth century, immigrants from Syria, Lebanon, Greece, and the Balkans (all parts of the crumbling Ottoman Empire) also went to Mexico, Guatemala, El Salvador, Colombia, Chile, and other destinations in the Americas. I told Mayra Levy that while on a trip to southern Chile I once stopped briefly (for a couple of hours) in Temuco, and there is a dwindling Jewish community there that descends from immigrants from Monastir, a city on the central coast of Tunisia, about 165 kilometers south of Tunis. The Temuco Jews originally spoke Ladino. In 2015 a Chilean doctor called Jacob Cohen Ventura, himself part of the community, wrote a lucid history of it, which served me as a guidebook.

Temuco is where Pablo Neruda lived in his youth after he left his native town of Parral and before he settled in Santiago—where before reaching the age of twenty, he wrote *Twenty Love Poems and a Song of Despair* (1924). During my visit to Temuco I traced his footsteps. I juxtaposed my effort with a visit to a local Jewish cemetery, since Cohen Ventura included in his book a list of all the Sephardim buried there. It was different from the Sephardic cemetery in Cuba in that it was better kept. The stones also had a more distinct Ottoman style.

In a department store in Tamuco, I talked to a sixty-five-year-old woman who said she was Sephardic. I told her about my trek through the Jewish communities in Latin America. And about the dream I had about my childhood home that prompted my trek. I said I was interested in language and mentioned that I had read Cohen Ventura's book. She knew him personally. She said she had been a teacher. Switching to Ladino she told me all sorts of words used by Temuco Jews of the immigrant generation. I wrote them down. *Aferrar* meant "to grasp, to take away." *Gameo*, "dumb." *Catran*, "evil." *Intiñido*, "dirty, drunk." *Cafrar*, "to argue." *Embesar*, "to teach." And *Jamor*, Hebrew for "donkey."

The woman also shared a few expressions in Ladino, such as *An este se fizo un buen judío*, "This one became a fine Jew." *Mercar la zarzaba*, "to buy vegetables." *Esto está de alabar al dio barujú*, "This is enough to praise the Almighty." And *Ansina se face: Así se hace*, "That's how it's done."

"Listening to the way she pronounced these terms," I told Mayra Levy, "a whole universe unfolded before my ears."

Since the first Sephardic center in Cuba, Chevet Ahim, had been closed for years, I asked Mayra Levy if through her influence I could visit the building. She would let Ruth Behar know. That afternoon Behar called. "Mayra was successful. We'll get a chance to visit," she told me.

The following morning Behar and I made our way to Old Havana. A beautiful young woman waited for us at the door. The abandoned location is still kept up for visitors. It has a few of the ornaments still in place. The building reminded me of my visit to the agricultural colonials in Entre Ríos. The Sephardic synagogue in Cuba was in somewhat better condition, though given the general decay of Havana where buildings look always as if they are about to collapse, it felt as if the synagogue's very physicality was in peril.

Behar also arranged for us to visit the kosher butcher nearby. This, for me, was an unforgettable experience.

Meat in Cuba is scarce. Kosher meat is even more of a privilege. As we walked through the labyrinthine streets, from afar I saw a queue forming outside a closed metal garage door. There were about twenty people, women and men, chatting with each other. A few had grocery bags. We too stood in line.

A few boys were playing baseball in the street. A couple of passers-by looked at them and at the line. If you didn't know about the butcher's, as it was in my case, you would be suspicious of what looked like a mini-rally in the middle of Old Havana.

At a certain time a smaller adjacent door opened up. A woman was behind it. She wanted to see how many people were waiting. Then she said that, as everyone knew, there was an established list of rations. Each buyer needed to show their monthly booklet to make sure they were due a meat portion.

A dozen people were allowed inside. Behar asked if she and I could also enter, saying that someone from Chevet Ahim had called in advance. The woman smiled. We would only be allowed in if we stood in the back row, from where we could watch the whole action.

Inside there was an older butcher and a younger apprentice. They had sharp knives. There were stacks of beef on several shelves. Depending on a person's booklet, they would fulfill an order, weigh the meat, and then wrap it in newspaper.

This was, we were told by the woman, kosher meat specially prepared for the Cuban Jewish community. It was available for a couple of hours one day every two weeks, which meant that the butcher's was almost always closed.

For my last Friday night in Havana I attended Friday night Shabbat services in the Sephardic Hebrew Center, located at Calle #17, Esquina E, not far from the Meliá Cohiba. The temple is very small. I calculated around fifty or sixty people could fit in the sanctuary. There were about forty people in attendance, a number of them tourists from the United States. The service was conducted in Spanish with a few words of Hebrew. Many of the young Cuban Jews in attendance were mulattos.

I was told the congregation was composed of eighty families. They have an Israeli dance group as well as a choir.

There is no permanent rabbi, let alone a cantor. A rabbi—I believe from Santiago, Chile, or else Canada, Mexico, or Argentina—comes for the High Holidays.

There was something performative about the synagogue service. A mature man led the ritual. His daughter went to the Bimah to recite various prayers in Hebrew. It felt as if the event was catered for me and other visitors, proving to us how resilient Cuban Jews were in their devotion.

Afterward there was a community dinner at El Patronato. It was in the activities hall. There were Cuban and Israeli flags in one corner. There probably had been a party recently because the walls still had festive decorations on them. I also saw photographs of community members.

The dinner was made to coincide with sundown. There must have been one hundred people. Again, lots of foreigners: Americans, Canadians, Israeli, French, and others. Salad, pasta, and dessert on plastic plates. Adela Dworin wasn't present, but there were various members of the Cuban Jewish community in attendance, coordinating the seating and serving the meal.

There was a Kiddush to let everyone know Cuban Jews were more than surviving. Lots of young people were around.

I heard about the athletics team representing Cuba in the forthcoming

Maccabi Games in Israel. Even though there are no diplomatic relations between the two countries, Cuban athletes were participating. In fact, this wasn't the first delegation to participate. I got the impression that, for political reasons, the Cubans traveled with the athletes from another country's delegation, perhaps Panama or Mexico.

I sat next to a Cuban engineer and his wife who was a doctor. They were in their mid-fifties. He told me they had a daughter waiting to move to the United States, if only they could find an American who could sponsor her. They were not on speaking terms with their relatives in Miami. Would I know of anyone? She had studied accounting.

The wife worked at a hospital in Havana. She described her routine to me. "The emergency room is different from those in the United States. In Cuba there are no weapons. We take care of ailments of all kinds, malnutrition, alcohol poisoning, and so on." She gave me a sense of what her doctor's monthly salary was in Cuban currency. It was less than I had already paid Juan Pablo for driving me around.

She talked about having colleagues who had worked in Algeria years ago. Now a whole cadre was in Venezuela. When Hugo Chávez, Venezuela's president, was diagnosed with cancer, at Castro's invitation he moved temporarily to Havana where he was treated. Such is the quality of Cuba's medical care.

As the dinner came to an end, I looked again for Señor Sefsovitch. He was gone. The sofa where he had been sitting was empty.

11.

On my last day in Cuba Ruth Behar arranged for me to meet with the island's most popular science-fiction writer whom she had met on a previous visit. We got together for a Coca-Cola at a pleasant outdoor Havana restaurant. He goes by the pseudonym of Yoss. His real name is José Miguel Gómez Sánchez. I had not heard of Yoss until Ruth Behar recommended him to me and suggested that I talk to him, as she thought his work might be of interest for my Restless Books imprint.

He dresses on a regular basis as a punk rocker: jeans, sleeveless T-shirt, leather vest, and a red bandana holds up his long black hair. He belongs to a music group. One of the nights before I heard him play in a bar. He makes his living giving writing workshops, writing books about all kinds of obscure topics (for instance, varieties of swords in King Arthur's age), and composing an array of phantasmagoric novels. Among his books are *Se alquila un planeta* (*A Planet for Rent*, 2015), a series of stories inspired by Ray Bradbury's *The Martian Chronicles* (1950) that features in comedic form an assortment of Cuban stereotypes, and *Super Extra Grande* (2016), a novella about a gigantic monster who suffers from digestive problems. In Yoss's own words, his work is about "how things are always about to happen in Cuba, though they never actually do." The two books were translated into English by David Frye, a first-rate translator who also happens to be Behar's husband.

Yoss talked about what makes Cuban science-fiction unique. The island's sci-fi literature was shaped by two influences—the Anglo-Saxon, which is ingenious, preoccupied with narrative, and the Soviet, which is denser, attracted to ethics and morality, and obsessed not with the cause of change but its effect. There was hardly any influence of Spanish or Latin American science-fiction. The amalgamation of these two influences, to which the Creole humor was added (more specifically, the art of *choteo*, meaning that nothing should be taken seriously) resulted in a light, irreverent, engaging style that is very Cuban and very sci-fi.

In the months before my most recent trip to Havana, President Obama had announced the reestablishment of United States–Cuban relations. I asked Behar and Yoss what they thought. Yoss argued that "the normalization of US-Cuban diplomatic relations is something three generations of Cuba have kept on waiting for without much faith. Barack Obama brought change. But it was short-lived. Without the blockade, who will Cuba blame for its economic inefficiency? What will Cubans do without the United States as a scapegoat?"

"Our island could have been for sale and we'll hand it to the best buyer," Yoss added. "The state-run monopolistic capitalism we have now could have given place to a simpler form of capitalism, more efficient but also more barbaric."

In contrast, Behar was less bleak about the consequences of normalized relations. In her view, "the Cuban people's endurance and resourcefulness as well as their spirit of independence will enable them to resist Americanization." She argued that many Cuban Jews in Miami wanted to return now to invest in and rebuild the island's infrastructure. Moreover, this "new flow of people, ideas, and money" will help reenergize Cuba's Jewish community. "Synagogues and Jewish cemeteries around the island will be repaired," Behar predicted. "Jewish elders will receive additional care and attention. And most importantly, if economic prospects improve, Jewish youth will be motivated to stay in Cuba, rather than making *aliyah* to Israel, or trying to emigrate to the United States."

Since my principal interest was in Jewish life in Cuba, I asked Yoss to give us his impression of Cuban Jews. To my amazement, he started by discussing a few canonical Jewish authors who, he said, had shaped his welt-anschauung: Saul Bellow, Joseph Heller, Michael Chabon. He spoke highly of Norman Mailer's *The Naked and the Dead* (1948) and spent twenty minutes discussing the moral juncture in *Catch 22* (1961). Then he talked about having spent time recently browsing the Talmud ("fascinatingly complex!") and The Book of Enoch ("hallucinating!"). It was only after this detour that he finally focused on my questions.

"During colonial times," he said, "the Americas provided a safe haven for Crypto-Jews. But life in the colonies wasn't much easier. In Cuba, these secret Jews lived incognito. They didn't build synagogues. They didn't eat kosher food. They didn't celebrate Bar Mitzvahs and other rituals. To the point that they forgot they were Jews. Then, in the nineteenth century, Ottoman Jews and Jews from Eastern Europe came to the island. They brought their families with them. They arrived penniless and soon became well-off. Yet they remained a small community. And they assimilated. Their children became Cuban. They didn't keep their own traditions. There are a few tragic, shameful episodes connected with Jews in Cuban history, such as the voyage of the *MS St. Louis*. After Fidel came to power, a large portion of the Jewish community left for Miami and elsewhere in the United States. The ones that remained are a source of envy. However, I must say there are also a lot of *judío-jineteros*, Jews that whore themselves. They put on the *kipá* (the yarmulke) in the hope that a Jewish tourist will give them money. Yes, being Jewish in Cuba is like being a Bahai: a curiosity."

I asked Behar and Yoss if Cuba could be described as a "paradise lost." Yoss responded: "Cuba today is a museum, or maybe a theme park, of what actual Socialism once was. Unlike North Korea, tourists can come without fear of being devoured by some ideological beast. It is also a favorite destination for ex-Communists from the Third World, for Latin Americans who have a messianic vocation and like to wear Ché Guevara T-shirts. It is also attractive for people who are looking for sun, rum, tobacco, *mulatas*, and salsa. It is really a parallel universe, not in Asia but only ninety miles from Key West and a seventy-five-minute flight from Miami. In other words, for a European, and especially for an American, to come to Cuba is like using a time machine."

"Why, in the face of so much deprivation, do Cubans continue to smile and dance and be happy? Why, if the Cuban regime is obviously a dictatorship, does no one rebel against it? Why do many Cubans leave the island?

What does the future hold for us? I don't know. No one knows. After foreigners come, they try to offer answers. But they are always wrong. Truth is, this is indeed a paradise. Or maybe a pre-paradise. I say it because in Cuba sólo vivimos, we just live. Cuba es el aquí y ahora, sin futuro, it is the here and now, without a future. We dance in order to forget. On the street there's easy cheap sex. Abortion in the island is a form of birth control, a kind of day-after pill. In Cuba we don't want to know about the future because we don't want to plan for it. It's better just to enjoy what we have right now."

He concluded: "Wait, Ilan. Let me give that question you asked another spin. Cuba is indeed a paradise. Or at least the right place to build it. I think we are a deliciously imperfect paradise. I could list a thousand things that don't work, from the Internet to the banking system, salaries, public transportation, even our pseudodemocracy. Yet, in spite of all this, we have the Cuban people. And that's a huge asset. Generous, affable, gracious, good-humored, Cubans have the gift of knowing how to make friends. We were promised the fruit of Eden but were given a ticket to hell. But we didn't die. We're still alive. At some point every Cuban has had the same dream. Not the socialist dream but the dream that this is all a movie set, that we're being acted upon, that life itself isn't ours but someone else's. What do we do in response? We plow on. What else is there to do?"

Upon listening to Yoss's reflection, Behar said: "Actually, that's a very Jewish attitude."

"Really?" asked Yoss. "Then I'm happy. I like to be equated with Jews."

12.

A few hours before my flight, Juan Pablo picked me up at Meliá Cohiba to take me to the José Martí airport and then we went to the apartment to pick up Behar.

We talked about an assortment of topics. At some point during the drive we passed an accident. A biker had been hit by a car. The bicycle was on the ground, in bad shape. Near it was the biker. He looked as if he had severe pain in his left leg.

I heard Juan Pablo murmur something about the number seven. He had counted the number of people congregated around the accident. "They are seven. Whenever I see an accident, I count the number of people that come, supposedly to help the victim. They are always seven. That's before the police come. Their arrival changes the math altogether. It can be one policeman. Or two. On a rare occasion you'll see three, although they don't come all at once. Anyway, that's normal. What isn't normal is the number seven.

Seven passers-by. I don't understand why but it's always the case. That's in the first seven minutes. A while later, the group will either grow or dwindle out, depending on the gravity of the accident."

This particular one didn't seem too serious. And yes, seven bystanders were surrounding the biker.

We came to a standstill. I looked at my watch, fearful I would miss my flight.

"Don't worry," Juan Pablo said. "You'll make it on time. Accidents in Cuba are more performance than anything else. We really don't have the wherewithal to create a sophisticated traffic accident."

I laughed. For some strange reason a story by Isaac Bashevis Singer came to mind. Called "A Wedding in Brownsville," it is about an old doctor in Manhattan who emigrated from Eastern Europe decades earlier. His entire world—his family, his friends and acquaintances, his first loves—were wiped out by the Holocaust. While the doctor sometimes thinks about his past, he prefers to keep it buried. The narrative describes the journey the doctor makes on a particular day to Brownsville, in Brooklyn, to a wedding he's been invited to. His wife decides not to go. The doctor takes a taxi. As it crosses Central Park, the doctor, from inside the taxi, sees a traffic accident. He doesn't put too much thought into it. He finally makes it to the Brownsville site where the wedding is about to take place. Soon he recognizes a number of guests. They aren't people he has seen recently. They all belong to his past, the pre-Holocaust past. As he talks to them, he realizes they are relatives, family, and acquaintances. And he also notices that one of his first loves is among the crowd. The story concludes with the realization that the doctor is attending his own wedding—to the woman he passionately loved before he emigrated to the United States. And that it was he who had been the victim—in fact, he had died—in the Central Park accident. In other words, the wedding in Brownsville was his visit to paradise.

"Why seven?" I asked Juan Pablo.

"Dunno." He paused, then continued. "Years ago, while I was in school we read about a theory by a psychologist who argued that, on average, people have the capacity to remember more or less seven items. That's what the human mind is capable of. You're wasting your time if you want them to remember more."

To me the comment felt like it came out of the blue. Juan Pablo added: "Aren't phone numbers usually made of seven digits? Then you have seven days of the week. The seven colors. The seven wonders of the world. The seven deadly sins. The seven seas. Bizarre, eh? Well, for some mysterious reason whenever people in Havana gather around an accident it's also seven. Go figure."

The two of us were quiet for a while. What if I had died in this accident and the rest of my life was that hallucination I had in the *memento mori* that things were fine, that life was on course? I told myself that dying in Cuba wasn't unappealing. But I would prefer that it did not take place right now. I still had a bunch of chores to do. For instance, finishing my book about traveling around Jewish sites in Latin America.

"Isn't there an idea that there are seven heavens?" Juan Pablo asked.

I told him I'd heard about it.

"That's the Cuban version of heaven," he said. "You never quit making it there. Lots of delays, lots of bureaucratic hurdles. You need to wait, to be in line."

His words made me think of Yoss's comments on Cuba as a paradise. "You think you're there, which makes you a fool. Truth is, you will be in line for hours, maybe days. Then, when you least expect it, you will make it to the Sancta Sanctorum or whatever the place, where you are finally in. And you know what? It will be a rather plain, uneventful room. The whole thing will be a performance. In other words, they will have sold you a bill of goods. That's what I think about the seven heavens."

The car finally started moving. "I promise. We will make it to the airport on time."

5   RAT ROUTE

1.

There's a song in the Spanish-speaking world by Los Fabulosos Cadillacs that goes by the title *"Desapariciones"* (Disappearances). It is by an Argentine ska band and is included in the 1992 album called *El león*. Most people don't refer to the song by its title but by its celebrated refrain: ¿Adónde van los desaparecidos? Where do the desaparecidos go? I don't like the version sung by Los Fabulosos Cadillacs. I once was at a concert where the popular Panamanian salsa musician Rubén Blades, its author, performed it. But the version I prefer is by the Mexican rock band Maná.

The song's inspiration, of course, is the desaparecidos of the Dirty War, a period framed within the larger Cold War narrative. Aside from Argentina, other Latin American countries—Chile, Uruguay, Bolivia, and Paraguay— also cleansed their populations. The premise at the time was that the region wasn't yet ready for democracy. It was too immature. The military identified Communists, anarchists, and other left-leaning youth as a threat.

The song lyrics deliberately leave a lot unsaid. That silence ends up creating a haunting effect. The desaparecidos, we're told, don't just die like the rest of us. They stay behind, hiding behind bushes and near water reservoirs. The lyrics also ask why they were disappeared. Answer: because all of us aren't equal. When do the desaparecidos come back? When we remember them *con la emoción apretando por dentro*, with emotion gripping you inside.

In my head I kept repeating these few lines from "¿Adónde van los desaparecidos?" as I walked into a sparse, imposing architectural structure that rises up near the metro station Quinta Normal, close to the Parque Las Palmeras, in Santiago, Chile.

My wife, Alison, was with me. So was Eliah Germani, a handsome, fifty-eight-year-old Chilean Jewish doctor on staff at a pediatric intensive care unit in Concepción, Chile's second largest city. Concepción is located on the northern edge of what is known as Patagonia, a sparsely populated region of the Andean Mountains at the southern end of South America—grasslands, pampas, and deserts divided into two parts, a smaller western part in Chile and a far more substantial eastern part in Argentina.

Married to a German woman, Germani found his Jewishness in the medical profession. He taught himself Yiddish and has become more devout with age. He is the author of *Personal Objects* (2015), a collection of short stories about Jews caught in the act—and art—of searching. Reading his stories, you feel as if Germani is a friend of Kafka.

Germani and I met years ago in Chile's capital. Over the years we see each other whenever I'm in Chile, which if possible I try to visit every year. I have a deep affection for the country, to the point that I often tell people if I'd had a choice of where to be born I would have selected Chile.

A few days earlier, the three of us had made plans to visit the Museo de la Memoria y los Derechos Humanos together. Inaugurated in 2010 by President Michelle Bachelet, the first woman president in Chile's history and at one point a political prisoner under General Augusto Pinochet's military junta, the museum is part of a series of national projects in Latin America devoted to keeping alive the memory of the desaparecidos and other victims of state violence.

After a coup d'état that pushed the elected president Salvador Allende to commit suicide at the official presidential residence, La Moneda, Pinochet was in power in Chile for seventeen years, from 1973 to 1990. It was a period of horrible repression. An estimated three thousand people were killed by the government on suspicion of being communists. Thousands more were arrested, imprisoned, and tortured. Some two hundred thousand Chileans went into exile.

The museum is a large, cold, concrete structure. To enter one needs to descend a long ramp. Once inside, the visitor comes on large photographs,

TV screens, and other graphics of the coup that brought the country to a halt on September 11, 1973. For the rest of the visit one must go up, level after level, via a series of staircases. The feeling is of ascendance.

"As if we're going to heaven," Germani said. "There's something Kabbalistic in the idea, which is found in the *Sefer ha-Zohar*, one of the canonical books in Jewish mysticism. In looking for the desaparecidos, we are reaching different *Sephirot*, different celestial spheres according to Kabbalah, each allowing us to appreciate another facet of human life."

Alison asked him where he had been during the dictatorship. "In Germany toward the end of it. I was doing my medical training, first in Münster and then in Berlin. I was there between 1987 and 1990. It was a difficult period. The country was in a state of siege. I have never been a political animal. Mine was an 'interior emigration.' While abroad I became acquainted with Bach, Beethoven, Schumann, and Brahms."

"Were Jews targeted with special emphasis?"

"Not in Chile. In Argentina, yes."

In the museum one comes across different galleries, some featuring diaries written in prison, others collecting children's drawings imagining the places where their fathers or siblings were held captive. Press clippings, recordings, and videos place the exhibit material in historical context.

Germani hadn't been to the museum before. "Somehow I preferred not to go through the experience again," he told me. "But it's good to see it with you, too. A foreigner's perspective is less impartial."

We came across a display of *arpilleras*, brightly colored patchwork pictures made by women depicting violent moments of confrontation. And another section is about the large numbers of Chileans who were forced to live in exile.

And then we saw a section on Pablo Neruda, Chile's most important poet, whose voice was a clarion call to the resistance in the dictatorship's early days before Neruda died of cancer. The exhibit explored the connection between Neruda's poetry and the people. His funeral was attended by hundreds of mourners. It was among the first acts of resistance of the population against General Pinochet. His poems were memorized as a form of defiance.

Over the years I have explored Neruda's oeuvre as devotedly as I have read Borges's essays and stories. The two were polar opposites on the ideological spectrum. Most of his life Borges claimed to be apolitical. Indeed, his oeuvre resists (to the degree that this is possible) any overt political message. In his forties Perón targeted him because Borges refused to endorse him, instead describing the elected military man as a second-rate ruler. In the first half of the 1970s José López Rega—a notorious anti-Semite and Perón's minister of social welfare who later on fled from Argentina to Spain as an itinerant ambassador and became an admirer of Libia's ruler Muammar Qaddafi—did everything in his power to get Jews out of Argentina's public spheres. Borges made his opposition very clear. However, in his old age Borges accepted Chile's presidential medal from General Augusto Pinochet. Rumors have it that it was this move that meant he was not awarded the Nobel Prize.

Neruda, on the other hand, was a devoted Communist. He served as senator and ran for president, opting to move out of the way in order for Allende to get the nomination. One of the most enduring of contemporary poets, Neruda received the Nobel Prize in 1971. His books are perennial best sellers all over the world. Young readers in particular identify with him. In protests in Berlin against the World Bank, during the Arab Spring, and in dozens of other belligerent moments, they are caught with one of Neruda's volumes in hand.

Just as I have wandered through Buenos Aires looking for signs of Borges, every time I'm in Santiago, Isla Negra, Valparaíso, Temuco, and other Chilean cities, I return to places where Neruda lived.

"Do you remember the segment in his 'I Explain a Few Things' where he impugns the military for the massacres they've perpetrated?" asked Germani.

"I do," I said.

He was referring to the last stanzas of one of Neruda's most famous poems, which deals with the Spanish Civil War. He lived in Madrid in 1936 and was friends with Federico García Lorca. The poem directly accuses General Franco's forces of destroying the country. I particularly like the last stanzas:

> Traitors,
> generals:
> look at my dead house,
> look at Spain broken:
> from every house burning metal comes out
> instead of flowers,
> from every crater of Spain
> comes Spain
> from every dead child comes a riffle with eyes,
> from every crime bullets are born

that one day will find out in you
the site of the heart.

You will ask: why doesn't his poetry
speak to us of dreams, of leaves
of the great volcanoes of his native land?

Come and see the blood in the streets,
come and see
the blood in the streets,
come and see the blood
in the streets!

In the museum, these verses felt pertinent. What makes "I Explain a Few Things" essential is its capacity to speak to the ravages of war regardless of location.

"To me, Neruda teaches us an astonishing lesson," I said. "The pen is mightier than the sword. Maybe at the very moment of destruction, a bullet will inflict deeper pain. But the poet's words survive. They are still read. That's the best revenge!"

I asked Germani if he knew the song "¿Adónde van los desaparecidos?"

And on the upper level of the museum, the visitor sees a list with the names of the three thousand victims engraved in glass. The arrival feels cathartic.

A few years ago in New York City I had talked about the museum at length with Ariel Dorfman who is a professor emeritus at Duke and is the author—among dozens of novels, studies, and movie scripts—of the Broadway play *Death and the Maiden*. The play deals with Chile's effort at national reconciliation, which took place a few years after democracy was restored. The play, turned into a film and directed by Roman Polanski, is about a woman who is thrown into an existential dilemma when on the street one day she recognizes the man who raped, tortured, and vilified her during Pinochet's time. She wonders if she should engage in revenge.

I had seen the stage version with Glenn Close, Richard Dreyfuss, and Gene Hackman. In fact I attended the Broadway show with Alison and a couple of friends, one of whom was the daughter of one of Central America's most vicious tyrants. When I first met her, I didn't know her family history. I discovered the connection only later, after putting two and two together.

Dorfman had worked for Salvador Allende and went into exile with his family to save his life. He was one of Pinochet's most vocal opponents. He wrote an autobiography, *Heading South, Looking North* (1998), about this period. Although Dorfman praised the country's willingness to face its own ghosts, he was also critical of the ways in which Chile's Reconciliation Commission handled its task. He told me that building the Museo de la Memoria was a step in the right direction.

I was surprised that Dorfman's name wasn't prominently displayed.

"People have mixed feelings about him," said Germani. "While they appreciate his courage to speak out against oppression, the feeling is that he did it to call attention to himself."

Alison was impressed by the fact that the museum was built in lieu of revenge, with a desire to transcend hatred.

After our visit the three of us walked a few blocks in search of a place to eat. We found a modest Peruvian restaurant. As we ate we delved into the topic of memorials. Germani compared the museum of Yad Vashem in Israel, devoted to the victims of the Shoah, and the US Holocaust Museum in the Washington Mall.

I mentioned my visit to the B-movie museum of the Spanish Inquisition in Mexico City and the conversation I had afterward with Angelina Muniz-Huberman in Mexico.

"Memory is like real estate," I said. "It has value. Governments invest in that value."

Alison agreed. "I found the museum wonderful. Although the suffering of the desaparecidos has been institutionalized, the place still feels as if it belongs to the people."

"To me having a single place where collective memory is 'housed' is dangerous," I added. "National memory, memory that belongs to everyone, has no address. That's why I like the lyrics of '¿Adónde van los desaparecidos?' People sing it spontaneously. There's nothing official about it."

The conversation was no longer about the duty to remember a cataclysmic event. It was about how the remembering is done and by whom.

"Endeavors like the Museo de la Memoria are founded on the premise that memory is a tool to avoid similar tragedies in the future," I said. "Truth is, the idea is naïve. After the Shoah, genocide hasn't disappeared from the face of the earth. On the contrary, it is more present than ever, from Guatemala to Sarajevo, from Rwanda to Syria."

"Do Chilean Jews remember the victims of Pinochet in any particular way? In memorials? During religious services?" asked Alison.

"It's complicated," Germani answered. "The dictatorship wasn't anti-

Semitic. While a few anti-Semites were insiders, as a whole the regime didn't target the Jewish community. In fact, on a couple of occasions the authorities received invitations to attend Yom Kippur services. In other words, the Jewish community in Chile had three sides: a hefty presence in the resistance as well as those that went into exile, like Dorfman himself; those who stayed and maybe cozied up to the regime; and those who were murdered for having held important positions in the Allende administration."

"A decade ago, I talked with David Grossman, the Israeli writer, about what I felt was an ambivalence in Israel about memory," I said. "He told me something he had said to the British playwright David Hare, who was interviewing him for a theatrical monologue he was working on about the Israeli-Palestinian conflict called *Via Dolorosa* (1997)."

"We saw the monologue at the West End, Ilan," Alison said.

I reminisced. "If I remember right, Grossman told Hare that after the Six-Day War, and more emphatically in the aftermath of the Yom Kippur War, in October 1973, Israel went from being a nation looking into the future, devoted to building a new era for the Jewish people, to a nation obsessed with memorializing the soldiers who had died in the war. Grossman said that before the war stones were just stones. After the war they became shrines, sites through which to honor those who had fallen. Grossman said to me that in a landscape reconfigured by a secular ideology such as Zionism, 'the soil in the Holy Land again became sacred.'"

"Either the soil itself or a museum," Germani added. "One way or another, memory inserts its claws into us all the time." He paused. Then he added, "South America is a landscape where memory is hotly contested. From Concepción, where I live, and throughout Chile's Patagonia, German communities are ubiquitous. German immigration started in the mid-nineteenth century. The communities were links in the so-called Rat Route, the influx of former Nazis to the region after the Second World War. They protected them. And even now they nurture groups with neo-Nazi sentiments. They too want to have a claim on the memory real estate."

"Are these groups against the Museo de la Memoria?" I asked.

"Not openly. It is easy to stereotype all Chilean Germans, just as Chilean Jews are often typecast. Some in the German community were close to the Pinochet regime."

We finished our meal. Germani needed to catch a plane back to Concepción. On the way to the metro station Alison said, "A rose is a rose is a rose. . . . Well, a stone is never just a stone."

I told Alison and Germani an anecdote I had heard about Rabbi Meyer, who helped families of the desaparecidos in Argentina in the 1970s. "A father came to him for advice. The man was at an impasse, waiting to receive news of his son, who had been kidnapped by the military. The father wanted to know if he should recite Kaddish.

'If we can't prove your son is dead, you must wait,' the rabbi said.

The father rolled up his sleeve and showed Rabbi Meyer the tattooed numbers. 'For this I was saved from Auschwitz?'

'Your presence here is proof that there is hope,' stated Rabbi Meyer."

2.

A few months later I went to Buenos Aires again. I wanted to meet once more with Marcelo Brodsky, the photographer and human rights activist. I knew his brother was one of the desaparecidos. Brodsky was also one of the masterminds behind an official memorial dedicated to the victims of state terrorism. He had promised to show it to me.

There was another reason, too. The last time we saw each other, on our trip to Entre Ríos, Brodsky had mentioned an unusual little tourist guide called *Memorias de Buenos Aires: Signos de Terrorismo de Estado en Argentina* (2009). I knew about it: it is a heart-wrenching volume. In fact, I had been involved in the English-language version: *Memories of Buenos Aires: Signs of State Terrorism in Argentina.*

Back at home I spent time studying it. I now wanted to revisit Buenos Aires with the tourist guide in my hand. The book is full of detailed information and photographs of all the places in the city where members of the opposition were harassed, kidnapped, tortured, and killed.

In hindsight, the fact that all these places were turned into memory sites was a response to the conversation I'd had with Alison and Eliah Germani in the Peruvian restaurant after our visit to the Museo de la Memoria in Santiago.

I kept repeating to myself: collective memory has no address.

On my previous visit to Buenos Aires I had been to neighborhoods such as Balvanera, Palermo, Belgrano, and Recoleta. They are all in the guide. In fact, every so often I remember seeing paving stones, known in Spanish as *baldosas*, on street corners and in park grounds. I also remembered seeing plaques on building facades, invoking the time, circumstance, and protagonists of a particular historical event.

I hadn't paid much attention then, though. It was different this time around. The frequency of the *baldosas* was overwhelming.

I started in Palermo and Recoleta. On the Carlos Pellegrini Advanced

School of Commerce building, at Calle Marcelo T. de Alvear #1851, I saw a plaque with the names of thirty-two students and two teachers who were detained and disappeared. At the Plaza Houssay I saw the names of students, teachers, and staff of the Universidad de Buenos Aires and the José de San Martín Clinical Hospital.

Then I came across a sculpture called "Applause," at Calle French #3617, above the entrance to the headquarters of the Antonio Cunill Cabanellas Department of Dramatic Arts. It is in memory of actors who disappeared. And the Patricios First Infantry Regiment, at the crossroads of Avenida Bullrich and Avenida Santa Fe, functioned as a detention center between 1976 and 1977.

Moving on I stopped at the corner of Avenida San Juan and Avenida Entre Ríos. This is where the journalist Rodolfo Walsh, a prominent member of the Montoneros, was killed on March 25, 1977.

I took the metro to the neighborhood of Almagro. On the corner of Calle Acuña de Figueroa and Avenida Corrientres, a *baldosa* stated that Graciella Mellibovsky, a graduate from the Buenos Aires National School with a degree in political economy, was kidnapped on her way to meet friends. She was never seen again.

Also in Almagro, I stopped where Hugo and Abel Stejilevich were attacked at Avenida Corrientes #3860. Hugo Stejilevich was an actor and a union delegate. The tour guide says that on the day of his kidnapping he committed suicide by swallowing a cyanide pill. The information on this particular event stated that Abel had studied at the Carlos Pellegrini Advanced School of Commerce and that he was injured in the leg as he tried to escape his kidnappers.

Needless to say, these horrors didn't suddenly appear, in a vacuum. Unfortunately, Argentina has a long and terrible history of repression. Among the most tyrannical regimes was that of Juan Manuel de Rosas between 1835 and 1852. Any sort of opposition was crushed ruthlessly. Domingo Faustino Sarmiento, the author of *Facundo: Civilization and Barbarism*, had to go into exile in Santiago, Chile (where he wrote his book), in order to survive Rosas's mighty first.

As part of that opposition Esteban Echeverría, a mordant nineteenth-century polemicist, wrote a short story that is at the heart of the nation's literary tradition: "The Slaughterhouse" (1838–1840). The story takes place during Lent, as meat is being prepared by one of the city's butchers. An opponent to the regime passes by the place, and those in the slaughterhouse, like stray dogs, start to bully him. Soon a mass of people is cheering. The crowd quickly loses control, and the regime's opponent becomes a sacrificial lamb. Echeverría's message is itself cutthroat: dissent is made to pay a heavy price in these lands.

Unquestionably the most haunting sites I visited, on the riverfront on the north side of Buenos Aires, was the Navy School of Mechanics, known as ESMA, at Avenida del Libertador #8151. This was the largest, and most infamous, of the clandestine detention centers during the Dirty War. A military training center since 1924, it is now a museum housing a number of human rights and cultural organizations, including the National Memory Archive, the Nuestros Hijos Cultural Center of the Mothers of the Plaza de Mayo Association, and the Latin American Initiative for the Identification of Persons.

There is an L-shaped room in the attic, known as *capucha*, where people were handcuffed and shackled on mattresses, black masks covering their eyes and hoods over their heads. They were repeatedly tortured, in part in order to alert the authorities about friends, relatives, and other subversives. The word *capucha* was insistently repeated, as a warning whenever someone anywhere else in the building did something deemed reprehensible.

Other aspects of ESMA also showcase the way in which language itself was a tool for torture. On the premises, systemic murders were called *traslados*, meaning "transfers." The forced-labor area was called *la pecera*, "the fishbowl." Prisoners who were told they were going on "outings" understood the euphemism to mean operations that facilitated other kidnappings. Along these lines, the word *desaparecido* meant "illegally detained." And, according to survivors, the term *algo*, "something," was a recurrent motif in the parlance of torturers: *algo habrán hecho*, "they must have done something."

All of which makes a comparison with Nazi detention camps controversial. Robert S. Wistrich—author of *A Lethal Obsession: Anti-Semitism from Antiquity to the Global Jihad* (2010) and, until his death in 2015, a professor of modern European history at the Hebrew University in Jerusalem—knew very little about Argentina. The ESMA wasn't a place exclusively for Jews. Yet their presence was substantial. It is possible to estimate that around 20 percent of the inmates were Jewish. Indeed, Wistrich believed "there is little doubt that Jewish opponents of the military regime were subjected to special treatment, or that a Nazi-like anti-Semitism existed in sections of the Argentine armed forces and police."

My visit to ESMA left me in a state of exhaustion. It is not a figure of speech to describe ESA as *el infierno mismo*, hell itself, since it is estimated that about five thousand detainees were in there, most of whom ended up as desaparecidos.

I agreed: in the atrocities perpetrated by the Argentina junta, there were echoes of Nazi savagery.

3.

Still in Buenos Aires, next afternoon I met again with Marcelo Birmajer at Café La Biela, in the La Recoleta neighborhood.

Heartbreakingly, since my last visit when Birmajer and I walked around El Once a terrible personal tragedy had befallen him. A few months prior, on December 23, 2015, his brother Eduardo had been stabbed to death by a Palestinian in Jerusalem.

I was sitting at one of the tables outside the restaurant in the plaza. As soon as Birmajer arrived, I expressed my condolences. Eduardo had lived with his family near Jerusalem. As a young man he went through an intense spiritual search, looking for an answer in Oriental religions. After a while he found what he was looking for in Judaism, and he became orthodox. He moved to Israel, raised a family, and was an active member in a yeshiva.

He and Birmajer had had a difficult relationship. Since in Jewish tradition a person must be buried the same day, Birmajer and his mother couldn't attend the funeral. But the two of them were getting ready to travel to Israel shortly and spend time with Eduardo's family.

I asked him how his life had changed after Eduardo's death. He talked about the enormous amount of emotional outpouring he had received from people. And he immediately linked his reaction to the AMIA attack.

Birmajer didn't have any relatives that perished that day. But it had taken place in his beloved neighborhood. His brother's killing occurred thousands of miles away. Yet he felt that the dagger that upended his brother's life had penetrated his own heart. It had spilled into the same river of blood that connected to the AMIA tragedy. His anger was deep.

Months earlier, when I heard about the stabbing, I had sent him a note. Now I told him I had written a short story, "Yom Kippur in Buenos Aires," inspired by our friendship. It is about the inner turmoil that the sibling of a terrorist victim, himself not a strong believer, goes through during Kol Nidre—the most sacred night of the Jewish year, at the start of Yom Kippur—as the gates of heaven supposedly open for people who are about to confess the sins of the previous year. I also told him I had read his column in *Clarín* about his brother. It was called "Mi hermano Edu" (My brother Edu), published on January 2, 2016. To me it seemed discreet, full of empathy. The expression in Spanish is *dolida* (wrenching) in its emotional tone. Politically, he didn't support an outright eye-for-an-eye approach of the Israeli military against Hezbollah, Hamas, and other Islamic fundamentalist organizations. In fact, he was in favor of a two-state solution in the Middle East.

Birmajer wrote: "Independently of these types of Palestinian 'Islamfascist' assassinations, which have no relationship with any territorial conflict, I continue to believe that the best solution to the Israeli-Palestinian conflict requires leadership on the side of Israel and is about accepting the Jewish state on the Palestinian side. That will enable them to accept for the first time the construction of a Palestinian state. Peace depends on the Palestinian leaders neutralizing rather than stimulating the Palestinian assassins."

I told him that, though I agreed with him ideologically, I also appreciated the way in which he channeled his pain. And I wondered if I could ask him a question: Was it difficult not to turn Eduardo's death into a pose? I mentioned a lecture by Elie Wiesel about the Holocaust that I had attended, which to me had felt grandstanding and sanctimonious. Throughout his career, Wiesel had been accused by a small cadre of critics of making a career out of the Shoah.

As a writer addressing personal tragedy Birmajer responded that it meant breaking through the gap between the private and public spheres. Regardless of one's temperament, he said, this presented a quagmire. All tragedy is local: it happens to someone in a specific time and place. Since 2001 he had written scores of columns, in all kinds of venues, about the Middle Eastern conflict. I could Google his views: they were always consistent; Eduardo's death hadn't made him change his mind. He was hopeful. The anger between the two sides was too deep. One needed to believe in the future. Otherwise things would be too bleak.

4.

The following day, with my guide book still in my hand, I reached what was the culmination of my tour, the Parque de la Memoria. This memorial is in Costanera Norte, near an ecological reserve in the Nuñez neighborhood, alongside the main campus of the city's public university. It is the equivalent of Santiago's museum: the institutional site where locals and tourists alike go to remember the victims of state terrorism.

I had an appointment there with Brodsky, who was a leading voice in building the site.

Created in 1998 by legislative decree, the memorial sits on over thirty-five acres next to the River Plate. Unlike Chile's Museo de la Memoria, this one is an open space, with grass and concrete paths on which a variety of modern sculptures are exhibited. At its core is a wall, which, according to Brodsky, was built "in dialogue with Maya Lin's sober Vietnam Memorial in Washington, DC, and Daniel Libeskind's fractured—in Z shape—design of the Jewish Museum in Berlin." The wall lists nine thousand names of those who disappeared between roughly 1969 and 1983.

Coincidentally, just a week after my visit President Barack Obama came to the Parque de la Memoria. A few months later, the German chancellor Angela Markel followed.

Brodsky was wearing jeans, a colorful blouse, a light jacket, and Birkenstocks. He looked as joyful as ever. He is also part of Buena Memoria, a human-rights group in Argentina dedicated to keeping the memory alive of those who were targeted by the military junta. They do this with the purpose of fighting for freedom and justice and fortifying the country's democracy.

"Those nine thousand are only the ones we've been able to name," Brodsky said. "The total is closer to thirty thousand."

He and I walked through the park. "The military used all sorts of linguistic subterfuges to avoid talking directly about the state-sponsored atrocities they were engaged in," Brodsky said. "It's a long-standing Argentine sport that, in my view, reaches its climax during this period. For instance, they referred to the death sentence as *traslado*, 'transfer.' They didn't talk directly of death."

I asked if Jews were particularly targeted during the Dirty War. At first, he was cautious. "Not more than other minorities."

I mentioned Wistrich's comment on "the special treatment" Jews received during the dictatorship.

"Well, since many Jews were left-leaning," Brodsky stated, "and had been involved in antimilitary activities, the number was high among the desaparecidos, around two thousand of the nine thousand confirmed victims, which represents 22 percent of the confirmed victims, or 6.6 percent of the estimated total of thirty thousand. That is, more than six out of every hundred."

"An enormous number," I posited.

"Yes," Brodsky continued. "This is an exorbitant price, given that Jews in Argentina account for less than 1 percent of the total population."

He said the military junta went after opponents, and if they were Jewish, then this was added ammunition.

"Was your brother targeted because he was Jewish?"

"It is difficult to say," Brodsky responded. He thought for a minute. "Not likely. But once he was in the concentration camp, the fact that he was Jewish gave his executioners *otra excusa para flagelarlo*, another reason to brutalize him."

Brodsky said that in the transcript of his imprisonment, which Brodsky was able to recover after the heir of a torturer donated his library to an institution, his brother Fernando, when asked his religion, responded Jewish.

Brodsky opened a book of photographs he had published a few years before called *Nexo* (2001). Pages 54 and 55 displayed the facsimile of an official document. His captors had written the answer in capitals: *RELIGIÓN: JUDÍA*. RELIGION: JEWISH.

As Brodsky's recounting became more vivid, I felt a pull in my stomach. He told me that during the military period, he himself was forced into exile. He lived in Barcelona for eight years. Only when Raúl Alfonsín, the first elected president, was in command did he return home.

"I left after becoming the target of a kidnapping attempt. A Navy task group caught me on the street while I was out on a date. It was on May 17, 1977. It happened in Buenos Aires's Plaza Flores. I was only able to escape—I ran away desperately—after a bystander intervened. I heard three shots. One bullet hit me in my left thigh. When I realized I was wounded, I jumped into a taxi. For several days I couldn't walk."

After my visit to the Parque de la Memoria, we jumped into Brodsky's car and he drove us to his house in Belgrano. His photo studio is adjacent. He wanted to show me a series of images.

On the way, we talked about the most famous Argentina Jewish dissident during the dictatorship, the journalist and editor Jacobo Timerman.

"Frankly, I don't think of him as a dissident," Brodsky said. "He was no Nelson Mandela or Vaclav Havel."

"Why?"

"I don't know," Brodsky replied. "There's something phony about him. Initially *La Opinión*, the newspaper he was at the helm of, supported the coup. Since you've written about him, Ilan, you know he was a kind of Argentine narcissist, which means a narcissist twice over. In my view Timerman was also a bit of a hypocrite, though I must confess he was true to his principles."

The founder of the weekly *Primera Plana* and editor in chief of the daily *La Opinión*, Timerman was known for supporting in-depth reportage about government corruption. A few months after the coup, he published all sorts of exposés on anti-Semitism and the habeas corpus to the courts by the families of the desaparecidos. Naturally, the Argentine army became furious.

Timerman's arrest came on April 15, 1977, as some twenty civilians obeying orders from the army besieged his apartment. At the scene Timerman was described by his captors as the scum of the earth: a Zionist, an impostor, and a usurper.

He was subjected to beatings, solitary confinement, and electric shocks. His interrogation sessions lasted between twelve and fourteen hours. Although the charges against him were never made clear to him, publicly the Argentine junta accused him and other people, among other claims, of having ties to David Graiver, a banker who purportedly managed the money accounts of the guerrilla group Montoneros that was intent on bringing down the nation's central government. His torturers questioned his loyalty as a Jew toward the Ukraine, his place of birth; toward Argentina, to which he immigrated at the age of five; and toward Israel, a state where, stripped of his Argentine citizenship, he was flown when the Argentine junta, under international pressure, finally set him free.

But Timerman was at odds with the Argentine Jewish community as well. He judged them to be complicit in the nation's tragic state of affairs. In *Prisoner without a Name, Cell without a Number*, he writes in regards to anti-Semitism: "Many times I've been asked whether a Holocaust is conceivable in Argentina. Well, that depends on what is meant by a Holocaust, though no one would have been able to answer that question affirmatively in Germany in 1937." He adds: "There are no gas chambers in Argentina, and this leaves many with a clear conscience. Yet between 1974 and 1978, the violation of girls in clandestine prisons had a peculiar characteristic: Jewish girls were violated twice as often as non-Jewish girls."

And then Timerman posits—parenthetically: "(Must all anti-Semitism wind up in soap? If so, then anti-Semitism does not exist in Argentina, and it becomes a matter of accidental, coincidental situations, as the leaders of the Argentine Jewish community claim. But can there be anti-Semitism without soap? In that case, the Jewish community leaders are no different from the *Judenrat* of the Hitler ghettos at the beginning of the Holocaust.)"

"For Timerman, his Jewishness was a political act," Brodsky stated. "This was difficult for his captors to understand. For them it is a religion, or else a conspiracy."

"He learned from Shoah survivors, though," I replied. "If he saw himself as a victim, then others would see him as such. So he resisted."

"But he was phony. When he finally went to Israel, he spoke badly of Israel. Not that I'm a defender of the Israeli government's policies. It was 1982, the time of one of the Lebanon invasions. Timerman wrote a little book criticizing it. He was consistent in his animosity toward dictatorship, that's true. But Israel had saved him from prison. Anyway, he became persona non grata. He also wrote volumes of reportage on Chile and Cuba."

5.

After Brodsky showed me around his house, we went to his studio. It was a large space. One of the walls had shelves from ceiling to floor that were full of photography books.

Brodsky's oeuvre is in world-class institutions such as New York's Metropolitan Museum of Art, Houston's Museum of Fine Arts, London's Tate Collection, and Argentina's Museo Nacional de Bellas Artes. He likes to work with his own images and with archival material, in which he intervenes in a variety of ways. For instance, he showed me a series of old family photos, which he had enlarged and on which he had written all sorts of comments in different colored pencil.

One of them was a class photo from when Brodsky was in high school. He circled in different colored pencil a few of the members of his class, writing next to the circles a comment on how they fared during the Dirty War. Two of them had disappeared. A few others had gone into exile.

There was also a photo of Brodsky in a telephone booth in Spain. He said to me he used to frequent that cabin to speak without charge with his parents in Buenos Aires.

"The Spanish telephone company was poorly managed at the time. You could find public phones where you could make long-distance calls without paying a peseta."

I told him I remember doing that on one of my trips to Madrid in 1980.

"It was during one of those phone calls that my parents told me about Nando," Brodsky stated. (In Spanish, Nando is short for Fernando.) "He had been kidnapped by a clandestine military task force. There was no sign of him anywhere. Not at the Department of Psychology at the private university he attended, nor in the usual spots he frequented with friends.

He paused. "We all suspected the worst. One of his neighbors apparently witnessed the kidnapping. After others confirmed the sighting, my parents went to the police. They got no response. And so they started going from one police station to another. And they talked to leaders of the Jewish community, Rabbi Marshall Meyer among them. To no avail. People wanted to help but couldn't. The state is almighty."

He looked for some photos he wanted to show me. "To this day, his absence haunts us all. Just thinking of him keeps his memory alive . . ."

In one image Nando is a young man. He is alone on his bed in a room, sitting cross-legged, his fingers intertwined. It is probably his room. The bed is well made, with a wool cover on top. His hair is longish, uncombed. He wears elegant suit pants and a white button-up shirt. The top button of the shirt is buttoned. Although Nando's face is blurry, it's clear he's looking down. At his hands? Is he depressed? Or is he simply posing in front of his brother's camera?

This is the best photograph Brodsky has of his brother. It is also the first photograph he ever took with an old camera his father gave him as a present when he was fourteen years old.

In another image Nando is at the family's dining-room table. "This is our house in Caballito," Brodsky explains, "a neighborhood in Buenos Aires's western side. That's where the family lived, in front of Parque Rivadavia, on the eighth floor of an apartment building."

There is a party going on. Nando looks elegant in a Prince of Wales–type jacket. A fancy flower arrangement on a table takes a third of the photo's lower portion. The table displays half-empty glasses of wine. Nando's head is turning around. Again he seems to be looking down, although in this case his eyes are closed. He looks like the heir of an aristocratic Buenos Aires family.

Nothing in this or other pictures I see suggests the family is Jewish. I asked Brodsky if he grew up in a Jewish household. "Certainly, although you don't see it in the pictures. There were mezuzahs, menorahs, and plenty of other paraphernalia. A Star of David. Souvenirs from the Jerusalem Arab *shuk* (the Arab market)." A plate honoring Brodsky's father, Dr. Mauricio Brodsky, who was head of the Hospital Israelita's Department of Ophthalmology.

Finally, Brodsky showed me the most vivid of all the existing photographs. It is also in black and white. It shows Nando—thin, with long hair, wearing an undershirt. His left eye shows he has been beaten up. "He looks like Christ."

Brodsky found it at the Archivo del Juicio a las Juntas, the tribunal for military criminals. This photo was given to the judges by Victor Basterra, a prisoner who survived the dictatorship, working as a slave in the detention center.

"Nando's kidnapping took place on August 14, 1979. He was twenty-two years old. From the ESMA, he was allowed to call on a couple of occasions. The phone calls were a form of extortion."

When the trials against the military junta took place in 1984, the photo became very important. It had been given to Victor Basterra's prosecutors and was used to convict Nando's torturers. In court Brodsky's mother, Sara Brodsky, showed the photo to her son's torturers as she accused them of kidnapping him without any legal reason.

"Possibly Nando was one of those thrown into the waters of the River Plate," Brodsky stated.

He told me the sibling relationship had been complicated. "Nando was the more relaxed one. We shared the same room until the age of eighteen. He loved music. He played the guitar. The last time my family spoke with Nando was in January 1980."

He paused. "My brother lived in São Paulo for a while with a Japanese girlfriend, an ophthalmologist, Alice Miyata, who loved him dearly. In 1978 or the beginning of 1979, he thought the political climate in Argentina had improved, so he came back. It was bad luck. It was one of the last disappearances."

Nando had been an activist, though this didn't define him. He was close to a Marxist group called Grupo Obrero Revolucionario. "It was mainly for purposes of discussion," Brodsky said. "He wasn't a prominent militant. He participated in some organizations but wasn't a leader. Youth is by definition about rebellion. About wanting to change the world. The folks he socialized with had such dreams."

Whenever he talked about his brother's final moments, I would notice a change in Brodsky's style as a raconteur. "Nando was tortured by a man called Oscar Rubén Lanzón. With the return of democracy Lanzón disappeared. He changed his name, a bit like those he persecuted. Or like the Nazis after the Second World War who went to Chile and Argentina. But Lanzón was found, in spite of his pseudonym. A Mexican journalist working for the newspaper *Reforma* located him. Lanzón was put on trial. He was found guilty and, as a result of declining health, was placed on house arrest. One day he was found dead. Asphyxiated."

In an essay Brodsky published in 2011 in the newspaper *Página 12*, he wrote about the photograph of Nando at the ESMA: "The photograph has no end."

6.

About 100,000 Jews reached Latin America and the Caribbean between 1933 and 1942. In comparison, about 160,000 came to the United States between 1933 and 1942. Yet, as historians have argued, these numbers are deceitful. Only after Kristalnacht, on November 9, 1938, did the United States actually fulfill its annual quota, in 1939, of German Austrian immigrants, in large part as a response to the violence against Jews in Germany.

While I was in Chile and Argentina, I kept coming across references—from Eliah Germani, Marcelo Brodsky, and others—to the Rat Route. I knew that former Nazi officers (*Nacis* is another common spelling in Spanish) such as Klaus Barbie, Josef Mengele, Gerhard Bohne, Erich Priebke, Josef Schwammberger, and Adolf Eichmann were known to have sought refuge in Argentina, Brazil, Paraguay, Chile, and Bolivia. A number also made it to Canada, the United States, and elsewhere. Arguably the most notorious Nazi hunter was Simon Wiesenthal. At one point he estimated that the number of Nazi criminals in Argentina was close to a hundred.

Eichmann was the most famous case. As soon as I delved fully into it, I realized that the Eichmann case—his escape to Argentina, his kidnapping by the Israeli secret service Mossad, the international celebration that came after his arrest, and the sour aftertaste it left in Argentina and elsewhere in the region—was a double-edged sword. To explore it in full I went to as many locations as possible in Buenos Aires. I found little that was of interest. The places where Eichmann was kidnapped, where he was kept incommunicado while the Israeli government decided his fate, and so on, are either gone or are not available for public viewing.

The South American climax of the Eichmann saga took place on Wednesday, May 11, 1960. Bus 203 was due to make its usual stop at 7:40 p.m. on Calle Garibaldi in the neighborhood of San Fernando, in the northern part of Buenos Aires. Agents for Mossad had carefully studied the pattern.

Two passengers usually came down off the bus, a man and a woman. The woman disappeared after a few steps while he continued, sometimes stopping at a kiosk to buy cigarettes, then walking on until he reached his home. His name was Ricardo Klement. His previous name had been Otto Heninger. But the name that mattered was his original one: Adolf Eichmann. He had been the man in charge of orchestrating the Nazi genocide of millions of European Jews during the Second World War.

When it became known, Operación Garibaldi (to my ears the name still rings in Spanish) was a global sensation.

On this particular night the bus was taking longer than usual, to the point that Mossad agents almost called off the entire endeavor. It finally arrived a bit after eight o'clock. They quietly kidnapped Eichmann, put him inside a Chevrolet sedan, and took him to a temporary address where one of them interrogated the former Nazi.

David Ben Gurion was Israel's prime minister. The Jewish state had declared its independence in 1948. Soon afterward a war took place in which its Arab neighbors, unhappy that the United Nations had supported the Jewish state, sought to eliminate the new country by "throwing the Jews into the sea." The Israeli Army Forces fought back, claiming Jerusalem as the nation's capital. Almost a decade and a half later, Zionism was still a powerful ideology.

The rationale behind the creation of Israel was the Holocaust. A nationalist bent had shaken the diaspora. Jews wanted to "normalize" their existence.

The Nuremberg Trials took place between November 1945 and October 1946. Members of the Nazi apparatus were put on trial by an international tribunal. But Ben Gurion wanted to bring some of the Nazi perpetrators to justice in Israel.

Eichmann lived in the San Fernando neighborhood in a humble, unassuming house, with his wife and three children. He was an employee of Mercedes-Benz. Before that he had worked at the gas corporation Orbis. On the day of his capture he was returning from a day's work.

Ben Gurion got his wish. The intrepid way in which the Mossad kept Eichmann incommunicado for days, then made him sign a release statement accepting transport to Tel Aviv, is all part of the narrative. El Al, the relatively new Israeli airline, made its first (and so far only) arrival in Buenos Aires on May 18, 1960. Abba Eban, a celebrated Israeli diplomat, was on that flight, heading a delegation to the celebration of 150 years of the 25 de Mayo, the beginning of the Independence struggle. The departure was set for a few days later, on May 20, 1960.

By then the captive was cooperating. The agents sedated him. He was dressed up in the uniform of an El Al guard. They made arrangements in the terminal and finally brought him on board. When the plane finally took off, only a handful of people on board knew who this passenger was. Until someone said, "The passenger traveling with us is Adolf Eichmann." There was disbelief on the plane.

Eichmann was indicted on fifteen counts, including crimes against the Jewish people and crimes against humanity, and was found guilty and sentenced to death. On June 1, 1962, he was executed by hanging. His body was cremated, his ashes spread at sea, far from Israeli waters.

The impact of the trial was enormous. The testimony of Holocaust survivors was televised worldwide. In fact the spectacle became a kind of collective expiation. People who had gone through the war and had kept their experiences to themselves suddenly felt the right to speak. On a larger scale these testimonies forced nations to acknowledge their participation during the war.

Hannah Arendt wrote a controversial book about the trial, *Eichmann in Jerusalem: A Report on the Banality of Evil* (1963). It was an expanded version of a series of articles she had published in the *New Yorker*. A German philosopher and student of Martin Heidegger (who was a Nazi sympathizer), Arendt's argument was that Eichmann was a mere apparatchik, a bureaucrat who followed orders from the higher Nazi commands and, thus, was not necessarily guilty of the counts for which he was indicted. Arendt didn't altogether exculpate Eichmann. She simply portrayed him as a being small fish in a large ocean.

The events in Jerusalem eclipsed another controversy: the Argentine government was ignored. Indeed, neither the government nor the police knew anything about it until the El Al flight had landed in Tel Aviv and Ben Gurion officially announced the news to the Knesset.

In accounts published later it was clear that, after two of Eichmann's children realized their father had been abducted, they hesitated to contact the authorities for fear of calling attention to their precarious situation. The same went for former Nazis, as well as German exiles in Argentina.

Eventually, Eichmann's children got in touch with the Tacuara Nationalist Movement (MNT), a radical neo-Nazi organization that was anti-Semitic, militaristic, and fascist. The MNT was modeled on the Spanish Falange led by José Antonio Primo de Rivera. Its members stormed into a synagogue not far from where Eichmann lived, convinced that he was being held hostage in the basement. They came out empty-handed.

I visited Calle Garibaldi #6067, in the San Fernando neighborhood near Ruta 202 and the Mitre railway. Although the knowledge that Adolf Eichmann had been kidnapped there made the journey momentous, truth is there was little to see. Eichmann's house, a three-room chalet, was demolished in 2001. I knew that until a few years earlier, there was a neighbor, Guillermo Gómez, who went out of his way to deter visitors from staying in the area, including journalists and other media people, and especially Israelis, who often arrived on bus tours.

I also knew that, after his kidnapping, Eichmann's house showed up in the San Fernando municipality as belonging to Marta Valinotti de Eichmann, the wife of one of Eichmann's grandchildren. Nicolás, Eichmann's older son, abandoned his wife and daughter, Mónica, after the kidnapping and returned to Berlin. Mónica became a Hare Krishna devotee, supported herself by buying and selling art, and lives in the United States. Another one of Eichmann's sons is an archeologist who is now also living in Berlin.

At any rate today the place looks rather mundane. There are no historical markers. Passersby didn't have anything to say. No one was interested in the topic. Finally, an old woman told me she knew that a German officer had lived in the area and that he had been caught. But she couldn't remember his name. "You know how many in the Argentine government should be caught, too? There wouldn't be enough room in prison for them," she said.

I felt her sentences had an ideological agenda she hesitated to articulate. I asked her about Tacuara. Was the movement active?

"Ah, that's a long time ago. I'd rather not talk about it."

"Is there anti-Semitism in Argentina?"

"Of course there is," she replied. "And there should be. Jews control the bank industry. Israel, a murderous state, is in cahoots with Argentine Jews."

I thought to myself that, immediately after the Eichmann incident in Buenos Aires, life for Argentine Jews must have felt precarious.

I experienced a similar situation in Mexico in the early 1980s, when the country's Jews suddenly became targets of animosity. The police didn't seem ready to defend them. Did Argentine Jews organize? Was there a movement inside the community—in line with what the American rabbi Meir Kahane did in the United States in the late 1960s with the Jewish Defense League—to take justice into Jewish hands? It was a dangerous act. Was it also courageous?

At the time of Eichmann's kidnapping, the president of Argentina was Arturo Frondizi. He was known for encouraging foreign investment in oil and steel. When Frondizi's regime found out about Eichmann, it accused Israel of transgressing against foreign borders. It said the young Jewish state was now using Nazi tactics to achieve its goals. It threatened to break off diplomatic relations.

The consensus among Argentineans was that Israel had intruded on their territorial rights. The country's Jewish community was divided. On the one hand it celebrated Operación Garibaldi, saying it was a statement of astute Israeli spying; on the other hand it felt vulnerable to the critique, expressed in newspapers, on TV, and in political circles, that Jews believed themselves to be above the law.

To absolve itself Israel sought ways to distract attention from the operation. Among other things, the details were largely kept quiet for years. The Ben Gurion government argued that the operatives were not actually Israeli employees but "Jewish volunteers, some of them Israelis." In 1961 Israel officially began to recognize its involvement in the operation.

The tension culminated on June 23, 1960, when the US Security Council adopted Resolution 138, asking Israel to make reparations for its infraction of Argentine sovereignty. Israel demurred, responding that such a request was beyond the jurisprudence of the security council and that any reparation would need to be negotiated bilaterally.

An unsuccessful part of Operación Garibaldi was the late attempt by the Israeli operatives to kidnap Josef Mengele, the famous "Angel of Death," the physician at Auschwitz known for his role in sending victims to the gas chambers and for doing experiments on his patients.

There had been sightings of Mengele in Buenos Aires. Eichmann himself offered some information to the Mossad about him, since Mengele at one point had helped him as a doctor. But the information came to nothing. Apparently, Mengele had escaped without trace a few weeks earlier. He made his way to Brazil and drowned while swimming in 1979. His body was buried under a fake name. His remains were eventually disinterred and identified by forensic experts.

The dark shadows these Nazi figures project might overstate the Nazi presence in Latin America. Through a variety of secret channels, the region welcomed them. It is true that their impact is insignificant in comparison to their actions on the European stage. Still, the impunity with which they were sheltered remains a shameful episode.

7.

In truth, the impact of Eichmann's kidnapping in Buenos Aires has not been properly understood in the Jewish world outside Argentina. I for one didn't quite grasp its significance until I spent time wandering around the city's working-class neighborhoods.

From my conversation with the old woman, I wasn't convinced that people didn't know who the former high-command Nazi officer was. They simply didn't want to talk to me about it. The Rat Route was a well-known historical chapter. Talking to me was incautious, they probably thought.

In my excursions into Nazi territory in South America, I came across a concept I knew little about: Plan Andinia. It was mentioned to me casually in conversations, often in connection with Israel's military power not only in the Middle East but in the world at large. I also stumbled upon Plan Andinia in reference to the aftermath of the *comunas* established at the dawn of the twentieth century in Entre Ríos and Santa Fe by the Jewish Colonization Association. Somehow Plan Andinia had become a treacherous afterthought.

While in this frame of mind, when I was back home I came across a copy of Roberto Bolaño's novel *La literatura nazi en América* (*Nazi Literature in the Americas*, 1996), in my own personal library, of all places. Bolaño is among my favorite Spanish-language authors of the late twentieth century. His style feels inspired by Dashiell Hammett, Raymond Chandler, James M. Cain, and other American hard-boiled writers. Bolaño's third novel had been published in 1996, when this enfant terrible was still utterly unknown.

I had read it when the English translation came out. But somehow I had forgotten about it. The narrative is shaped as a lucid, cohesive catalog of authors and books belonging to a spurious intellectual tradition in the Southern Cone that lionizes Adolf Hitler, his hideous Aryan theories, and the stream of neo-Nazi activities from 1930 to 2010 in Chile (where Bolaño was from), in Argentina, Bolivia, Colombia, Cuba, Venezuela, Brazil, and Paraguay, as well as in the United States.

At one point, in the "Epilogue for Monsters," Bolaño lists a series of publishing ventures in South America devoted to Nazi literature. One of them is a magazine called the *Fourth Reich in Argentina*. He describes it as "verging on insanity, illegality and idiocy." He goes on to say that "the magazine was outlawed but transformed itself into a publishing house. Some titles appeared under the imprint of the Fourth Reich in Argentina, but the majority did not. In its new guise the Fourth Reich continued to make its erratic way until the year 2001. The identity of the publisher remains a mystery." While Bolaño's book is strangely soft on references to anti-Semitism, my new reading of *Nazi Literature in the Americas* suddenly made me realize that I had never before encountered any neo-Nazi literature from the region. Should there be any, I asked myself?

I'm not sure Bolaño had encountered any either. Every entry in his book, without exception, is bogus. This, precisely, is what fascinates me: its tongue-in-cheek approach. A fine novel achieves its success by creating believable characters whose emotions readers are able to empathize with. Bolaño had achieved something arguably more difficult: he had invented an entire bookshelf dedicated to what he describes as an illustrious literary tradition—which is totally nonexistent.

His inspiration was likely a similar book of speculative fiction by Borges, *Universal History of Infamy* (1935), also encyclopedic in nature, in which a number of entries are real and others are fictional. But Bolaño's is far more inventive. In fact I see it as a "machine of irreality," such is the way in which creations by him give way to other creations. For instance, there is one fictitious biography of a Chilean called Carlos Ramírez Hoffman, which serves as the point of departure of Bolaño's next novel, *Distant Star* (1996). Ramírez Hoffman is portrayed as a right-wing performance artist who is also a serial killer.

Before my trip I asked an assortment of colleagues devoted to Latin American literature if they happened to know if everything in Bolaño's volume was truly fictional. The consensus was that every iota in it was indeed concocted.

Every iota? I wasn't so sure. The fact that Bolaño had created a fictional magazine called the *Fourth Reich* made me wonder if there wasn't a larger canvas I was missing in my explorations in Latin America.

This and the constant references to Plan Andinia prompted me to schedule the next portion of my travels in the Chilean Patagonia. Throughout my treks there, I continuously looked for possible references—on streets, in newspapers, in bookstores—to Edelmira Thompson de Mendiluce, Zach Sodenster, Harru Sibelius, Italo Schiaffino, and Max Mirebalais, alias Max Kasimir, Max Von Hauptmann, Max le Geuele, and Jacques Artibonit, all characters in Bolaño's *Nazi Literature in the Americas*. I never came across any.

Still, I came across a strong undercurrent of anti-Semitic and, in stronger measure, anti-Israeli animosity. The way I entered this realm of hatred was through another book I also had in my personal library, which I found when I returned Bolaño's volume to its place. It was Jacobo Timerman's *Prisoner without a Name, Cell without a Number*.

Timerman wasn't in my mind since I had thought about him while I was wandering around El Once. By happenstance, I opened the book to page 73. On that page he includes the following about a specific instance in which he was asked about a spurious scheme known as Plan Andinia:

> For many years, Argentine Nazi ideologues have claimed the existence of a Jewish scheme for seizing Patagonia, the southern zone of the country, and creating the republic of Andinia. Books and pamphlets have appeared on this

subject, and it's extremely difficult to convince a Nazi that the plan is, if not absurd, at least unfeasible. Naturally, my questioners wanted to know more details than were presently available to them on this matter.

Question: We would like to know some further details on the Andinia Plan. How many troops would the State of Israel be prepared to send?

Answer: Do you actually believe in this plan? That it even exists? How can you imagine four hundred thousand Argentine Jews being able to seize nearly one million square kilometers in the southern part of the country? What would they do with it? How would they populate it? How would they defeat twenty-five million Argentines, the armed forces?

Question: Listen, Timerman, that's exactly what I'm asking you. Answer me this. You're a Zionist, yet you didn't go to Israel. Why?

Answer: Because of a long chain of circumstances, all personal and familial. Situations that arise, one linked to the other that caused me to postpone it time after time . . .

Question: Come on, Timerman, you're an intelligent person. Find a better answer. Let *me* give an explanation so that we can get to the bottom of things. Israel has a very small territory and can't accommodate all the Jews in the world. Besides, the country is isolated in the midst of the Arab world. It needs money and political support from all over the world. That's why Israel has created three power centers abroad . . .

Answer: Are you going to recite *The Protocols of the Elders of Zion* to me?

Question: Up to now, no one's proved that they're untrue. But let me go on. Israel, secure in these three centers of power, has nothing to fear. One is the United States, where Jewish power is evident. This means money and political control of capitalist countries. The second is the Kremlin, where Israel also has important influence . . .

Answer: I believe the exact opposite, in fact.

Question: Don't interrupt me. The opposition is totally fake. The Kremlin is still dominated by the same sectors that staged the Bolshevik Revolution, in which the Jews played the principal role. This means political control of Communist countries. And the third center of power is Argentina, especially the south, which, if it were well developed by Jewish immigrants from various Latin American countries, could become an economic emporium, a food and oil basket, the road to Antarctica.

As he states it later on, Timerman repeatedly tried to convince his captors that such a plan was a figment of their imagination.

The reference convinced me I needed to looked deeper into Plan Andinia. Thus, the next leg of my travels, with Alison again, was to Patagonia—from Santiago to Puerto Montt and on to Punta Arenas—to see for myself.

In my youth I had read Bruce Chatwin's travelogue *In Patagonia* (1977). The sparse style left a deep impression on me. It is a reflection on nomadism. To this day I see it as a model of travel writing: sharp, succinct, inspired. I took a copy with me. It had an introduction by Nicholas Shakespeare who argued that the Patagonian people didn't like Chatwin's book because it wasn't accurate. For narrative purposes he had misconstrued information. This didn't make a dent on my thoughts. Isn't that the travel writer's prerogative? One doesn't travel the way one writes and vice versa. The travel writer isn't a historian. He has a duty toward the truth. But the truth in a journey belongs as much to him as it does to the surroundings he sets foot in. For these reasons, rereading *In Patagonia* as I went along with Alison was just as satisfying as it had been before—and perhaps even more so.

Before we set off I phoned my Israeli friend Eliezer Nowodworski. He didn't disappoint. As an Argentinean with deep knowledge of his country's Jewish history, he immediately stated that this hideous plot amounted to a full-fledged competitor—at least in its deceptiveness—to *The Protocols of the Elders of Zion*. The two offer a theory of how Jews are committed to taking control of the world—in the case of this plan, of a specific portion of land in Patagonia shared by Argentina and Chile.

"How old is the myth?" I asked.

"Relatively recent," Nowodworski replied. "Maybe at most from the 1960s."

Since he was in a rush and couldn't attend to my questions, he promised to send me a bunch of materials by email.

By the time I landed in Puerto Montt, located in the northern end of the Reloncaví Sound in Chile's southern Llanquihue province, I had them in my server. I was able to access a number of illuminating documents that granted me a unique window into the region. Reading them felt apropos since Puerto Montt and its surroundings are the by-product of the wave of German colonization that took place in the second half of the nineteenth century.

"Why is it called 'Plan Andinia' and not 'Plan Patagónico'?" I asked Nowodworski.

"The Patagonia is a region," he responded. "It is at the bottom of the continent, divided between Chile and Argentina, and therefore having two coasts, a Pacific coast and an Atlantic coast, respectively in each country. It comprised the southern section of the Andean cordillera as well as grass-lands, deserts, and pampas. But the Andes, which is the longest mountain range in the world (some 4,300 miles long and from 120 to 430 miles wide), starts in Venezuela, Colombia, and Ecuador, and reaches almost to the southernmost tip of American land."

Nowodworski said in an email that he had been away and had only just found the time to send me a link to a manifesto called *The Andean Plan and the New Jewish State* (1965), the Plan Andinia or the New Jewish State. The manifesto, often quoted as historical proof by promoters that argue that the Plan Andinia is the result of "a cabal of Jews" intent on taking Argentina away from the Argentine people, is available online.

The moment I read it I realized I could have found it on my own, except it was only because I was in southern Chile that I realized what I was looking for. What I read gave me pause. Every word resonated as if amplified by a loudspeaker. In Puerto Montt I was staying in a hotel on the edge of the Reloncaví Sound. Walking at night I saw an abundance of businesses with German names. Supermarkets sold German products. On the street there were German cars. At one point I ate at a cafeteria that on its menu featured Frankfurter Würsts and other sausages with mustard, an assortment of beer, and apple strudel. The deeper I traveled, the more intense the feeling became of being in a transplanted Alpine region.

I felt anxious. As I walked along the street, the gaze of passersby looked ominous.

According to the manifesto, the cabal supposedly met on March 23, 1969, between seven and nine o'clock, at the Templo Israelita, in Paso Street #423 in Buenos Aires. The meeting was led by one Rabbi Gordon and the purpose was to machinate the creation of a Jewish state in the Southern Cone. He stressed the importance of keeping such a plan absolutely secret.

Rabbi Gordon argued that "our great prophet doctor" Theodor Herzl, through his book *Der Judenstaat* (1896), orchestrated the creation of a Jewish state in Palestine and that fifty years later another Jewish state would be founded in Argentina, which has "the richest land in the world."

The reason to make this second Jewish state in such a remote land, argued the manifesto, is that Argentina is "strategically invaluable" because "it keeps Jews away from the major points of global conflict." That distance is an asset: Jews are tired of being at center stage. Thus, they are looking for an ideal remote location, a place where they will hardly be noticed.

At any rate, the ulterior motive of the Jews is to destabilize the world order. To achieve such an objective, the document stated, it is crucial to

PROFUNDIZAR EL CAOS YA EXISTENTE, FOMENTAR LA CONFUSIÓN, INTENSIFICAR LA CORRUPCIÓN, ESPECIALMENTE EN EL CAMPO POLÍTICO, ADMINISTRATIVO, CULTURAL, ECONÓMICO Y SOCIAL. "It is essential to deepen the already existing chaos in the country, generate confusion, intensify corruption, especially in the political, administrative, cultural, economic, and social realms."

The use of capitals is deliberate. The authors want the document to feel like an authentic official transcript. Plus, it plays with tone.

The state of absolute unruliness, it is posited, will bring about a need by the international community to intervene in order to stabilize Argentina. The result will be the dismembering of the nation. Jews will then take possession of the portion of land in Patagonia that belongs in part to Chile and in part to Argentina. The objective, according to Rabbi Gordon, will be accomplished: the foundation of a new *Judenstaat*, a new Jewish homeland.

Needless to say, all this propaganda is offered in the manifesto with absolute disregard for the truth, although it uses a handful of elements to insinuate its plausibility. For instance, nowhere in the document is it explained exactly who Rabbi Gordon was. And who the other attendees at the meeting were. Still, the document seemed knowledgeable of the fact (one seldom remembered in historical accounts) that, during various meetings of the Zionist Congress, there was mention of establishing a Jewish state in one of three different locations.

The first one was Palestine, the ancient biblical land. This was the choice that the World Zionist Congress would ultimately make. The other two possibilities were Argentina and Uganda. Clearly, the promoters of the Plan Andinia used the information to concoct another chapter, one in which Argentina wasn't entirely abandoned as an option. Instead, ostensibly, it was quietly pursued, especially after the realization that, in the Middle East, Israel was surrounded by Arab enemies devoted to destroying it.

In a bookstore in Puerto Montt I was able to purchase a copy of Walter Beveraggi Allende's book *Del yugo sionista a la Argentina posible: Esquema económico de la dependencia y la liberación argentina* (*From Zionist Oppression to a Possible Argentina: Economic Strategy for Argentina's Dependence and Liberation,* 1976). It is a despicable anti-Semitic rant. Nowodworski had mentioned it to me as being a source of Plan Andinia. "A lawyer, economist, and political thinker with palpable anti-Semitic and anti-Peronist views, he is the plan's architect," he stated. "And its principal propagator. He's your man, Ilan. Through him, you'll get a full picture of the anti-Zionist feeling in Patagonia."

Beveraggi Allende's academic style was rather dry. In order to understand his ideological argument, it was crucial to link two apparently disparate historical trends, belonging to two historical periods—the arrival of thousands of shtetl Jews in Entre Ríos at the end of the nineteenth century and the surreptitious welcome of former Nazi generals to South American countries such as Argentina, Chile, Brazil, Paraguay, and Bolivia after the Second World War.

That a massive Jewish migration to the colonias in the Pampas had taken place between 1880 and 1910 served as evidence to proponents of Plan Andinia that the acquisition of land was a strategy for Jews to control the region. If it had been done in Entre Ríos and Santa Fe by the Jewish Colonization Association on behalf of Baron Hirsch, why couldn't Patagonia be the next step?

My next objective was to find out more about Beveraggi Allende. I wrote to Nowodworski again while Alison and I were in transit from Puerto Montt to Puerto Varas, an idyllic lake town also known as the City of Roses. We stayed at Hotel Bellavista, in Avenida Vicente Pérez Rosales #60, on the shore of Lake Llanquihue.

People in Puerto Varas were warm, convivial, and openhearted. From my hotel window I could see the Osorno Volcano. At one point I traveled to it. I had read about it in the autobiography of the Chilean poet and activist Marjorie Agosín, *A Cross and a Star* (1995), in which Agosín assumes the voice of her mother, Frida, the daughter of European Jewish immigrants. Frida spent the Second World War in the region. Growing up Jewish in the area must have been challenging.

If Puerto Montt had a strong German presence, Puerto Varas almost felt Aryan. It was famous for its German traditions including Kuchen Day, a day devoted to German cakes and other pastries and gateaux. It seemed to me that with the passing of time immigration hadn't given place to full-fledged acculturation. Pockets of anti-Jewish resentment were potentially explosive. Suddenly, it crossed my mind: Patagonia, at least this part of it, was a portal to an alternative Jewish narrative, one on the outskirts of history.

Alison and I went to the Restaurant Casavaldes, which served a superb Argentine *asado*. After dinner I asked a couple sitting next to us about Beveraggi Allende. They didn't know who he was.

"It's an Argentine thing," I said. Although they depended on regular Argentine tourists, in their response I got the sense the couple perceived their neighbors as rogues.

On the way back to Hotel Bellavista we stopped by Café Cassis, a hub that specializes in ice cream, pastries, and chocolates. I told Alison about my correspondence with Nowodworski and about Plan Andinia. She laughed. "Anti-Semites are far more resourceful than Jews," she said. "Coming up with such idea takes ingenuity."

I told her that the idea made me think of Michael Chabon's novel *The Yiddish Policemen's Union* (2007), about the creation of a Jewish state in Alaska. Plan Andinia was somewhat similar: an isolated landscape where Zionism starts from scratch. It also made me think of Philip Roth's *Operation Shylock* (1993), which has a similar premise. Among other things the plot is about how Israel is no longer a viable place for the Jews to live. As a result a diplomatic dialogue is established with Poland to explore the possibility of Israelis relocating there. And *Neuland* (2016), by the Israeli writer Eshkol Nevo who is the grandson of Levi Eshkol, Israel's third prime minister. In Nevo's book, a son searches for his father who decides to create a new Jewish state in Moisés Ville, Entre Ríos, in the true spirit of Theodor Herzl.

"There is something novelistic about Plan Andinia," I said.

Alison replied: "More than novelistic, it is science-fiction. 'Science' because it is about social engineering. And 'fiction' because it is utterly absurd."

That night at the hotel I surfed the Internet for biographical information on Beveraggi Allende. I came across information about more than three decisive decades, between 1944 and 1976. Allende sounded like he was one of the fictional characters straight out of Roberto Bolaño's *Nazi Literature in the Americas.*

The pages said that Beveraggi Allende was born in 1920 in Buenos Aires and studied jurisprudence at the Universidad de Buenos Aires. He went to Harvard for a postgraduate degree in economics, which he completed between 1944 and 1945. Upon his return to Argentina he was a militant in the center-left Partido Laborista, which supported Juan Domingo Perón in the 1946 elections.

Like other intellectuals Beveraggi Allende opposed the party's ideological line, and in response Perón's government detained and tortured him. This didn't convince him to endorse the official ideological line, however. He left for Montevideo and then went to Boston. He stayed there from 1949 to 1950, teaching for a while. Among other things, he worked as a lexicographer, collaborating in the *Diccionario Appleton Revisado Inglés/Español Español/Inglés* (1953).

His views rapidly changed, though. In 1951 he was the first Argentine-born citizen (and the only one so far) to be stripped of his citizenship. Such a measure occasionally happened to immigrants but not to natives. In 1953 with his brother Domingo, he drove across Mexico and made it to Guatemala. In Guatemala he became friends with Ernesto 'Ché' Guevara, among others. Soon after, Beveraggi Allende returned to Boston. Since he didn't have US citizenship, he could lose his teaching job at any point.

With the coup d'état against Perón, Beveraggi Allende's citizenship was restored. He returned to Argentina and taught at the Universidad de Buenos Aires and other institutions. He also became affiliated with the extreme-right nationalist group of the magazine *Azul y Blanco*, edited by Marcelo Sánchez Sorondo and Pedro Curutchet. He shared with them their nationalism and anti-Semitism.

All of them believed there was a Jewish world conspiracy, with New York and Tel Aviv as dual headquarters. And so, with the deepening of an Argentine crisis in 1969, the Plan Andinia came into existence. It was quickly endorsed by other extreme-right Argentine figures.

I wrote another email to Nowodworski. I told him I had purchased Beveraggi Allende's book in Patagonia. I said I was also about to tell him I didn't find much by way of anti-Israel rhetoric in the Chilean Patagonia when in a restaurant on the outskirts I came across an announcement: "No Zionists allowed." The restaurant was closed and I couldn't ask for details.

Nowodworski wrote back saying he remembered a motion in 1971 "to turn October 12 into the day to *hacer patria y matar judíos*, be patriotic and kill Jews." He stated: "Remember, Ilan, in Argentina, October 12 isn't a holiday called *Día del Descubrimiento*, Discovery Day, or *Día de Colón*, Columbus Day, as is the case elsewhere in Latin America. Argentines know it as *Día de la Raza*, Race Day."

I read online that, by the early 1970s, Beveraggi-Allende's views had had an enormous impact in Argentina. Might he himself have been the author of the anonymous *El Plan Andinia y el nuevo estado judío* (*The Andinian Plan and the New Jewish State*)? Its power was like that of Hitler's *Mein Kampf*, *The Protocols of the Elders of Zion*, and other anti-Semitic literature.

"It is essential to remember that the plan isn't exclusive to Argentina," Nowodworski wrote me. "There are also extensions of it in Chile and Paraguay. But the mainstream media in those countries never openly talked about it."

Nowodworski said that things got bad in 1971. There were various attacks perpetrated by Tacuara. They used bombs with tar and other explosives to attack the Argentine Yiddish newspaper *Di Idishe Zaitung*. It was all in response to the Eichmann kidnapping by the Mossad.

"At the time, the Tacuara Nationalist Movement splintered into a number of other organizations. A few ex-Tacuaras founded the Montoneros, a leftist terrorist group. The result was that left and right no longer were distinguishable, which is typical of Argentina. These were small-scale right-wing operations, though. The Montoneros became famous when the group kidnapped and killed the ex-president Aramburu, at the end of May 1970. Beveraggi Allende was close to a number of the Montonero leaders."

Mention of the plan in various media outlets increased. In 1973 a brand new magazine called *Cabildo*—inspired by the Nazi publication *Stürmer*—regularly referred to it. In another message Nowodworski added that, around 1976, while he was studying at the AMIA on Calle Ayacucho every so often one would hear someone shouting outside, "Stop the factories, *judíos de mierda*. Stop making plans to control our Patagonia!" and "The homeland shall be homeland when no Jews remain in it." Nowodworski wrote: "Do you know the 'Lionel Messi' line—'he's the best player in the world and one of the best in Argentina'? Think about it in the context of Argentine anti-Semitism: it is bad that Jews are plotting to take over the world; yet that isn't as bad as their desire to control Argentina."

All this was making me anxious.

"Why are Jews so vehemently hated?" I asked Alison one night.

"It is psychological. People have to find a scapegoat," she replied.

"What do you prefer: to hate or to be hated?"

She laughed.

8.

With Chatwin's *In Patagonia*, Alison and I took a boat south. We traveled to Puerto Natales and onward, stopping in all kinds of sparsely populated villages. The landscape was sublime. As we wandered around, the idea of Plan Andinia grew even more far-fetched. These areas were esthetically pleasing but I couldn't visualize them as a suitable stage for any nationalist revival.

After several weeks we went back to Puerto Varas. One afternoon at Café Cassis in Puerto Varas, she and I came across a young couple. I never asked what their names were. He was a singer and guitar player who delivered his idiosyncratic version of Beatles songs. She served as his booking and publicity agent and went around the tables collecting money.

At one point when he was smoking a cigarette outside and resting between songs, I talked to her. She was Israeli whereas he was Scottish. She said she had finished her army service a few months back and was enjoying her freedom. I asked if she had heard about Plan Andinia.

"Yes," she answered. "A nutty theory in this neck of the woods. A few locals think Israelis are buying Patagonia." She laughed. "Can't you see how rich I am? With the ten-dollar bill you gave me I'll buy an acre near Frutillar, Llanquihue, or Puerto Octay. That's where the new Knesset will be located. And the new Tachana Mercazit? It will be near the Teatro del Lago."

She began to laugh. Then she added: "Do you know about another similar plot called Plan Sefardia?"

"No, I don't."

"Aha . . . It is said to circulate in Costa Rica, where purportedly Jews are intent on creating a new Jewish state. There has been information spread through social media about this plan. Even the winner of the Nobel Peace Prize Arturo Arias, who is Catholic, is said to 'act like a Jew.' Yes, acting like a Jew makes others go crazy. That's why I'm in Patagonia. Israel is enough of a loony house. I've been on two incursions into Gaza. I'm tired of acting out. But I can't escape my fate. Perhaps no one can. Anyway, I don't tell my parents where I am. I don't want them to trace me. At least I'll spend the next few years with a semblance of freedom, although anti-Zionists are convinced my freedom is their demise."

I told the Israeli woman I was looking for Walter Beveraggi Allende's anti-Zionist work. She didn't know about him. "But I'm happy to recommend to you two other Jew haters: Norberto Ceresole and Miguel Serrano."

Ceresole I knew well. I had talked about him with Martha Shiro, my Venezuelan friend in Miami. Serrano, on the other hand, I had never heard of.

On the way back home we stopped in Santiago and stayed at the Hotel Park Lane, Calle Ricardo Lyon #207, in the Providencia neighborhood. In a local bookstore I took the opportunity to buy one of Ceresole's books, *El nacional-judaísmo: Un mesianismo post-sionista* (*The National-Judaism: A Post-Zionist Messianism*, 1997).

Years ago I had written about Ceresole. I thought I remembered his ideological bent. I was wrong. Ceresole's particular mix of nationalism, populism, and anti-Semitism was potent. Delving again into his oeuvre allowed me to connect him with Beveraggi Allende.

Ceresole was best known outside South America as a Holocaust denier. But although his anti-Semitism was clear-cut, his political loyalties weren't always easy to sort out, nor was the time line of his career. Like Beveraggi Allende he embraced the far right and the far left, identifying, for example, with anti-Soviet causes but also spending time in Moscow where he taught and became a member of the Academy of Science.

He opposed the terminology that came from Marxism, Communism, and even the postcolonial theories of Frantz Fanon and Edward Said, for being ineffective in describing the contradictions at the heart of the Spanish-speaking world. He embraced a racialist and religion-filled approach that established a tension between oppressors and oppressed based on ethnic background and theological belief.

This led him to see Latin America as a landscape of missed opportunities. He believed that elites whose tentacles are the pseudo-democratic political parties falsify the region's history, trapping people in a blissful state of ignorance. In his work utopian philosophies such as Marxism are suspect both because they are foreign and because they simply substitute one set of lies for another. What Latin America needs in order to wake from its slumber, Ceresole believed, are charismatic military personalities who are in touch with authentic nationalist feelings. As a result he worked tirelessly to shore up the military and to install charismatic military leaders in three different countries: Peru, Venezuela, and his native Argentina.

He began his career on the left, in Argentina, as a Peronista. Peronism was associated both with left-wing populism and with right-wing fascist groups, including an offshoot of the Tacuara Nationalist Movement.

After Perón died in 1974 Ceresole joined an offshoot of the Trotsky-inspired guerrilla group Ejército Revolucionario del Pueblo (the People's Revolutionary Army), an urban guerrilla group. At that time he made contact with the Cuban government, although he was already developing an acute anti-Communist allergy. When sentiment in Argentina began to turn strongly against Peronism, Ceresole left for Spain. It was in Spain that he became close to neo-Nazi groups.

He was also involved with the Carapintadas, a group of disgruntled army mutineers led by the ultra right-wing lieutenant colonel Aldo Rico. In 1994 Ceresole met Hugo Chávez in Buenos Aires, ostensibly through a mutual contact with the Carapintadas. Years later Ceresole described their initial encounter as enlightening: "When I met Chávez," he declared, "I felt a revelation, that is, I saw a character that somehow I had imagined. . . . I had imagined [him] as a possibility. I had a negative experience with some Argentine military and when I saw Chávez it was, frankly, like a breath of fresh air. I immediately understood his left-wing line, which I didn't like, and therein emerged the fraternal struggle between Chávez and Ceresole."

He was often asked in public if he was an anti-Semite, a fact he only occasionally bothered to deny. His idol, Perón, had harbored Nazi refugees in Argentina, which, for Ceresole, is a country that, in geopolitical parlance, "sits in the periphery of Western Civilization." By his own account, his anti-Semitic stance found its grounding in Buenos Aires in 1992, with the attack on the Israeli Embassy and more prominently in 1994, when the AMIA was the target of a terrorist attack.

After Argentina under pressure considered breaking diplomatic relations with Iran, Ceresole published in the periodical *Amanecer*, on May 29, 1998, an "Open Letter to My Iranian Friends." In his article he quarreled with the view that Iranian intelligence was behind the attack, suggested that breaking off Argentine-Iranian relations was desired by the Jewish lobby in the United States, and claimed that "the fight against the Jewish state should not be limited geographically to the Middle East." Ceresole argued that the Jewish lobby in the United States was in command of *el poder norteamericano*, a North American power force that controlled the entire world. He also stated that Zionism had undergone a metamorphosis "so radical in the last few years that today it is practically something else: a nationalist-religious messianism. The classic dichotomy between religious Judaism and secular Zionism is an equation that belongs to the past."

Embracing a radical Arab cause, Ceresole pointed to the Israeli secret services as the culprits of the AMIA attacks. For him the "Jewish problem" today, not only in Argentina in particular but in the world at large, corresponds, as he argued, "with an internal crisis of the State of Israel." Argentine Jews, among whom he had nurtured strong relationships, became in his imagination a menacing agent. "I suddenly discovered them not as I had known them until then," he wrote. "That is, not as individuals distinct from one another, but rather as elements for whom individuation is impossible, a group united by hatred, and, to use a term that they like, by ire." Ceresole stated that he received death threats from "the internal Jewish-fundamentalist connection" and, as a result, was prompted by his lawyer to leave Argentina.

In quick succession he transformed himself into a spokesperson for anti-Jewish causes. His attention wasn't focused on the Middle Eastern conflict per se (although the topic certainly concerned him) as much as it was on the Jewish influence in the world at large. He published a series of volumes where he described the Holocaust as a myth and painted Israel as a threat.

His line of argument is labyrinthine. Ceresole often contradicts his own abhorrent views, or else he cannibalizes his own previous oeuvre. Overall, he argues that Judaism purports to be a tolerant religion but at its core it eliminates any possibility of dialogue. (By the way, he was critical of Edward Said, for instance, whom he described as "committing a grave mistake" when considering that Palestinians might find in Jews a partner for dialogue.)

He presents the AMIA attack as a by-product of fundamentalist Jewish forces that infiltrated Israel's Shin Bet. He persuades his readers that the actual 1994 tragedy was *un autoatentado*—a self-inflicted wound made by the Argentine Jewish community, especially the ultra-right within that community, with the help of Israeli intelligence in order to showcase the fury of "the so-called enemies" of the Jewish people.

Ceresole goes into detail analyzing the car bomb and the way that Israeli intelligence planted evidence in order for Iran to be accused of plotting the explosion. Intriguingly, he meditates on the question of what happens when Jews kill Jews, using as an example the assassination of Yitzhak Rabin just a year later. His interest is when rabbinical response determines such Jew versus Jew behavior is acceptable.

I was fascinated. The AMIA incident was the ignition in Ceresole's machination of hatred. The sediment of that hatred was buried in mud. Ceresole reasoned that while Argentina was traditionally seen as a European country (that is, Caucasian), the white population was, in essence, a minority. He then claimed that the Jews, using the Bible, colonized Argentina in such a fashion that other ethnic groups, demographically larger, were marginalized.

According to Ceresole, a similar strategy took place in the colonization of the United States and Israel, enabling Jews and their allies to usurp a white minority. Other races, including other Jewish racial populations originating in Spain, were thus pushed aside. The outcome of this Jewish supremacy was the kidnapping of world history and the creation of the Holocaust narrative, which he calls "The Myth," with none other than Elie Wiesel as its foundational father.

That's how Ceresole became a Holocaust denier. He defined the Holocaust as "a destabilizing creation" and the Achilles's heel between Western civilization and the state of Israel. He calls it "the greatest lie ever told by humans since the Old Testament." He praises the German scholar Ernst Nolte, a controversial scholar of Hitler's rise, but subscribes mainly to the ideas of three prominent French Holocaust deniers, whom Ceresole depicted as pals: Roger Garaudy, Paul Rassinnier, and Robert Faurisson.

In June 1995 Ceresole was expelled from Venezuela by the DISIP, Venezuela's secret police, on the grounds that he had been an instigator in Chávez's 1992 failed coup against Carlos Andrés Pérez and that he had links with Arab terrorists. Publicly Ceresole turned the expulsion on its head: he claimed that the expulsion was actually the work of the Israeli Mossad because DISIP and Mossad were partners.

Interestingly, being expelled did nothing to lessen his links to Chávez. When Chávez came to power through a general election in Venezuela in December 1999, Ceresole reemerged as his consultant. It is at this point that Ceresole's anti-Jewish views became tangible in Venezuela.

A couple of weeks after Chávez' election Pynchas Brener, the rabbi of Venezuela's Unión Israelita, published a piece in the newspaper *El Nacional* called "The King Is Naked." In it he linked Chávez's demagoguery to that of Adolf Hitler and Joseph Stalin and expressed hope that things would change sooner rather than later.

Ceresole saw Brener's critique not only as an affront to the emerging leader, whom he believed had redeeming powers to reorganize the infrastructure of Venezuelan society, but also as proof that, as in Argentina, Venezuelan Jews were traitors with whom it was impossible to establish a dialogue. Ceresole responded to Brener's letter by depicting the rabbi as "a prophet of Zionist hatred" and maintaining that Brener's opinion wasn't his alone but represented the Venezuelan Jewish community in its entirety. In his eyes they formed a Zionist wedge in Chávez's land.

Reading about Walter Beveraggi Allende and Norberto Ceresole in Chile left me in a state of profound despondency. Allende promoted Plan Andinia as a tool of Zionist domination. Ceresole argued that the AMIA attack was a hoax. Together they constituted an axis of anti-Semitic ideas in Latin America. That their work was almost unknown outside of a small circle of passionate supporters might be due to its lack of importance. But ignoring such anti-Semitic cells strikes me as dangerous.

9.

One night at Hotel Park Lane I fell deeply asleep and had a nightmare:

I was in a dark humid room that felt like a dungeon. I had been imprisoned there for a crime I couldn't remember. I knew it would be impossible to get the lawyer representing me to make a strong argument in my favor. I resigned myself to a life behind bars.

Outside my cell window I could see an outside ladder that was beyond my reach. Given the position of the ladder, I was forced to look at it almost all the time.

At some point my cell door opened. A guard in his sixties came in. To my surprise he said I would soon be free. In choosing my path, he recommended my best option to be the ladder. "It would get you to the upper floor," he said. "But don't be dismayed. There will be people going up and down the ladder. They are all dead."

"How did they die?" I asked.

"I don't know. In all sorts of ways. Illness. Accidents. Lack of nourishment. Some are adults, others are children. You might recognize a few."

"From where?" I asked.

"From your life."

"People from my life aren't dead . . . ," I said.

At that point, I woke up.

I told Alison about the dream. The first thought she had was that it was a reference to the biblical passage in *Genesis* 28:10–12, popularly known as "Jacob's ladder."

"In Jacob's case, the staircase is understood to be reaching to heaven," she said. "He sees angels walking up and down. But I don't think yours makes those connections. My impression is that your explorations on Jewish hatred are pushing you to the edge. You need to relax."

10.

Unfortunately I couldn't relax as fast as I wished. In Santiago I had ice cream in the Providencia neighborhood with Patricio "Pato" Tapia. He is a journalist who for years wrote in the cultural section of *El Mercurio*, Chile's right-wing newspaper, which, during the military dictatorship, was aligned with General Augusto Pinochet. Tapia, whom I have known for years, is an erudite *conversateur*.

I asked Pato about Bolaño's *Nazi Literature of the Americas*. I told him that before my trip to Patagonia I asked my colleagues if anyone thought Bolaño's list of neo-Nazis in the volume was based on reality. None did. Yet in my travels I had come across characters—despicable ideologues—who could easily have been included in the encyclopedic book.

Pato described Bolaño as astute. "Could there be an undercurrent of hidden meaning in the pages of *Nazi Literature of the Americas*?" He also said that Chile had an ambivalent connection with Bolaño. "He is unquestionably one of its most distinguished sons. But he made his career for the most part abroad. And he is quite critical of Chile in his oeuvre."

The answer reminded me of Cervantes's *Don Quixote*: it is the most Spanish of books, yet when read closely it is obviously anti-Spanish.

Maybe Pato was onto something. Among the most striking aspects of *Nazi Literature in the Americas* is the almost total absence of Jews. And, also, of anti-Semitism. "In my eyes, the fact that Bolaño doesn't feature these topics is startling," I suggested. "It is the equivalent, roughly, of discussing the rainbow without mentioning its colors."

Pato and I then talked about the absence of any tangible discourse in Latin America about the Shoah. The catastrophe is almost never part of the official school curriculum. Movies such as Steven Spielberg's *Schindler's List* (1993) lack context. This is not to say that figures like Anne Frank aren't known. But even she, and others like her, don't command sustained attention.

I mentioned that Alison and I had just come back from Puerto Montt, Puerto Varas, and other places in Patagonia. I said I was struck by the German presence there. He knew quite a bit about the topic, especially in regards to Argentina. Although Chile was also a magnet, between 1885 and the First World War, he said, about three million German immigrants made their way to Argentina alone, settling mostly in the southernmost region of Patagonia. They settled in colonias, just as the Jews did in Entre Ríos and elsewhere, keeping to themselves, using the German language for private and business transactions, and engaging in cultural exchange. German colonization continued unabated until around 1945.

Pato added that German immigration to Argentina has been a prime motor of progress. Just as Jews in the country are described as *rusos*, meaning that people are referred to not by their religious affiliation but by their national background and they are dumped into a single group even when they don't belong to it, a *Deutschargentinier*, a person of German ancestry in the country, might be not only German but also from Austria, Switzerland, France, Poland, Romania, Russia, Hungary, and the former Yugoslavia.

He proceeded to discuss the Rat Route, the Eichmann case, and more recent incidents involving German colonias in southern Chile. In particular he talked about Colonia Dignidad, which was founded in 1961, about 215 miles south of Santiago, by Paul Schäfer, a German lay preacher, a former soldier, and a convicted pedophile who fled Germany for Chile after the Second World War. Over three decades more than thirty thousand boys were raped in the colonia. Schäfer was a nefarious leader. He brainwashed his victims and enforced a vow of secrecy.

"There's a movie called *The Colony* (2015), with Emma Watson, directed by Florian Gallenberger, based on these incidents," Pato stated. "General Augusto Pinochet used Colonia Dignidad as a torture camp. His regime hid weapons in it, including poison gas."

The conversation switched to neo-Nazi rallies. He said that neo-Nazis, known as Tropas Nacistas de Asalto, constituted a movement of approximately twenty thousand members.

"Don't think this is exclusive to Chile, Ilan. They are also active in Argentina, Paraguay, and Bolivia. And, I hasten to add, in the United States."

"Chile has its share. One of their rallies took place in Santiago on April 20, 2009. As a journalist I wanted to attend it. The lead speaker was Miguel Serrano. But something, I forget what, came up that day and I ended up assigned to another story."

Since this was not the first time I had heard the name Miguel Serrano, I asked Pato for details. He said Serrano was a prominent Chilean diplomat who served as his country's ambassador in a number of places. Pato also said he was Chile's most significant neo-Nazi ideologist.

Once we finished our ice cream, Pato and I walked just a few steps to one of the best bookstores in Santiago. "You will find Serrano's books on its shelves," he assured me.

11.

Reading Miguel Serrano's oeuvre opened another window into neo-Nazism in Latin America.

Among the ones I was able to get my hands on was his most important book, *The Hero's Resurrection* (1986). In it Serrano developed his theory, which he called Esoteric Hitlerism. His central argument is that Adolf Hitler wasn't human like the rest of us. Instead, he was an avatar incarnated in human flesh. To explain this, Serrano used elements from Buddhism, Hinduism, and other Oriental philosophies to embrace the concept of the reincarnation of the soul.

In his view Aryan blood comes from outer space. He explains this through a far-fetched vision of evolution. The Cro-Magnon man gave place to his Neanderthal successor, but somewhere along the line fallen angels took over and created supernatural creatures by means of galactic forces.

To develop this view Serrano submerged himself in Cathar mysticism. The Hitler avatar, he states, was primordial. In other words the Führer has metamorphosed into a place, Shambhala, an underground center in Antarctica, where he connected with the hyperborean gods. Hitler's primary reason to exist was his opposition to the Jews who, according to Serrano, represent the forces of evil in the world through the demiurge Jehovah. Throughout time the hyperborean gods might suffer tragic setbacks. But ultimately they shall return with a fleet of UFOs to inaugurate the Fourth Reich.

All this sounded ridiculous to me. Yet hatred, I know, has no obligation to be logical.

In part to make sense of it, I met with Raúl Zurita in a breakfast buffet at the Hotel Park Lane. Zurita is Chile's most important poet. His politics are difficult to pin down. Author of *Zurita* (2011), a magisterial poetic exploration of religious, ideological, and spiritual motifs in his own life, he was in part the inspiration for the protagonist of Roberto Bolaño's novella *Distant Star* (1996), who at one point during the Pinochet dictatorship rents a small airplane in order to write anarchist poetry in the Santiago sky.

Zurita, who won Chile's National Prize of Literature in 2000, knows better than anyone else about the constellation of South American anarchists, anti-Semites, neo-Nazis, and nihilists. Active against the Pinochet dictatorship, he understands how hatred is institutionalized in Chile and Argentina.

I told Zurita about my meeting with Pato Tapia. Since they hadn't been on good terms for some time, he changed the topic. I then said I was interested in finding out more about Miguel Serrano's influence in Chile. When Zurita heard me utter that name, he smiled.

"He was a charlatan," he said. "A Chilean diplomat who died in 2009 at the age of ninety-one, he was infatuated in equal measure with Nazism and Oriental philosophy. Throughout his life, he came up with a concoction not even Bolaño could have invented."

"Is Serrano popular?" I asked.

"Yes, among a small cadre of followers. His visions spring out of the Movimiento Nacional Socialista, created in 1932 by General Díaz Valderrama. After a few years the movement lost steam and was dissolved around 1938. Serrano still caught a glimpse of it, though. He was born into a well-to-do family in Santiago in 1917 and worked as a journalist and diplomat. Between 1953 and 1962 he was Chile's ambassador to India. He held similar posts in Yugoslavia, Romania, Bulgaria, and Austria. Salvador Allende, the socialist president elected by popular vote and sworn in during 1970, immediately dismissed him from the diplomatic service. His dismissal made Serrano sour. He turned his energy to writing books (becoming quite prolific), a bunch of which have been translated into English. He authored a four-volume autobiography called *Memorias de él y yo* (Memoirs of him and me [1996–1999])."

Zurita added that on YouTube there were videos of Serrano at neo-Nazi rallies, giving the Nazi salute, and reading in German.

"You will find also a photograph of Serrano with India's prime minister Jawaharlal Nehru, from Serrano's time as ambassador to India. And a photo with Herman Hesse in Hesse's last residence in Montagnola, Switzerland. Serrano befriended Hesse as well as the pyschoanalyst C. G. Jung, whose work emphasizes the role of a collective unconscious and whose ideology was connected to Nazism. In *El círculo hermético: de Hesse a Jung* (*C. G. Jung and Herman Hesse: A Record of Two Friendships*, 1965), he described his friendship with them."

I told Zurita that in the past month I had been reading the work Walter Beveraggi Allende and Norberto Ceresole.

"Ah, the ugly side of Latin America! Miguel Serrano was different. His Esoteric Hitlerism is truly astounding. I don't know anyone capable of making sense of it. Yet it has an allure among those who believe the Fourth Reich is destined to take place in the Southern Hemisphere."

I pressed him to develop his thought. "If I get any of it, the Fourth Reich represents the return of Hitler's avatar. Its arrival will amount to a destruction of evil, represented by the Jews. Serrano believed it would also give room to a new era for South America, where various dualisms keep the region from finding its center. But please don't panic, Ilan. These are fabulous theories with no footing in reality."

12.

"¿Adónde van los desaparecidos?" Where do the desaparecidos go?

On one of my last stops in Buenos Aires I decided to take a ferry bus to Montevideo, Uruguay, where I stayed for a couple of days. It is some 280 kilometers away from the city on the River Plate, so it took me a while to get there. The name Monsieur Chouchani had come up enough times—starting with my original dream—for me to see the writing on the wall. The words of Shaul, the Talmudic student I met in Buenos Aires, still resonated in my ears: "Maybe you're looking for him without knowing it. He might be your man."

I wanted to see the tomb for myself. It was not only the sole connection I could establish with Monsieur Chouchani. It was also a way to engage with him in spirit in response to the dream I had about my childhood home. My journey was intuitive. I had read all sorts of journalistic pieces, scholarly articles and books about him during my travels. Maybe by being at his resting place I might come to terms with his prohibition.

Uruguay—originally known as Banda Oriental del Uruguay (the eastern bank of the Uruguay), for its location east of the Uruguay River and north of the Río de la Plata River—has the fourth-largest community of Jews in South America after Argentina, Brazil, and Chile. Jewish immigrants to the country came from Hungary, Italy, Germany, Greece, Turkey, and France, among other places. After the Arab-Israeli War of 1948 that followed Israel's declaration of independence, a large group of Ottoman Jews arrived from the Arab world as well.

But many Uruguayan Jews moved to Israel in the second half of the twentieth century. In fact per capita Uruguay is the country from which the most people have made aliyah. The majority emigrated in the 1970s and, affected by an economic crisis, between 1998 and 2003. When I visited Uruguay I was told there were around twenty thousand Jews in the country, mostly in the capital. My impression is that the number is considerably smaller now.

In Montevideo I visited the Comité Central at Río Negro #1308 and the Memorial del Holocausto del Pueblo Judío, a memorial inaugurated in 1994 on the banks of the Río de la Plata, at the Rambla Presidente Wilson, in the neighborhood of Punto Carretas. The memorial is designed as a long structure made of pink granite that symbolizes Jewish history. The structure—which includes a handful of inscriptions, one of them by Elie Wiesel—at one point is interrupted by a sharp break, an allusion to the Holocaust. Nothing to write home about. These are small, parochial sites. (The memorial was vandalized in 2017, about a year after my visit.)

My destination was the Cementerio Municipal, Montevideo's Jewish cemetery between Avenues César Mayo Gutiérrez and Tomás Aldabalde, in the neighborhood of La Paz, not far from the Cantera Cópola. I was looking for Monsieur Chouchani's burial place. People used a variety of names to refer to him. They called him Ben-Chouchan or Shushani. I had heard that the name could be a variation of Mordechai, although this seems improbable.

I read a chapter in Elie Wiesel's book *Legends of Our Time* (1968). Wiesel was forty years old when it was published. In the chapter "The Wandering Jew," he never calls Monsieur Chouchani by name. Yet it is clear he is talking about him.

Wiesel, who won the Nobel Peace Prize, describes Chouchani as mysterious. He met him in Paris after the Second World War. "He popped up everywhere, always unexpectedly, only to disappear a week later, a year later, without leaving any trace." Elsewhere, Wiesel says that "his birthplace was, now Marrakech, now Vilna, then Kishinev, Safed, Calcutta, or Florence. He produced so many proofs, so many details that he managed to be convincing about each place as the final verity. But the next day the edifice would crumble: he would describe, in passing, the enchanting atmosphere of his native town, somewhere in China or Tibet. The vastness of his exaggerations exceeded the level of falsehood: it was a philosophy."

Wiesel also says that "he mastered some 30 ancient and modern languages, including Hindi and Hungarian. His French was poor, his English perfect, and his Yiddish harmonized with the accent of whatever person he was speaking with. The *Vadas* and the *Zohar* he could describe by heart. A wandering Jew, he felt at home in every culture."

Indeed, this was a mysterious figure whose traces I've sought for a long time. I had heard him mentioned by a philosopher from Jerusalem. An acquaintance from Belgium also suggested that I look him up, "since he might hold the clue to some of your journeys."

Years before, I had met Wiesel, who died in 2016, at a lecture he delivered in Northampton, Massachusetts. Unfortunately, I didn't know at the time anything about Monsieur Chouchani. In his book Wiesel maintained that "for three years in Paris I learned from him, in terror." He had paid for Monsieur Chouchani's tombstone in Montevideo.

Indeed, little is known in concrete terms about Monsieur Chouchani, other than the fact that, as a biblical and Talmudic scholar, he might have had one of the most portentous minds of his generation.

I also read about him in the work of Emmanuel Levinas, the French philosopher who was a descendant of the Gaon of Vilna. His *Nine Talmudic Readings* (1990) is a vast book I return to regularly. Levinas states that it was Monsieur Chouchani who inspired him to study the Talmud. He is also evasive about his master, in large part because this was the mystique Monsieur Chouchani built around himself.

Nobody knows his exact name. At times it is argued that he was Hillel Perlmann, a disciple of Rabbi Abraham Isaac Kook, the chief rabbi of British Mandatory Palestine. Otherwise, he is Mordechai Rosenbaum or Rozenblum. Monsieur Chouchani might have been born in Lithuania or in North Africa. Apparently, the year was 1895. He died in 1968. Some theories state that he adopted the Hebrew name Shushani.

Throughout his adulthood he looked like a beggar. I know he traveled to Israel, as there is an article from the newspaper *Ma'ariv*, on October 16, 1952, that describes a group of passengers from France to the Holy Land that includes him. "The man is unkempt in his outward appearance," it read, "dressed in rags, and at first glance you would not give a penny for him. . . . This is a Torah scholar, the likes of which there are not many, who swims like a champion swimmer in the sea of the Talmud, the midrashim, the earliest and later [biblical] commentators and external sciences."

Could he have been from the Ottoman Empire? He memorized Maimonides's *Guide of the Perplexed* (from the twelfth century) in full. He was capable of offering a whole variety of insightful midrashim—hermeneutical commentary, at times using storytelling as a tool—yet was humble to the degree of being self-effacing.

Monsieur Chouchani, people believed, had survived the Holocaust, although, as in other biographical information, alternative anecdotes prevail. An Israeli filmmaker who made a documentary about him shows that at one point, it was said, he was arrested by the Gestapo. He told the Nazi officer in charge that he was Aryan from the Alsace region and a mathematics professor at the University of Strasbourg. The officer responded that he wouldn't be fooled, since in civilian life he himself was a mathematics teacher. Monsieur Chouchani countered by saying that he would offer a mathematical riddle and if the officer could solve it, he should indeed be executed. Soon he was set free and made it to Switzerland.

In another version of the story Monsieur Chouchani was arrested in Paris. The Nazis asked him to undress. When they realized he was circumcised, they prepared to send him to a concentration camp. But he told them he was Muslim. They asked if he knew the Koran. He proceeded to recite various parts with such detail that an imam who was present validated the claim and Monsieur Chouchani was let go.

He died in Montevideo. Apparently on his last Friday night, he was part of a B'nei Akiva seminar where a few Talmudic sources were discussed.

It took me a while to locate the stone. It was made of marble. While a bit dusty the day that I arrived, it was extraordinarily polished. The Hebrew inscription read in part: "The wise Rabbi Chouchani of blessed memory. His birth and his life are sealed in enigma." No dates were given.

I found a few pebbles nearby. I put them on the marble.

A few other visitors were walking at a distance in the graveyard. After a few minutes a young man who looked like a hippie came to where I was. He was wearing heavy glasses and a yarmulke. I didn't ask his name.

He wanted to know if I was visiting the burial ground of a relative. I mentioned Monsieur Chouchani.

"This is his tomb. Was he family?"

"No. For a while now I have felt compelled to come to his resting ground. I'm not sure why."

The man said I wasn't alone. Strangers regularly came to visit Monsieur

Chouchani's tomb. I said that, in some sense, Monsieur Chouchani reminded me of Rabbi Judah Lowe (the Maharal), credited for creating a Golem, a man made of clay or mud. In Prague there is a statue of him with a long curly beard, a long tunic, and a hat in the form of an inverted pot.

"Elie Wiesel set money aside in perpetuity to keep Monsieur Chouchani's tomb clean. Do you think Monsieur Chouchani could have make a Golem, too?" asked the hippie.

I laughed. "I'm a rationalist. But he was known to possess astonishing intellectual powers."

The hippie then told me a story about a rabbinic student who went to meet a rabbinic master.

"Rabbi, my mind ruminates without stop," the student said. "It dwells, it frets, it worries, and it agonizes. I don't know what to do."

The rabbi responded: "What do you ruminate about?"

"About whether everything in the Torah is meaningless."

"What does it matter?"

"What does it matter to me? Nothing else matters."

"Well, if it matters to you that much," the master said, "then you're a devout Jew after all. It is alright for a devout Jew to ruminate. That's what faith is about."

He paused. "I like your Hasidic story," I said. "What do you know about Monsieur Chouchani?"

"There isn't much to know . . ."

"Why not?"

"He didn't leave anything behind. Only his tomb remains. But it has become a shrine. In fact, it might be a portal."

"A portal to what?"

"To heaven."

"In what sense?"

"I don't know. Do you know about *le septième ciel*, the Seventh Heaven? The Jewish heaven is called *shamayim*. It is made up of seven layers. Each of them has different texture, a different consistency. Those in search of meaning, those reaching the Seventh Heaven, are often lost along the way. They find chaos in the previous six heavens. The first one is Malkuth, kingdom. It generally comes in the form of dreams. The second one is built as a land of milk and honey but eventually shows its true worth: a life that is barren, unessential. It is about Yesod, origins. The third is about Tiferet, adornment, that is, about hiding what the true self really is. The fourth is about reaching paradise and about Da'at, knowledge. The fifth is about hatred but also about Binah, understanding. The sixth is about ascendance and also about wisdom, Chokhmah. And the seventh. . . . That's the most perplexing, the most hidden of all hidden stages. It's about almost touching the *Keter*, the regal crown. At that point you get the sense that you've reached the end, that your journey is over. But then you find out you're only at the beginning. Even more cumbersome is the fact that you realize—suddenly, unavoidably—that what you were looking for is altogether different. At that point you become humble, maybe even pure. Your senses become clear. You're finally free to be yourself."

As the hippie spoke I felt I was being granted a much needed dose of meaning. I wanted to ask him lots of questions. I wanted to know if he himself was in the middle of such a journey. I wanted him to explain in more detail what he was saying. But just as he appeared out of nowhere, he disappeared in a blink.

I turned around in all directions: he was gone.

I felt desolate.

I stayed near Monsieur Chouchani's grave.

Why had I come here? I didn't know. He had shown up in my dream. I had disobeyed him, visiting my childhood house in Mexico City. It had been a mistake, though. The feeling I was left with was of fracture.

Maybe it wasn't beginnings that the dream was about but, rather, about the end. Why was Monsieur Chouchani buried in Montevideo? My feeling was that it was an accident. A person's life is ruled by serendipity. After the Holocaust he stayed in Europe—until an inner force took him to Latin America.

Where would I be buried? Although I had lived a large chunk of my life in Mexico, it was no longer my home. My place now was near my immediate family. They would be the ones to ultimately decide.

The cycle of Jewish life is unpredictable. The line you create in your odyssey forms a design whose twists and turns contain the secret of your existence.

Suddenly I could sense that being near Monsieur Chouchani was giving me an inner strength that was rejuvenating. My explorations of the neo-Nazi world had left me depressed. But this place was holy. It refreshed in me a sense of purpose.

The dream I had wasn't about origins, about where one comes from. It was about how those origins define your mission.

I walked toward the exit of the cemetery with a sense of joy I hadn't felt for some time.

6   MAKING ALIYAH

1.

I was at Café Aroma in the Ayalon Mall of Ramat Gan, a city near Tel Aviv, sitting with a couple of friends. The two made their living as translators and interpreters.

Ury Vainsencher is an engineer by training. He was born in Uruguay. In the past Vainsencher had told me he slip-slid into the translation field in 1986. It has been his job ever since. Although he knows other languages, he works almost always with English, Hebrew, and Spanish.

My other friend was Eliezer Nowodworski, and I had been in close touch with him via email while I visited El Once in Buenos Aires, Entre Ríos, Patagonia, and other places in South America. He provided me with information about Plan Andinia and about Walter Beveraggi Allende. Nowodworski once told me that "translators are boring people with interesting lives." He is from Argentina, the grandchild of Samuel Rollansky whose mammoth Judaica library at the IWO in AMIA's building in Buenos Aires was destroyed in the 1994 terrorist attack. Fluent in a panoply of languages he is a generalist with all kinds of information at his fingertips. Jewish life for him is a web of information.

Nowodworski and I have been close for a couple of decades. Years ago, as I was writing *Resurrecting Hebrew* (2008), he accompanied me during a trip in search of his namesake, Eliezer Ben Yehuda, who was credited with orchestrating the revival of Hebrew as a modern language. He went with me to the offices of the Academy of the Hebrew Language, to the street in Jerusalem where Ben Yehuda lived with his family, to a series of conversations I held with philologists, politicians, writers, columnists, and activists, Jewish as well as Palestinian.

I love Israel. I find it jazzy and inspirational, in the way it faces its challenges, and restless in its desire to innovate. Although I often have trouble with its governmental policies I know it is surrounded by enemies. Born out of desperation after the murder of six million Jews in Europe, the country was forced on the Arab dwellers who lived there for centuries, a thorn whose injury is unlikely to heal, at least in the foreseeable future. Yet the six million Jews in Israel today—yes, the same amount as were murdered by the Nazis, in the only place on the globe where Jews are a majority—have coped with adversity through imagination. Israel became modern at an astonishing speed, to the point of vertigo. That vertigo is palpable everywhere one goes.

For some reason, the country reminds me of Julio Cortázar, the masterful Argentine author of *Rayuela* (*Hopscotch*, 1963). A jazz aficionado, he spent his life looking for ways to make literature less rigid, more improvisational. This novel is about a group of South American exiles in Paris in the 1960s, the life they lead, aimless, marked by a nostalgia for the countries they left behind for political reasons. While they know what they want, they let intuition define their days. Israel is also made of exiles—Jews and others uprooted from other parts of the world. The difference is that, for the most part, they don't long to return. When they actually travel around outside their immediate confines, they recognize a condition that is essential to all humans: we are all temporary visitors. Life moves too fast. It is crucial to enjoy every moment as if it is the last one, because death, in whatever form, might suddenly pop up out of nowhere.

Every time I'm in Israel I spend time at theaters, bookstores, galleries, and concerts. Art is vibrant on the streets. In fact it often feels to me as if nowhere on the planet are people more expressive, more tuned in to the obsessions of modernity than they are in Tel Aviv, Haifa, and other cities.

At any rate, this time around I was visiting Israel—and would return to it at least twice—on an altogether different mission: to explore the connections between Israel and Latin America. I wanted to know the nuances in regards to the immigration of Jews from Argentina, Brazil, Mexico, and other countries. How long do Latin American Jews in Israel identify as such? Does this identity disappear with the children of those who made aliyah? What are the countries of provenance for most Latin American Jews in Israel? Do Latin American Jews in Israel tend to live together, like the Russian immigrants who arrived with the fall of the Soviet Union? Are there specific neighborhoods? Cemeteries? And particular professions they went into? What kind of presence overall do the Spanish have in the Israeli population?

For instance, I knew that Latin American *telenovelas* are immensely popular in Israel. They are broadcast in Spanish with Hebrew subtitles. Does their popularity inspire people to learn the Spanish language in full? And how about Latin American Jewish cuisine in Israel? I also knew that Israeli musicians are influenced by salsa, samba, and bossa nova, that Israeli scientists from Argentina, Brazil, and other countries are world famous, and that fútbol from South America is fashionable.

Like Argentina, Israel is a multiethnic society. Immigration has played an enormous role in its development. It is one of the newest nations on the globe. In 1969 Borges wrote, "The oldest of nations / is also the youngest." He failed to add that it is also one of the most beleaguered. Immediately after its creation, in 1948, by a UN resolution the Arab neighbors that surround it swore to throw all the Jews into the Red Sea. In all sorts of ways they have been at it—some more, others less—since then. At the core of the discord is the imposition of borders they feel Western civilization has forced on them throughout modern times.

Israelis and Palestinians have a claim to the same portion of land, more or less. The birth of a Jewish state in the middle of the twentieth century was greeted with enthusiasm by Jews all over the world, especially after the death of six million of their peers during the Holocaust. What the early founders of Zionism failed to acknowledge when opting for Palestine as their choice location because of its biblical history was the local population, whose roots in the land were ancestral.

The Israeli-Palestinian conflict has single-handedly redrawn not only the Middle Eastern map but also Jewish identity in the diaspora and people's loyalties all over the globe. Thirteen countries in Latin America voted at the UN General Assembly in 1947 in favor of establishing a Jewish state in Palestine, including Brazil, Ecuador, and Venezuela. Only Cuba voted against. Six countries abstained: Argentina, Chile, Colombia, El Salvador, Honduras, and Mexico.

Ironically, some of those that abstained have become a source of immigrants to the young nation. According to the historian Judith Elkin in her book *The Jews of Latin America* (1980; rev. 1998), between 1948 and 1986 there were 73,045 people who made aliyah from the Spanish- and Portuguese-speaking Americas. The largest number of these were from Argentina (42,389), although not all of them stayed. She claims that 47,900 Israeli citizens by 1995 were known to have been born in some country of Latin America.

In Spanish, there is a difference between *israelita* and *israelí*, Israelites and Israeli. Over espresso I started by asking Nowodworski to explain that difference to me.

"It was established after 1948," he said. "The first edition of the *Diccionario de la Lengua Española* that includes *israelí* is from 1956. At that point, the Academy stated that the word is derived from *Israel*, meaning it refers to a citizen of the modern state, whereas *israelita* comes from Latin and is connected with 'the people of Israel' in the Bible. It is important that this difference is made because many Israelis don't want to be confused with Israelites and vice versa."

I asked Vainsencher and Nowodworski about the status of Spanish in Israel. Vainsencher said that there probably are between seventy and one hundred thousand Spanish speakers in the country. Most of them came after 1948, when the state became independent. A number of kibbutzim were founded by Jews arriving from South America: Argentina, Uruguay, and Brazil. Then came smaller immigration waves (Vainsencher called them *olitas*, "little waves"). They coincided with military coups and economic and political crises.

He described his formative years in Uruguay. He was raised in a Zionist household. At the age of sixteen he went to Majón Grinberg—an institute created in 1956 in Jerusalem by the education department of the World Zionist Organization to foster a Zionist education among teachers that culminated in massive aliyahs. The experience left a deep impression, and he dreamed of returning for good, which happened about twenty years later.

Vainsencher said the capacity to retain their Latin American Jewish roots varies from family to family. A few create a space (*una colectividad*) that perpetuates their similarities while others seek to erase those similarities by becoming full Israelis. The Tzahal, the Israeli defense forces, serve as an equalizer. Vainsencher served briefly in the army as well, *con algo de pena y por suerte sin nada de gloria*, with some hardship and, fortunately, without any glory. Everyone who passes through it (with the exception of the ultra-orthodox) becomes an Israeli through and through.

Nowodworski jumped right in. He said those making aliyah come mainly for one of two reasons: their attraction for Israel and the uncertainty in their countries of origin. Anti-Semitism has been a constant factor, too. In Argentina, there was the anti-Semitic wave after the Eichmann affair, the coup d'état in 1976, the threat of a return to Peronism in 1983, the possible victory of Duhalde in 1999, and the terrible crisis of 2002–2003. It is important to remember that the uncertainty in one's own country of origin often causes immigrants to return once things become stable. He himself made aliyah as a result of his Zionist education and because there was a feeling of optimism after the peace treaty signed between Menachem Begin and Anwar El-Sadat of Egypt in 1979.

Vainsencher talked about Spanish-language periodicals that are published in Israel. He describes them as "somewhat parochial." He added that the Internet quickly deems those publications irrelevant because people have access to Argentina's *La Nación*, Spain's *El País*, Chile's *El Mercurio*, and so on. "Stories are local but readers are global," he announced. His own family sought to assimilate wholeheartedly into Israeli culture. "I didn't make aliyah to become a member of an ethnic community. I'm Israeli, although I have a linguistic and cultural heritage that doesn't only make me proud but defines me as well."

"My children are an altogether different story," Vainsencher continued. "They came very young. My daughter doesn't have any memories of her life prior the aliyah. My son entered kindergarten in Israel and at the beginning experienced some difficulties. In the end they both assimilated to such a degree that the two now live in the United States. They understand Spanish but they don't read it, and I don't believe the language is part of their identity. My grandchildren are *pequeñitos*, little ones. But it isn't hard to divine how they are likely to see themselves: their ancestors' connection from Latin America won't be more important for them than the narrative of the departure of the Jews from Egypt in Passover Haggadah."

It was Nowodworki's turn now. He described how his own children are interested in *lo latino*, things Hispanic, and that they give the impression of understanding Spanish. "After all," he said, "they listen to my wife and me talk to our respective parents in Spanish and therefore feel some sort of connection, albeit a tenuous one. But my son has been vegetarian since he was three years old. Nobody believes his parents came from Argentina. At the same time I lament the fact that to a large extent I'm the last straw of Yiddish in my family and wasn't able to teach them anything of it."

He emphasized that it was mostly in the kibbutzim and *moshavim*— that is, Israeli towns based on cooperative agricultural labor—where Latin

American Jews settled originally in Israel. "If you have time, Ilan, I will take you to one or two."

I reminded him that in my youth I had lived in a couple of kibbutzim.

"Quite similar," said Nowodworski. "As you know, many of them no longer function as kibbutzim. And no, there aren't cemeteries that are exclusive to a Spanish- or Portuguese-speaking community, although people might end up buried next to kin because of their home address. The vast majority of burials," he explained, "are done in state-run graveyards, according to one's religious beliefs, unless the deceased opted for a private cemetery because of their secular views. This means that in Hedera, for instance, there is an x percentage of Russian immigrants. In the Hedera graveyards, the same percentage will be reflected in those who are buried. But not because of certain burial quotas. It is simply a result of where people chose to live. And while Russians do stick together in Israel, Latin Americans by norm do so less frequently."

I asked Nowodworski if there were rivalries among Latin American Jews in Israel. "Nah," he responded:

> Unless we're talking about fútbol. Are you going to pretend you don't care when Argentina plays Uruguay? In contrast, every so often after an international game, when their national teams are playing, there are confrontations between Ukrainians and Russians that result in injuries. But Latin Americans in Israel consume less alcohol and in general are less serious about these matters. Are you really going to remember the score the morning after? People know it is only a game. Interestingly, lots of fans tune in to watch a classic between Kibbutz Mefalsim (near the Gaza Strip, established in 1949 by a youth movement with immigrants from Argentina and Uruguay) or Kibbutz Or HaNer (created in 1957, in southern Israel, near Sderot, with a majority of Argentine players) "*chicaneando*," the word in Argentine Spanish for dribbling, against Bror Hayil (founded in 1948, also near Sderot, and with a large Brazilian constituency). In the end, though, they all drink beer together.

Nowodworski alerted me to the fact that years ago Florinda Goldberg, a professor at the Hebrew University and an Argentine by birth, along with a colleague, had collected interviews with Latin American Jewish immigrants to Israel with influential lives. He mentioned others as well, like Irene Stoliar, who wrote about the Socialist-Zionist secular youth movement Hashomer Hatzair in Cuba, and Ivonne Lerner, who focuses on the linguistic transition. I took note of these references.

On the topic of language Vainsencher, who knew of my passion for the mix of Spanish and English called Spanglish, added that among native Spanish speakers there is a tendency to switch back and forth between Spanish and Hebrew. "In general, they speak a hybrid tongue and by default chose Hebrew quickly because they find it difficult to use a pure Spanish in a conversation. I suppose this is proof of assimilation, don't you think?" He said that in Israel ethnic humor is accepted. There are frequent jokes about Iraqis, Kurds, Russians, French, and so on. Yet there practically aren't any jokes about Latin American Jews. "I asked a professor who specializes on humor why this is the case. 'I don't know,' he replied. Perhaps because they are like the Poles. There is never anything new to say about them.'"

Nowodworski was less tolerant of this phenomenon. "As a translator, I try not to mix languages. But code-switching is inevitable. Thanks to TV, radio, movies, and the Internet, nowadays it is easy to keep one's own native language. Telenovelas in particular are immensely appealing to some. I tend to be critical of those who forget their mother tongue and also didn't learn the vernacular as they should have. Honestly, the *enano purista*, the purist dwarf, often pops up in me!"

I switched to another topic: Israel's role as a weapons provider. Since the 1970s the country has provided military assistance to a number of Latin American countries, sometimes in the form of arms sales, sometimes as training and strategic advice. A number of the region's dictators became admirers of Israel, including Paraguay's Alfredo Stroessner, Chile's Augusto Pinochet, Nicaragua's Anastasio Somoza, and El Salvador's Roberto D'Aubuisson. It is one of the top five arms-exporting nations in the world.

Vainsencher argued that the defense ministry strictly controls the technology, military services, and who it sells weapons to, and that when it comes to Latin America those items are for national defense and not for internal repression.

He posited that, given the neighbors Israel is surrounded by, its survival depends on its military might. "Without power, we would be devoured in a second by the sharks. We need an independent military manufacturing capability to ensure we have the type and quantity of weapons we need, when we need them. A country of eight million can't support such an industry based solely on local demand—it needs exports. Moreover, one of the components of this might is the capacity to offer military advice and hardware to others."

Nowodworski said he approached this topic with mixed feelings. "Weapons are one of the prime exports for Israel, indeed. Some of the buying governments (in Africa, Asia, and Latin America) are usually among the lowest ranked in terms of civil rights. For instance, we sold weapons to South Africa during their darkest period. History shows that these sales are a great investment in the short term and a loss in the long term, when these items are used against their own citizens, civilians."

It was getting late, and Vainsencher had an appointment elsewhere in Tel Aviv. He said goodbye. Nowodworski and I stayed behind.

We ordered another round of espressos. I told him I had recently been in Buenos Aires and described my experiences exploring El Once and my tracing of Borges's path in the city. He reminded me that Borges visited Israel twice. The first trip was in 1969. It came at the invitation of the first prime minister, David Ben Gurion. In an autobiographical essay written for the *New Yorker* Borges wrote, "along the shores of Galilee, I kept recalling these lines from Shakespeare: 'Over whose acres walk'd those blessed feet, / Which fourteen hundred years ago, were nail'd / For our advantage, on the bitter cross.'"

He wanted to know about my travels through Latin America. He was amused by the fact that I had used S. Anky's *The Enemy at His Pleasure* as my excuse to survey what I described to him in an email as "a landscape where superficially everything looks stable." I told Nowodworski I had reached a point of saturation in my travels. Maybe the correct word is *diffusion*. What I was finding out was illuminating. But at this point the approach felt mechanical. Notebook in hand I would spend a long time in a certain location, soaking up the customs, talking to people, eating their food, visiting far-flung sites, exploring the nuances of the place, all in order to build a weblike picture of Jewish life in Latin America.

I had mixed feelings. I felt egotistical, which is the critique often targeted against anthropology: the anthropologist zooms in, harvests a well of information, and leaves. . . . Thank you very much! At times I even wanted to *tirar la toalla*, throw in the towel, drop my attitude of eyewitness, and somehow find a different point of entry to the reality around me.

"Add the fact that I myself am part of the world I am exploring," I said, "at once the observer and the observed. This means that my impartiality is less a mantra than a façade. It awakens in me a sense of being an imposter."

I told Nowodworski that, on one of my returns home, I was in an antique bookstore in Wellfleet, Cape Cod, when I found a copy of Konstantin Stanislavski's manual *An Actor Prepares* (1936). I reread it with gusto. The legendary Russian theater director—creator of "the method" whereby actors are able to identify the emotions that allow them to model a character ("Love the art in yourself and not yourself in the art," Stanislavski famously said)—liked to talk about "the invisible fourth wall" separating the stage from the audience. In my explorations, I always respected that fourth wall separating me from the people I encountered. But now I was eager to break it down.

"It must not have been easy for Ansky to witness the decay in which he found Volhynia and Podolia. That's what the ethnographer goes through: as he describes the changes before him, he himself undergoes changes." Nowodworski paused. "I don't think anyone else has looked at the Jewish communities of Latin America the way you've been doing it, Ilan. But have people looked at you in return? The teller contains, within himself, the tale."

I said that finding a wealth of information about Plan Andinia had been particularly upsetting. "I didn't know how deep the animosity against Jews in the Patagonia really is. Europe was the theater of the 'Final Solution.' So far there has not been ethnic cleansing in Latin American in connection with the Jews. But there has been plenty of ethnic cleansing for racial reasons. In the Dominican Republic against the Haitians, for example. In Mesoamérica (Mexico and Central America) against the indigenous population. Surely the theoretical apparatus is there for a systematic attack against Jews."

Nowodworki said that I needed to use Stanislavski's fourth wall as a shield. "'You're the one who has gathered the knowledge, Ilan. Others will be in charge of interpreting it."

We decided to meet again a few days later in Jaffa, the southern and oldest part of Tel Aviv. My son Isaiah was flying to Israel to join me. He would be with us, too.

2.

I was staying at the Dan Tel Aviv Hotel, at 99 Hayarkon Street, which is not only comfortable but also quite central.

Next morning I decided to visit Beit Hatfutsot, the Museum of the Jewish People. Dedicated in 1978, it is on the campus of Tel Aviv University. I had been there years ago. I still have mixed feelings about it.

The impression I got this time around was also dissatisfying. The material had clearly been updated, though not enough. I saw panels discussing American Jewish comedians from Groucho Marx to the Borsch Belt in the Catskills to the age of Jerry Seinfeld. There were references to Columbus's New Christian translators, to Jewish pirates in the Caribbean, to the capture of Adolf Eichmann in Buenos Aires, and to Operation Moses, which evacuated Ethiopian Jews from Sudan during a famine that resulted, in part, from a civil war.

Still, as I walked for an hour, the museum's agenda became obvious. Unapologetically, the objective still seemed to be to perceive Zionism as the destination of diaspora Jewish life. Everything led to it! What didn't was either ignored or left unexplored.

That was my impression the first time around, too. There had been mannequins, enormous maps, archeological reconstructions, and so on. The narrative started in biblical times, suggesting that although the characters in the Bible are myths it is possible to use them as anchors to understand the period in which they lived. The same approach was used with the Davidic Kingdom, the destruction of the temples in Jerusalem, the first exile in Babylon, the second exile in Rome, the Talmudic period, La Convivencia in Spain, and onward to the Ashkenaz (the Pale of Settlement), Germany, France, and other European countries, the emergence of Zionism, mass migration to America, the Shoah, and poof! the creation of the Jewish state.

In other words, the restoration of exile was the principal leitmotif. Could Israelites—that is, Jews—make their way back to the land of milk and honey? In what way? How would they justify their return home? For, in the end, there was only one home: Israel. That home was permanent. It was eternal. All other homes were transitory and therefore of secondary importance. Just like in the Museo de la Memoria y los Derechos Humanos in Santiago de Chile, to achieve this Beit Hatfutsot used a gimmick. The architectural structure made visitors descend as the journey through the diasporas evolved, only to conclude with an ascension, an aliyah, that was achieved through an elevator that announced the arrival to *Eretz Israel*. Another way of describing this is through social engineering: ideology begets culture. Or one might simply call it manipulation.

The relationship between Israel and the diaspora is a complex one. True, Zionism is a nineteenth-century movement predicated on the rejection of the diaspora. But Israel has been around for three-quarters of a century. It is time to recognize that the diasporas aren't disappearing. Instead, they remain a vital stage. But Beit Hatfutsot is not interested in nuances. Its mission is to look at Jewish history from one single prism: the triumph of Israel against adversity.

In the past, in general, the information on the Latin America Jewish was rather thin and often erroneous. The same could be said for the present. There was something about Argentina and the Dirty War, about Curaçao, about Brazil and other places this side of the Atlantic. It felt like an afterthought, though.

At some point I saw a brief section on Venta Prieta. As in other parts of the museum, it seemed as if ideology was behind the curatorial drive. Nothing from my experience in this town near Toluca, Mexico, resonated with this museum exhibit. Nor did the voyages I made to meet the Jewish converts in Bello, near Medellín, Colombia. Or what I knew about the so-called Indian Jews in Iquitos, Peru, although they also don't like to identify themselves that way. Or in Belém, on the Brazilian side of the Amazon River. The museum featured Venta Prieta as an *exotic* community. But it never explored it in depth. The message was: Look how fanciful diaspora Jews can become. Yes, they are everywhere. But do they have a goal? Do they simply vegetate in order for the museum to exhibit them as circus creatures?

By the time I made it back out to the street, the juxtaposition of my two visits to Beit Hatfutsot left me upset. For a while, I thought of Jewish life in the United States. Even more than British-mandated Palestine, the United States was the veritable magnet of Ashkenazi and Sephardic immigration at the turn of the twentieth century. Wasn't America the real promised land? In the Beit Hatfutsot exhibit, the United States constitute a major chapter. Still, the information feels skewed, one-sided. I thought of Latin American Jews. America (not Israel) was where a large number moved during the Dirty War and in the financial and political debacles of the 1980s and 1990s. There is no word in Hebrew that is the equivalent of aliyah, because the United States didn't represent an ascent. Instead, for the Latin American Jews it was a longitudinal move: from one diaspora to another. Still, life to a large extent was plentiful there.

I thought of the small enclave within the United States, a minority within the minority, who are Latino Jews. These are people who immigrated to the United States from Argentina, Cuba, Mexico, and elsewhere. I am one of them. I have seen statistics suggesting a total of two hundred thousand perhaps. From my experience I would say that number is disproportionate. Maybe one-third is closer to the truth. Yet that amount is sizable. It constitutes about one-third of the total population of Jews in Latin American countries.

Throughout the decades I have socialized with a large number of them: doctors, lawyers, scholars, therapists, artists, businessmen, teachers, activists, and so on. Based on my experience I'd say they are fighters: restless, engaged, ambitious. In fact, as I looked back on my travels through Jewish Latin America, I realized that many of my companions belonged to this group. Latino Jews concentrate in large southern cities such as Miami, New York, San Francisco, San Diego, Houston, and Los Angeles. Latino Jews are highly educated, part of the American middle, upper-middle, and upper classes. Why wasn't there anything on us Latino Jews at the museum? Maybe because our loyalties are torn: at times we identify as Jews, at other times as Latino, and still at other times as Latino Jews. But Zionism isn't a big story among us.

In fact, it could be said that, in choosing the United States, we opted not to make aliyah. This is certainly true for me. As I told Ury Vainsencher and Eliezer Nowodworski in our conversation a few days ago, in my youth I lived in two kibbutzim, Ma'ale HaHamisha, in the Judean hills in the outskirts of Jerusalem, and Tel-Katzir, in the north, near the Sea of Galilee. I write about my experience in *On Borrowed Words* (2001). For a while I even contemplated becoming an Israeli citizen. But I came to understand that it wasn't for me. The diaspora is my place. I like being a minority. I like living "in dispersion," so to speak. It gives me gravitas. It grants me a voice and a raison d'être.

After my visit to Beit Hatfutsot I had an appointment for lunch with the historian Raanan Rein, who was serving as vice rector of Tel Aviv University. He has taught at the institution since 1991. He is extraordinarily prolific. His research on Argentine and Spanish politics and the integration of Jews to those societies has resulted in a hefty shelf of scholarly books. The Argentine government awarded him the title Commander in the Order of the Liberator San Martin for his contribution to Argentine culture. And the Spanish king Felipe VI awarded him the title Commander in the Order of the Civil Merit. Rosalie Sitman also joined us for about half an hour. She coordinates Spanish courses at Tel Aviv University and has written extensively (among other topics) on Victoria Ocampo, the grande dame of Argentine culture in the first half of the twentieth century. Ocampo edited the journal *Sur*, where Borges published his best work in the 1940s.

The three of us met at the Green House, Tel Aviv University's faculty club. Over prix fixe, I asked them about their careers as Latin Americanists in Israel. Most of their undergraduates are native born. Several were *mochileros*, backpackers who wandered through South America after completing their military service. Many graduate students are of Latin American origin, either born there or children of Spanish-speaking immigrants. A good knowledge of Spanish is a prerequisite for the Latin American history program, which makes the presence of first- or second-generation immigrants more pronounced.

Sitman reflected on her upbringing in Chile and her education at Oxford. She is in her sixties, short, amiable, married with three children. She made aliyah in 1978. I asked her about the role of larger-than-life magazine editors in the shaping of intellectual life in Hispanic civilization and the extent to which their periodicals have been supportive of Jewish causes.

"Ocampo is unique," Sitman stated. "Borges described her as *la mujer más argentina*, the quintessential Argentine woman. She was the daughter of a high-society couple. A French governess taught her French at an early age. She audited Henri Bergson's courses at la Sorbonne but never matriculated because women didn't pursue academic degrees at the time. Still, Ocampo invested her family fortune in culture. It's impossible to think of women editors like her at that time."

I said this was especially true for the Jewish world. In fact, I could only think of a similar example: "Abraham Cahan, the founder of the *Jewish Daily Forward* (in Yiddish, *Forverts*) in New York City, which he edited from 1887 to 1946," I said. "Such was its importance that *Forverts* became synonymous with Ashkenazi immigration to America. Cahan was also a novelist—among others, he wrote *The Rise of David Levinsky*—and a temperate Socialist and Yiddishist."

"Has any other Jewish editor of printed media rivaled his flamboyant personality?" I wondered. "There are plenty of examples in the Spanish-speaking world. For instance, José Ortega y Gasset, the Spanish philosopher, who exerted enormous influence through his journal *Revista de Occidente* more or less simultaneously as Victoria Ocampo did with hers. In retrospect, Ortega y Gasset didn't fare well in ideological terms. At times his views were semi-Fascist, even anti-Semitic. In contrast, Octavio Paz in the monthly *Plural*, which he edited after he returned in 1968 from his years in India where he was a Mexican diplomat—he was truly broad-minded. Irving Howe, Alfred Kazin, Susan Sontag, Daniel Bell, and other New York Jewish intellectuals collaborated in it; and *Vuelta*, the monthly he opened after the Mexican government censored *Plural* and its principal sponsor, the newspaper *Excelsior*." I said that I remembered reading pieces on the literature of the Holocaust in *Vuelta*. "These types of pieces contributed to the perception of Mexico as being a meeting ground for all sorts of cultures. Curiously, Paz, who won the Nobel Prize for Literature in 1990, was, to use one of his own images, 'a philanthropic oger.' He wrote profusely about all sorts of imaginable topics. His complete works run to thirteen bulky volumes. But Jewish themes are completely absent."

Sitman said that in its first epoch from 1931 to 1955 *Sur*, Victoria Ocampo's journal, was a bridge between Argentine culture and the rest of the world. Not only Western civilization but also Indian. Ocampo, who herself had little interest in writing (though she left behind a multivolume autobiography), invited contributions for *Sur* from international authors such as Albert Camus, Pierre Drieu La Rochelle, Roger Caillois, Rabindranath Tagore, and others. "She made Buenos Aires the literary capital of Latin America," Sitman said. We talked about the fact that Igor Stravinsky, André Malraux, Indira Gandhi, and Antoine de Saint Exupéry were Ocampo's recurrent guests. And that Graham Greene dedicated his novel *The Honorary Consul* (1973) to her.

"Jewish life was a topic of interest to Ocampo," Sitman announced. "It was part of her cosmopolitanism, which Borges exemplified." In that sense, *Sur* was evangelical. It promoted a desire to make Argentina the epicenter of cultural life in the Americas. Waldo Frank, the American Jewish novelist and literary critic who lived in New York's Upper West Side and wrote for the *New Yorker* and the *New Republic*, was the son of a wealthy Wall Street attorney. His lifelong interest in Latin America was nurtured through his collaborations in *Sur*. We discussed the stand the magazine took against Nazism, which wasn't de rigueur in Argentine intellectual circles. "Ocampo was the only Latin American writer who attended the Nuremberg Trials in 1946."

Sitman had to leave. I stayed with Rein for a while longer. Born in 1960, he has a boyish look and a demeanor I've come to associate with Israelis: self-assured, laid-back, and a bit cocky. He was born in Israel to a family that has lived there since the 1870s. He knew no Spanish before starting his university studies. We talked about a couple of topics deemed controversial in academic circles. One is the theme of *yeridah*, a Hebrew word meaning "descent." An antonym to aliyah, it refers to Israelis—those born in Latin America, or else their children—who have chosen to return to their original home countries. "It is a reality Israelis tiptoe around," he said. Rein called it *la migración de retorno*, return migration. "It's a shhhh topic. Israel wants to be seen as a trophy. For that reason, 'ascent' is seen as a natural progression. Renouncing Israeli life, even when you keep a double passport—that is, when you're American but you also vote in Israeli elections—is a kind of defeat. Better discussed in private."

I asked him how many Latin American Jews in Israel took part in this return migration. "There is no data," he posited. "My student Adrian Krupnik is doing a doctoral thesis about it. If we start from 1960 onward, I calculate that we're talking about thousands and thousands of people."

What I mostly wanted to hear from Rein was about organized groups of Jewish self-defense in Argentina, another topic that verges on anathema. In 2011 he cowrote with his student Ilan Diner an article based on material found at the Israeli State Archives as well as on extensive interviews with Jewish recruits of paramilitary groups organized by the Argentine Jewish community to defend itself against a growing wave of anti-Semitism.

We talked about how the capture of Adolf Eichmann in Buenos Aires in 1900 had been greeted with a wave of resentment inside Argentina and in neighboring countries. Ultra-right factions such as the Movimiento Nacionalista Tacuara, which emerged among the conservative sectors of the Peronist movement, look at the country's Jews as being allies of Israel, which thus turns them into a target of animosity. In response Jews, with advice from the Israeli government and armed forces, formed entities in the 1960s such as Irgún, Bitajón, and others, designed to protect Jewish interests.

I told him I had been to Calle Garibaldi #6067, in Buenos Aires, where Eichmann was taken away by Mossad agents. At the time, I thought about the anti-Semitic wave it must have generated. I wondered if Argentine Jews had organized.

"These were fists of solidarity," Rein said. "They sent an irrevocable message. To anti-Semites, it was about Jews no longer accepting punches without reaction. And for other Jews, it was about fortifying the social fiber, telling the young to stand up for themselves. Since the Argentine government looked the other way, it was left to the Jewish community to shape up."

However, the situation nearly got out of hand. As he and his student stated in their article: "In late 1963, the Argentine foreign ministry expressed its concern to Israeli diplomats about several matters 'that might disturb relations between the two countries.' Specifically, it referred to 'military training' that Jewish youth were receiving in camps in the province of Buenos Aires under the supervision of Israeli instructors. 'It's a real underground,' said an Argentine official. This concern of Argentine authorities was caused by the formation of Jewish self-defense groups in the Argentine capital, determined to confront the provocations of anti-Semitic, nationalist right-wing bullies." Rein continued: "Diplomatic relations between Argentina and Israel were at risk."

I was fascinated. The question of Jewish self-defense is a complex one. I told Rein that the topic touched me in a personal way because, in the late 1970s in Mexico, I too had been part of such Jewish militias. As in the case of my kibbutz experience, I wrote about this in my memoir *On Borrowed Words*.

In 1982, early during my sophomore year in high school, I was recruited by older friends who were already part of the paramilitary troupe. The invitation was wrapped in mystery. These were trying times for Mexico, I was told. In September, in a crippling economic recession, the country's Presidente José López Portillo had nationalized the banking industry. In trying to find a target to blame for years of inefficient governmental oversight, López Portillo claimed that it was the fault of the upper crust, Mexico's rich elite, who constantly exchanged their pesos for US dollars. He threatened to publicize a list of *sacadólares*, people who invested in dollars saved in remote locations, such as the Caiman Islands. It was stressed that such a list had an abundance of Jewish surnames.

The atmosphere in the country was dangerous. Anti-Semitic rhetoric was on the rise. There were frequent opinion pieces published in newspapers that described Jews as foreign agents. Swastikas and Nazi references showed up in graffiti. One could hear high-pitched anti-Jewish attacks on the radio.

I still remember one of the recruiters saying to me that it was foolish for Mexican Jews to expect protection from the police. If push came to shove, we needed to take the law into our own hands.

I accepted. A few of my friends were already part of the militia.

Training took place late at night. I would drive to Centro Deportivo Israelita, arriving there after ten o'clock. A number of other youths would gather at an agreed location from which we would walk to the training site. The operatives in charge of the organization came about half an hour later. The ones at the top command would always have their faces covered with a white pillow case. As in the case of Argentina, they would speak in Spanish with a heavy Hebrew accent.

In inspirational speeches they would talk about Jewish self-defense in the Warsaw ghetto, among the Vilna *Partisaners*, and in other places at the end of the Second World War. Decades later, Jews in the diaspora remained a fragile minority. We could no longer allow our enemies to treat us as cattle on their way to the slaughterhouse.

Then these operatives left, and we were left with young leaders, many of whom we knew personally. They trained us to perform a variety of acts, such as covering up Nazi-inspired graffiti while no one noticed, or settling scores with a vituperating anti-Semite on his way back from work. The physical exercises we performed were strenuous. A few members also worked with weapons.

I don't know how many of us were part of the endeavor. Was there recruitment done not only in my Jewish school but in others as well? I remember an equal number of boys and girls participating in it, although, if memory serves me well, the chain of command, judging by their voices, was made up exclusively of men.

The morning after a certain operation had been performed, as one of us would show up at school with a black eye or a broken arm, the rest would secretly know not to ask how it happened. To keep the secret was our code of conduct.

I didn't think much of Bitajón while I participated in it. Given the number of relatives of mine who had perished in concentration camps, it made sense to be a member. Only years later, when I was an adult, did it dawn on me that I was involved in an activity that might have verged on illegality.

In retrospect, I can see the experience defined me in profound ways. I'm not proud of everything I did in the Mexican Jewish militia. But as Rein spoke of similar endeavors elsewhere in Latin America, I felt proud.

If not this, I wondered as my conversation with Rein continued, what kind of response should anti-Semitic attacks bring about? Muted stoicism? Rebellion against submissiveness and against a docile attitude of community leadership, characterized by the Hebrew word *shtadlanut*? Revenge?

"There is no single way to face anti-Semitic bullies," he posited, "but being part—and a successful one—of Mexican, Argentine, or Brazilian societies, it is important to develop a local strategy, instead of importing a 'foreign' attitude that might result in your being considered another country's agent."

Anti-Semitism in the Americas is as old as modernity. Its sources have changed over time. In certain periods it has been sponsored by the Catholic Church. In others it has sprung from the dissemination of stereotypes in popular culture, such as *The Protocols of the Elders of Zion* and other propaganda. And anti-Semitism has been linked to Arab nationalist movements as well as left-wing anti-Zionist ideologies. Needless to say, these sources aren't mutually exclusive.

In the history of responses, the Shoah represents a watershed moment. Although there were Jewish revolts in ghettos like those in Vilna and Warsaw as well as organized partisan Jewish militias in various parts of Europe during the Second World War, the conventional image is that, during this period, millions of Jews went to their deaths in a docile, gregarious way, without standing up to their victimizers. Zionism and the creation of the state of Israel in 1948 were direct reactions to this attitude. They promoted an active, vigorous, "masculine" stand that predicated unapologetic assertiveness. Since then, the image of the Israeli army as bold, forceful, even hostile, has been built as a reversal of the stereotype of Jews as being compliant.

Not that things have become less complicated ever since. Zionism was predicated on the premise of the end of the diaspora. Instead, seventy years later, Jewish life outside Israel is vigorous, although it often requires negotiations with the Jewish state on political, economic, religious, and cultural matters in order to find a balance. This is particularly true when it comes to self-defense. Living within sovereign states, Jewish communities (in particular in the Americas, which reach from Canada to Argentina) need to negotiate a delicate line between autonomy and dependence in order to survive. These negotiations are frequently at two levels: vis-à-vis the national state (for example, the United States) and vis-à-vis the Jewish state.

It is possible to talk of three major periods in the history of Jewish self-defense: (1) from the Second World War to the 1970s, which featured strategies by various types of organized Jewish groups against right-wing forces; (2) from the 1980s to the beginning of the twenty-first century, when the enemy was Arab nationalists; and (3) from September 11, 2001, in which the challenge has simultaneously been from two fronts, right-wing groups and Muslim fundamentalists, now linked with left-wing causes portraying Israel as a colonialist nation.

The methods of these Jewish self-defense groups vary greatly from one ecosystem to another. On one hand, in the United States there have been ultranationalist Jewish militias whose purpose is to seek revenge against attacks and, by doing so, reverse the stereotype of diaspora Jews as being helpless. The result has been an ideology infatuated with violence. On the other hand, self-defense groups in Argentina have been orchestrated around the concept of support toward the country's Jewish institutional life as well as toward Israel.

In either case, Israel hasn't been an innocent bystander. It has offered specific organizational advice, and at times its investments have been deeper.

The root of the modern concept of Jewish self-defense is found in the work of Russian Zionist leader Ze'ev Jabotinsky. Founder of the Jewish Legion of the British army during the First World War as well as right-wing Jewish organizations such as Beitar, Ha-Tzohar, and Irgun, he argued that if Jewish life in the diaspora was to continue it required a Jewish paramilitary force capable of avenging anti-Semitic attacks. Jabotinsky once famously stated: "Whoever doesn't repay a blow by a blow is also incapable of repaying a good deed in kind."

After the independence of Israel, in whose foundation Jabotinsky played a major role, his ideas reverberated across continents. In the United States they were incarnated in the ultranationalist ideology of Rabbi Meir Kahane, who, among other things, created the Jewish Defense League in 1968 to "protect Jews against aggressors by whatever means necessary." In contrast, self-defense mechanisms acquired a more muted yet equally powerful strategy in countries such as Argentina, Chile, and Mexico where paramilitary groups coalesced after the kidnapping of former Nazi general Adolf Eichmann in response to a nascent wave of anti-Semitic attacks. Jewish youth organized into organizations like Bitaján, which worked closely with members of the Israeli army in training and intelligence.

I asked Rein if he believed Jewish self-defense groups would be crucial in the twenty-first century. His short answer was yes. However, he insisted on "not doing it alone." Instead, he talked of "the need to develop strategies, based on alliances with other social and ethnic sectors of society, to oppose the growing tide of fundamentalism, racism, xenophobia, and other forms of intolerance."

3.

I said good-bye. I was tired and wanted to return to my hotel. My conversation about self-defense with Raanan Rein reminded me of a verse in the Bible: "But ye shall break down their altars, and dash in pieces their pillars, and ye shall cut down their Asherim" (*Exodus* 34:13). God appears in a cloud to Moses on Mount Sinai, giving him the second set of tablets. This is a divinity that describes itself as gracious, merciful, forgiving, and abundant in goodness. In contrast, Moses portrays the Israelites as stiff-necked, sinful, and even unworthy. Still, God replies that He is making a covenant with them. As long as God is obeyed, "Before all thy people I will do marvels" (*Exodus* 34:10).

The difference of the two partners in this covenant, at least in terms of their portrayal, is striking. As it turns out, both of them are capable of showing another side. On the surface, God will be less benevolent than it appeared at first sight. And the Israelites will rise to the occasion by finding a humility in themselves that isn't visible in the majority of their desert performance.

But then, ipso facto, comes the act of mercilessness. In return for choosing God, the Israelites will be protected from the Amorite, the Canaanite, the Hittite, the Hivite, and the Jebusite. His wrath won't stop there, though: he commands that their altars, their monuments, and their sacred trees be destroyed.

In other words, this is no peaceful or accommodating God. On the contrary, He is uncompromisingly violent. A God striving for revenge.

Shouldn't Jews seek revenge, too? The thought scared me. In my youth I had participated in Bitajón. In other words, I had been part of this attitude. Today would I do the same acts I engaged in? No. I prefer to think of myself as peaceful.

I caught a taxi. As often happens with me, I ended up understanding as much from the driver as from anyone else.

He and I talked in Hebrew for a while. When it became obvious to him that I speak as a foreigner, he asked me where I was from. Mexico, I responded. He quickly switched to Spanish, telling me he was born in Paysandú, on the banks of the Uruguay River that borders Argentina. I asked him how long ago he had made aliyah. He said in 1972. The following year Uruguay's president Juan María Bordaberry suspended civil liberties. By now he felt completely Israeli, although he still thought "South American women were hotter (*son más calientes*) than Israeli women." In a span of about fifteen minutes, he talked to me about his three marriages. The first was to a woman from Ashkelon he preferred not to name. They had two daughters, both of whom live in New York. The second was to a well-rounded Brazilian shiksa from São Paulo, who came to live with him in Tel Aviv but ended up not liking Israel. He still dreamed of her. His third and current wife was from Romania. The taxi driver told me that although he had made a home in Israel, frankly he wished he had remained in Uruguay his entire life.

I thought of Rein's doctoral student writing on Israelis' return immigration to Latin America. The taxi driver would be a suitable person to interview.

"Israel is always on the verge," he murmured in Spanish. "Everyone hates us." Then, suddenly, he seemed to change gears. "But what are we gonna do? Only one thing: *enseñarles quién es el rey, verdá*?" he asked. "Show them who's da king?"

In the state in which I was, after my conversation on Jewish self-defense with Rein and my rambling thoughts on vengeance in the *Book of Exodus*, the statement felt eerie to me. I was unnerved.

That night, when I talked to Nowodworski on the phone and mentioned my talks with Sitman and Rein and my exchange with the taxi driver, I could hear him laughing. "Israel is a rollercoaster," he stated. "In no time it gets your adrenaline running."

4.

A few days later a former student of mine, Benjamin "Benji" Sklar, came for breakfast at the Dan Tel Aviv Hotel. It was a sumptuous buffet, the kind that Israelis know how to throw. We had not seen each other in a couple of years. I was delighted to see him healthy and full of life.

Benji is a Houston native. His mother is from Mexico City, so he grew up hearing Spanish, but he didn't commit to it fully until he was in college. He was wearing his army fatigues. The Tzavah, as the Israeli defense force is called, plays a central role in the nation's culture. Regardless of its actions, which to foreigners are often questionable (especially its incursions into neighboring nations or to Ramallah and other parts of the Occupied Territories), it is thoroughly revered by all segments of society. Strangers stopped by our table to thank him for his service. He smiled at them in response.

In his mid-twenties, Benji is a sweet, bright, sociable, handsome young man. He played football at Amherst. He took a couple of courses with me. Having much in common, we became friends. My impression was that after graduation he would follow a typical route for upper-middle-class men at the college and go into the New York banking industry. These men get a well-rounded liberal arts education (Shakespeare, poststructuralism, the perils of democracy, and so on), which, to a large extent, serves as a platform for their vision to dominate the world financially. But he surprised me early in his senior year when he told me he was contemplating joining the Tzavah. His parents would surely disagree, he said, but he was inclined to do it, because it was "a matter of honor."

He had been raised Jewish. The family was affiliated with a congregation near Rice University while he was growing up. His parents met in law school and have been working together at their own law firm for decades. Benjamin's grandfather, Doctor Jorge Mario Magallón, taught law for over sixty years in Mexico City. And his great-grandfather was a respected governor.

In Hebrew school, Benjamin learned Israeli history and sang Israeli songs. A crucial element in these was the heroism of those who sacrificed themselves for the Jewish state. Then, in his sophomore year as an undergraduate, he lived in Tel Aviv for ten weeks under the auspices of the Birthright program, which, among other things, pays for young Jews in the diaspora to travel to Israel at a formative time in their life. The experiences opened Benjamin's eyes. "If I'm not standing on the border with Lebanon, Gaza, or the West Bank, someone else is . . . and it might be the enemy." He believed he had the physical ability, mental toughness, and ambitious vision needed to become a soldier.

My son Isaiah was with me. He asked Benji what prompted him to join the Israeli army right after college. "It was Wall Street or nothing," he replied. "I believed that any job that wasn't at an investment bank in New York did not make the cut. For me as a college kid, Goldman Sachs was king. Even though I knew nothing about finance, Excel spreadsheets, or how money really worked, I was one of 160 interns out of 17,000 applicants to work in sales-and-trading at Goldman Sachs for the 2013 summer in New York. I would wake up at a quarter to five every morning, make it to the office, and sit at a desk like a chicken with its head cut off. Throughout the summer, I remember staring out the window and thinking to myself, 'There is so much for me to see and do in this world.'"

"Were you scared?" Isaiah wondered.

"No, I wasn't," said Benji. "I wasn't put on this planet to just buy low and sell high. I wanted to flap my wings and fly. I had dreams of jumping out of helicopters and planes, performing risky operations, and wearing a military uniform with honor! Moving to Israel, learning Hebrew, and enlisting in a combat unit could be quite exciting. A while later, I convinced myself that anything else would really be a step backward. Needless to say, my family and friends discouraged me. But my heart was itching. I wanted to do something special, something bigger than myself. . . . I was willing to sacrifice everything to chase that dream. I can say now, after all the sweat, blood, and tears, the days without food and the nights without sleep, that it has been unbelievable. I'm a proud member of the Israeli Paratrooper Brotherhood."

I wanted Benji to explain how the Israeli army introduced him to the country's culture. "The army is a fundamental pillar of Israeli society—like high school in America. If you don't graduate from high school, people think you've missed the boat. The land in Israel was paid for in blood. Through the army, I met ultra-orthodox soldiers as well as Ethiopians, Russians, French, Arabs, Bedouins, and Druze. Israel has countless building blocks. When I lie on the beach in Tel Aviv, I tip my hat to the thousands of soldiers grinding away, suffering so that people can feel safe. You know you're Israeli if you appreciate clean silverware and air-conditioning."

"Have you met other Spanish speakers living in Israel?" I asked.

"I had two other Spanish speakers in my platoon. Out of twenty-five soldiers, three of us spoke Spanish. Freddy was from Peru, Alberto from Madrid. Alberto was well educated. He spoke French, English, and Hebrew. He knew how to move around. Freddy, on the other hand, only spoke Spanish. He had no idea about the world he was living in. The three of us were a little clique. We would yell Spanish *groserías* when we were pissed off and needed to let off steam. And we had each other's back because, even though we weren't best friends, we had a connection on a Latin level that overrode any cultural or socioeconomic differences. Peru, Spain, and Texas are very different, yet everyone smiles when you can say in front of your commander, *No mames, güey!* Don't mess with me!"

"Do you have two citizenships now, US and Israeli? Or is it three, including Mexico?"

"I have two citizenships. I became an Israeli citizen the day I moved to Israel. When I was born my mother did not want me to be a Mexican citizen. She feared I would be an American in Mexico and a Mexican in America."

A couple of years after our conversation in Tel Aviv, we saw each other again in New York. After finishing his service he enrolled in a master's program at Tel Aviv University. But before he started, he was offered a job in Brisbane, Australia, running a drone services business for the oil and gas industry. "I said, 'Goodbye Israel, hello Australia.'" But when he made a pit-stop in Houston on his way to Brisbane, Benji went to war with his father. "How could you not move to New York City and work on Wall Street?" his father asked him. "You're shooting yourself in the foot." And Benji followed his father's advice, though not fully. Rather than working on Wall Street, he fund-raised for lone soldiers in the Israeli Defense Force.

5.

In Jaffa my son Isaiah and I met with Nowodworski. He showed us around. During the British Mandate, Jews were just building Tel Aviv as a modern city. Jaffa was where they congregated. There was also a substantial Christian population there at the time.

Today the population of Muslims is smaller, yet most of the cafés and clothing stores are owned by them. We had Turkish coffee at an Oriental café on one site. Nowodworski described for us the uneasy tension that exists between Jews and Arabs. "We are part of the same country but really we live worlds apart. Things might explode at any time. Arabs in Jaffa have benefited from the Jewish economy. This isn't a terror hub. Yet democracy is a precarious affair."

During our conversation I told Nowodworski about my visit to the grave of Monsieur Chouchani in Montevideo and my quest to understand his role in my dream. I described my encounter with the hippie. I asked Nowodworski why he thought Monsieur Chouchani had become such a legend. He said he had been interested in him for a very short while.

I said that to me there is a bit of Socrates in Monsieur Chouchani. His reputation was based on hearsay. He was perceived as a martyr. He supposedly had a prodigious memory capable of remembering the entire Talmud and quoting it at will. But apparently he left no writings whatsoever, no correspondence, no interviews. All this was a shame. We are unable to decipher him because he only embraced orality, and nothing is known of him in the written form.

We concluded that perhaps he was one of the thirty-six righteous men, the so-called *Lamedvavniks*, whose faith, according to Jewish lore, keeps the world going. While every generation has exactly that number, nobody knows who they are. Maybe I had been in search of one of those Lamedvavnik. The legend has its source in the Book of Proverbs, in the Mishnah (*Tosefta*, Sofa 10:1), and in the Kabbalah, where the number thirty-six refers to the number of saints.

After the Oriental café, we visited the Tabeetha School. Founded in 1863, it is owned by the Church of Scotland and provides education in English for Christians, Jews, and Muslims. While we were wandering through the school, it looked like an institution that could do work toward understanding across religions.

"Lots of organizations have that goal," Nowodworski affirmed. "But can it be achieved?"

He then took us through the Old City to a restaurant specializing in delicious *shakshuka*, a Middle Eastern dish made of eggs and sauce. Isaiah and I each had a different kind.

Isaiah wanted to know to what degree Eastern European food was still eaten in Israel. "It depends," replied Nowodworski. "It reminds too many people of the diaspora. This land was built as a refutation of all that, so many people adopted Middle Eastern cuisine as an expression of their integration into society. But there is a trend of going back to the roots."

That afternoon in Tel Aviv we had tea with Irene Stoliar, who was on the faculty at Bar-Ilan University. Nowodworski had mentioned that she was the author of a study on the youth movement Hashomer Hatzair in Cuba. She had a copy of her book for me.

The conversation ended up being an enlightening lesson on the role played by Jewish youth groups in Latin America as stepping stones toward Israel. I myself had belonged to one: the Jewish Boy Scouts of Mexico.

Stoliar explained how this organization functioned as a source of community building and Zionist recruitment in Havana. Other youth organizations were Maccabi, Betar, and Hanoar. The members of Hashomer Hatzair are called Shomrim. They were active for approximately three decades, from the early 1930s until 1961 when, as a result of Castro's revolution, the majority decided to make aliyah or emigrate to other countries. Stoliar emphasized the role played by youth organizations in Jewish communities all over, including in Latin America. They fostered a cultural identity, at times mixed with religion, although in most cases these organizations were secular. Ideology, on the other hand, played a major role. "Hashomer was an invaluable tool through which Zionism entered the consciousness of young Cuban Jews. A few made aliyah. And even those who didn't ended up shaping their Jewish identity around the existence of the state of Israel."

"Do you think they remained Zionists in their adult life?" I asked.

"Yes," replied Stoliar. "Even when it isn't easy to love Israel for those outside it. And even inside, one's emotions are sometimes turbulent toward it."

She explained that the Shomrim in Havana would gather regularly after school on a weekly basis, sometimes even more frequently. There would be weekend activities such as camping. They would dress in uniform, carry ID cards, talk about the current state of world affairs, study Jewish history from a Zionist perspective, sing songs, cook together, and engage in other forms of social interaction. They would declare a dual loyalty: to Cuba and to Israel. There was a pledge of allegiance, a code of honor, and a manual for a fruitful life that included devotion to the land. Agriculture was stressed. This is important because most Shomrim were urban people, yet the Kibbutz in Israel was presented as a decisive strategy to build a new nation, particularly in an arid climate.

All of us looked at Stoliar's book together. It is full of black-and-white photographs of camp sites, reproductions of ID cards, and other memorabilia.

Isaiah asked me about Hashomer Hatzair in Mexico. I said plenty of my friends were members. The organization served as a mating ground. Many of my acquaintances there ended up getting married. I said that a substantial number ended up moving to Israel.

"Were the boy scouts Zionists?"

"Not particularly," I responded. "Yet Israel was in our consciousness. I remember that our pledge of allegiance was in Hebrew." I recited it for him.

He wanted to know what happened in my youth if you spoke against the Israeli government.

"Nothing," I responded. "But you have to remember that by 1980, when I entered college, Israel was seen only as a do-gooder. This was after the Yom Kippur War but before the 1982 invasion of Lebanon. The tide was changing, but that change hadn't quite reached Mexican Jewish youth organizations yet. Grandmothers still came back from Israel with little glass bottles containing sand from the Holy Land. Buying yourself a *dubon* (an Israeli army winter jacket) was cool. As a sign of heartfelt solidarity people used *kova tembel* (kibbutz hats). And kitschy Israeli songs like "Yerushalaim shel

Zahav" (Jerusalem of gold) as well as lyrics by Naomi Shemer and Chava Alberstein were sung by Jewish choirs throughout the diaspora. All this changed dramatically in the 1980s."

From Isaiah's gestures I saw that the past in which Israel was an all-do-gooder seemed almost incomprehensible.

6.

I was scheduled to be in Jerusalem for several appointments. Isaiah stayed in Tel Aviv. He came along later.

I took a bus from the Arlozorov station to Jerusalem's Tachana Mercazit, the central terminal. It took forty-five minutes. Not too far from me were a father, a mother, and their five-year-old daughter. I vividly remember the girl's face as she passed by near me when the passengers were still finding their places. She smiled at me in an overly theatrical way, to the point that I was puzzled.

The family spoke Spanish. I tried identifying their accent. Maybe Peruvian. Or Guatemalan. The father almost from the very start took out a tablet. I could hear the sound the movie made until his wife asked him to quiet it down.

A little while after the bus starting moving, the daughter began to cry. It took a while for the mother to calm her down.

I made small talk with the mother. She told me they were from Colombia on their way to a Bar Mitzvah in Haifa. Currently they lived in Miami, where a considerable portion of the Colombian Jewish community had moved in the 1980s at the height of the drug war.

I asked her where her family was from, since there are four major Jewish centers in Colombia: Barranquilla, Medellín, Cali, and Bogotá.

She responded Barranquilla. There were about six hundred Jews there, she said. "It's a small community. We keep to ourselves. Mostly secular business people. You know that Colombia is really two countries, right? East and West. East is marked by the Caribbean spirit. And Bogotá. People there are called *cachacos*. Have you been to Cartagena?"

I told her I was a fan of *One Hundred Years of Solitude*. Years ago I had written a biography of Gabriel García Márquez's first forty years, up until the moment he wrote his novel and when it was translated into English in 1970. It's a gorgeous expression of Colombia's Caribbeanness.

I asked her if she knew of the Indian Jews in the community of Bello, not far from Medellín.

"They're a fraud," she responded. "Why convert to Judaism? It makes no sense. You're always a target of anti-Semitism. Why would anyone want to be a Jew? Unless, of course, you're born one, in which case *hay que cargar la cruz*, you must carry the cross."

Feeling comfortable in our exchange, I inquired if Jews were involved with the drug kingpin Pablo Escobar. I knew this was officially the case.

"Ese es un cuento chino," she responded. "It's a tall tale." She said Jews always kept themselves out of the drug trade.

Next to us, an ultra-Orthodox Jew stood up to pray.

And about fifteen minutes later, a portion of the people were already asleep, and I heard a sudden shriek.

"¡Ayuda! Por favor, auxilio . . ." The mother was shouting. "Help! Someone please help!" I turned around. She and her husband were attending to their daughter.

"Help!" said the father in English, with a heavy accent.

There was a commotion. The mother was crying. Words were coming out in Spanish, English, and Spanglish.

Two soldiers began attending to the girl as people became agitated. A couple of passengers proceeded to the area where the family was sitting. One of them was a doctor. She looked for the girl's life signs, then made a positive gesture.

At this point, the ultra-Orthodox man asked me if I was related to the family.

"No," I replied.

I became restless. My mind became set on the possibility that the girl's situation wasn't a medical emergency after all but a terrorist attack. I visualized a couple of Arab-looking men stabbing the driver and taking control of the bus. My heart was beating fast. Was I in a terrorist attack like the dozens I had seen on TV?

It was all in my mind, though. I looked around: everyone was perfectly calm. Fear was provoking in me an apocalyptic vision.

When the bus finally arrived in Jerusalem, medical personnel jumped in before anyone was allowed to leave. The girl was taken out on a stretcher. The father followed nearby, and then the mother who, as she was about to get off the bus, looked at me in distress.

I felt her pain. I was also relieved the incident hadn't involved terrorism.

7.

A few hours later I was in Mea Shearim, one of the oldest neighborhoods in Jerusalem, which is mostly populated by ultra-orthodox—that is, Haredi

Jews. They were dressed up in costumes. My visit to Israel coincided with the festival of Purim, which invokes the reckoning narrated in the Book of Esther about a Persian king, Ahasueros, and his evil minister, Haman, who was intent on killing all the Jews in the kingdom. The plan was foiled by Mordecai and his niece and adopted daughter, Esther, who eventually became queen of Persia. While the historical nature of these events has long been disputed, Purim is celebrated with such enthusiasm, issues of accuracy become secondary.

To their long beards the male Jews around me added fake white goatees, whiskers, and other stubble. They wore enormous Disney-like triangular hats in the form of a *hamentash*, a fill-pocket pastry that is the traditional Purim food and that Haman supposedly wore. Little girls were dressed in tutus. Walking around Machane Yehuda Market and then onto Shikun Habad, I was inspired by the joyful atmosphere. I was also taken by its subdued, dignified nonconsumerism.

I couldn't avoid comparing the costumes to Halloween. The celebration is connected with a Christian holiday dedicated to remembering the dead. The roots might be Celtic and, therefore, pagan. At any rate the day has become commercialized to such a degree, its origins are now foggy. Humor is at its core. In that sense, it is now closer to the carnival than to All Hallows' Eve ("hallows" means saints), which is when, around the twelfth century, parishioners wandered through European streets, which reminded Christians of the souls in Purgatory.

In the United States, for young and old, Halloween is an excuse to dress up like gothic- and death-connected popular characters: witches and demons, Draculas and Frankensteins. It has evolved into an opportunity for satirical depictions of the international leaders du jour, such as Donald Trump, Hillary Clinton, Pope Francis, Kim Jung-un, Fidel Castro, et al. These portrayals are irreverent, even buffoonish.

In comparison there was something at once disheartening and reassuring about the ultra-Orthodox. Their Hamans were flat, monotonous, uncreative. Yet their unpretentious festivity serves as an opportunity to appreciate their isolation from world affairs. The festival's dismissal of secularism with its multiple gods as dangerous is admirable. Seventy-five years after the Shoah, it has granted them continuity.

At one point I came across a group frantically singing and dancing in jubilation on the street. Every time the word *Haman* was pronounced, *graggers* (Yiddish wooden noise-makers) made a hullabaloo. For a few minutes I imagined myself joining the Hasidim, not only in their Purim activities but in their way of life. Deep inside I've always nurtured a quiet envy of the ultra-Orthodox. That envy is somewhat connected with the idea that ignorance is bliss. They don't have to deal with fashion. They don't have to make daily decisions based on a surplus of choices. They don't have doubt as a core emotion imbuing everything they do. Their life is based on absolute conviction.

I know I'll never embrace such absolutism, simply because I'm a skeptic at heart. Which doesn't stop me from wishing I did. Would things be simpler?

A couple of Haredi women passed by near me. I tried looking them in the eye but they avoided my eyes. Well, maybe bliss is underrated. What would I do without daily eye-to-eye contact?

8.

In Jerusalem, while Isaiah visited the Wailing Wall with the daughter of an acquaintance, I talked with Florinda Goldberg, who teaches in the Department of Romance and Latin American Studies at the Hebrew University, in Mount Scopus. Among other works she is the author of studies on the Argentine Jewish poet Alejandra Pizarnik, whose path is similar to that of Sylvia Plath. She lived a tormented life, which ended very early with suicide.

Goldberg and I had corresponded with each other in the past. Nowodworski reintroduced us. Born in 1943 and having made aliyah from Argentina in 1977, she specializes on the topic of aliyah from Latin America. Years ago she edited an anthology, sponsored by the organization of Latin American *olim* (immigrants). It featured archival material, publications, and interviews. The objective was to map out this wave of immigration.

When I asked her about the number of Latin American Jews in Israel, Goldberg responded that the government periodically offers statistics on the matter. But she said they were based on the country of birth and not on self-identification.

"Let me give you an example of my own family," suggested Goldberg. "My mother was born in Poland and therefore doesn't count, even though prior to emigrating to Israel she lived more than forty years in Argentina. My children were born in Buenos Aires and thus they count, but they arrived in Israel at the ages of three and six. Culturally, they are first and foremost Israelis. If you allow for any give-and-take between these two categories, perhaps the official numbers aren't exact."

She talked of how assimilation was almost total, although food remains a feature of the "second culture," and to a lesser extent language does too. "Argentines often identify themselves through their Spanish (e.g., Argentine) accent in Hebrew," Goldberg affirmed. "Also, Jewish writers from Latin America who made aliyah almost always write in Spanish, not in Hebrew."

She mentions that her children were Israelis but felt *la argentinidad* as part of their identity. Her grandchildren did not, in part because their other parent was Israeli.

I told Goldberg that Nowodworski had mentioned a couple of kibbutzim that identify as either Argentine or Brazilian. She mentioned approximately seventy where Latin Americans lived at some point. Of the seventy the majority had an Argentine Jewish population, since this was the largest migration and among the most deeply Zionist. She said that, in this regard, the most famous kibbutzim were Mefalsim, Gaash, Ein Hashloshah, Or Haner, and Bajan. "Bror Hail is Brazilian, although it also has a strong Argentine presence." Goldberg talked of the Latin American moshavim, which she said were seven, of which she mentioned four: Kojav Mijael, Mevo Betar, Nir Tzvi (originally known as Kfar Arguentina, or Argentine village), and Tzur Natan.

"During the first decades of aliyah from Latin America, until the late 1960s, the kibbutz and moshavim were the primary destination for immigrants," she affirmed. "After that, cities became a magnet. And people who had lived in kibbutz and moshavin moved to urban centers as well. In the 1970s there were some twenty-two thousand Latin American Jews in Israeli cities and some eight thousand in the rural settlements."

Goldberg told me that scores of immigrants from Argentina came from the agricultural colonies sponsored by Baron Hirsch. Then she surprised me with the fact that a whopping 25 percent of Uruguay's entire Jewish population made aliyah.

"Has Israel ever gone through a period of anti-Hispanism of any kind?" I asked.

"On the contrary," responded Goldberg. "There is enormous interest—and empathy—for all things Hispanic: food, literature, music."

9.

Back in Tel Aviv, Isaiah, Nowodworski, and I were invited for dinner to the house of Ivonne Lerner, who was a docent at the Instituto Cervantes.

In a taxi I asked Nowodworski if he had heard about the *cagots*.

He had. "They lived in the French corridor from northwestern Spain to the English Channel. Other names for them are *gahets* and *gafets* (Gascony), *capots* (Languedoc and Anjou) *agotac* or *agotes* (Basque country), and *caqueux* and *cacous* (Brittany). Unlike the Jews, about whom there is an overabundance of literature, little is known about them. They were neither a religious sect nor a political group. In some historical documents they are described according to their deformed features: webbed hands and feet, baby hair on adult heads, ingrown nails, missing earlobes, yellowish skin, and so on, although these might be more the product of mythology. It was said they were incarnations of the devil itself."

"Just like us," I said. "I read once that, to distinguish them, the *cagots* were asked to use specially made doors in buildings. Some folktales suggested their descendants were dogs. Others argued they were from a line of Visigoths defeated by King Clovis in the sixth century. And another theory posited that they were the first to convert to Christianity in Gaul."

I had also seen the word *chrétiens* ("cretins" in English) as a derivation from *cagot*.

"Maybe," said Nowodworski.

"What strikes me as extraordinary is how little is left of them, and about them. They were a most persecuted people. Their existence at once proves and disproves Sartre's thesis. On the one hand they are yet another example of a group that is ostracized for no other reason than to serve as scapegoat. The rule is simple and straightforward: everyone needs an enemy. On the other hand the animosity the *cagots* inspired doesn't appear to have given them any special traction in terms of survival skills. It was the French Revolution, with its principles of *liberté, égalité, fraternité* that gave the *cagots* what others also received: equal rights. In time this meant acculturation to modern society. In other words they became indistinguishable from everyone else. Why didn't the Jews become like everyone else?"

Nowodworski laughed. "Would you really want that, Ilan?"

Also an Argentine, though born in the United States, Lerner is married to an Israeli. They have two children. She is fascinated with languages. In our conversation, she described her journey often emphasizing the way different languages shaped her worldview.

We ate al fresco. She made pasta, chicken, and salad.

While Isaiah talked with Lerner's daughter who was home on leave from the army, I asked Lerner about her decision to immigrate to Israel. "I was born in the United States, in a small town in Illinois, where my parents opted to live for a few years. That's where I spent my first eighteen months. The family returned to Argentina afterward."

"In Argentina, I wasn't sent to Jewish school. That is, I didn't learn Hebrew. I also didn't have a Bat Mitzvah. I don't regret it. That's the advantage of growing up in Argentina, in contrast with other Latin American countries where the Jewish communities are smaller and have a more closed mindset. It is so big in Argentina you can choose what kind of Jew you want to be. I think it's crucial to interact with people of other backgrounds and have friends of all religions."

At the age of twenty-four Lerner and her Israeli husband moved to New York, where they lived with three other Israelis. Interacting with them was her introduction to Hebrew. "A week after arriving in Israel, where we decided to settle, I started my Ulpan (Hebrew training school). I quickly was able to communicate in Hebrew, in spite of my heavy Argentine accent, which I still carry today, three decades after immigration." She stated that she had never made aliyah. "I just came to Israel *y me fui quedando*, and I just prolonged my stay," she said. "I'm not a Zionist, nor do I come from a Zionist family. I came to Israel because my husband—then my boyfriend—was Israeli. I arrived after having lived for five months in the United States. Truth is, I wasn't happy about it. It was tough to try to adapt to two different countries in such a short time."

Lerner invoked a popular Spanish song: "No soy de aquí ni soy de allá" (I'm neither from here nor from there). "That's every immigrant's dilemma! This is clear in one's language. I neither speak nor write like my childhood friends and in general we have a foreign accent in the country of residence that places us rather quickly. If I have to define who I am, I will say I'm an Argentine who lives in Israel. I have a lot in common with other Argentines dispersed throughout the world and with my own life for twenty-five years in Buenos Aires. My adult life is interwoven with Israel in the last three decades, yet I'm an Argentine."

"A family's identity is built up through habits, traditions, cuisine, humor, and the way emotions are expressed," in Lerner's view. "With regard to food, in Israel it isn't common for families to have dinner together every night, and in my house dinner is essential, an event I defend to death." (This happens to me but with differences I notice here. Given the contrast, I fight for them tooth and nail: food, manners, and so on.) "Not only is dinner sacred. I try to make *comida casera*, home-cooked food. I know my daughters with keep that habit."

Nowodworski joined us in the conversation, as did Isaiah. Someone mentioned the Israeli sales of weapons in Latin America. I had discussed this in the café with Nowodworski and Ury Vainsencher.

At this point Lerner described Israel as a money-driven country. "If there's money to be made, the opportunity won't be missed. There are no scruples. Just as Israel collaborated with South Africa during apartheid, it has been close to several Latin American dictatorships. In the case of Argentina during the dictatorship, on the one hand Israel was looking to save Jews who were in danger and achieved its goals, and on the other hand it sold weapons and uniforms (for instance, *dubonim*, a type of Israeli military jacket used during the Falkland War) to those dictatorships. Nowadays, with the wave of global terrorism, Israel is the sought-after advisor. Yet no one questions that role."

I switched the topic back to language. Lerner described the Spanish spoken by many Latin American Jews in Israel was "impoverished." "My hypothesis is that Hebrew exercises in Israel a higher penetration (because of its ideological and historical load) compared to other countries defined by immigration. Only a month after arrival, an immigrant will say *ótobus* and *universita* instead of *autobús* and *universidad*." Lerner affirmed: "I don't ask people to say *granja colectiva*, collective farm, instead of kibbutz. That would be ridiculous. But if there is a native Spanish word for something, why not use it? For me all this is quite puzzling."

"Do you speak both Hebrew and Spanish at home?" I wondered.

"Yes, mine is a bilingual household. I speak to my children in both languages. That's a feature of immigrants like me who came to Israel in the 1980s. I don't allow my children not to know the Spanish word for *mother*. Thanks to this and to the frequent guests we have from Argentina, and thanks to our trips there, they both speak Spanish at a very high level— though with a Hebrew accent—and feel that it is an inseparable part of their identity. At family meals, whenever there is a non-Spanish-speaking guest, we all have to make an effort to speak only in Hebrew. We'll see what happens with the grandchildren. My oldest daughter has already told me she isn't planning to speak to her own children in Spanish because it isn't natural to her, except for a few untranslatable words and the ubiquitous *sana sana colita de rana* ("Heal, heal, little frog's tail") when they're injured. As for me, I plan on speaking Spanish to the grandchildren."

I asked about telenovelas. "They've been a powerful source of linguistic sustenance in Israel, both for those who want to learn Spanish from scratch and for those who want to maintain it. About the latter, it is through telenovelas that they have appreciated again a treasure they have in themselves and might have overlooked because of the prevailing melting pot ideology. It's astonishing what the interest that others might have in something of yours all of a sudden increases its value in your own eyes—and ears."

10.

During our trip Isaiah and I frequently talked about Jewish-Palestinian relations. The topic touched close to home. Back in the United States he was dating a girl whose parents were Syrian immigrants.

While we were relaxing one day at the hotel, in our conversations Isaiah asked me at one point if I had any Arab friends in Mexico when I was growing up. I couldn't remember any. In fact I couldn't remember any interaction between Arabs and Jews in Mexico, although I knew there was a solid community of Syrians, Lebanese, and other Arabs. On the way to school my school bus often passed near the Centro Libanés, the Mexico's Lebanese Cultural Center. Yet I had never been in there. Nor could I remember any young Lebanese being invited to CDI, the Jewish sports center.

"My feeling is that the relationship between Arabs and Jews in Latin America is seldom explored," I added.

Yet as soon as I returned home, I found out that, outside of the Arab world, the largest Arab diaspora anywhere on the globe is in Latin America. There are between seventeen million and thirty million altogether, which is about twenty times the number of Jews in the region. Some areas in Latin America had received a bigger number of Arab immigrants than others. I read at some point that one out of ten people in São Paulo, Rio Grande do Sul, in Brazil, claimed to have their origins in the Middle East. Actually, the population of Lebanese descent in Brazil is larger than the entire population of Lebanon.

Likewise, Colombia has over three million, the majority also from Lebanon and from Syria, including the singer Shakira. There are more Palestinians in Chile than anywhere else except the Occupied Territories. And the numbers in Argentina are equally large. Argentina has close to five million. This means that for every Argentine Jew there are forty Argentine Arabs.

Why didn't I know any of this before? In New York City I spoke with Naief Yehya, a Mexican intellectual best known for his explorations into pornography. A Druse, he has been living in Brooklyn since 1991. He is married to a Puerto Rican and has two children.

"This is a huge topic, Ilan," he said. "Be careful because *te puedes ahogar en un vaso de agua*." The expression is cute. It really means "a tempest in a teapot." But Yehya used it with another meaning, to convey the sense that the topic could swallow me whole.

And then, after I explained that I was coming close to concluding a series of travels throughout Jewish Latin America in the span of four years, he used another popular expression: *La manzana de la discordia*, the bone of contention. The expression in Spanish, I believe, is about Greek mythology, a reference to Paris awarding the golden apple, inscribed "to the fairest of all, Aphrodite."

"Mexico, your own Mexico, has about a million Arabs," he affirmed. "This minority came with the crumbling of the Ottoman Empire in the 1920s."

Yehya's father was eighteen when he arrived in Mexico from Syria. He and other Arab immigrants were called Turks, a term they thoroughly disliked. Yehya's mother is Lebanese. She was born in Mexico. He said his parents' generation wanted to assimilate at all costs. His father, upon arriving in Mexico, refused to speak for an entire year. He didn't want to be a Syrian in Mexico. He wanted to be Mexican. His silence was a way to recalibrate: to learn the language and along the way a new identity.

As a result Yehya doesn't speak Arabic. He can understand a few words. But Arabic isn't a homogenized language. It is used differently throughout the Arab world. Lebanon and Syria use a similar language. But the further you travel into the Arab peninsula, the more heterogeneous the language becomes.

Yehya remembers his parents' generation speaking a mix of Spanish and Arabic. The hodgepodge didn't have a name. "Basically, it was a language created by the absence of a complete vocabulary and laws of grammar. But also there was some nostalgia and a need of having some kind of private dialect that gave a sense of belonging, maybe a notion of identity."

Mexicans saw him as different. He doesn't remember being excluded in middle and high school. But at university he was often distinguished from the rest. He felt as a minority in Mexico.

As a Druse he is a minority within a minority. He remembers a proportion of fifty-fifty between Christian and Muslim Arabs. The Druse were always the smallest percentage.

His forebears didn't see religion as central. Instead, it was politics that mattered to them. His father and uncles were Marxists.

Arab immigrants arrived in Yucatán, Veracruz, Nayarit, Tamaulipas, Nuevo León, Sinaloa, and other states. The trades were mostly business.

The influence of Arab Mexicans is felt in a number of spheres, including cuisine. One of its features is *tacos al pastor*, a type of taco in which the meat is grilled in a vertical rotisserie, as in the Turkish kebab, the Greek gyro, and the Arab *shawarma*.

Arab Mexicans include one of the richest men on the globe, Carlos Slim. And also one of the country's best poets, Jaime Sabines.

Yehya's oldest son, a college student, went through a period in which he identified with his Arab ancestry. It was a form of rebellion. His first day of classes had been on 9/11. The impact of that day, the way Americans stereotyped Arabs, became an essential feature of his personality. "The war against terror turned every Muslim into a possible terrorist," Yehya argued. "It created an atmosphere of fear, resentment, and intimidation."

When I talked to him a few months later, he added: "All these elements became much worse with Donald Trump in the White House. He verbalized the usual racist and paranoia innuendo, becoming the voice of those who have radicalized their opinions about Arabs and Mexicans as a threat. For my family, the new reality became sordid."

Lebanese Christians had an easy time assimilating. In no time they went from being Maronites to *Guadalupanos*, followers of Mexico's patron saint, the Virgin of Guadalupe.

I asked Yehya what he felt toward Jews. "It's a vague, impossible question," he answered. "Living in New York as I do, at a personal level I don't think of 'the Jews' as a unified entity. It's an incredibly diverse group. In fact, I feel utterly incapable of pointing at something that unifies them."

He remembered a harmonious relationship with his Mexican Jewish counterparts. He went to school in Polanco, in the northern part of Mexico City, first at American schools and later at the French *lycée*. "This area was heavily populated by Jews," he reminisced. "Half of my classmates were Jews and half were Christian. I was usually the most politicized kid in my class. This means that I was very aware of the Middle Eastern conflict while most of my friends seemed oblivious to it. Still, as a whole there were never any issues. Some Jews preferred to socialize in cliques, although I remember visiting Jewish friends in their own houses and having them at my own home also."

He paused: "At any rate, the Palestinian-Israeli conflict ended up pushing Jewish-Arab relations over the edge." Israel's War of Independence of 1948 pushed many Arabs to leave Lebanon. Scores of them moved to Mexico, arriving in Veracruz. In the 1930s Arabs made up less than 5 percent of the total immigrant population. Yet they contributed with half of the immigrant economic activity."

"In downtown Mexico City, Jews and Arabs who worked in business interacted daily," he stated. One of Yehya's uncles had a *comedero*, a working-class restaurant. He remembers Jews coming in frequently. "But the various wars put a dent in those visits," he posited. After the Yom Kippur War in October of 1973, his uncle came back home one day to say that Jews were no longer eating at the restaurant. "I have never practiced a religion," he stated.

"I can't make myself believe in God or in any organized system of magical beliefs," he concluded. "Nevertheless, I identify as a Druse. All my life I have followed the conflicts, wars, and politics in Israel and Palestine. I visited Israel as a journalist. I have written about the situation when things looked bad. I have also made my voice heard when there was an open window after the Oslo Accords." He sighed. "But now I'm completely pessimistic about the future. I've always admired progressive Jewish thinkers like Tony Judt and Tom Segev, among many others. I have thought of them as a big part of the solution. They have brought hope for peace and justice in the region. In contrast, the Arab states have been ruled by dictators who can hardly claim any kind of moral authority. The Arab world is a mess and will remain that way for decades to come. Interestingly, new and very strange alliances are being formed between unexpected partners, which results in the multiplying of new and bloody wars. At the same time, right-wing groups in the United States and Israel are more empowered than ever. They are growing in size and influence. In other words, the situation with the Occupied Territories seems almost impossible to resolve. Racism and intolerance are on the rise. It's a terrible time for the Arab world."

After my conversation with Yehya, I called Rose Mary Salum. Of Lebanese descent, she is the editor of the digital magazine *Literal*, devoted to Latin American arts and letters. Salum lives in Houston. She was born in Mexico City. A descendant of Christian Arabs, she remembers a harmonious relationship between Arabs and Jews when she was growing up. Her uncle was president of the Centro Libanés and often talked of cordial communication with the Jewish community. "Ellos son como nosotros," she remembers her uncle saying, "They are like us."

"In certain crucial moments of the Arab-Palestinian conflict," Salum stated, "Christian Arabs have been supportive of Israel, as in the Lebanon War. But that support evaporated. The 2006 invasion of Ramallah created an abyss between the two sides that to this day feels almost insurmountable."

She talked of the disparaging way in which the Spanish language was used by those around her to refer to people of various ethnic groups. Salum mentioned that even at the time she emigrated to the United States with her family in 1998, her grandmother still referred to the non-Lebanese Arabs as *nacos*.

"My grandmother would say that Lebanese people were different from the rest of the Arabs," Salum added. "Marrying one of them wasn't encouraged."

I told her something similar took place among Mexican Jews. "It was believed that an Ashkenazi and Sephardi couple was a formula for failure. Ashkenazi Jews talked of Sephardic Jews derogatively as *shajatos*."

When I asked Salum to delve deeper into her views of Jews, she recalled that, for a variety of reasons, the Jewish community was always present in talks at family reunions. "Either because the Lebanese and the Jewish cultures were perceived as similar by the rest of the country," she posited, "or because Middle Eastern countries were always at war with each other, or perhaps because we had the same values although expressed in different ways. In that regard I have always felt a certain attraction to the Jewish culture, either by understanding it or by criticizing it."

Was it easier for her to identify as a Lebanese in the United States than in Mexico? She responded that, for her, identity is defined by tradition as well as by history and social customs. "I feel at peace with my heritage now, yes. I am at home in my own skin. After a long time I've finally come to understand that I can embrace the Lebanese, Mexican, and American ideas and traditions at my own pace and convenience without any concern of how others identify me. I can mix them and integrate them in my daily routine without the feeling of confusion I used to experience when I was younger—though, honestly, I'm at times defiant of people who, out of laziness, try to place me in a category that threatens their own perspectives."

Salum said that her two children, a son and a daughter, follow Mexican and Lebanese customs. "They have the same identity conflicts as your own children, Ilan. For a long time I myself was confused in regards to my Arab Mexican identity. But maturity has granted me clarity and peace. Hopefully these are felt by my children, just as they have probably been felt by yours."

She changed the subject. "When he was little, my son had a *cedrito*, a little cedar tree. After 9/11, my husband hid it as a precaution at a time when anti-Muslim feeling was running rampant. He is Arab on his father's side. But my son insisted that he wanted to have it, that it defined him, that it made him who he is. And so he kept the *cedrito* next to him."

11.

I wanted to talk to a Palestinian from Latin America. When it comes to the Middle Eastern conflict, their view, obviously, is as unique as that of Israel. The region has almost one and a half million. Chile alone has half a million.

A mutual friend put me in touch with Lina Meruane. Born in Chile in 1970, she teaches at New York University and is a decorated writer, the recipient, among other awards, of the Anna Seghers Prize and the Sor Juana Inés de La Cruz Award. Her books include the novel *Seeing Red* (2012). I had read a few articles of hers as well as her book *Volverse Palestina* (2014), which translates as *Becoming Palestine*, a fascinating exploration of how she decided at one point to assume her Palestinian identity openly. Among other things, that moment involved a trip to Israel and the Occupied Territories in 2012.

Meruane was about to depart for a semester-long stay in Berlin. This meant that our dialogue was done via email. It ended up being a revelatory exchange.

I started by telling Meruane we all shape our character—at least, I have done so—based on an "anti-me" that I imagine circulating around.

"It's not at all surprising that so many Jews carry this feeling of opposition," said Meruane. "There's a history to this and a present life determined by long-lasting prejudice. They are not alone, though. There are lots of people experiencing prejudice, being determined by racial and other forms of hate. But perhaps for each one of us it is also a given that we are who we oppose, we seem to define ourselves by what neglects us or opposes us. . . . And I wonder where this us-versus-others might take us. How willing are we, or you, to defend what defines your identity negatively? For instance, do you feel you need to constantly perform and protect your Jewishness so as to respond to anti-Semitism? Furthermore, do you feel you must defend Israel because you are a Jew, no matter what its government does, no matter how it defines anti-Semitism for its own political sake? Do you believe you betray Israel if you're critical?"

My own opinion is that being Jewish is no excuse for closing one's eyes. I strongly believe in the role of criticism as a constructive endeavor. I have spent my entire life advocating an open, engaged critical eye. On one hand, the policies of Israel toward Palestinians infuriate me. To a large degree, the Israelis are responsible for the rise of anti-Semitism in the last fifty years, at least since the Six-Day War. On the other hand, I support the existence of a Jewish state, where I have lived and which is a magnet to me.

"Being critical, even for Jews who believe in an exclusionary Jewish state, does entail being seen as an anti-Jew, as someone against their own people—Jewish identity is being turned into a political identity." If you're a Jew, rejecting Israel's policies will often land you on the list of Jewish self-haters—a hefty list that includes Hannah Arendt, Noam Chomsky, Daniel Barenboim, Judith Butler, and so on. But I believe there should be room for dissent. Otherwise, the very enterprise of modernity—that is, to think critically—is doomed.

In Meruane's view, though, modernity has failed. "We can still be critical. . . . In any case, it isn't the rise in anti-Semitism that we are seeing today so much as of anti-Zionism: a critical stance on Israel's colonial politics."

I talked about my admiration for the Jewish Argentine pianist and composer Daniel Barenboim who, along with Palestinian literary scholar Edward Said, founded the West-Eastern Divan Orchestra, a youth orchestra based in Seville that featured players from Israel, Egypt, Iran, Jordan, Lebanon, Syria, and Lebanon, as well as Palestinians. I also told Meruane that in my opinion there are three types of anti-Semitism: religious, economic, and political. It isn't easy to separate them. Anti-Zionism, on the other hand, is mostly political.

She said, "I belong to this last group: those who oppose Zionism on political grounds. I've been accused of anti-Semitism as a result of this position, but I've learned that anti-Semitism is used widely to discourage critical positions. And you can never prove that you are not anti-Semitic, especially if you're part Palestinian."

"You talk of yourself as 'part' Palestinian," I continued. "What does that mean? What part is that?"

"The part where I struggle! What does it mean to be a Palestinian for one who wasn't born in Palestine, who hasn't lived there? One who doesn't speak Arabic? One who doesn't belong to the Muslim majority? One who got to Palestine by chance and was only there once? Can blood or genes be said to be Palestinian? Are a few last names enough to grant you an identity?"

It was my turn: "Maybe it is like a Jew who doesn't live in Israel or speak Hebrew. Are blood and genes the stuff of identity? Yes, along with the imaginings we infuse them with. Names are ID cards: they tie us to clans, to myths, to lineages. By rejecting them, we create alternatives: other clans, other myths, other lineages. Identity is pregnant with meaning because we can't live without meaning. I sometimes imagine what it means to be a Palestinian."

"Being a Jew might be difficult enough," Meruane posited.

"Being a secular Jew, maybe even an agnostic Jew (which is different from an atheist), sometimes placed me on a collision course with orthodox Jews. Actually, there are countless ways of being a Jew, to the degree that I sometimes ask myself why we don't splinter into parallel religious sects. Does being a Palestinian Christian put you at odds with Palestinian Muslims?"

She responded: "I have a harder time thinking of myself as a Christian, the faith I was educated into and have rejected completely, than as a Palestinian. I do find these questions of identity difficult. They invoke an essentialist vision of the self. How we define ourselves seems to call for a politics of belonging, a politics of engagement. If we refuse to engage blindly, then we're seen as betraying *our* identity even if we aren't sure it belongs to us."

"You seem rather conflicted about identifying yourself as a Palestinian."

"Not with being a Palestinian," she told me, "but with identifying, with identity as something unique and forever fixed. Although I was born in Chile, I haven't lived there for some twenty years. And while I'm constantly returning, I can't say my identity continues to be as Chilean as it used to be; it has been contaminated with other belongings. Later in life I've connected with the fact that I'm also half Palestinian in descent, which, politically speaking, makes me a Palestinian in the diaspora. If I thought of myself in an oppositional manner, as you suggest you have, I would have just too many enemies, more than I could deal with. Likewise, I can't help imagining that you don't define yourself only as a Jew. I sensed this in your *Resurrecting Hebrew*, a sort of layered identity. In fact, you and I share a likeness in titles, where the notion of identity as a process is central—mine is *Becoming Palestinian*."

Meruane wanted to know how I belonged to a people when I don't fully identify with all of its tenets?

"By keeping your individuality," I answered. "By not losing yourself in an ideology. There are members of my family with whom I strongly disagree. Zionism, when I was young, was an epochal movement. It had culminated in the creation of a Jewish state after almost two millennia. The diaspora is over, it announced. The Shoah was the catalyst. Jews no longer needed to be pariahs. But the euphoria was blinding. It resulted in tragedy: success came at the expense of others."

She said: "A success that required for Israelis to turn a blind eye to excess, violence, and injustice. It also required a transformation of the Jewish identity. The new Israelis rejected what had previously defined them, the identity of the victim. A change of names signaled this transformation: David Gruen became Ben Gurion, Golda Meyerson Golda Meir, etc."

I argued that it was a thorough reinvention: vulnerability gave place to implacability.

"The metaphor of the *sabra* (Hebrew for the thorny cactus that resists the harsh conditions of the desert) was embraced," Meruane added.

I mentioned that nowadays Yiddish (the language of the Ashkenazi diaspora, which in the early years of Israel was looked down on as unworthy) is seen as feminine whereas Hebrew is masculine: vigorous, athletic. However, to me the creation of Israel in 1948 also gave place to a new kind of Jew, I mean a figurative one: the Palestinian. They are now the ones victimized, the new pariahs: expelled, homeless, in need of utopia.

"As if to overcome their own victimhood, Jews needed to subject others to that fate," Meruane asserted. "To me it's shocking how quickly they've forgotten their own past. Or perhaps it's not so much forgetting but reshaping the present in order to turn Palestinians into enemies. Not all Israelis and not all Jews, but sadly, a large majority."

It was my time to speak. "In turn Palestinians have speedily figured out how to play the role of victims too. For it takes two to tango. We are two sides of the same coin. Do we need each other? Does resolving the conflict require the recognition that the other side is an integral part of who we are as individuals?"

"I wish it were so, Ilan. But these sides aren't the same. There is an enormous power differential, which is too often sidelined in representations of the conflict. Palestinians don't have a state of their own. They control very little power, even inside the wall. They aren't free to decide on what's left of their land, which, by the way, has been increasingly taken from them by settlers beyond the green line established on the West Bank in 1967. They are subjected to constant dispossession of their homes and rights. And their voices are seldom heard in the international forum. There is no tango here, no symmetry."

"Once in a while, Palestinians perhaps play victim," Meruane added. "They ask for compassion when violent resistant hasn't fared well. Very few have benefited from the occupation. Palestinians would much rather stop being under colonial power."

I assured her without hesitation that from my countless conversations with Israelis, many would do anything to stop playing their role as well. No one wants to be an oppressor.

"Surely, this is true," she said. "No one wants to be called an oppressor, no one wants to think of themselves as one. It's a negative form of identity, for sure. I also know many Israelis who are weary of conflict and want it all to come to a happy end. But wanting is not enough, simply because wanting can be very passive politically speaking or else insufficient."

I wondered if she was as critical of Hamas and the Palestinian Authority the way I am of the policies of the Israeli government. Or does her criticism only go one way?

"I'm critical of both," she replied, "but not as critical as I am of Israel. The Palestinian Liberation Organization (PLO) and Hamas are so weak in comparison. They are responding to decades of growing oppression with periodic bouts of violence that have not fared well for them. After the failure of the Intifadas, the Palestinian Authority tried a conciliatory strategy toward Israel. It made concessions that weren't in the Palestinians' best interest, hoping that by doing so they would get a better deal. It didn't work out and it won't. In the meantime, people lost faith in the possibility of an agreement led by the PLO. Now we have Hamas, which has found no way out of occupation other than by responding violently to Israel, since their demands will not even be heard. They don't get to negotiating even after winning internal elections. The story of despair and violence gets repeated over and over again while Israel sits back or sends more bombs over Gaza or puts more Palestinians in prison. The idea that both sides are equal—equally violent, equally victimized—is far from true."

I hadn't said they were equal. I said they are two sides of the same coin. One is at times on top. But things flip over. My life as a Jew has taught me that. We are caught in a conflict in which we have taught ourselves that, in order to function, we need an enemy. This happens because our psyche functions through antipodes. Is this an essential part of human nature?

I wanted to know if she was suspicious of people like me—simply because I'm Jewish. "Not at all," Meruane said. "I don't know you so I wouldn't tell you anything private, but that would be the case with any writer I wasn't personally close to. Your being a Jew doesn't reveal to me anything specific about you. And it doesn't make you my enemy, if that's what you're asking. I understand why you ask, though. I think not assuming anything, not mistrusting you has a lot to do with the education I received. I did not grow up making religious distinctions. I never thought of my Chilean Jewish classmates as Jews. Honestly, I didn't quite understand what being a Jew or an Arab meant until much later. As far as I was concerned, we were all Chileans, and quite literally we were all simultaneously from and in the same class. I stress this because the distinction was of income, not of racial origin or belief. In school there was no calling out of Jewish students, or at least I wasn't aware of it. There were plenty of students of Arab descent too. They were sometimes called *turcos*, meaning Turk. But I never gave a thought to all this. I'm not trying to idealize Chilean society, which, in fact, is extremely conservative, as well as racist and classist, and of course misogynistic. Yet social class at the time seemed to matter more than religious differences."

"So you were a *turca*," I said.

"I was, although I wasn't dark-skinned and my last name didn't sound Middle Eastern, which means not everyone realized I was. But once in a while I got called *turca*. It was a paradox. Our families had arrived at a time when most Christian Arabs were escaping the Ottoman Empire, with Turkish passports. And here we were called by the name of our former enemies. . . . I was being stereotyped, I guess, but it didn't feel abusive. Just as I was *la turca*, my best friend was *la rusa*, since she was blond. Somehow *rubia* derived into *rusa*, although this was still at a time when the USSR was solidly in place. Turks and Russians were not in our mental maps, back then."

"Curiously, I was *el güero*, the blondy—that is, I could have been your friend," I said. "I went to a Jewish school all my life. I was in college when I discovered Mexico. At that point I became a Jewish stereotype to others. Actually, stereotypes, in my view, are useful."

Meruane wanted to know how useful. I said I don't believe that the mind is able to function without them. They are intellectual devices, what Plato called "universals." It is also how language works. For instance, when we see three different types of chairs, one with one leg, one that unfolds, and one that is painted in multiple colors, we don't call each of them by a different name. The word "chair" refers to them all because at an early age we form a mental image of what a chair ought to be. But when encountering examples that deviate from the norm, we still apply the same word, "chair." That's how stereotypes are made: by compressing into a universal a series of preconceptions that ends up erasing the differences.

"The Palestinian part of my identity was always present in a silence of sorts," Meruane continued. "It did not represent a problem, nor was I suffering from it. The Palestinian community in Chile is the largest outside Palestine. It is old, and it assimilated into Chilean society easily because the majority of Palestinians in the country are Christians. When I was young, it was harder to be a woman than it was to be a *Chilestinian*. In truth my Palestinianness only became an issue when I arrived in the United States, in 2001."

I said that it worked the opposite way for me. In Mexico I was Jewish because I mostly moved among Jews. In New York, where I landed in the mid-1980s, I suddenly became Mexican, because I spoke Spanish and didn't quite fit into the mainstream model of Jewishness.

"Do you fear that by befriending a Jew like me your intellectual position might be compromised?" I asked.

"Even if you were my opponent," Meruane posited, "which you can't be by *simply* being a Jew, my intellectual position wouldn't be compromised. I don't believe that by talking to someone I might disagree with I am being turned over. I grew up in a divided world. Even families were divided. You never just stopped talking to people. On the contrary, you argued. You even shouted and banged doors once in a while, though always under the same roof. Even if you disagreed you had to come to terms with living together. That's the basis of politics: discussing, disagreeing, negotiating. . . . But your question has raised my suspicion now: are you having second thoughts about talking to an atheist and half Palestinian anti-Zionist? Might *your* position be compromised?"

"Not in the least," I said. "I, too, am an atheist. Or at least I thought I was one for years. These days I'm less certain. Maybe I'm a skeptic, which is different from an atheist. My religion is built around doubt."

12.

An incident on my return flight from Tel Aviv served as a coda to this visit to Israel. It didn't involve Arabs. Otherwise, the country's gender, political, and religious tensions were all summed up together.

Isaiah was sitting in another section of the plane. I was on an aisle seat at the rear of the plane. To my left, in the window seat, was an ultra-orthodox man.

We were still boarding when a young female passenger arrived. She put her jacket on the middle seat. She looked Israeli.

She proceeded to place her belongings in the overhead compartment. I noticed the ultra-orthodox man becoming nervous. Suddenly he stood up and stormed out in the direction of the entrance.

A few minutes later the ultra-orthodox returned along with a male attendant. The flight attendant asked politely if the woman would mind changing her seat.

"It's a religious custom," he stated. The ultra-orthodox was uncomfortable sitting next to her.

With a *sabra* accent, she replied, "Absolutely not!"

The attendant looked resignedly at the ultra-orthodox. A young man in his twenties on the other side of the aisle to my left, wearing jeans and a sweatshirt, who was sitting next to another gentleman, offered to exchange seats with the ultra-orthodox.

The switch was done. Once everyone was comfortable, I heard the twenty-five-year-old say out loud: "I was born a woman. I transitioned a few months ago . . ."

Everyone laughed.

A few minutes later the ultra-orthodox again stood up. After collecting his belongings, he walked—serenely this time—toward the front of the plane.

People applauded.

7   THE PUSH

"What does *el séptimo cielo* mean?" asked my oldest son, Joshua.

He and I were waiting for a few minutes outside the Polish consulate in midtown Manhattan, near the Morgan Library.

"It is Spanish for the Seventh Heaven," I replied. "It refers to a state of bliss. According to the Talmud, the universe is made of seven heavens, *shamayim* in Hebrew."

"Why not just one?" he said. "One heaven should be enough. People fight to get into it. Although, on second thoughts, having more than one would open up possibilities to those who are left behind because they aren't affiliated with any particular religion."

I continued our conversation. "Well, everyone visualizes heaven in a different way. I've always thought human visions of heaven are shaped by those in charge of the visualization. Heaven for food lovers is a five-star restaurant. For librarians, it is a library. For fútbol fans, an exciting match. . . . Truth is, most maps of heaven have multiple layers. Dante's paradise is made of nine concentric spheres surrounding the earth. Each sphere is represented by another planet. A particular group of people is found there. For instance, the first sphere is the moon. The inconstant are there. The second sphere is Mercury. It houses the ambitious. The third is Venus. It is reserved for lovers. And so on. The human ascends to God through these various stages. Another way of looking at it would be like Russian dolls: each heaven has others inside it."

"Judaism doesn't have a heaven, though. Am I right?" Josh wondered. "I've always known it to be concerned with the here and now."

"But there *is* a Jewish heaven. It has the shape of a waiting room."

"Surprise, surprise."

"Why?"

"Aren't Jews always waiting?"

"There is the *shamayim*, with its seven. This is where the divine and other heavenly beings dwell. *Sheol* is the realm of the dead. And *eretz*, meaning earth, is home to the living."

A few minutes later, Josh and I were entering the consulate. After a security guard went through our bags, we made our way to a couple of seats in a small waiting area on the first floor. Our appointment was in about twenty minutes. We were given a queue number.

As we sat waiting, after a couple of minutes of niceties, something, I forget what, prompted me to tell him about the dream I had that set in motion my explorations through Jewish Latin America because the present is too fidgety, too unstable.

"You look exhausted and nervous. Are you okay?" Josh asked.

I said I was fine. But he was right: I was tired. The approximately four-year-long trek had drained me of all energy. I was in a state of discomfort. My body felt weak, uneasy. My sleep was strange. I would fall asleep deeply only to wake up a few hours later in a sweat, my heart beating a mile a minute. I would go to another room and sit in the darkness for half an hour until I regained my calm.

Josh and Isaiah were an integral part of my trips to Jewish Latin America. On occasion one or other of them joined me in some of my treks. Otherwise every time I came back I would summarize my adventures through a series of anecdotes about what I had seen, who I spoke to, and to what degree my preconceptions about this or that topic had been shattered.

Now I had reached the end and was back home on a steady basis, and I needed to set my thoughts in order. The journey had been as much about the history of Jewish Latin America as it had been a quest of self-discovery. I could see how all the pieces, dissimilar in their nature, each formed a part of a larger puzzle. I wanted to turn them into a narrative. But all of a sudden, I felt as if the earth beneath my feet was shaking. That's because a lot had changed in the United States in the four-year period I had dedicated to my quest. When I started the country was in a dramatically different mood. I had come back to an altogether different reality. The forces of fear had been unleashed.

It was January 2017. The unimaginable had happened: Donald Trump was in the White House.

I told Josh that in the last few days I had been rereading Ansky's *The Enemy at His Pleasure*, which was, along with the dream I had about not being able to return to my childhood home, what had inspired me to explore Jewish Latin America. "I remember telling myself, when I opened the book for the first time almost half a decade ago, that a civilization that is apparently healthy in one moment might vanish into air in the next."

"Obviously, you didn't have to go that far," Josh said. "I am nervous, too. The real change is happening here. Who knows how far it will go. It can unleash a civil war. Or it will fade as a mere hiccup in American history."

"In time we hate that which we often fear," Charmian tells Cleopatra in Act I, Scene 3 of Shakespeare's *Anthony and Cleopatra*. The instability brought along by Trump was unlike anything I had experienced since my years in Mexico, when I made a choice to join Bitajón, the Jewish self-defense militia. In my early twenties I became a member because the atmosphere of xenophobia, intolerance, and anti-Semitism in Mexico was rampant.

I mentioned that just a few months before, in Patagonia, I had explored neo-Nazi activities, encountering theoreticians like Walter Beveraggi Allende, Norberto Ceresole, and Miguel Serrano whose oeuvre frightened me.

"They might be linked to the alt-right that brought Trump to power," Josh posited.

"They aren't different at all," I stated.

Our conversation switched back to Jewish visions of heaven. I told Josh I had visited a considerable number of graveyards during my trip. In Havana a taxi driver called Juan Pablo Escobar had talked to me about cemeteries having a direct line to God. It was roughly the same idea I had heard in Montevideo, where a hippie said to me that a specific tomb was a Jewish portal to the world beyond. It was the tomb of Monsieur Chouchani who, without my realizing it, had become the leitmotif of my quest.

A Talmudic scholar had first mentioned his name to me in Buenos Aires. It seemed to me an obscure reference at the time. That mention prompted me to look for further clues. I had gotten many of them along the way. Finally, I had gone to Montevideo to see Monsieur Chouchani's final resting place. I had found the tomb well kept. I learned later on that its upkeep was paid for with money left behind by Elie Wiesel, the Shoah survivor and

Nobel Prize winner. At any rate, my visit was uneventful until I met a hippie near Monsieur Chouchani's tomb. He talked to me about *le septième ciel*, about the meaning of each of the seven heavens: kingdom, origins, adornment, understanding, wisdom, knowledge, and the divine crown.

It was this exchange that persuaded me Monsieur Chouchani was the same mysterious man dressed like a hobo whom I had seen in my dream waiting outside my childhood house. The man in the dream stopped me from going in.

"Why didn't he allow you in?"

"I don't know. . . . But I disobeyed him. In Mexico City, I went to Colonia Copilco and looked for my old house. It was a strange experience. I did return to my childhood home. Maybe I shouldn't have."

I described the feeling of foreignness I had experienced in the house at Calle Odontología #85. "The woman, I assume the current tenant, was suspicious of me. After much insistence she finally let me in, in part because she knew my father and had seen him act in several telenovelas. I walked around inside, but to be honest, it was useless. It all looked very different. Unrecognizable. Why hadn't I paid attention to the dream? It would have been better to keep the memory of my house intact. Now it is meshed with current memories of the neighborhood as it has become in the last few decades: overpopulated, chaotic, hostile. . . . Yes, I have been thrown out. That's what childhood is about: a pastoral period, to which there is no way back. Yet my insistence had also paid off somehow, because with all my feelings of exile and longing I had reached some of the furthest corners of Latin America in search of Jewish life—from the "Indian Jews" near Medellín, Colombia, and the legend of the Lost Tribes of Israel expounded by the Spanish missionaries in the New World from the sixteenth century onward to the activism during the Dirty War in the 1970s, which resulted in a large number of desaparecidos.

"Do you have an overarching vision now?" Josh asked.

I said I was now looking at my four-year journey as a quest for self-discovery, mine and of those around me. I was full of voices, images, and ideas. To a large extent my quest had been about the concept of home: my own home and the home of Jews in the Hispanic world. I also said I was weary. Indeed, I had a vision: Jewish Latin America was a Diego Rivera–like mural, replete with intriguing characters. The challenge was to bring all those voices and images and ideas into a narrative now that the world had changed dramatically.

"Funny! When I started, my impression was that where I was going, south of the United States–Mexico border, could change at any moment and its Jews might not survive the schism. But it is here that things have changed more dramatically. Bigotry is in the air as well as intolerance and xenophobia. Perhaps my endeavor wasn't so much a trip abroad but a trip inside. The hippie in Montevideo told me that Monsieur Chouchani's tomb was a portal. He also said that, just when you get the sense that you've reached the end of your journey, you understand that what you were seeking is something else altogether."

One thing I learned was that in Latin America the health of Jews was a sociopolitical thermometer. For one reason or another, whenever there was upheaval, Jews, physically and metaphorically, were always present. Corsairs, apostates, entrepreneurs, and in general just plain dreamers, they arrived in the New World to escape the Inquisition. Regardless of the turmoil, they have kept true to their ancestral faith, and for this they have paid a heavy price. A few were persecuted while others practiced their religion in secret. Maybe all this turned a few of them into freedom fighters. It is known that the wars of independence in Latin America featured a number of judaizantes enamored with the concept of freedom.

Centuries later, Ashkenazi and Sephardic immigrants, speaking Yiddish, Ladino, and other languages, arrived in the Americas from Eastern Europe, the Balkans, and the Arab world. Once again they came in search of liberty because people in their homelands were repressive, biased, and despotic. Within a few decades these immigrants thrived. They opened businesses, schools, synagogues, and community centers while also keeping to themselves and refusing full assimilation. Naturally, that stubbornness, that endurance generated animosity. In tense times that animosity turned into hatred. Still, they plowed on. Maybe Jean-Paul Sartre was correct in *Anti-Semite and Jew*: rejection is useful when you are stubborn. You need a no to turn it into a yes.

Josh and I moved on to discuss the fragility of life in the United States as well. Just as it did me, the anti-immigrant, anti-black, and anti-Jewish rhetoric of the Trump camp frightened him deeply.

"Is that why you've been thinking of heaven?" he asked.

"Maybe."

"Does Latin America have a heaven too?" he wondered. "I mean, people in it have different religious views. Catholics, Protestants, Jewish, Muslim, Buddhist, Hindu. . . . And I'm sure the indigenous population before Columbus had their own vision."

"The Aztecs, for example, divided the world into thirteen heavens and nine netherworlds. The Mayas had a different cosmogony and so did other pre-Columbian civilizations."

"Perhaps your dream was not so much about being excluded from your home as about seeking your own heaven."

I smiled. In the consulate a woman behind a window called our number. We stood up, proceeded to where she was, and gave her a folder full of official documents.

More than a year before I had decided to apply for Polish passports for me and my two children, Joshua and Isaiah. Alison, my wife, wasn't eligible. In fact, I decided to apply for Polish passports after my encounter with Isaac Pérez in Santa Fe, New Mexico, when we discussed the repatriation of conversos and other Jews by the Spanish government. At the time I was critical of the venture, and of Spain in particular, which, in my mind, looked opportunistic, given that the country had been going through one of the most troubled financial crises in its history. Why now, I thought, more than five hundred years after the Alhambra Decree, which officially expelled the Jews in 1492? Yet the thought of seizing such an opportunity kept on coming back to my mind.

It returned as an aftermath of my encounter with the Cuban bureaucrat in the José Martí Airport in Havana, who tried to shame me for having my Mexican passport with proofs of Israeli visits and how I thought at the time how preposterous passports in general were. Yet rather than giving up any passports that I and my family already had, I decided to multiply them. Call it an exit strategy.

Or else, call it *the push*, as it was referred to at the dinner table.

Isaiah, my second son, said at the dinner table at the time: "Should we try getting Spanish passports?"

"Nah," I responded. "We don't have Sephardic ancestry. I feel ambivalent toward Spain."

"And not toward Poland?"

He was right. If Spain generated ambivalence in me, Poland awoke outright animosity. My grandparents would probably be turning over in their graves if they knew of my efforts. As a result of poverty and anti-Semitism they had left—or better, "were aborted from"—Poland, Ukraine, and Belarus. They never looked back: Mexico became their new home. Now I was soliciting a return to Poland for me and my children. Call it irony.

Or else, revenge. "Is that why we're doing it?" Isaiah asked me at one point when Josh was also around. "Like in one of those Hollywood movies in which the protagonist presses a button and, poof! the past is redone."

"That's dumb. I would never erase the past. The past is never gone. In fact, as Faulkner used to say, it is not even the past. That past is what made us who we are. . . . I'm an accidental Mexican because it was Mexico that opened the doors to my ancestors. No, this effort is more like a restitution. The environment no longer defines me as it did your great-grandparents. I am Mexican *and* American *and* Polish. You and your brother are now allowed to choose what you want to be as well."

I told Isaiah that, with a Polish passport, he could work at will in the European Union. Who knows where his life will lead him? I have no intention of living in Poland. I simply wanted to give all of us a head start—though it was also, as Josh put it, "a sign of paranoia." Throughout history Jews have been expelled from countless places: Egypt, the Kingdom of Israel, England, France, Spain, Portugal, and so on. "You think the United States is next, Pa?"

Our ancestors were chastened beyond their control, I told myself. As a result of Darwinian forces, I was now in a position to reverse history. In other words, I had something my ancestors lacked: control of my own destiny. But did I? The whole thing was preposterous.

"And not Israel?" asked Josh.

"What?"

"And you haven't applied for an Israeli passport?" he stated. "If you're a Jew, that's the passport to end all passports."

"Not for me," I replied. "I love Israel wholeheartedly. It is often the place where I feel most comfortable. I like its creative spirit. But I also like being a diaspora Jew."

My mother was the one who started the process of requesting Polish passports before me. She found a middle man in Mexico, Ronen Waisser, a bureaucrat specializing in reclaiming European citizenship for people in the Americas whose ancestry is traceable to the Old World. Waisser asked her to follow the paper trail. What my mother needed, he said, was proof that her father, Haim (in Spanish, Jaime) Slomianski, was Polish. Ever since she was little, my mother knew that in the ups and downs of history her father's birth certificate had disappeared. Or else that he had never gotten one, which isn't surprising since official government documentation in Eastern Europe didn't begin in earnest until after the First World War. Still, the absence of such a certificate jeopardized her chances of getting the process in motion. As a last resort Waisser suggested looking up in the Mexican registry of immigration my grandfather's year of arrival, 1921. Fortunately, my mother found a listing there. Jaime Slomianski was vaguely recorded there as *un ciudadano polaco*, a Polish national. This, according to Waisser, was sufficient for her purposes.

Soon, for a fee, she got Polish passports for herself and my sister who in turn got them for her children. The information was passed onto me so that I could do the same. That's what the appointment at the Polish consulate in New York City was about: the last step in the extended family's return. Isaiah, who was studying abroad, already had his papers with him.

The appointment was a few weeks after Donald Trump's presidential inauguration.

I had returned to the United States days before Election Day. Throughout the last legs of my trip, people wherever I was were obsessively tuning in to their TVs to follow closely every single step made by the two candidates, Trump and Hillary Clinton. Those steps, no matter how insignificant they were, were repeated to exhaustion by the media. When one of the presidential debates was broadcast, I was in Puerto Montt. All the streets were empty. More than a national election, this felt like a global referendum.

Trump's arrival in the White House unleashed a growing slew of xenophobic sentiments in the country. He had been endorsed by the far-right, including members of the Ku Klux Klan. Its followers were in recruitment mode in Texas, Missouri, Arizona, Ohio, Montana, Idaho, and Pennsylvania. Their estimated membership was between twenty thousand and sixty thousand. These numbers were growing. Trump seemed allergic to multiculturalism, a fact used by the far-right as a springboard for their view of an America ruled by white supremacy. Likewise, Trump dismissed cases of police brutality against blacks. He wanted to give more power to the police. And he wanted to deport close to a million Dreamers, young undocumented men and women up to the age of thirty who had been brought to the United States by their parents.

Indeed, in his speeches, Mexican immigrants in general were targeted. They had abused the system, he announced. In rallies Trump emphatically talked of building a wall between Mexico and the United States—to be paid for by the Mexican people.

It sounded like Juan Domingo Perón, Hugo Chávez, and other chauvinistic Latin American strongmen.

Election Day was a moment of reckoning. A couple of days beforehand, a spray-painted sign appeared on a prominent rock at the peak of Mt. Tom, not far from where I live, on the banks of the Connecticut River. It displayed a swastika along with anti-immigrant rhetoric.

Not that any of this is new. I have taught at American universities for decades, and anti-Semitic—more frequently, anti-Zionist—propaganda frequently shows up in the academic ecosystem. It is exacerbated when the Israeli-Palestinian conflict goes through one of its cyclical bursts. In this regard campuses in Latin America are even more explosive. In them one frequently hears that Zionism is an agent of colonialist forces; that its objective is to divide the so-called Third World; that Zionists control the world media; and that the Holocaust was a hoax. Even the word "Jew" had become inappropriate, even dangerous.

Trump's ascent made it all tangible. It was part of a populist crusade on the international stage. There was the fall of the city of Aleppo in Syria to the forces of the repressive dictator Bashar El-Assad. Terrorist attacks took place in Berlin, London, Paris, and elsewhere. The Russian ambassador was assassinated in the Turkish city of Ankara. Vladimir Putin in Russia is an autocrat. North Korea's Kim Jung-un toys with nuclear missiles. Are all these signs of another global cataclysm?

Fatefully perhaps, the Statue of Liberty was on my mind. Only one day before our appointment at the Polish consulate, I had seen on Twitter a photoshopped image of the Statue of Liberty in tears, immigrants in chains at its feet. It made me remember the time when I visited the statue for the first time. It was 1974, the year Richard Nixon resigned. I was spending a few weeks with relatives in Queens. My Aunt Bonnie, her third son, Richie, who was roughly about my age, and I took the subway to South Ferry. We bought tickets, took a boat, and climbed the staircase to the top, where the crown is located. Such heights were still allowed then. After coming down again we walked around Liberty Island.

I remember Aunt Bonnie stopping before the pedestal and proudly reading the sonnet inscribed in it: "The New Colossus," by Emma Lazarus. My English at the time was precarious, so I caught only a handful of words. I wasn't even sure what a sonnet was. And, of course, I couldn't for the life of me begin to imagine the significance of such verses on millions of immigrants to the United States.

A decade later, I became one. . . . To this day I remain wholeheartedly grateful to the United States for opening its doors to me. I am also disturbed by the rise of ultranationalism, which, since Trump, is felt in alt-right groups supported by a disenfranchised white, mostly rural population. I'm frightened by the ubiquity of the American flag. This incessant form of jingoism I find frustrating. Why do we need to display the flag with such zeal inside the country? Are we trying to convert anyone? Journalist Sydney J. Harris, a syndicated columnist for the *Chicago Sun-Times*, said that "the difference between patriotism and nationalism is that the patriot is proud of his country for what it does whereas the nationalist is proud of his country no matter what it does."

I myself have recited "The New Colossus" countless times in public: on Fourth of July ceremonies, in marches, on the radio, in the classroom. It is a poem I know by heart. Strictly speaking, it isn't good poetry. That doesn't matter. It's the message conveyed in these fourteen lines that is extraordinarily resonant:

> Not like the brazen giant of Greek fame,
> With conquering limbs astride from land to land;
> Here at our sea-washed, sunset gates shall stand
> A mighty woman with a torch, whose flame
> Is the imprisoned lightning, and her name
> Mother of Exiles. From her beacon-hand
> Glows world-wide welcome; her mild eyes command
> The air-bridged harbor that twin cities frame.
> "Keep, ancient lands, your storied pomp!" cries she
> With silent lips. "Give me your tired, your poor,
> Your huddled masses yearning to breathe free,
> The wretched refuse of your teeming shore.
> Send these, the homeless, tempest-tost to me,
> I lift my lamp beside the golden door!"

The last six lines have become a national mantra. The Statue of Liberty—or, as Lazarus calls it, the "Mother of Exiles"—talks directly to Europe, asking that continent to allow those without material means but with plenty of dreams to travel across the ocean to the land of freedom and opportunity.

Curiously, for most people Emma Lazarus is just a name. She doesn't even register in the canon of American poetry. The fact that she wrote "The New Colossus" looks like a fluke: out of nowhere this poem by this nobody is ingrained in the American mind. Truth is, Lazarus is a fascinating figure. Part Sephardic and part Ashkenazi, she was the fourth of seven children. Her parents were Moses Lazarus and Esther Nathan. Moses Lazarus's family was from Germany, her mother's from Portugal, although they had been in New York since before the American Revolution. As an adult Emma Lazarus was friends with Ralph Waldo Emerson. She wrote the sonnet (it was published in 1883) to help raise money to finance the pedestal of the Statue of Liberty, which was designed by the French sculptor Frédéric Auguste Bartholdi and built by Gustave Eiffel, who is famous for another structure, the Eiffel Tower.

The statue was dedicated on October 28, 1886. The tower was a gift from France to the United States. This was the time when Italians, Jews, and other Europeans were arriving in large numbers on American shores, passing through customs on Ellis Island. Lazarus empathized with the plight of the immigrants, in particular with the hardship that poor Yiddish-speaking shtetl dwellers were experiencing on their journey across the sea.

Why did Lazarus refer to the Statue of Liberty as Mother of Exiles and not as Mother of Immigrants? Whenever I wandered into a different setting in Latin America, Israel, and elsewhere and pondered the question of immigration, I asked myself that question. Although I don't know a concrete answer, I came up with an explanation, which at least to me seems plausible. It was based on what could be described as an exercise in literary cloning.

At the time of Lazarus's writing, the vast majority of those arriving on Ellis Island were immigrants. Not exiles. Not refugees either. Just immigrants. But she called them exiles because when thinking of them she had a specific profile in mind. To understand this profile, it is important to know that shortly before she wrote this poem, Lazarus had composed another, about the expulsion of the Jews from Spain. It is titled "1492."

> Thou two-faced year, Mother of Change and Fate,
> Didst weep when Spain cast forth with flaming sword,
> The children of the prophets of the Lord,
> Prince, priest, and people, spurned by zealot hate.
> Hounded from sea to sea, from state to state,
> The West refused them, and the East abhorred.
> No anchorage the known world could afford,
> Close-locked was every port, barred every gate.
> Then smiling, thou unveil'dst, O two-faced year,
> A virgin world where doors of sunset part,
> Saying, "Ho, all who weary, enter here!
> There falls each ancient barrier that the art
> Of race or creed or rank devised, to rear
> Grim bulwarked hatred between heart and heart!"

Call them twins: the two sonnets have practically the same structure, the same motifs, and the same message. Indeed, they are essentially the same poem, to the degree that Lazarus travels instantaneously from one historical event to another. The Mother of Exile is here the Mother of Courage and

Fate. Those expelled from the Iberian Peninsula at the end of the fifteenth century were victims of the Inquisition, "the children of the prophets of the Lord, / Prince, priest, and people, spurned by zealot hate." In "The New Colossus," those children become huddled masses. Both yearn to breathe free.

Therein the answer to the question as to why Lazarus doesn't use the word "immigrant." For her Jews were not immigrants but exiles, eternally longing—even in America, yet another diaspora—to return to the place they were originally exiled from: the Promised Land. Conversely, exiles—that is, all immigrants—were Jews in metaphorical terms, finding another diaspora in their extended historical journey.

In my opinion Lazarus understood that America isn't only the United States. It is also *América*—that is, an entire continent. In this sense Lazarus's "virgin world" is a large expansion: from Alaska to the Patagonia. What distinguishes the two, America and *América*, is basic: America is arrogant, narcissistic, and forward-looking. It requests complete surrender from those around it. América is more modest and also more fragile. One is about the insatiable quest for success. The other is about adapting to defeat, knowing full well, as Montaigne put it in his personal essay "On Cannibals," "There are defeats more triumphant than victories."

It wasn't surprising that a few months after Trump's inauguration, a member of his administration announced that "The New Colossus" didn't represent the values of the Statue of Liberty. The statue "is a symbol of American liberty lighting the world. The poem was added later. It wasn't actually part of the original project." The bureaucrat added that, to be accepted into the United States in the twenty-first century, immigrants needed to speak English, "because the notion that speaking English wouldn't be a part of immigration systems would be very ahistorical." Needless to say, I was appalled.

Serendipitously, these reflections led me to consider the parallel status of Jews and Latinos in the United States. As of 2017 there were over five million Jews in the country. After Israel, this was the largest concentration in the world. Likewise, there were about sixty million Latinos, which is an even more staggering number. For every Jew, there were about twelve Latinos.

The connection between the two minorities is tenuous. Although there are dialogue groups in several cities, for the most part each of these minorities keeps to itself. A survey conducted by the Anti-Defamation League in 2002 showed that 35 percent of Hispanics in the United States harbored anti-Semitic views, a substantially higher number than average Americans, which, according to the same source, were at 17 percent anti-Semitic. Interestingly, the survey suggested that among Latinos, the anti-Semitic percentage was higher among foreign-born, at 44 percent, whereas Hispanic Americans born in the United States were at 20 percent. When it was released, the survey was at once enlightening and controversial. (By the way, no similar analysis is available on any anti-Hispanic sentiment among Jews.)

I thought of my visit to Beit Hatfutsot, the museum of the Jewish diasporas in Tel Aviv. After wandering around through an exhibit that felt slanted, biased, and unfriendly to anyone who doesn't identify as a Zionist, I left with a feeling of frustration. One of my first thoughts was of Jewish Latino life in the United States. This life is the bridge between disparate heritages.

I came to the realization that my entire exploration through Jewish Latin America was the journey of a double outsider: *ni de aquí, ni de allá*, from neither here nor there. Perhaps that's the best, most useful status a Jew may have: to be nowhere and everywhere.

Ironically, Trump was making me connect with my Jewishness and with my Mexicanness with renewed zeal. Images of Nazi Germany and of the Spanish Inquisition constantly popped into my mind. The fact that "The New Colossus" was rejected by the Trump administration was proof of my distress. Painful as it was, it was clear to me that the United States was no longer the sturdy enclave of freedom I had embraced as an immigrant in my youth.

In coming back, had I reached what the hippie described as *Keter*? Was there room now for clarity?

Being next to Josh, I somehow felt safe. I also felt an inner sense of vigor. I had traveled across Jewish Latin America. Like Ansky, my duty was to deliver a chronicle, to build a narrative out of light and darkness, sound and silence. I was ready to delve into the narrative.

My full last name was read in a loudspeaker: Stavchansky. It was a sign that our turn had come. Josh and I proceeded to a window behind which a woman greeted us with a smile and asked for all the paperwork: photographs, notarized certificates, letters, and a check.

She spoke Polish. I told her I know only a handful of words. It crossed my mind that such ignorance might disqualify us in the process. When I asked him Waisser recommended to feign ignorance and simply go along since knowing Polish isn't actually listed as a requirement on the Polish consulate's webpage.

I switched to English. So did the woman.

In my childhood home, Polish, German, and Russian were perceived through the prism of family history as languages of oppression. Upon listening to her, the effects of this perception suddenly came back. "She has me in her power," I thought.

Soon I was signing a series of documents and delivering her a check. I felt I was in a state. I felt like cowardly. I felt a traitor.

"Are you okay?" Josh asked.

Suddenly, in lieu of the Polish woman behind the glass window I saw before me Monsieur Chouchani. He was dressed in an old black suit. His hair was unkempt, his beard disheveled. One side of his thick glasses was held together with tape. On his forearm I saw a tattooed number. "It can't be," I told myself. "He is buried in Montevideo. I've been to his grave."

"Sus pasaportes polacos estarán en el correo en tres o cuatro semanas," Monsieur Chouchani announced—in stunning Spanish—after rubber-stamping the back of the check I handed him. "Your Polish passports will be in the mail in three to four weeks."

I giggled. "Dziękuję Ci," I answered in Polish. "Thank you." I know only about a dozen words in the language my ancestors lived in for centuries.

"Like me, now you'll have as many houses as you need," Monsieur Chouchani said. "Isn't that what you wanted?"

I turned around. Josh was also looking with perplexity at the glass window.

As we proceeded to leave the consulate, already close to the exit, he said to me, with a gesture of satisfaction: "Perhaps this is what the Seventh Heaven is: imaginary happiness."

ACKNOWLEDGMENTS

The sequence of events in my four-year voyage across Spain, Latin America, and Israel has been built to shape a coherent narrative line.

I wholeheartedly thank the extraordinary people I have been with along the way in the span of more than four years. Their generosity is boundless:

Argentina: Marcelo Birmajer, Marcelo Brodsky, Edgardo Cozarinsky, Daniel Divinsky, Ricardo Feierstein, Juan Gelman, Nora Glickman, Gisela Heffes, Guido Indij, Ricardo Piglia, Ana María Shúa, Eliahu Toker, and Osvaldo Quiroga.

Australia: Ian Campbell, Barry Carr, and Anna Lanyon.

Brazil: Luis S. Krausz and Moacyr Scliar.

Chile: Marjorie Agosín, Jacob Cohen Ventura, Ariel Dorfman, Cecilia García Huidobro Mac Auliffe, Eliah Germani, Rafael Gumucio, Iván Jaksić, Lina Meruane, Rodrigo Rojas, Patricio "Pato" Tapia, and Raúl Zurita.

Colombia: Azriel Bibliowicz, Jeffrey Cedeño, Hugo Chaparro, and Juan Fernando Merino.

Cuba: Ruth Behar, Javier Corrales, Adela Dworin, Jorge J. E. Gracia, Achy Obejas, Leonardo Padura, Gustavo Pérez Firmat, and Yoss (aka José Miguel Gómez Sánchez).

England: Glenda Abramson and Carlos Fonseca.

Germany: Verena M. Dolle and Susanne Zapp.

Israel: Alon Confino, Ruth Fine, Florinda Goldberg, Tal Goldfajn, Hillel Halkin, Annette and Shaul Hochstein, Ivonne Lerner, Tal Nitzan, Eliezer Nowodworski, Raanan Rein, Leonardo Senkman, Rosalie Sitman, Benjamin Sklar, Irene Stolian, Ury Vainsenchei, and Hana Wirth-Nesher.

Mexico: Betty and Homero Aridjis, Eko, David Enríquez, Hugo Hiriart, Myriam Moscona, Angelina Muníz-Huberman, Rosa Nissán, Rose Mary Salum, Guita Schifter, Katia Schkolnik, Jacobo Sefamí, Abraham and Ofelia Stavchansky, Liora Stavchansky, Mónica Unikel, Juan Villoro, Jorge Volpi, and Naief Yehya.

Peru: Guillermo and Mónica Bronstein, Isaac Goldemberg, Sonia Goldenberg, Raquel Obregón, Mario Vargas Llosa, and Miguel-Ángel Zapata.

Spain: César Alegre, Isabel Durán Giménez-Rico, Patricia Ehrle, Felipe Fernández-Armesto, Juan Carlos Marset, and Antonio Torres.

United States: Gloria Abella Ballen, Lisa Ades, Verónica Albin, Frederick Luis Aldama, Diana de Armas Wilson, Isaac Artenstein, Alan Astro, Zachary Baker, Wendy Barker, Jay Bolotin, Sara Brenneis, Jonathan Brent, Justin Cammy, Jules Chametzky, Martin A. Cohen, Santiago Cohen, Justin David, Lawrence Douglas, Ron Duncan, Catherine Epstein, Carlos Flores, Irma Flores, David Frye, David Gitlitz, Mathew Glassman, Carol Green, Yael Halevi-Wise, Jim Hicks, Stanley M. Hordes, Catherine Infante, Ben Kaplan, Steven G. Kellman, Stacy Klein, Aaron Lansky, Taryn and Ray La Raja, Jeffrey Lesser, Fran Levine, Carol and Joel Levy, Jonathan Lewis, Luis Loya, Adál Maldonado, Linda Marshall, Leonard Milberg, Martin Miller, Susan Miron, Daniel Olivas, Max Page, Isaac Pérez, Nancy Pick, Mark Protti, Alvin H. Rosenfeld, David G. Roskies, Barbara and Sheldon Rothblatt, Rachel Rubinstein, Max Rudin, Stephen A. Sadow, Austin Sarat, John Sayles, Ken Schoen, Daniel Shapiro, Steve Sheinkin, Neal Sokol, Doris Sommer, Leo Spitzer, Alejandro Springall, Carlos Uriona, Gerardo Villacres, Dalia Wassner, Allen Wells, and James L. Young.

Venezuela: Alicia Freilich, Jacqueline Goldberg, Elisa Lerner, Antonio López Ortega, Margara Russotto, Ariel Segal, Martha Shiro, Federico Sucre, and Irina Troconis.

It has been sheer pleasure to work with my editor at University of Pittsburgh Press, Joshua Shanholtzer. Amy Sherman did stellar work managing the manuscript. And many thanks go to copyeditor Pippa Letsky for her sharp, clearheaded approach.

Thanks also to Alane Mason at W. W. Norton, Reed Malcolm at the University of California Press, Patrick Alexander of Pennsylvania State University Press, Nancy Toff at Oxford University Press, Deborah Gershenowitz at Cambridge University Press, Beth Bouloukos and Rafael Chaiken at SUNY Press, Elise McHugh at University of New Mexico Press, and Miriam Angress at Duke University, with whose help my explorations of Jewish and Latin American cultures have taken shape through the years.

Gracias to my beloved students at Amherst College.

I appreciate the invaluable support of my colleagues in Restless Books: Brinda Ayer, Alison Gore, Arielle Kane, Alicia López, Nathan Rostron, Benjamin Samuel, Jack Saul, and Rachael Guynn Wilson. And my colleagues at Great Books Summer Program: Paula Abate, Noah Rosenblum, and Any and David Ward.

Finally, *mi casa*, my true home, regardless of place, is with Alison Sparks, Joshua, and Isaiah. I adore you!

SELECTED READINGS

1. The Pull

Ansky, S. *The Enemy at His Pleasure: A Journal through the Jewish Pale of Settlement during World War I.* Edited and translated by Joachim Neugroschel. New York: Metropolitan Books, 2003.

Ansky, S. *The World of S. Ansky: A Russian-Jewish Intellectual at the Turn of the Century.* Edited by Gabriella Safran and Steven J. Zipperstein. Stanford: Stanford University Press, 2006.

Elkin, Judith Laikin. *The Jews of Latin America.* 1980. 3rd ed. Boulder, CO: Lynne Rienner, 2014.

Sartre, Jean-Paul. *Anti-Semite and Jew.* Translated by George J. Becker. New York: Schocken Books, 1948.

Stavans, Ilan, with Joshua Ellison. *Reclaiming Travel.* Durham, NC: Duke University Press, 2015.

2. Yiddish Gauchos

Aizenberg, Edna. *Books and Bombs in Buenos Aires: Borges, Gerchunoff, and Argentine-Jewish Writing.* Hanover, NH: University Press of New England, 2002.

Astro, Alan, ed. *Yiddish South of the Border: An Anthology of Latin American Yiddish Writing.* Albuquerque: University of New Mexico Press, 2003.

Avni, Haim. *Argentina and the Jews: A History of Jewish Immigration.* Tuscaloosa: University of Alabama Press, 1991.

Baker, Zachary. "The Streets of Buenos Aires: Jevel Katz and Yiddish Popular Culture in the Argentine Metropolis." Vol. 3, No. 8 of *Yiddish Theater Forum*, edited by Joel Berkowitz. 2004.

Bashevis Singer, Isaac. *Collected Stories.* Edited by Ilan Stavans. 3 vols. New York: Library of America, 2004.

Birmajer, Marcelo. *El Once: Un recorrido personal.* Buenos Aires: Aguilar, 2006.

Birmajer, Marcelo. *Three Musketeers.* Translated by Sharon Wood. New Milford, CT: Toby Press, 2011.

Bolaño, Roberto. *The Insufferable Gaucho.* Translated by Chris Andrews. New York: New Directions, 2013.

Borges, Jorge Luis. *Collected Fiction.* Translated by Andrew Hurley. New York: Viking, 1998.

Borges, Jorge Luis. *Selected Non-Fiction.* Edited by Eliot Weinberger. New York: Viking, 1999.

Brodsky, Adriana. *Sephardi, Jewish, Argentine: Creating Community and National Identity, 1880–1960.* Bloomington: Indiana University Press, 2016.

Brodsky, Adriana, with Raanan Rein, eds. *The New Jewish Argentina: Facets of Jewish Experience in the Southern Cone.* Leiden: Brill, 2013.

Burman, Daniel, dir. *Lost Embrace.* 2005.

Burman, Daniel, dir. *The Tenth Man.* 2016.

Cohen, Martin A., ed. *The Jewish Experience in Latin America: Selected Studies from the Publications of the American Jewish Historical Society.* 2 vols. Waltham, MA: American Jewish Publication Society/Ktav, 1971.

Cohn, Mariano, with Gastón Duprat, dir. *Todo sobre el asado.* 2016.

Cozarinsky, Edgardo. *The Bride from Odessa.* Translated by Nick Caistor. New York: Farrar, Straus, and Giroux, 2004.

Cozarinsky, Edgardo. *The Moldavian Pimp.* Translated by Nick Caistor. Afterword by Alberto Manguel. London: Harvill Secker, 2006.

Cozarinsky, Edgardo. *Urban Voodoo: A Sentimental Journey.* Translated by Ronald Christ and the author. Preface by Susan Sontag. New York. Lumen Books, 1990.

Cozarinsky, Edgardo, dir. *Carta al padre.* 2014.

Cozarinsky, Edgardo, dir. *La Guerre d'un seul homme.* 1981.

Feierstein, Ricardo. *Historia de los judíos argentinos.* Buenos Aires: Editorial Galerna, 2006.

Gerchunoff, Alberto. *The Jewish Gauchos of the Pampas.* Translated by Prudencio de Pereda. Introduction by Ilan Stavans. Albuquerque: University of New Mexico Press, 1998.

Godio, Julio. *La semana trágica: Enero 1919*. Buenos Aires: Hyspamérica, 1985.

Gurwitz, Beatrice D. *Argentine Jews in the Age of Revolt: Between the New World and the Third World*. Leiden: Brill, 2016.

Heffes, Gisela. *Judíos/Argentinos/Escritores*. Buenos Aires: Atril, 1999.

Heschel, Abraham Joshua. *Moral Grandeur and Spiritual Audacity*. Edited by Susannah Heschel. New York: Farrar, Straus, and Giroux, 1996.

Kriwaczek, Paul. *Yiddish Civilization: The Rise and Fall of a Forgotten Nation*. New York: Vintage, 2006.

Lesser, Jeffrey. *Jewish Colonization in Rio Grande do Sul, 1904–1925/Colonização judaica no Rio Grande do Sul, 1904–1925*. São Paulo: Centro de Estudos de Demografia Histórica da América Latina, Faculdade de Filosofia, Letras e Ciências Humanas, Universidade de São Paulo, 1991.

Lesser, Jeffrey. *Welcoming the Undesirables: Brazil and the Jewish Questions*. Berkeley: University of California Press, 1995.

Lindstrom, Naomi. *Jewish Issues in Argentine Literature: From Gerchunoff to Szichman*. Columbia: University of Missouri Press, 1989.

Plager, Silvia. *Mi cocina judía*. Buenos Aires: Sudamericana, 2014.

Sarmiento, Domingo Faustino. *Facundo: Civilization and Barbarism*. Translated by Mary Mann. Introduction by Ilan Stavans. New York: Penguin Classics, 1998.

Scliar, Moacyr. *The Centaur in the Garden*. Translated by Margaret A. Neves. Introduction by Ilan Stavans. Madison: University of Wisconsin Press, 2003.

Scliar, Moacyr. *Collected Stories*. Introduction by Ilan Stavans. Albuquerque: University of New Mexico Press, 2002.

Senkman, Leonardo, with Ricardo Feierstein, Isidoro Niborski, and Sara Itzigson, eds. *Integración y marginalidad: Historia de vidas de inmigrantes judíos a la Argentina*. Buenos Aires: Milá, 1985.

Shavit, Ari. *My Promised Land: The Triumph and Tragedy of Israel*. New York: Siegel and Grau, 2013.

Sinay, Javier. *Los crímenes de Moisés Ville*. Buenos Aires: Tusquets, 2013.

Sion, Brigitte. *Memorials in Berlin and Buenos Aires: Balancing Memory, Architecture, and Tourism*. Lanham, MD: Lexington Books, 2015.

Sofer, Eugene. *From Pale to Pampa: The Jewish Immigrant Experience in Buenos Aires*. New York: Holmes and Meier, 1982.

Sosnowski, Saúl. *La orilla inminente. Escritores judíos argentinos*. Buenos Aires: Legasa, 1987.

Stavans, Ilan. *Borges, the Jew*. Albany: State University of New York Press, 2016.

Stavans, Ilan, ed. *The Cross and the Scroll: 1,000 Years of Jewish-Hispanic Relations*. New York: Routledge, 2002.

Stavans, Ilan, ed. *Oy, Caramba! An Anthology of Jewish Stories from Latin America.* Albuquerque: University of New Mexico Press, 2017.

Stavans, Ilan, with Marcelo Brodsky. *Once@9:53am: Terror in Buenos Aires.* University Park, PA: Dimayot-PSUP, 2016.

Szifron, Damián, dir. *Wild Tales.* 2015.

Szwarcbart, Herman, dir. *Un pogrom en Buenos Aires.* 2007.

Rein, Raanan. *Fútbol, Jews, and the Making of Argentina.* Translated by Martha Grenzeback. Stanford: Stanford University Press, 2015.

Rozitchner, León. *Ser judío.* Buenos Aires: De La Flor. 1967.

Toker, Eliahu. *¿Nu? Reír en el país de ídish.* Buenos Aires: Milá, 2006.

Toker, Eliahu. *El pueblo elegido y otros chistes judíos.* Buenos Aires: Milá, 2003.

Toker, Eliahu, with Patricia Finzi and Moacyr Scliar. *Del Edén al diván: Humor judío.* Buenos Aires: Editorial Shalom, 1991.

Toker, Eliahu, with Marcelo Rudaeff. *La felicidad no es todo en la vida y otros chistes judíos.* Buenos Aires: Milá, 2001.

Vagnenkos, Alejandro, dir. *Jevel Katz y sus paisanos.* 2005.

Weisbrot, Robert. *The Jews of Argentina: From the Inquisition to Perón.* Philadelphia: Jewish Publication Society, 1979.

Winsberg, Morton. *Colonia Baron Hirsch: A Jewish Agricultural Colony in Argentina.* Gainesville: University of Florida Press, 1964.

3. Kahlo's Eyebrows

Aguinis, Marcos. *La gesta del marrano.* Buenos Aires: Planeta, 1991.

Artenstein, Isaac, dir. *Tijuana Jews.* 2007.

Avni, Haim. *Spain, Franco, and the Jews.* Philadelphia: Jewish Publication Society, 1982.

Baca, Jimmy Santiago. *C-Train and Thirteen Mexicans.* New York: New Directions, 2002.

Benchimol, Samuel Isaac. *Eretz Amazônia: Os judeus na Amazônia.* São Paulo: Valer Editora, 1998.

Ben-Dor Benite, Zvi. *The Ten Lost Tribes: A World History.* Oxford: Oxford University Press, 2009.

Bibliowicz, Azriel. *Migas de pan.* Bogotá: Alfaguara, 2013.

Bohm, Gabriel, dir. *The Longing: The Forgotten Jews of South America.* 2007.

Bokser, Benzion. *Abraham Isaac Kook: The Lights of Penitence, the Moral Principles, Lights of Holiness. Essays, Letters, and Poems.* Mahwah, NJ: Paulist Press, 1978.

Chuchiak, John F. IV. *The Inquisition of New Spain, 1536–1820. A Documentary History.* Baltimore, MD: Johns Hopkins University Press, 2012.

Cohen, Martin A. *The Martyr: Luis de Carvajal, A Secret Jew in Sixteenth-Century Mex-*

ico. Introduction by Ilan Stavans. Albuquerque: University of New Mexico Press, 2001.

Columbus, Christopher. *The Four Voyages.* Translated by J. M. Cohen. London: Penguin Classics, 1992.

Cordero Reisman, Karen, ed. *Another Promised Land: Anita Brenner's Mexico.* Los Angeles: Skirball Cultural Center, 2017.

Durán, Fray Diego. *The Aztecs: The History of the Indies of New Spain.* Translated by Fernando Horcasitas. Introduction by Doris Heyden. New York: Orion Press, 1964.

Entine, Jon. *Abraham's Children: Race, Identity, and the DNA of the Chosen People.* New York: Grand Central Publishing, 2007.

Feitler, Bruno. *The Imaginary Synagogue: Anti-Jewish Literature in the Portuguese Early Modern World.* Leiden: Brill, 2015.

Fernández de Oviedo y Valdés, Gonzalo. *Historia general y natural de las Indias.* Madrid, 1557.

García, Fray Gregorio. *Origen de los Indios del Nuevo Mundo e Indias Occidentales.* Edited by Carlos Baciero et al. Madrid: Consejo Superior de Investigaciones Científicas, 2005.

Gitlitz, David M. *Secrecy and Deceit: The Religion of the Crypto-Jews.* Introduction by Ilan Stavans. Albuquerque: University of New Mexico Press, 2002.

Glickman, Nora, with Ariana Huberman, eds. *Evolving Images: Jewish Latin American Cinema.* Austin: University of Texas Press, 2018.

Glusker, Susannah Joel. *Anita Brenner: A Mind of Her Own.* Austin: University of Texas Press, 2010.

Goldemberg, Isaac. *The Fragmented Life of Don Jacobo Lerner.* Translated by Robert S. Picciotto. Introduction by Ilan Stavans. Albuquerque: University of New Mexico Press, 1999.

Goldemberg, Isaac. *Remember the Scorpion.* Translated by Jonathan Tittler. Los Angeles: Unnamed Press, 2015.

Halevi-Wise, Yael. *Spanish Jewish History and the Modern Literary Imagination.* Stanford: Stanford University Press, 2012.

Harris, Tomás. *Cipango.* Translated by Daniel Shapiro. Lewisburg, PA: Bucknell University Press, 2010.

Hernández, Marie-Theresa. *The Virgin of Guadalupe and the Conversos: Uncovering Hidden Influences from Spain to Mexico.* New Brunswick, NJ: Rutgers University Press, 2014.

Herrera, Hayden. *Frida: A Biography of Frida Kahlo.* New York: HarperPerennial, 2002.

Herz, Cary. *New Mexico's Crypto-Jews: Image and Memory.* Essays by Ori Z. Soltes and Mona Hernández. Albuquerque: University of New Mexico Press, 2007.

Hordes, Stanley M. *To the End of the Earth: A History of the Crypto-Jews of New Mexico.* New York: Columbia University Press, 2005.

Jnohn, Tomas, ed. *Jewish Pioneers of New Mexico.* Foreword by Thomas E. Chávez. Afterword by Henry J. Tobias. Santa Fe: Museum of New Mexico Press, 2003.

Kaman, Henry. *The Spanish Inquisition: A Historical Revision.* 4th ed. New Haven, CT: Yale University Press, 2014.

Kedourie, Elie, ed. *Spain and the Jews: The Sephardic Experience, 1492 and After.* London: Thames and Hudson, 1992.

Kritzler, Edward. *Jewish Pirates of the Caribbean: How a Generation of Swashbuckling Jews Carved Out an Empire in the New World in Their Quest for Treasure, Religious Freedom—and Revenge.* New York: Anchor, 2008.

Kunin, Seth D. *Juggling Identities: Identity and Authenticity among the Crypto-Jews.* New York: Columbia University Press, 2009.

Las Casas, Fray Bartolomé de. *A Short Account of the Destruction of the Indies.* Translated by Nigel Griffin. Introduction by Anthony Pagden. New York: Penguin Classics, 1999.

Liebman, Seymour B. *The Inquisitors and the Jews in the New World.* Coral Gables: University of Miami Press, 1974.

Liebman, Seymour B. *The Jews in New Spain: Faith, Flame, and Inquisition.* Coral Gables: University of Miami Press, 1970.

Liebman, Seymour B. "The Mestizo Jews of Mexico." *American Jewish Archives* (November 1967): 144–74.

Martínez-Dávila, Roger L., with Josef Díaz and Ron D. Hart. *Fractured Faiths/Las fes fracturadas: Spanish Judaism, the Inquisition and New World Identities/El judaísmo español, la Inquisición y las identidades en el Nuevo Mundo.* Santa Fe: SF Design and FrescoBooks, 2016.

Moscona, Myriam. *Tela de sevoya.* Mexico City: Lumen, 2012.

Moscona, Myriam, with Jacobo Sefamí, eds. *Por mi boka: Textos de la diáspora sefardí.* Mexico City: Lumen, 2013.

Muñiz-Huberman, Angelina. *Los esperandos: Piratas judeoportugueses . . . y yo.* Madrid: Sefarad Editores, 2017.

Muñiz-Huberman, Angelina. "The Girl on the Balcony." *Halapid: Journal of the Society for Crypto-Judaic Studies* 15, no. 3 (Summer 2008): 4–5.

Muñiz-Huberman, Angelina, ed. *La lengua florida. Antología sefaradí.* Mexico City: Fondo de Cultura Económica–UNAM, 1989.

Muñiz-Huberman, Angelina. *El sefardí romántico.* Mexico City: Debolsillo, 2014.

Neulander, Judith S. "Cannibals, Castes, and Crypto-Jews: Premillenial Cosmogony in Postcolonial New Mexico." Ph.D. dissertation, Indiana University, 2001.

Neulander, Judith S. "Crypto-Jews of the Southwest: An Imagined Community." *Jewish Folklore and Ethnology Review* 16, no. 1 (1994): 64–68.

Neulander, Judith S. "The New Mexican Crypto-Jewish Canon: Choosing to Be 'Chosen' in Millennial Tradition." *Jewish Folklore and Ethnology Review* 18, nos. 1–2 (1996): 19–58.

Nissán, Rosa. *Like a Bride* and *Like a Mother*. Translated by Dick Gerdes. Introduction by Ilan Stavans. Albuquerque: University of New Mexico Press, 2002.

Payne, Stanley G. *Franco and Hitler: Spain, Germany, and World War II*. New Haven, CT: Yale University Press, 2008.

Paz, Octavio. *The Labyrinth of Solitude and Other Writings*. Translated by Lysander Kemp, Yara Milos, and Rachel Phillips Belash. New York: Grove, 1991.

Perera, Victor. *The Cross and the Pear Tree: A Sephardic Journey*. New York: Alfred A. Knopf, 1995.

Ray, Jonathan. *After Expulsion: 1492 and the Making of Sephardic Jewry*. New York: New York University Press, 2013.

Ripstein, Arturo, dir. *El Santo Oficio*. 1974.

Robb, Graham. *The Discovery of France: A Historical Geography from the Revolution to the First World War*. New York: W. W. Norton, 2007.

Sachar, Howard M. *Farewell, España: The World of the Sephardim Remembered*. New York: Alfred A. Knopf, 1994.

Salcedo Mitrani, Lorry, dir. *The Fire Within: Judeus na Floresta Amazônica*. 2008.

Salgado, David, dir. *Erezt Amazonia*. 2002.

Scliar, Moacyr. *A majestade do Xingu*. São Paulo: Companhia das Letras, 1997.

Scliar, Moacyr. *The Strange Nation of Rafael Mendes*. Translated by Eloah F. Giacomelli. New York: Harmony Books, 1987.

Segal, Ariel. *The Jews of the Amazon: Self-Exile in Earthly Paradise*. Jewish Publication Society, 1999.

Springall, Alejandro, dir. *My Mexican Shiva*. 2007.

Stavans, Ilan. *The Return of Carvajal: A Mystery*. University Park: PSUP, 2019.

Stavans, Ilan. *On Borrowed Words: A Memoir of Language*. New York: Penguin, 2002.

Stavans, Ilan. *Return to Centro Histórico: A Mexican Jew Looks For His Roots*. New Brunswick, NJ: Rutgers University Press, 2014.

Stavans, Ilan. *The Riddle of Cantinflas: Essays on Hispanic Popular Culture*. Revised and expanded ed. Albuquerque: University of New Mexico Press, 2013.

Stavans, Ilan, ed. *The Schocken Book of Modern Sephardic Literature*. New York: Schocken Books, 2005.

Stavans, Ilan. *Singer's Typewriter and Mine: Reflections on Jewish Culture*. Lincoln: University of Nebraska Press, 2012.

Stavans, Ilan, with Steve Sheinkin. *El Iluminado*. New York: Basic, 2011.

Tello, León Tello. *Judíos de Toledo*. 2 vols. Madrid: Consejo Superior de Investigaciones Científicas, Instituto D. Arias Montano, 1979, 1980.

Tibol, Raquel. *Diego Rivera: Great Illustrator*. Mexico City: Editorial RM, 2008.

Tobias, Henry J. *A History of the Jews in New Mexico*. Albuquerque: University of New Mexico Press, 1990.

Toro, Alfonso. *La familia Carvajal*. 2 vols. Mexico City: Editorial Patria, 1944.

Vargas Llosa, Mario. *The Storyteller*. Translated by Helen Lane. New York: Farrar, Straus, and Giroux, 1989.

4. Paradise Lost

Anders, Gigi. *Jubana!: The Awkwardly True and Dazzling Adventures of a Jewish Cubana Goddess*. New York: Rayo/HarperCollins, 2005.

Barnes, Julian. *A History of the World in 10 ½ Chapters*. New York: Alfred A. Knopf, 1989.

Behar, Ruth. *An Island Called Home: Returning to Jewish Cuba*. Photographs by Humberto Mayol. New Brunswick, NJ: Rutgers University Press, 2007.

Behar, Ruth. *Traveling Heavy: A Memoir in between Journeys*. Durham, NC: Duke University Press, 2013.

Bejarano, Margalit, with Edna Aizenberg, eds. *Contemporary Sephardic Identity in the Americas: An Interdisciplinary Approach*. Syracuse: Syracuse University Press, 2012.

Block, Elena. *Political Communication and Leadership: Mimetisation, Hugo Chávez, and the Construction of Power and Identity*. New York: Routledge, 2016.

Brustein, William I., with Louisa Roberts *The Socialism of Fools? Leftist Origins of Modern Anti-Semitism*. New York: Cambridge University Press, 2015.

Carciente, Jacobo. *Presencia sefardí en la historia de Venezuela*. Prologue by Santos Rodulfo Cortés. Caracas: Centro de Estudios Sefardíes de Caracas, 1997.

Corrals, Maritza. *The Chosen Island: Jews in Cuba*. Miami: Salsedo Press, 2005.

Freilich, Alicia. *Cláper*. Translated by Joan E. Friedman. Introduction by Ilan Stavans. Albuquerque: University of New Mexico Press, 1998.

Goldsmith, Martin. *Alex's Wake: The Tragic Voyage of the* St. Louis *to Flee Nazi Germany—and a Grandson's Journey of Love and Remembrance*. New York: Da Capo Press, 2015.

Gutiérrez Alea, Tomás, with Juan Carlos Tabío, dir. *Fresa y chocolate*. 1993.

Kaplan, Marion A. *Dominican Heaven: The Jewish Refugee Settlement in Sosúa, 1940–1945*. New York: Museum of Jewish Heritage, 2008.

Levine, Robert M. *Tropical Diaspora: The Jewish Experience in Cuba.* Gainesville: University of Florida Press, 1993.

Ogilvie, Sara A., with Scott Miller. *Refuge Denied: The* St. Louis *Passengers and the Holocaust.* Madison: University of Wisconsin Press, 2010.

Padura, Leonardo. *Heretics.* Translated by Anna Kushner. New York: Farrar, Straus, and Giroux, 2017.

Rosenberg, Stuart, dir. *Voyage of the Damned.* 1974.

Silverstein, Stephen. *The Merchant of Havana: The Jew in the Cuban Abolitionist Archive.* Nashville, TN: Vanderbilt University Press, 2016.

Timerman, Jacobo. *Cuba: A Journey.* New York: Alfred A. Knopf, 1990.

Wells, Alan. *Tropical Zion: General Trujillo, FDR, and the Jews of Sosúa.* Durham, NC: Duke University Press, 2009.

Whitney, Kim Abion. *The Other Half of Life: A Novel Based on the True Story of the MS* St. Louis. New York: Alfred A. Knopf, 2009.

Yoss. *A Planet for Rent.* Translated by David Frye. New York: Restless Books, 2015.

Yoss. *Super Extra Grande.* Translated by David Frye. New York: Restless Books, 2016.

Yovel, Yirmiyahu. *The Other Within: The Marranos, Split Identity, and Emerging Modernity.* Princeton, NJ: Princeton University Press, 2009.

5. Rat Route

Agosín, Marjorie, ed. *A Cross and a Star: Memoirs of a Jewish Girl in Chile.* Albuquerque: University of New Mexico Press, 1995.

Aizenberg, Edna. *On the Edge of the Holocaust: The Shoah in Latin American Literature and Culture.* Waltham, MA: Brandeis University Press, 2016.

Anonymous. *El plan andinia, o, El nuevo estado judío.* Buenos Aires: Nuevo Orden, 1965.

Arendt, Hannah. *Eichmann in Jerusalem: A Report on the Banality of Evil.* New York: Penguin, 1987.

Baer, Alejandro. *Holocausto: Recuerdo y representación.* Madrid: Losada, 2006.

Bard, Mitchell. *Death to the Infidels: Radical Islam's War against the Jews.* New York: Palgrave Macmillan, 2014.

Bascomb, Neal. *Hunting Eichmann: How a Band of Survivors and a Young Spy Agency Chased Down the World's Most Notorious Nazi.* Boston: Houghton Mifflin, 2009.

Beveraggi Allende, Walter. *Del yugo sionista a la Argentina posible: Esquema económico de la dependencia y la liberación argentina.* Córdoba: Confederación Nacionalista Argentina, 1976.

Bolaño, Roberto. *Distant Star.* Translated by Chris Andrews. New York: New Directions, 2004.

Bolaño, Roberto. *Nazi Literature in the Americas.* Translated by Chris Andrews. New York: New Directions, 2009.

Brodsky, Marcelo. *Nexo.* Buenos Aires: La Marca Editora, 2001.

Camarasa, Jorge. *Odesa al Sur: La Argentina como refugio de Nazis y criminales de guerra.* Buenos Aires. Planeta, 1995.

Camarasa, Jorge, with Carlos Basso Prieto. *América Nazi.* Buenos Aires: Aguilar, 2011.

Caro Grinspun, Isaac. *Extremismos de derecha y movimientos neo-Nazis.* Santiago: Lom Ediciones, 2007.

Caro Grinspun, Isaac. *Movimientos neonazis, antisemitismo y xenofobia en Chile.* Santiago: Universidad Arturo Prat, 2005.

Ceresole, Norberto. *Caudillo, Ejército, Pueblo: La Venezuela del Comandante Chávez.* Sevilla: Ediciones Al-Andalus, 2000.

Ceresole, Norberto. *La falsificación de la realidad: La Argentina en el espacio geopolítico del terrorismo judío.* Madrid: Ediciones Libertarias, 1998.

Ceresole, Norberto. *El Nacional-Judaísmo: Un mesianismo post-sionista.* Madrid: Ediciones Libertarias-Prodhufi, 1997.

Ceresole, Norberto. *Subversión, contrasubversión y disolución del poder: Guerra y sociedad en la argentina contemporánea. Un país entrópico en un mundo apolar.* Buenos Aires: Centro de Estudios Argentina en el Mundo, 1996.

Ceresole, Norberto. *Terrorismo fundamentalista judío: Crisis del "Nuevo Orden Mundial."* Buenos Aires: Centro de Estudios Argentina en el Mundo, 1996.

Cesarini, David. *Becoming Eichmann: Rethinking the Life, Crimes, and Trial of a "Desk Murderer."* Boston, MA: Da Capo Press, 2007.

Chabon, Michael. *The Yiddish Policemen's Union.* New York: Alfred A. Knopf, 2007.

Cohen Ventura, Jacob. *Los judíos de Temuco: Cien años de historia. El inicio de la comunidad judeo-sefardí en Chile.* Santiago: RIL Editores, 2011.

Darnay, John. *¿Fin de Argentina? ¿O una nueva república?* Buenos Aires: Editorial Brujas, 2004.

Dorfman, Ariel. *Death and the Maiden.* New York: Penguin, 1989.

Dorfman, Ariel. *Heading South, Looking North: A Bilingual Journey.* New York: Viking, 1998.

Feierstein, Daniel. *Genocide as Social Practice: Reorganizing Society under the Nazis and Argentina's Military Juntas.* Translated by Douglas Andrew Town. New Brunswick, NJ: Rutgers University Press, 2014.

Finchelstein, Federico. *The Ideological Origins of the Dirty War: Fascism, Populism, and Dictatorship in Twentieth-Century Argentina.* New York: Oxford University Press, 2014.

Fingueret, Manuela. *Daughter of Silence.* Translated by Darrell B. Lockhart. College Station: Texas Tech University Press, 2012.

Friedman, Max Paul. *Nazis and Good Neighbors: The United States Campaign against the Germans of Latin America in World War II.* Cambridge: Cambridge University Press, 2003.

Gallenberger, Florian, dir. *The Colony.* 2015.

Germani, Eliah. *Objetos personales.* Santiago: RIL Editores, 2015.

Goñi, Uki. *The Real Odessa: How Perón Brought the Nazi War Criminals to Argentina.* London: Granta, 2003.

Harel, Isser. *House on Garibaldi Street.* London: Frank Cass, 1997.

Levinas, Emmanuel. *Nine Talmudic Readings.* Translated, and with an introduction, by Annette Aronowicz. Bloomington: Indiana University Press, 1990.

Lindemann, Albert S., with Richard S. Levy, eds. *Anti-Semitism: A History.* Oxford: Oxford University Press, 2010.

Nevo, Eshkol. *Neuland.* Translated by Sondra Silverstone. New York: Vintage, 2016.

Pacheco, José Emilio. *Morirás lejos.* Mexico City: Joaquín Mortiz, 1976.

Page, Max, ed. *Memories of Buenos Aires: Signs of State Terrorism in Argentina.* Epilogue by Ilan Stavans. Amherst: University of Massachusetts Press, 2013.

Papiernik, Charles. *Unbroken: From Auschwitz to Buenos Aires.* Translated by Stephen A. Sadow. Introduction by Ilan Stavans. Albuquerque: University of New Mexico Press, 2004.

Patterson, David. *Anti-Semitism and Its Metaphysical Origins.* Cambridge: Cambridge University Press, 2015.

Patterson, David. *A Genealogy of Evil: Anti-Semitism from Nazism to Islamic Jihad.* London: Cambridge University Press, 2010.

Poliakov, León. *The History of Anti-Semitism.* 4 vol. Philadelphia: University of Pennsylvania Press, 2003.

Posner, Gerald L. with John Ware. *Mengele: The Complete Story.* New York: Cooper Square Press, 2000.

Rein, Raanan *Argentina, Israel, and the Jews: Perón, the Eichmann Capture and After.* College Park: University Press of Maryland, 2003.

Rein, Raanan. *The Franco-Perón Alliance: Relations between Spain and Argentina, 1946–1955.* Pittsburgh: University of Pittsburgh Press, 1993.

Roniger, Luis. *Anti-Semitism, Real or Imagined? Chávez, Iran, Israel, and the Jews.* Jerusalem: Hebrew University and Vidal Sassoon International Center for the Study of Anti-Semitism, 2009.

Rosenfeld, Alvin H. *Resurgent Antisemitism: Global Perspectives.* Bloomington: Indiana University Press, 2013.

Roth, Philip. *Operation Shylock.* New York: Simon and Schuster, 1993.

Semprún, Jorge. *The Long Voyage.* Translated by Richard Seaver. New York: Overlook Press, 2005.

Senkman, Leonardo. *El antisemitismo en la Argentina.* Buenos Aires: Centro Editor de América Latina, 1989.

Serrano, Miguel. *C. G. Jung and Hermann Hesse: A Record of Two Friendships.* Translated by Frank MacShane. London: Routledge and Kegan Paul, 1966.

Serrano, Miguel. *Él/Ella: Book of Magic Love.* Translated by Frank MacShane. New York: Harper and Row, 1972.

Serrano, Miguel. *Nos: Book of Resurrection.* Translated in collaboration with the author by Gela Jacobson. London: Routledge and Kegan Paul, 1984.

Serrano, Miguel. *La resurección del héroe.* Bogotá: Editorial Solar y Cía, 2003.

Serrano, Miguel. *The Serpent of Paradise: The Story of an Indian Pilgrimage.* Translated by Frank MacShane. London: Rider, 1963.

Serrano, Miguel. *The Ultimate Flower.* Translated by Frank MacShane. New York: Schocken, 1970.

Serrano, Miguel. *The Visits of the Queen of Sheba.* Foreword by C. G. Jung. Translated by Frank MacShane. London: Routledge and Kegan Paul, 1960.

Spitzer, Leo. *Hotel Bolivia: The Culture of Memory in a Refuge from Nazism.* New York: Hill and Wang, 1998.

Taguieff, Pierre-André. *La nueva judeofobia.* Barcelona: Gedisa, 2003.

Thomas, Gordon, with Max Morgan-Witts. *Voyage of the Damned: A Shocking True Story of Hope, Betrayal, and Nazi Terror.* New York: Skyhorse, 2010.

Timerman, Jacobo. *Prisoner without a Name, Cell without a Number.* Translated by Toby Talbot. Foreword by Arthur Miller. Introduction by Ilan Stavans. Madison: University of Wisconsin Press, 2003.

Toker, Eliahu. *Sitios de la memoria. Los cementerios judíos porteños de Liniers y Tablada en la historia y la cultura.* Buenos Aires: Milá, 2005.

Volpi, Jorge. *In Search of Klingsor.* Translated by Kristina Cordero. New York: Scribner, 2007.

Wiesel, Elie. *All Rivers Run to the Sea: Memoirs.* New York: Schocken, 1996.

Wiesel, Elie. *And the Sea Is Never Full: Memoirs.* New York: Schocken, 2000.

Wiesel, Elie. *Legends of Our Time.* New York: Rinehart and Winston, 1968.

Wistrich, Robert S. *A Lethal Obsession: Anti-Semitism from Antiquity to the Global Jihad.* New York: Random House, 2010.

Zurita, Raúl. *Zurita.* Santiago: Editorial Universidad Diego Portales, 2011.

6. Making Aliyah

Bahbah, Bishara A., with Linda Butler. *Israel and Latin America: The Military Connection.* New York: Palgrave Macmillan, 1986.

Bolaño, Roberto. *The Savage Detectives*. Translated by Natasha Wimmer. New York: Farrar, Straus, and Giroux, 2008.

Castaneda, Carlos. *The Teachings of Don Juan: A Yaqui Way of Knowledge*. Berkeley: University of California Press, 1968.

Cortázar, Julio. *Hopscotch, Blowup, We Love Glenda So Much*. Translated from the Spanish by Gregory Rabassa and Paul Blackburn. Introduction by Ilan Stavans. New York: Everyman's Library, 2014.

Goldberg, Florinda, with Iosef Rozen, eds. *Los latinoamericanos en Israel: Antología de una aliá*. Buenos Aires: Contextos, 1988.

Kaufman, Edy, with Yoram Shapira and Joel Barromi. *Israeli–Latin American Relations*. New Brunswick, NJ: Transaction Books, 1979.

Klich, Ignacio, with Jeffrey Lesser, eds. *Arab and Jewish Immigrants in Latin America: Images and Realities*. London: F. Cass, 1998.

Klor, Sebastian. *Between Exile and Exodus: Argentine Jewish Immigration to Israel, 1948–1967*. Detroit: Wayne State University Press, 2017.

Lispector, Clarice. *The Hour of the Star*. Translated by Benjamin Moser. New York: New Directions, 2011.

Meruane, Lina. *Volverse palestina, seguido de Volvernos otros*. 2nd ed. Santiago: Random House, 2015.

Moser, Benjamin. *Why This World: A Biography of Clarice Lispector*. Oxford: Oxford University Press, 2009.

Rein, Raanan. *Árabes y judíos en Iberoamérica: Similitudes, diferencias y tensiones*. Sevilla: Fundación Tres Culturas del Mediterráneo, 2008.

Rein, Raanan, with Ilan Diner. "Miedos infundados, esperanzas infladas, memorias apasionadas: Los grupos de autodefensa judíos en la Argentina de los años sesenta." *Estudios* (Centro de Estudios Avanzados, Universidad de Córdoba), no. 26 (July–December 2011): 163–85.

Stavans, Ilan. *Resurrecting Hebrew*. New York: Nextbook/Schocken, 2008.

Stoliar, Irene. *Los Shomrim del Caribe: Historia del movimiento Hashomer Hatzair en Cuba*. Tel Aviv: Yad Yaari, 2013.

Timerman, Jacobo. *The Longest War: Israel in Lebanon*. New York: Alfred A. Knopf, 1982.

Wistrich, Robert S. *From Ambivalence to Betrayal: The Left, the Jews, and Israel*. Lincoln: University of Nebraska Press, 2012.

7. The Push

Grosser Nagarajan, Nadia, ed. *Pomegranate Seeds: Latin American Jewish Tales*. Albuquerque: University of New Mexico Press, 2005.

Lazarus, Emma. *Selected Poems and Other Writings*. New York: Dover, 2002.

Lesser, Jeffrey, and Raanan Rein, eds. *Rethinking Jewish-Latin Americans.* Albuquerque: University of New Mexico Press, 2008.

Sadow, Stephen A., ed. *King David's Harp: Autobiographical Essays by Jewish Latin American Writers.* Albuquerque: University of New Mexico Press, 1999.

Schor, Esther, *Emma Lazarus.* New York: Nextbook/Schocken, 2005.

Stavans, Ilan. *On Self-Translation: Meditations on Language.* Albany: State University of New York Press, 2018.